For
Jeffrey Steinberg, 1947–1981.
Founder and publisher of Stonehill,
visionary & friend.

You that look pale
and tremble at this chance,
That are but mutes
or audience to this act,
Had I but time—
as this fell sargeant, death,
Is strict in his arrest—
O, I could tell you—
But let it be.

—Hamlet

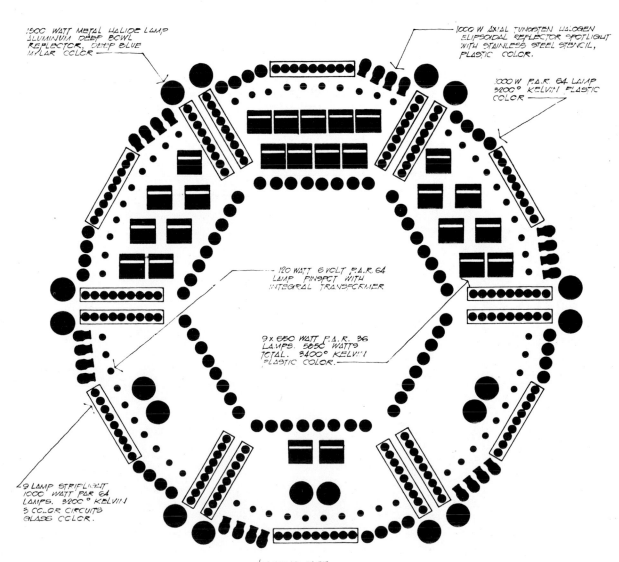

LIGHTING PLOT
ROLLING STONES TOUR

THE ROLLING STONES

The First Twenty Years

Written & edited by
David Dalton

ALFRED A. KNOPF
NEW YORK
1981

ARCHIVISTS

Tom Beach
James Karnbach

CONTRIBUTORS

Kenneth Anger	Andrew Oldham
Chris Barber	Anita Pallenberg
Victor Bockris	Coco Pekelis
Stanley Booth	Lisa Robinson
Barbara Charone	John Sievert
Connie De Nave	Elsa Smith
Pete Erskine	Patti Smith
Giorgio Gomelsky	Gloria Stavers
Brion Gysin	Terry Southern
Nick Kent	Andy Warhol
Alexis Korner	Cathy McGowan
Scott E. Kutina	Miles
Sue Mautner	Jim Morrison
Charles Shaar Murray	
Ted Newman-Jones III	

If there are any errors of a factual
nature in this book, please address
your corrections to Mr. Tom Beach,
Backstreet Records, 11218 Grandview
Ave., Wheaton, Md. 20902.

MEMORIES

At the beginning of this undertaking
(then appropriately called *Stones Un-
earthed!*), Tom Beach helpfully hinted
that if we were to do the thing properly
we must first pinpoint what each Stone
was doing every day from their residency at the Crawdaddy Club at the
beginning of 1963 until the virtual dissolution of the band's First Incarnation
at the end of 1966. We listened in-
credulously, trying not to register
alarm at his compulsive attitude, but
soon we too were completely possessed
by rampant curiousity and voracious
vicarious voyeurism. We amalgamated,
annotated, correlated and integrated
millions of trivial and momentous facts
and dates quite indiscriminately. Egyptian scrolls some 30 feet in length, having their origin on the kitchen cabinets,
snaked their way through the hallway,
meandered through the living room
past the Shroud of Turin and ended in
swirling eddies at the bedroom door.

We had unwittingly joined the ranks
of leaf counters, bottle cap collectors,
train spotters (Brian's occupation before joining the Stones), baseball card
horders and marble swappers. This
only confirmed that we had become
part of the recent breed of obsessed
rock archivists, hopelessly regressed to
a stage of development experienced
primarily by male adolescents, known
as latency. We found in James
Karnbach the final flowering of this
terrifying condition that all involved in
this book were at one time or another
reduced to.

When we insisted we must find out
the astrological sign of Keith's dog,
Bumble, Beach looked at us with the
sort of quizzical and concerned gaze
people usually reserve either for the
temporarily deranged, the hopelessly
infatuated, or for cats on a full moon.
We knew then it was time to stop but
alas it was too late. One more clipping,
found under something witty, simply
had to go in. If there was no real information to speak of in a particular
item, it made no difference. Everything
about it held an almost hallucinatory
fascination. There was the quaint diction from that bygone era, the banal
syntax of Fleet Street hacks, even the
type itself held a special meaning for
us.

Four hundred galleys later, our publisher Jeffrey "too bad if you can't take
a joke" Steinberg, had resorted to locking himself in his office as we piteously
howled outside his door for more
pages. We tried flattery ("bound to be
a visionary and groundbreaking event
in publishing"), cajolery ("what if we
set it in six point type and included a
free magnifying glass in the slipcase"),
finally descending to boldfaced maudlin sentiment ("remember when we
drove up to Newport in you dad's car
to hear Dylan play his electric?").

Although we could attribute this
fanaticism (to others, of course) as a
drive for texture and authenticity, we
secretly knew ourselves to be in the
steely grip of galley fever. Fortunately,
we were saved (and you too, dear
reader) from a fate worse than doubt,
by the ruthless cuts made by Editress
Coco Pekelis, whose philosophy of
finding the *mot juste* is simply to omit
it. The sometimes cranky and always
pithy Pekelis weeded, worded and rewrote the massive MS., injected tasty
typos ("the greatest rock 'n roll bank in
the world"), typed, Ko-Rec-Typed, and
heroically transcribed interviews conducted under controlled substances
and on the blink of oblivon, rescuing
near aphasic in-uh-coherent utterances
from the Planet of Lost Phonemes.

We should like to decorate Jon
Goodchild, Commander of the Flow
Charts, who flew into battle when all
seemed lost. His savagely graphic
mind brought all creation under his design in seven days.

We thank all those who tirelessly
and generously contributed to this
project. Especially, Mary Laverne
Dimmick whose *Annotated Bibliography of the Rolling Stones* (University
of Pittsburgh Press) and donations of
material from her collection were the
start of this book.

Our never-ending gratitude goes to
the folks at Stonehill Publishing: to
Saint Betty of the Books Lux, sinuey
and sassy Deborah Lansing, ample,
goodnatured and droll Diane Brodie,
and the indescribable Heather White.
To Thomas Landshoff of Rogner &
Bernhard for saving the day on more
than one occasion.

An undying debt also goes to Marta
Hallet, Paula Greif, Richard Henderson, Jane Coke, Deborah Kooperstein,
William Burroughs, Skye Vermont,
Sugar Blue, Antonia, John Smead,
Robin Rothman, Steve Dossick, Lynne
Edelson, Wendell Niles, Jane Rose,
Art Collins, Kathy McGinnity, Allen
Klein, Iris Keitel, Al Steckler, Freddie
Sessler, Jim Taibi, Ron Furmanek,
Mark Johnson and Susann Dalton.

Thanks especially to Bill Wyman,
the archivist's archivist.

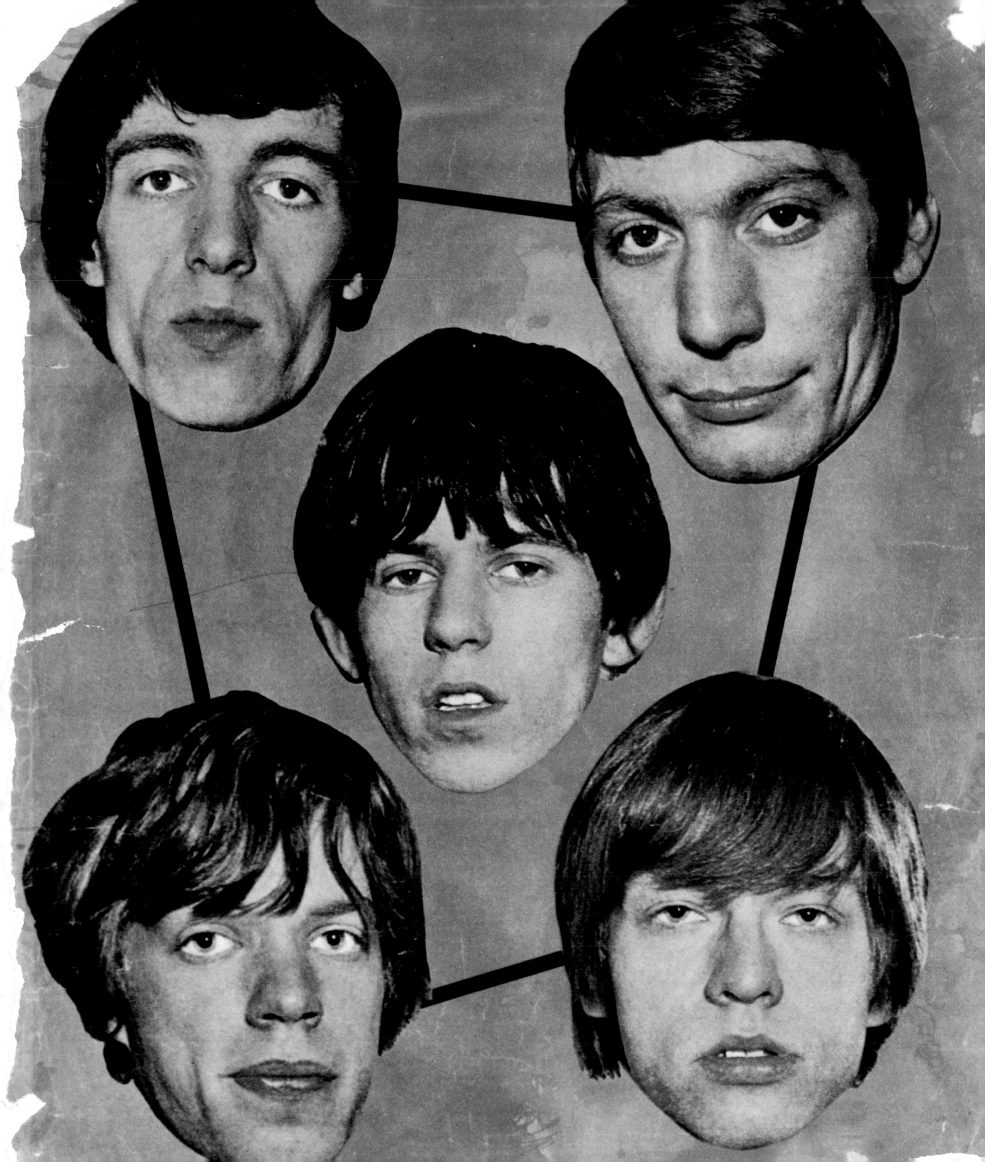

PREFACE

Gentle Reader,

What, you may ask, was the origin of this book?

Though the answer to this question may at first seem to border on the absurd, reflection will show that there is a good deal more in it than meets the eye.

Long ago, when the goddess Nü-wa was repairing the sky, she melted down a great quantity of rock and, on the Incredible Crags of the Great Fable Mountains, moulded the amalgam into thirty-six thousand, five hundred and one large building blocks, each measuring seventy-two feet by a hundred and forty-feet square. She used thirty-six thousand five hundred of these blocks in the course of her building operations, leaving a single odd block unused, which lay, all on its own, at the foot of Greensickness Peak in the aforementioned mountains.

Now this block of stone, having undergone the melting and moulding of a goddess, possessed magic powers. It could move about at will and could grow or shrink to any size it wanted. Observing that all the other blocks had been used for celestial repairs and that it was the only one to have been rejected as unworthy, it became filled with shame and resentment and passed its days in sorrow and lamentation.

One day, in the midst of its lamentings, it saw a monk and a Taoist approaching from a great distance, each of them remarkable for certain

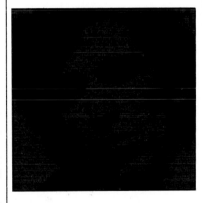

eccentricities of manner and appearance. When they arrived at the foot of Greensickness Peak, they sat down on the ground and began to talk. The monk, catching sight of this lustrous, translucent stone—it was in fact the rejected building block which had now shrunk itself to the size of a janpendant and looked very attractive in its new shape—took it up on the palm of his hand and addressed it with a smile:

"Ha, I see you have magical properties! But nothing to recommend you. I shall have to cut a few words on you so that anyone seeing you will know at once that you are something special. After that I shall take you to a certain

    brilliant
    successful
    poetical
    cultivated

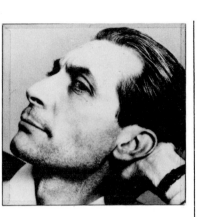

    aristocratic
    elegant
    delectable
    luxurious
    opulent
    locality on a little trip."

The stone was delighted.

"What words will you cut? Where is this place you will take me to? I beg to be enlightened."

"Do not ask," replied the monk with a laugh. "You will know soon enough when the time comes."

And with that he slipped the stone into his sleeve and set off at a great pace with the Taoist. But where they both went to I have no idea.

Countless aeons went by and a certain Taoist called Vanitas in quest of the secret of immortality chanced to be passing below that same Greensickness Peak in the Incredible Crags of the Great Fable Mountains when he caught sight of a large stone standing there, on which the characters of a long inscription were clearly discernible.

Vanitas read the inscription through from beginning to end and learned that this was a once lifeless stone block which had been found unworthy to repair the sky, but which had magically transformed its shape and been taken down by the Buddhist mahasattva Impervioso and the Taoist illuminate Mysterioso into the world of mortals, where it had lived out the life of a man before finally attaining nirvana and returning to the other shore. The inscription named the country where it had been born, and went into considerable detail about its domestic life, youthful amours, and even the verses, mottoes and riddles it had writ-

ten. All it lacked was the authentication of a dynasty and date. On the back of the stone was inscribed the following quatrain:

Found unfit to repair the azure sky
Long years a foolish mortal man was I.
My life in both worlds on this stone is
    writ:
Pray who will copy out and publish it?

Cao Xuequin, *The Story of the Stone*, (translated by David Hawkes).

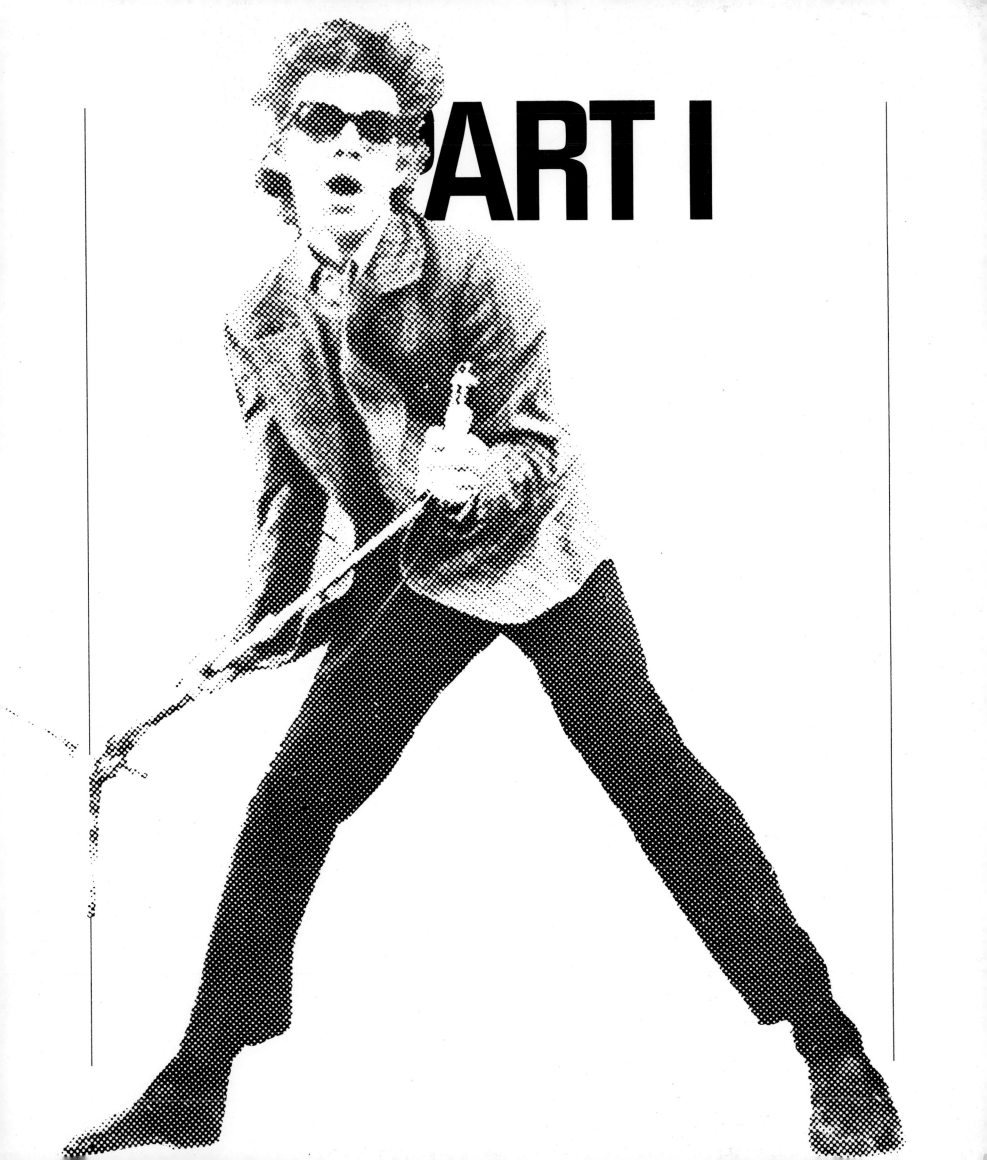

PART I

1
QUINTS

BY THEIR MUMS

Mick's mother thought he would become a politician. Keith had a pet white mouse and used to play truant from school. Mr. Watts helped Charlie buy all his clothes until he was 17. Brian was expected to become a dentist. Bill was once turned away from a dance because his trousers were too tight. These were some of the family stories learned about the internationally famous Rolling Stones by interviewing the people who know them best—their mothers. (Reprinted from *Everybody's* magazine).

Mick Jagger

Memories of Mick as a boisterous boy came flooding back to Mrs. Eva Jagger as she poured out a cup of tea in the lounge of their Dartford, England, home. A very nice house it is, too, with pebbled walls and French windows opening out onto the garden where Mick and his brother Chris used to spend hours swinging from the trees.

"We went through a Tarzan period when the boys would swing from branch to branch, giving out loud cries and screams. They used to terrify me sometimes, sitting for what seemed like hours, high up in some tree. I was always afraid they would fall," laughed Mrs. Jagger.

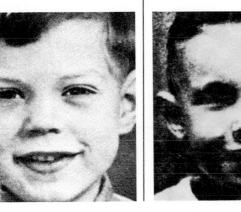

couldn't budge him.

"For a long time, Mick seemed destined for a steady office job; that was why he went to the London School of Economics to study accountancy. But he was always interested in pop music and used to play records for hours. After leaving a song on the record player only a couple of times, he knew the words and could sing it," Mrs. Jagger continued.

"But I don't think Mick considered making music his career until he started practicing with Keith Richard and Dick Taylor, who is now with the Pretty Things. I was very worried when Mick first started out with the Rolling Stones. Sometimes they all came around here to practice. A nice bunch of lads. But you couldn't help worrying. Then suddenly it all came right and they were a success.

"Mick's studies are coming in useful, now that they are making money. He knows how to look after it. But he isn't mean. For Christmas, he bought me a lovely watch."

Mrs. Jagger showed an album of early photographs of Mick, too pre-

"Quite honestly, I expected Mick to become a politician. He was a leader even when he was at school. If he believed in something, he would defend it against anyone. Not that he was argumentative. It was just that when Mick made up his mind, you

cious to even lend for publication. "He was a good boy most of the time," she said reflectively. "Except for one period when he was about four. Then he had a phase of hitting people for no reason at all. I remember once on holiday we were walking along a beach one day when Mick knocked down every single sandcastle we came across. Even ones that other little boys were still building. I gave him a spanking."

Bill Wyman

Like his fellow Stones, Bill Wyman has always been close to his family, though he has changed his name—he was born William Perks!

"I can't remember him ever losing his temper," his mother, Mrs. Kathleen Perks, said. "We found out later that when something annoyed Bill, he would go up to his bedroom and read the Bible. He was closely connected with our local church and was a member of the choir for 10 years."

Bill's musical education began at four, when he started piano lessons. "The trouble was he would never play at the right tempo, and was always messing around with the music. In the end, we got so fed up we gave the piano away," recalls Mrs. Perks.

Another instrument Bill used to play was clarinet, and a favorite trick was to put a pajama cord in a wastepaper basket and make it rise up like a snake while he sat cross-legged on the floor playing his clarinet.

"Bill had a good sense of humor and got up to all manner of things. I don't think anyone ever got the upper hand of him, either. I remember once he went to a dance with Diane, who is now his wife, and was turned away because his trousers were too tight. So the next week Bill went along again wearing a fairly wide pair of trousers. They let him in all right, and the first thing he did was to go into the cloakroom and take them off. Underneath were the same ones he had worn the week before.

"Bill had been keen to join a group ever since leaving school," says his mother. "When he met up with the other Stones, we weren't too happy at first, because he had a wife and baby to support, though all that was a secret at that time.

"We helped out a little, as it was a struggle at the beginning. Not that the hard work did them any harm—I always think it is a help if you have to struggle a bit at the start."

Keith Richard

Mrs. Doris Richard had no such problems with her son, Keith. "He was a bit of a mother's boy, really," she recalled. "When he started school, he used to get panic-stricken if I wasn't there waiting for him when they all came out."

Keith's mum came out of the canteen at the Dartford store where she works as a demonstrator to talk about her son. "I was one of a family of seven girls, and Keith was the first boy. With six aunts, he was a bit spoiled, and he really was a sweet-looking kid. Chubby and sturdy—and always with a red nose."

Now that he is older, Keith tends to spoil his mother! His latest gift was an Austin 1100 car for her birthday. This was typical of his generosity. Keith has also bought several other valuable presents for her, including an antique silver fob watch and a gold cigarette lighter.

"He was just the same as a child," recalls Mrs. Richard. "Always giving people presents. He would save up his pennies until he had enough money, and then buy me a box of chocolates. Rather spend money on others than himself. Never forgets anyone's birth-

day. He phones me frequently. When he is on tour, he writes regularly to let me know he is all right.

"Keith was always very fond of animals, and once brought a white mouse home because he said the boy it belonged to was going to kill it. We kept it in a cage and Keith looked after it very carefully until one day, while we were all out, the mouse escaped and we never saw it again. Keith was heartbroken.

"Keith was always worrying for a guitar of his own," remembers Mrs. Richard. "When he was 15, I bought him one for 10 pounds. From that day, it has been the most important thing in his life. My father, who used to run a dance band before the war, taught Keith a few chords, but the rest he has taught himself. One of his great ambitions is to be able to play really well."

Keith's last years at school were spent under a cloud, and he frequently played truant. With Teddy Boy dress all the rage, Keith used to wear pink socks and tight drainpipe trousers. When he went to Sidcup Art College, he became even more bohemian. But meeting Mick changed his life. From then on, he spent every possible hour practicing.

Has life with the Stones altered Keith at all? His mum thinks it has.

"He has become very independent," she says. "I used to do everything for him, and I was afraid that when he left home he would be hopelessly lost; but it isn't like that at all. He looks after himself perfectly well. He's a man now."

Brian Jones

Mrs. Louisa Jones also had doubts when her son, Brian, decided to make pop music his career. "He sometimes talked of becoming a dentist, and we were all behind him—especially when Brian did so well at school. He passed nine subjects in his G.C.E. at Ordinary level when he was only 16, and two years later gained Advanced-level chemistry and physics.

"Although he was quite clever, Brian was always full of fun and very attached to his sister, Barbara. Once they were racing about the house, and both came running into the kitchen. Somehow, they knocked the kitchen cabinet, and it crashed over with all our best china, including some we had as wedding presents. There was hardly a single piece that wasn't cracked or smashed. Brian was so abashed that we quickly pretended it didn't matter."

One of Brian's favorite hobbies was marquetry. He made up many pictures, using different colored woods. "I have only one left now," says Mrs. Jones, "and that is unfinished. It is a picture of a boat, and was the last one he did. He was about 13 or 14 when he started it, but he never did get around to completing it."

Brian's constant companion was his family's cat, "Rollader." It was Brian's idea to give her that name. Mrs. Jones says, "I've no idea why he chose it. We had her for 10 years, and she died when Brian was 15. He was terribly upset. He has always been terribly fond of cats. He likes all pets, but cats are his favorites. He has another one now which he keeps in London. It is a Manx cat, given to him by a fan when the Stones were in the Isle of Man."

As soon as he left school, Brian decided to learn the guitar. "At first, I thought it was only a hobby," says Mrs. Jones. "He had always been keen on music, and started piano lessons when he was six or seven. When he was 12, Brian joined his school orchestra and learned clarinet, but I don't think he has played that much since he left. He was keen on several sports at school, particularly table tennis and judo. One thing he really excelled at was diving. He wasn't particularly interested in swimming, but was constantly charging up the ladder to the high board."

Mrs. Jones doesn't think success with the Rolling Stones has altered Brian much. "If anything, he seems more helpful when he is at home these days," she says. "Before, he would help with the washing up on a Sunday and things like that, but now he is even better—making cups of tea and things like that. Of course, I am very glad that he has done so well. But, as a typical mother, I think it would have been nice if he had become a dentist."

Charlie Watts

Keith and Charlie Watts were opposites in childhood. Whereas Keith loathed school and organized sports, Charlie's thoughts were filled mainly

with football boots and cricket bats.

"He loved games, especially football, and was forever coming home with dirty knees and muddy clothes. Charlie was a big boy with strong legs. We often thought he would become a footballer. Even now, he will still walk across the road to kick a stone," recalls Mrs. Watts.

At school, Charlie won several prizes for Art and English. "His father was even more proud when he won those than he is about his success with the Stones," says Mrs. Watts. "We wanted Charlie to go in for graphic art or draftsmanship, and were very pleased when he went on to Harrow Art School.

"Charlie always wanted a drum set, and used to rap out tunes on the table with pieces of wood or a knife and fork. We bought him his first drum set for Christmas when he was 14. It cost 12 pounds. He took to it straight away, and often used to play jazz records and join in on his drums. The neighbors were very good; they never complained."

Charlie, who has a reputation for being a smart dresser, takes after his father. In fact, his dad used to go with him to buy all his clothes until he was about 17. And, until he met the Stones, Charlie had short hair!

"He has always taken pride in his appearance," says Mrs. Watts. "Until recently, his sister Linda always did his hair—Charlie would never trust a barber. She doesn't do it now, though, because he is away a lot.

"I was worried when he gave up his job to join the Rolling Stones," Charlie's mother explained. "He lived at home and we had to keep him. Of course, I hoped that the group would do well, but I never imagined they would be this big.

"Success hasn't changed him much, nor does being married. He does sometimes give people the impression that he is moody, but he isn't being moody at all, really. It's just that he gets very involved in his own thoughts. Charlie is very warm-natured, and he's given us several lovely presents."

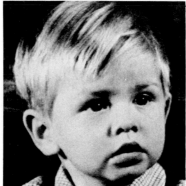

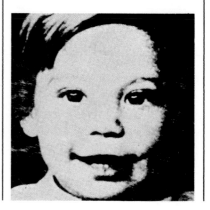

CHILDHOOD LIVING

Basically the thing at that period was that you used to just try and find girls that would screw. The rest of it was just . . . yer know, I mean, it wasn't quite as easy then as it is now. Since the invention of the Pill, it's become so much easier. In those days it was a big deal. You were just discovering yourself and your own body . . . Kinda weird. I was very emotional at that time, but then most adolescents are, like overdramatizing situations and that's why there's always been a very big market for adolescent love songs. You know, those songs that are based on the frustrations of the adolescent. Anyone who understands that, consciously or unconsciously, and writes fantasies based on that premise gets hits. *Mick.*

I used to pose in front of the mirror at home, I was hopeful. The only thing I was lacking was a bit of bread to buy an instrument. But I got the moves off first, and I got the guitar later. *Keith.*

I certainly can't claim that I came from a musical family. My dad was a lorry driver for British Railways and I reckon the only instrument any of them could play at home was a gramophone! *Charlie.*

My mum is very working class, my father bourgeois, because he had a reasonably good education, so I came from somewhere in between that. Neither one nor the other. *Mick.*

You have to remember that part of the hero image is making it from the bottom. It's more of a hangup makin' it if you're from the bourgeoisie, 'cause if you're on the bottom, like penniless, you've got nothing to lose. *Mick.*

Basically I think my parents wanted me to study piano just because we had one in the house. The fundamental music lessons in school were actually quite good, the theory lessons. They were good for teaching you about crochets [eighth-notes] and minims [half-notes] and all of that. I was always messing about on the piano instead of doing the right things. I used to speed them up and slow them down and put twiddly bits on and all of that, and my parents used to get very angry. *Bill.*

Musically, I was guided by my parents. Later, there were several piano teachers in Cheltenham. I struggled to get the notes right early on, but eventually I found I had a "feel" for music. I guess I knew that I was going to be interested only in music very early on—and that was because I quite honestly didn't feel much of an urge to do anything else. I just thought about different sorts of jobs and just rejected them because I knew I'd be bored stiff. *Brian.*

When I was thirteen the first person I really admired was Little Richard. I wasn't particularly fond of Elvis or Bill Haley . . . they were really good but for some reason they didn't appeal to me. I was more into Jerry Lee Lewis, Chuck Berry and a bit later Buddy Holly. There was a lot of TV then, *Cool for Cats, 6-5 Special, Oh Boy,* and I saw a lot of people on those shows. But rock started over here around 1955, which was a bit before all that. I mean, I missed all that Teddy Boy era, I wasn't into that at all. I never even saw it, 'cept for the tail end, and I wasn't particularly impressed. *Mick.*

I was into Little Richard. I was rocking away, avoiding the bicycle chains and the razors in those dance halls. The English get crazy. They're calm, but they were really violent then, those cats. Those suits cost them $150 which is a lot of money. Jackets down to here. Waistcoats. Leopard skin lapels . . . amazing. It was really "Don't step on mah blue suede shoes." It was down to that. *Keith.*

I was just a teenager when I first got interested in drums. My first kit was made up of bits and pieces. Dad bought it for me an I suppose it cost about £12. Can't remember anything that gave me greater pleasure and I must say that the neighbors were great about the noise I kicked up. They had a sort of tolerant understanding . . . "boys *will* be boys" kind of thing! I don't think I ever wanted to play any other instrument instead of the drums. I marvel sometimes even now at the way guitarists can get such tricky little phrases by just quietly using their fingers, but drums are for me. Someone like Max Roach . . . well, he's a real idol of mine. Maybe only another drummer can understand exactly what he is doing and how well he does it. But I can listen to a brilliant drummer for hours on end. *Charlie.*

I was crazy over Chuck Berry, Bo Diddley, Muddy Waters and Fats Domino, not knowing what it meant, just that it was beautiful. My father used to call it "jungle music" and I used to say, "Yeah, that's right, jungle music, that's a very good description." Every time I heard it, I just wanted to hear more. It seemed like the most real thing I'd ever known. I became interested in blues firstly when I found out that it was as much as existed. It was never played on the radio and, if it was, it was only by accident. Things that were hits in America, but never over here. I subsequently became aware that Big Bill Broonzy was a blues singer and Muddy Waters was also a blues singer and they were all really the same and it didn't matter. There were no divisions and I'd realized that by the time I was fifteen. *Mick.*

If you would listen to the BBC in those days there was really nothing on there. The first person I heard who I thought was really amazing was Les Paul. He was the one who turned me on to the sound of guitar music. I was listening to singers before that, mostly English ones doing covers of American hits by people like Frankie Laine and Kay Starr. Johnnie Ray was one of the first to make me really open my ears. That was like two or three years before Elvis. A few jazz records made it across and, though I'm not really interested in jazz, I do have some nice memories of some records by Dizzy Gillespie at the time and by a band led by Kenny Graham called the Afro-Cubists. I was in my late teens, I guess. Then rock and roll appeared, and it was a whole other thing. Just about then I was called up for the National Service and had to serve two years in the Royal Air Force in Germany. When I got there I started listening to American broadcasts, which we used to pick up in the British sector. Suddenly I was hearing things like the *Grand Ole Opry* show when I'd never heard country music before. I used to really like waking up at 6:00 A.M. before we'd go on duty and lie in bed and listen to all the great singers like Roy Acuff and Flatt & Scruggs. I'm still a great collector of that kind of music. Then we started to hear things by Bill Haley and Elvis, and then Little Richard and Chuck Berry. Little Richard and Berry really blew me away. I saw Berry in a film called *"Rock, Rock, Rock"* where he was playing "You Can't Catch Me," and I was completely won over. *Bill.*

I just couldn't take to games. Don't really know why, except that all that running around for no real reason seemed a waste of time. I skived off whenever it was possible and my regrets were that I simply had to turn up and play on some occasions. Even now, you'll never catch me at a cricket or soccer match. I mean, what is the point of it all. But the funny thing was that, almost despite my own attitude, I wasn't bad at badminton. At least there was a bit of action at this sport. Mostly though, it was just that I couldn't stand being bored . . . *Brian.*

I was O.K. until I got on to Rugby football. This was much too rough and energetic for me. But I wasn't really interested in all the practice and running about that went with playing for the school teams. It wasn't so much laziness, *I don't think.* It just seemed a waste of time. *Mick.*

I suppose I wasn't bad at football, though I never really got all that interested. But what I hated were the gym classes. All that drag about getting changed and leaping and running and jumping. I mean it didn't get you anywhere. *Charlie.*

I couldn't stand wearing a school uniform. I mean, what fun was there in being turned out exactly the same as everybody else. You felt just like the others and that didn't suit my attitude to things. I hated suits, too. But my mum made me wear 'em. *Bill.*

Working class. English working class . . . struggling, thinking they were middle class. Moved into a tough neighborhood when I was about ten. I used to be with Mick before that . . . we used to live close together. Then I moved to what they'd call in the States a housing project. Just been built. Thousands and thousands of houses, everyone wondering what the fuck was going on. Everyone was displaced. They were still building it and already there were gangs everywhere. Coming to Teddy Boys. Just before rock and roll hit England. But they were all waiting for it. They were practicing. Rock and roll got me into being one of the boys. Before that I just got me ass kicked all over the place. Learned how to ride a punch. *Keith.*

My dad bought me suits and I wore them as smartly as I could. A kind of Little Lord Fauntleroy, I suppose. But I do remember that I didn't like jeans and sweaters in those days. I thought they looked untidy and didn't feel somehow as good as I did in my little suits with the baggy trousers. *Charlie.*

It's strange, 'cause I knew Mick when I was really young . . . five, six, seven. We used to hang out together. Then I moved and didn't see him for a long time. I once met him selling ice creams outside the public library. I bought one. He was' tryin' to make extra money. *Keith.*

Charlie by Keith

You don't have to partake in the whole affair of the pop business—I don't anyway. I think Charlie fits in the group and the business as much as anyone.

He fits in well really because you only don't fit in if you're awkward. And Charlie ain't awkward.

He hasn't changed much since I met him first except that he's a lot happier since he got married.

Charlie's a very deep thinker. It's hard to tell if he's listening to a conversation or thinking about something else. Then, when you think he hasn't heard a thing you've been talking about, he'll start discussing the subject a couple of hours later.

But he's not that deep that we don't know him—although he still surprises us.

When I first met him he was playing with Alexis Korner, and later with this hilarious group called Blues By Six. We asked him over to join us when we were earning £2 a night each. I'm glad he came—he's a good bloke.

Keith by Mick

Very untidy and very forgetful —that's Keith. I've known him longer than anyone else in the group. I went to school with him.

I still don't know what he's thinking at any time and he really is one of my closest friends. We live close to each other.

From time to time, we've had little arguments. In fact we disagree quite a lot but we usually come to a compromise. There's never any hard feeling. As I said, he's forgetful and so he doesn't remember to bear a grudge.

He's very good at his songwriting now and we've got a relatively efficient way of going about it.

But Keith's so awful in the mornings. We don't have to talk to him and so really it's an asset. But occasionally he changes and is so bright. That's a drag because it's out of character!

The rest of the time he's so lively. He can stay awake much longer than

me. And I always admire him for being able to sleep on aeroplanes!

He's very good about the group. Very optimistic. This cheers me up when I'm feeling low.

I think people find it difficult to know Keith. Sometimes he's shy and other times he can't be bothered to take an interest in people.

Bill by Brian

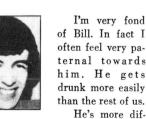

I'm very fond of Bill. In fact I often feel very paternal towards him. He gets drunk more easily than the rest of us.

He's more difficult to understand because he's married and until recently lived a very reserved home life. But now he and his wife are coming out more. I'm really pleased to be able to socialise with him and his wife because Bill and I socialise a lot on tour.

I think I'm considered the mad raver of the group and he's the op-

posite. He's older than the rest of us and more stable. Rather matter-of-fact.

He's a very likeable guy and an excellent musician. He picks things up more easily than the rest of us.

We take the mickey out of Bill a lot but he takes it well. He's pretty well-organized.

Bill was always the Rolling Stone that nobody ever knew.

When Bill first joined us he wasn't like the rest of us. He had greasy hair and dressed rather peculiarly. Keith and I used to laugh at him and not take him very seriously.

Bill is very concerned with money and he's very precise with things.

Brian by Charlie

The first time I met Brian he had a guitar in his hand. My first impression of him was just of a very good guitar player.

He's basically a very quiet bloke. He likes being left alone—not on his own, though.

He's really a very soft person. His biggest fault is the same as mine—people don't know him.

I know him really only as someone I play with. He can be very funny though—when he feels like it.

He's one of these people who, if he's feeling a bit ill or tired, likes to be left alone. He gets annoyed at people putting themselves on him when he doesn't want to know.

He's fairly quick-tempered but he gets over it. Like all of us, he's a bit moody.

I think he's generous to people he wants to be generous to. He's very wary of people he doesn't know. This business makes people that way.

At the start in particular he worked very hard with great determination for the success of the group.

When the only place he could learn and rehearse was from records, he used to sit there for hours listening to LPs.

Mick by Bill

I met Mick first at the Wetherby Arms in London's World's End three years ago. At the time I'd just broken up my group, the Cliftons, and Mick, Keith and Brian were already together.

He's changed considerably since then—he was a lot quieter and less confident. He was very friendly when I first met the group. In fact he was the only one who spoke to me for the first couple of hours.

Now he's more difficult to get on with. He's automatically on guard with people he's not sure about—if they're trying to hang on.

He's always been very close to the rest of the group and at no time have we been scared that he was going to quit and turn solo.

Why does Mick send people up? I think he puts these send-ups on as his way of being a comedian. He's not a born comedian and so he finds it's a way out for him to make people laugh.

He gets depressed sometimes and we have to bear with it.

He's a bit careful with money—not extravagant like Keith.

I also think Mick's a romantic—very much so.

When the group eventually breaks up I think he'll do something completely different.

A CONCISE HISTORY OF THE ROLLING STONES TOLD FROM A PERSONAL ANGLE BY A FAN: ELSA SMITH

My real knowledge of the Stones comes from much nearer home here, my husband not being the best provider. Gran Scotts had a pretty daughter, Eva, a lovely girl with real golden hair, a slim figure. She still has bright blue eyes that smile as she talks. We shared the same boyfriend as a girl. But while I went on to University, she stole the heart of a dour Northerner, Basil "Joe" Jagger, then a teacher of physical education at a local secondary school. They married, and July 26, 1944, in a small house in Brent Lane, Dartford, their son was born: Michael Phillip Jagger.

He was a big and bonny baby from the start, so big he didn't walk until he was a year, but all the mums admired him for his gingery hair and bright blue eyes and his cheeky smile, and still do, in Brent Lane, where their grand-daughters are fans. His father did war service, so it was later brother Chris was born. And Joe got an improved job, which enabled him to move to Dartford West, where Mick attended Wentworth primary school.

Here I was sent as a temporary teacher, my own son having now started at grammar school. I looked at the class of thirty boys and girls, and of those children all dressed alike: gray flannel shorts or skirts, white shirts and blouses, red and gray ties, all so alike but one so different, first it was his name: who could forget a child called Mike Jagger? A spiky name for a bright and spiky personality, ask a question whose hand is the first to shoot up and wave furiously, who is out of his seat to collect books to say "Please Miss can we have some football it's a lovely day," and when this same boy has short ginger hair, and I had a weakness for ginger nuts, and the same brilliant blue eyes that his mum has, no need to say Mike Jagger. It was easy to see he was destined for our ancient grammar school, a red brick ivy clad building. By now he was five foot ten tall with the same blue eyes, but his hair (he likes to call mousy) I should call light chestnut, and with just the hint of a wave.

By now the Jaggers are quite well off, with a pleasant house in the village of Wilmington, a white stucco house with lots of twisty old apple trees where Mike and brother Chris played Tarzan. Mike must have been great fun as a boy doing his thing to the telly. He had early shown skill at impersonations and did Cliff and Elvis, Eva said. I would watch my lovely boys sitting so neat and clean watching that dreadful Cliff Richards, that awful hair and that sexy dancing, and she laughs to think of her boys now still my lovely boys but they make Cliff look like milk and water.

Mike wasn't an ideal pupil. The now retired headmaster, Mr. Hudson, a small but bossy man known to the boys as "Lofty," he didn't take to Mike, who had the making of a fine athlete but didn't exert himself at school. Why risk life and limb at rugger, the school game? But he did make the team at basketball. After a shaky start and a good ticking off from "Lofty," he did get seven passes at ordinary level. Unpopular with many masters, he was liked by the French and History masters; but if you ask at the school, they practically disown him now. As the boy who threw away his opportunities as he got the necessary "A" level classes to get a university place, not full university, but the famous London School of Economics. This was a lucky break for Mike, as with his best friend, Keith Richards, he was now deeply interested in pop music with a Negro base.

Keith was also born in Dartford, in Morley Avenue, next door to their or Mike's old art master, who remembered the black-haired boy, born to Doris Richards December 1944. He first went to the primary school at the end of his road but later was with his friend, Mike of Wentworth. But there he was: a complete loner, hating school and often in tears, his mum, the pretty Doris said, "You must remember my Keith if only because he was such a cry baby." But he was in lower class and I didn't know him, but the small rebel against authority is still the rebel, even more than his best friend, Mick Jagger. His only real interest was music and he learnt quite a lot from his granddad. He was thrown out of the Dartford Technical College, and studied art at Sidcup with no better results except that he met Dick Taylor of the Pretty Things, also a pupil of Dartford Grammar School. But this also was not his thing.

Mick spent his days studying, his nights singing. He had used all his power of persuasion to get his parents to stake him to the equipment necessary, and it says a lot for Joe and Eva that they finally agreed, for at this time money was tight as Chris, unlucky with his teacher, failed to get a free place at grammar school and his dad was determined he should have the same start as Mike (whom he so closely resembles). Joe paid for him to go to a boarding-school, where he ended with the same good results as his brother, plus the medal for champion of sport, this meaning much to his father, now director of physical education at a large college, and complimented on his work by the Duke of Edinburgh.

One day when the fan mail was becoming too much to deal with Keith spoke to a pretty girl in the audience, a girl about his age with long brown hair and blue eyes. "Who are you, your name? Shirley? Well, Shirley, we need a girl who will help with the fan mail, what do you say?" and she said yes, and stood by the boys for the next nine years.

Mike had now taken his first year examination, failure not for our Mick, he passed and well, but it was the moment of choice, to stay on and perhaps rise to be a manager of a big firm or bank, or to live his life of music. He knew he must follow his star, but when money came rolling in, first he paid his grant money to the K.E.C., then repaid his parents for the loan for the equipment: good economics and good principles.

But around Dartford, they were already loved by the girls; a rash of "Mick," "Keith," "Brian" appeared on the personal belongings of most school girls, and some more daring wrote "I love Mick Jagger" in the front of their exercise books. So often I grew curious, the name was familiar but not the boy I had known, not this crazy chap I saw on the telly in creased white pajamas, or was it? Such a funny face but I loved it and him and when I drew his portrait, a friend of the family laughed and said: "Why draw my horrible little nephew?" Indignant "No indeed, it's Mick Jagger." "Well, he is my nephew, I'm afraid, let me tell my sister."

So after many years I met Eva again. "Of course, I know you. We bought sweets at your dad's shop," but I was there to talk about Mick. Instead I get Chris. He changes his jeans, unzips a banana, and looks at my drawing: "Too pretty—make him horrible and flog them dear!" "But Eva and I don't think he is horrible, we both think he is beautiful as a baby, a child, and now, we find we have many friends in common and one great interest: Mike." "Take no notice of Chris; he is a wee bit jealous." But after their TV show, it seems she and I were the only adults who thought all the Stones were beautiful, and *she* didn't like the music which I loved so much. Had now seen two shows and Mick, always kind, had written on my painting, "I really like this, Elsa," and "thanks for everything." Being a personal gift for him and chocs to share with the others.

I made myself known at the office, Shirley, very secret, but never a sight of the boys—they were usually on tour. Mick and Keith came home on rare occasions, Mick always with presents—and girls—for his mum. Once a very elaborate doll, silly boy, now a nice leather handbag, that I'd have liked. But he posed for family photos in the garden, some with Chris and some with Chrissie. He had given Chris a mini-minor car for his birthday and a white one to Chrissie, whom Eva liked a lot. But the times were changing for me; with illness and retirement, it seemed the end to me. The *Stone* mag and my own local paper all folded, and Marianne took Chrissie's place. A lady in the next hospital bed showed me the photo and a French magazine gave all the details of the romance.

I was cheesed off, to take it easy: no more shows, but I can still write, if badly, and I send a set of sketches to the office with an almost illegible letter. But Mick must have read it and sent them back all signed with love. Someone notices my name in a music paper and lo I'm in the circuit of the oldest, most faithful fans. Lovely! They come to see me and, later, when I make myself better, I go to town and meet the Stones.

2

PREHISTORY

HOW BRITAIN GOT THE BLUES, 1960-1961

There are three men responsible for the massive R & B revival in England at the beginning of the sixties: Barber led one of the biggest dixieland ("trad") bands in England. Within this unit Barber incorporated a blues segment featuring Alexis Korner on electric guitar and Cyril Davies on harmonica. Korner and Davies played Barber's blues break for a year and a half before forming the first English R & B band, Blues Incorporated—Charlie played drums, and Mick, Brian and Keith sat in occasionally. Giorgio Gomelsky, documentary filmmaker and Diaghilevian impresario, was the Stones' first manager.

He was responsible for giving them their first club residency at the Crawdaddy in Richmond, and thus unleashing them on the world.

Giorgio Gomelsky

Q: Aside from the obvious connection, the language, how else did England have such an enormous headstart in R & B and rock 'n roll? Even today the Europeans are only beginning to catch up.

GOMELSKY: It was more organized in England. *Melody Maker* started to be published in the thirties. There was a big industry for dance bands, about 30 or 40 Roselands in England. They loved ballroom dancing. So things were definitely more advanced than on the continent. Before the war, New Orleans and dixieland were very big. Funny again, talking about social classes, George White put together a band and Humphry Lyttleton was the trumpet player. Well, thank God he was an aristocrat, third cousin of the Queen or something. In England, the fact that Lyttleton started playing this music made it a sure thing for everybody to listen to. And traditional jazz, or trad as it got to be called in the late fifties, became very big in England. Chris Barber used to be as big as the Beatles were, used to play to seven, eight, nine, ten thousand people at the height of his career.

So anyway, immediately R & B started getting played in clubs there was the controversy between traditional jazz and modern jazz, because trad had by that time gathered a big enough following to have the upper hand and we had to go underground.

This would eventually bring us back to the blues. An interesting thing about the blues . . . even the Stones didn't like to be called a rock band because it was a dirty word. It meant Helen Shapiro, Adam Faith, Furey, all that. The jazz people, who *should* have been on our side, were, except for a very few, against us because they thought it was rock 'n roll.

"So I get on this train one morning and there's Jagger and under his arm he has four or five albums. I haven't seen him since the time I bought an ice cream off him and we haven't hung around since we were . . . five, six, ten years. We recognized each other straight off. 'Hi, man,' I say. 'Where ya going?' he says. And under his arm, he's got Chuck Berry and Little Walter, Muddy Waters. 'You're into Chuck Berry, man, really?' That's a coincidence. . . ." *Keith*

By that time, the beginning of the sixties, attendance was going down in the jazz clubs because *everyone* had jumped on the trad bandwagon. The quality was so . . . plastic, the audiences didn't go to jazz clubs anymore. So we had to go back to something authentic which is always what happens in these things . . . the blues were something authentic. In 1959, 1960 there were twenty people in the whole of London who were interested in the blues.

The Stones were London kids—compare New York to any other city in America, I mean there's no other city like London in England . . . of course anybody outside London is always the object of fun *in* London . . . when people had accents you just imitated their accents and everybody laughed . . . even the Stones used to do that . . . Brian was even more like Oxford than London was . . .

The Stones weren't the first people into the blues in England, Alexis Korner and Cyril Davies were, but the Stones were the first ones who were young, you know? Dave Hunt? He was an abortive attempt to go from the jazz world to . . . he was older than the Stones too. Why were the Stones more popular than the Animals? Mick. He's a lot sexier than Eric Burdon. Mick had a kind of gift of nature. To a great extent he didn't get into the exaggerated performance thing until he came back from America and saw James Brown and after that, man, he *was* James Brown, (*imitates moves*) Mick came off the fucking plane like this (*tap tap tap*). Mick was a little bit spastic all over . . . But still he had his moments where he would win everybody back because his singing was so *felt* . . . I said, "Hey man this is too much, this guy is really great, you know," and he *was* great . . . but what was so good about the Stones was you could rely on them for performance

Little Boy Blue and the Blue Boys: Dick Taylor, Keith and Mick, rock out, Dartford 1960.

in those days, every performance was a masterpiece . . .

Q: The groups playing R & B in the early days, did they see themselves as the chosen people?

GOMELSKY: Exactly! Like the existentialists in Paris or the beat generation, Kerouac's people. Every minority springs out of a desire to go back to a form of authenticity and hence it creates a logarithmic process, it multiplies itself. Four people the first night, eight the second. When you sense that, you know you're on to a sensibility, wavelength that you cannot go wrong on.

Chris Barber

BARBER: See, the period as I see it really starts in the fifties, not the sixties. I started my band in '54 . . .

We used to do this thing which was meant to be country blues, more or less. We called it skiffle music because we got the word skiffle which came from a record called "Hometown Skiffle" made in 1928 or so by the Paramont Record Company which was a race label of the 1920's.

Skiffle was popular because it was a very easy music. I mean, you can't take up playing disco music without skill, you can't take up rhythm and blues without quite a bit of technical skill and amplifiers and that sort of stuff. But with skiffle, people were making basses out of tea chests, you know, with a broom handle and string. Any old guitar that you can get, you can strum a G on it. You might rather pick a tune on it, it doesn't matter, you didn't have to. And you sang these rather easy songs. Skiffle suddenly took off because the guitar style was not very complex. You just strummed like playing rhythm on

an acoustic guitar—no amplification— with a kind of a tubey bass and a drum rhythm behind it.

Anyway, the thing that is the foundation for the blues being popular is the lyrics. First of all, to get a mass public interested the problem with jazz always is lyrics. There is no lyric, they are melodies. They are instrumental and instrumentals do not have the mass appeal of songs. People want to sing the song as they go along, the words of it. They can't remember melody. And the improvisation, they don't understand. They're prepared to accept it if it's exciting, but they can't understand it. The songs they understand, words, so of course blues hit them like that, which went along with the jazz they liked, so they became very very big. We began featuring, we began doing Muddy Waters' numbers at the end of our show anyway, from '58 onwards. We were doing "Mojo" to finish the show from the end of '58, before Muddy even came to Europe in '58, we were using it, and were still using it when Long John Baldry discovered it in '61 and started using it.

The only guy playing electric guitar blues at that time in England was Alexis Korner.

So I said come and join up with us. Alexis played guitar and Cyril Davies harmonica and they joined in with us and we did a half an hour rhythm and blues set at the end of every show. We were at the Marquee which was run by myself and Harold Pendleton playing once a week on Wednesdays.

I think Alexis already had Mick's address. Alexis knew him. Alexis knew everybody. Alexis is a guy who makes a living—his raison d'etre in

life is to bring people together. To get groups together. It isn't his own playing—he sings pretty good sometimes. That's Alexis' scene. He gets things together and get things going. He's put a lot of people in contact with other people and made a lot of things happen.

The whole thing, the social thing behind R & B in England was being attuned to it, being able to relate to it. You see, someone like Fabian was a rather American, a rather foreign thing to Britain. Somehow, this traditional jazz thing was definitely an indigenous style, it was rather British. And the skiffle thing was certainly British in sound and the British blues were very British in sound really. We were trying our darndest, Mick tries his darndest to sing like Muddy Waters and Bo Diddley, but he still sounds like Mick Jagger. I mean we are, after all, English, we can't help it, or change it, no matter what we do.

R & B is American, but it's a different part of the American culture. I have a feeling that the black culture is closer to the English culture than the American white culture is. Actually, I have a definite feeling about that, I don't know quite why. But I've often said that an Englishman feels more at home in New Orleans than he does in New York.

I've a feeling that to a certain extent the blues message, the way it's presented, seemed more close to people's consciousness here than the white American rock 'n roll which was stolen from it. Maybe it was more direct and down to earth and they were looking for something not tricked up with million dollar suits—you know? In the era of the traditional jazz concert in the '50s, God, we sold out show after

"When I left Beckenham Grammar School, I didn't have the faintest idea what I wanted to do. I didn't excel at anything, except math. Funny that, being good at math . . .

"We went through loads of tunes and messed about a lot. It wasn't a real audition. They didn't like me, but I had a good amplifier, and they were badly in need of amplifiers at that time! The two they had were broken and torn inside. Sounded great really, but we didn't know that then. I had a good amp, a Vox 130. But quite honestly I didn't like their music very much. They were into pure R & B. I had been playing hard rock. Anyway, they kept me on. Later, when they were going to get rid of me I think I clicked or something, and I stayed. I must have just fitted in . . .

"We were playing the Flamingo Club on Mondays, and very shortly afterward we got hold of a deadpan, dog-faced boy called Charlie Watts to play drums.

"We also played the Marquee Club with Cyril Davies on Thursdays, the Red Lion, Sutton, on Fridays and the Ealing Jazz Club on Saturday nights. I suppose that we were getting about 5 each after paying off all our equipment.

"I still felt very out of place with the others and often thought about throwing it all in and just being normal. Then all of sudden I decided that I'd try and conform, so one Saturday I washed my hair, brushed it just like the rest, and went down to Ealing. All the Stones were in the ABC Cafe and when I walked in they almost collapsed with laughter.

"At last, I was really one of them!"
Bill

show, where rock 'n roll really But the rock 'n roll sold the records. R & B is, of course, what you want to see *live*. I think to a great extent, a lot of the thing with the Stones was a *live* thing. You wanted to see them —it's something *to be there*.

We opened the door, which was then wide enough open for the Stones and the other bands to get in and do those gigs afterwards. Otherwise there would have been nowhere to work.

Alexis Korner

"I met Cyril Davies, the harp player, in 1953, and we started playing together as a duo all over the place; and various friends would play with us at a club we started in a pub—John Baldry would come around, and Davey Graham, people like that.

"And all the visiting American

blues players would come around. There was a long string of solo blues players coming over from the States, the cats who I suppose got tired of not being able to work much at home and who heard rumors that things were beginning to open up in Europe. Sonny and Brownie started coming over, Jimmy Cotton, Little Brother, Memphis Slim, Roosevelt Sykes.

"Big Bill Broonzy was the first one in. I love Bill. I learned one really important thing, the fact that audiences don't want to hear the kind of music you're playing doesn't mean they're right and you're wrong. It could be that you're the only person in the world that's right, at the moment, and you have to go ahead and tell people that you're right. I suppose that was why by the end of the '50s and the beginning of the '60s the young cats, like Mick Jagger and

▬▬▬▬▬▬▬▬

"Alexis Korner and Cyril Davies were the start of rhythm and blues in this country. If things were as they should be, Alexis would be right at the top. I met Alexis in a club somewhere and he asked be if I'd play drums for him. A friend of mine, Andy Webb, said I should join the band, but I had to go to Denmark to work in design, so I sort of lost touch with things. While I was away, Alexis formed his band, and I came back to England with Andy. I joined the band with Cyril Davies and Andy used to sing with us. We had some great guys in the band, like Jack Bruce. These guys knew what they were doing. We were playing at a club in Ealing and they [Brian, Keith, and Mick] used to come along and sometimes sit in. It was a lot different then. People used to come up on the stand and have a go, and the whole thing was great." *Charlie*

▬▬▬▬▬▬▬▬

Keith and Brian and Eric Burdon were with me in this, because they felt that way about it—that blues is a personal protest, by you and about you, and you're concerned with who you are and how you feel, and color doesn't matter. It was really Chris Barber who got it all started, not me. But Chris never gets any credit for it. In that period, between 1956 and 1960, when Cyril and I were playing duos and things, I was still just semi-pro. Trad jazz was the big pop music here, and Chris Barber was the big trad jazz band. Chris asked us to come back again, and he used us as an electric rhythm and blues unit within the band. He also started bringing over electric blues players from the States: Otis Spann, John Lee Hooker, Muddy, people like that. And he was

cutting his own throat and killing the trad jazz scene by having this R & B unit within the band. He knew exactly what he was doing, fostering the thing which was going to come next in music. It had to come next because trad jazz by then had become so formalized—not that it was real Mickey Mouse music by then.

"The other thing was I felt a very strong sense of responsibility towards

▬▬▬▬▬▬▬▬

"Living with Mick and Keith there wasn't much room for any high jinks. In fact, space was so limited that we even had to regulate our breathing—and that's no kidding. We talked mostly about getting ourselves organized into a proper R & B group. Talk didn't cost anything. If we weren't talking, we just played records by people like Muddy Waters, mostly records we'd begged and borrowed from friends. I worked in a record store for a while. At least, I was getting advance news on American discs being released here and I could play over records to my mates. Anyway, it's hard to concentrate when you're almost too hungry to think. Often, we'd get back to our little apartment and think about silly things like tearing up the blankets and making sandwiches of them." *Brian*

▬▬▬▬▬▬▬▬

the cats because they were 10 or 15 years younger than I. I considered that my job in a very tribal sort of thing—music as a sort of tribal living—and my job was to look after the other cats so they could start properly. After that, it's their own business. You've got to try and point them in the right direction and let them run, because they're going to run faster than you anyway.

"The band at that time was Charlie Watts on drums, Dave Stevens on piano, Cyril Davies on harmonica, a friend of Charlie's called Andy Hoogenboom, who was replaced after a fortnight by Jack Bruce on bass, Dick Heckstall-Smith on tenor sax, and me on guitar. The singers were Cyril Davies and Mick Jagger, and John Baldry was a fairly regular singer with us too. Mick used to sing three songs a night, his total public performance repertoire at the time. He learned more but was only really sure of three, one was a Billy Boy Arnold song, *Poor Boy* I think it was, and he used to sing one of Chuck's songs, and a Muddy Waters song. It was a weird band at that time because Brian Jones was still sleeping on our floor and Keith Richard used to come up from Dartford with Mick. And Charlie, on drums, when we finally decided to go pro all the way,

didn't want to come along. He was working in the advertising agency and didn't think it was secure enough. So we got Ginger Baker in instead of Charlie.

"We began playing at the Ealing Club, which was a drinking club. The Ealing Club was Mick's and Keith's first appearance on the scene. We played R & B there, which always had one night a week of trad jazz, and the jazz people didn't like us at all. We drew most of our support from the folk area because people into folk

▬▬▬▬▬▬▬▬

"Just a few months earlier I wouldn't have given their offer a second thought, because I was all for modern jazz. But I suppose I had a theory that R & B was going to be a big part of the scene, and I wanted to be in on it . . . The Rolling Stones were great, so I joined." *Charlie*

▬▬▬▬▬▬▬▬

began to come into blues bit by bit. The club held only 200 when you packed them in, and there were only about 100 people in all of London into the blues, and all of them showed up at the club that first Saturday night. Within four weeks it was packed, people traveling down from Scotland for the one-night session and traveling back the next day. Our membership lists had gone up to 800 at the end of the fourth week with more people showing up than could get in. The word started getting around London that there was something strange happening at this club in Ealing opposite the Irish pub.

"By the end of that fourth week, Harold Pendleton, who managed the Marquee, came round to take a look. He had a spare Thursday night at the Marquee, where nothing worked to bring in the audience, so he offered it to us. We took it. What happened on that first Thursday night was the original 120-odd members of the Ealing Club showed up, but the Marquee was bigger and they didn't look like very many people. But bit by bit it began to look encouraging, because the people who started coming in were young kids who didn't dig the trad jazz scene or the pop scene, and who wanted the excitement of something pretty raw. And that's exactly what we provided. They used to stand on the tables and rock and dance and shout, and by the eighth week or so, we were doing 350 on Thursday nights and feeling pretty good.

"Round about June, the BBC radio asked us to do a broadcast. There were seven of us in the band, including Mick, but they'd only pay for six for this broadcast. We had a band

meeting and I said to Mick, 'Look, we'll turn it down.' And he said, 'No, no, don't turn it down, because if you do that broadcast we'll have twice as many people in by next week.' That's what everybody thought—wow, a broadcast, they're going to be flocking in by the millions. So we decided that we'd go ahead with the broadcast and Mick, Brian, Keith, Ian Stewart and a friend—I don't remember who—would get together a group to work the Marquee that night as a support group; John Baldry would get together the lead band. The support group called themselves the Rolling Stones, the first time the Stones ever played publicly in London.

"By then we were packing in up to 1,000 on a Thursday night, and the communication between the audience and the stage was absolutely incredible. The doors would open at seven o'clock and by half-seven when we went on stage, the doors would close leaving people out on the street because there was no room. But even with a quarter hour before the end of the show people were offering £1 to get in, which was ridiculous and a hell of a lot of money at that time.

"Then the Stones decided they wanted to get together and do things on their own. I didn't bug them because I thought, you know, 'They got things to do and they should go and do them.' So they slid off, Mick, Keith, Brian, and Ian Stewart on piano, I remember about a year later Charlie

▬▬▬▬▬▬▬▬

"Despite the fact that class was very important it never separated me and Keith. We're very similar because we come from the same place. Keith and I were always close. We still are. I've never known anyone as long as I've known Keith. Therefore I've got nothing to compare it to." *Mick*

"The distance between me and Mick is a *very* subtle one. It isn't a tangible relationship. We go through distances because we have been and are so close. The fact that any distances occur at all is because of outside influences." *Keith*

▬▬▬▬▬▬▬▬

Watts, who was still not blowing regularly with anybody, came up to my old lady and said, 'The Stones have asked me to join them, what do you think I should do?' And she said, 'Well, if you're not doing anything else why don't you? What have you got to lose?' So Charlie joined the Stones."

(This interview conducted by Tony Scaduto first appeared in *Words & Music*, February 1973)

THE ALPHA WOLVES ASSEMBLE

On March 17, 1962, Blues Incorporated, the first white blues band (formed by Alexis Korner in late 1961) played its first gig at the Ealing Club, site of the historic meetings of Mick and Keith with Brian Jones and Charlie Watts. The lineup of Blues Incorporated was Alexis on acoustic guitar with electric pickups; Charlie Watts, drums; Cyril Davies, harmonica; Dave Stevens, piano; Dick Heckstall-Smith, tenor sax; and Andy Hoogenboom, bass. Two weeks later, when Blues Incorporated played the Marquee Club, Jack Bruce replaced Hoogenboom on bass.

The Ealing Club was the backroom of the ABC bakery which had formerly been rented out to "Trad" (traditional New Orleans) jazz bands. The ads in the *New Musical Express* read:

ALEXIS KORNER'S BLUES INCORPORATED

**The Most Exciting Event
of the Year.
G CLUB.
Ealing Broadway Station.
Turn left, cross at Zebra, and
go down steps between ABC Teashop
and Jewelers.
Saturday at 7.30 p.m.**

At the Ealing Club on April 7 Mick, Keith and Dick Taylor heard Brian (aka Elmo Lewis) for the first time, playing on his Hofner Committee with a green Elpico pickup. Keith described the encounter:

But Alexis was packin' 'em in, man. Jus' playing blues. Very similar to Chicago stuff. Heavy atmosphere. Workers and art students, kids who couldn't make the ballrooms with supposedly long hair then. Forget it, you couldn't go into those places. You gravitated to places where you wouldn't get hassled.

And suddenly in '62 just when we were getting together, we read this little thing about a rhythm and blues club starting in Ealing. Everybody must have been trying to get one together. "Let's go up to this place and find out what's happening." There was this amazing old cat playing harp . . . Cyril Davies. Where did he come from? He turned out to be a panel beater from North London. He was a great cat, Cyril. He didn't last long. I only knew him for about two years and he died.

Alexis Korner really got this scene together. He'd been playin' in jazz clubs for ages and he knew all the connections for gigs. So we went up there. The first or the second time Mick and I were sittin' there Alexis Korner gets up and says, "We got a guest to play some guitar. He comes from Cheltenham. All the way up from Cheltenham just to play for ya."

Suddenly, it's *Elmore James*, this cat, man. And it's *Brian*, man, he's sittin' on his little . . . he's bent over . . . da-da-da, da-da-da . . . I said, What? What the fuck? Playing bar slide guitar.

We get into Brian after he finishes "Dust My Blues." He's really fantastic and a gas. We speak to Brian. He's been doin' the same as we'd been doin' . . . thinkin' he was the only cat in the world who was doin' it. (*Rolling Stone*, August 19, 1971)

The week after his first visit to Ealing Mick sent Alexis a tape. Alexis: "Then some time after that, Mick Jagger wrote me a letter and sent me some tapes, I think that's how we made contact, and I told him to come on over. So he came up from Dartford and we talked about Chuck and Bo Diddley, and I talked about Muddy and Slim and Robert Johnson, people like that. We decided we dug each other and he used to come up with Keith and talk. I always was blowing with Charlie Watts anyway so he was coming pretty regularly. Brian also was coming in regularly to blow. I suppose another reason they came by was that there was likely to be a blues singer sleeping on the floor for that night, and it was something to come and talk to someone like that."

Brian, Ian Stewart (affectionately known as "Stew" or "Stu," depending on which side of Islington you happened to come from), Paul Jones (then P. P. Pond) and Geoff Bradford were already playing together.

On the BBC's history of the Stones, Alexis Korner asked Mick to recollect those early days at the Ealing Club:

MICK: I remember the Ealing Club . . . it was dripping off the roof all the time, wasn't it? It was so wet that sometimes we had to put a thing up over the stage, a sort of horrible sheet which was revoltingly dirty, and we put it up over the bandstand and so the condensation didn't drip directly on you, it just dripped through the sheet on you, instead of directly off the ceiling . . . It was very dangerous too, you see, 'cause all this electricity and all these mirophones and that . . . I never got a shock . . . it was incredibly primitive, you know, all these rock 'n roll groups were much more sort of up to date, they were sort of together, they had all these amplifiers. Someone amazed us all once by having this electric scene with three pickups, which we were all incredibly jealous of because we didn't have the money for a down payment on one, ho ho.

And I couldn't ever get in key. That was the problem. I was quite often very drunk 'cause the first time I was really nervous but I was never really nervous—afterward I was only nervous twice, you see. The first night I was with Alex in Ealing I was incredibly nervous 'cause I'd never sung in public before and the second time was singing the first time at the Marquee with Alex, which was like the same thing only a bit bigger. After that I never ever was nervous in my life, even in front of the queen of the Hellenes once in a crowd of forty thousand people in Greece I wasn't nervous due to the training with Alex Korner, and he didn't use to pay us much bread. Top act was Alex, yes it was fifteen bob. He used me Thursdays. We used to sing "Got My Mojo Working." John Baldry, Paul Jones, they were much taller than me. I was very small.

I remember Tuesday nights at Ealing. Six people used to come. It was so cold we'd have to play with our coats on. Eric Clapton used to

Dave Stevens, Dick Heckshall-Smith, Alexis Komer, Jack Bruce, Mick, Cyril Davies, and Charlie (hidden) at the Ealing Club

come and sing "Roll Over Beethoven," he couldn't play guitar then—he couldn't, it's very strange, he couldn't play guitar then—its probably very funny innit? He'd sing "Roll Over" with his eyes glued to the floor because he was too shy to look out to this audience of three people . . . and that was very draggy. Eventually Alex sort of got some more work together and we sort of got a group together. We got a drummer from Screamin Lord Sutch called Carlo and a bass player from SLS called Ricky and we used to play there on Saturday occasionally under the paternal auspices of Alex, who still had the cost of rent money because I still had to give him a bit of the take—not much of it. But it got very crowded, incredibly hot, and all kinds of rakes come down and demand these strange rock 'n roll

was incredibly hung up with form. Form was all-important. Anything else didn't matter at all, but form was important. Fantastic criticism down

MICK JAGGER FORMS GROUP

Mick Jagger, R & B vocalist, is taking a rhythm and blues group into the Marquee tomorrow night (Thursday) while Blues Inc. is doing its Jazz Club gig.

Called "the Rolling Stones" ("I hope they don't think we're a rock 'n roll outfit," says Mick), the lineup is: Jagger (vocal), Keith Richards, Elmo Lewis (guitars), Dick Taylor (bass), 'Stu' (piano), Mike Avery (drums).

A second group under Long John Baldry will also be there. (Jazz News)

be the leader, but nobody ever accepted him as such. I don't mean within the band, I mean with the kids.

Even if it wasn't *the* Rolling Stones, Mick had seen the future and it was them:

Q: When did you realise that it might be possible to make a living out of music?

MICK: At the time I didn't have any idea of how I was going to make a living. I remember the first time I played with Alexis Korner I made a pound or ten bob.

Q: What about the story that you didn't broadcast with Alexis because the Stones had a booking on the same night?

MICK: That's a lie. Alexis had a band and Charlie was the drummer. He had this BBC broadcast which was

"Ahm a kaang beh, behbeh . . ."
Stones in their first uniform, 1963.

Marquee Club, 1963.

numbers which they thought we ought to play, and then fighting them off with microphones sometimes and threatening them, right? Drunken people come up wanting to sing "Reddy Teddy"—they'd probably do better than me, I'm not very good at oldies . . . I can't remember an awful lot about it.

I used to sing "Don't Stay Out All Night," "Bad Boy," "Ride 'Em Down" sometimes, not mostly, with Keith. I

to the last tiny insane deail. We were all absolutely insane, I know I was completely, I mean whatever that means, insane, I was I'm sure.

Accounts of the origin of the Rolling Stones traditionally cite Thursday, July 12, 1962, as the first appearance of the Stones per se as a band. It's true they called themselves "the Rolling Stones" for this gig, but where's Bill and Charlie? Note Brian is still

using his *nom de blues.*

From the first there were inklings of the shape of things to come. Who was their leader, Mick or Elmo?

MICK: We only played down the Marquee about half a dozen times. As to who was the leader . . . Well, Brian used to want to be, but nobody really wanted to be the leader of the band —it seemed a rather outmoded idea.

Even though we were all working together Brian desperately wanted to

a big deal—but instead of having Charlie, who was in the band, he got someone else because he said Charlie wasn't a professional musician, 'cause he had some other job as well.

I didn't really expect to go on the broadcast because I was only one of his singers . . . Alexis used to sing, so did Cyril [Davies], Long John Baldry, Ronnie Jones, Paul Jones. But the thing is, we didn't have any gigs at all. We had a gig that night but it was one that Alexis had given us. I think that must have been our very first gig.

3

YESTERDAY'S PAPERS

EVERY DAY A TURN OF THE PAGE

It was love at first sight between the British press and the Stones—a marriage made in headlines heaven. The transition from smarmy pop and smoothy chops ballad boys like Adam Faith and Cliff Richard to this scruffy "cavemanlike quintet" giving the two-fingered salute (equivalent to "the finger" in the U.S.) was almost too good to be coincidental, as if the Bad Boy image had been handed to the reporter on a silver platter. And it had. They were unwittingly being spoon-fed propaganda by the group's manager and media maven, Andrew Oldham.

If they ever caught on that Oldham was stringing them along, the thought must have been fleeting. Who would *want* a bad press? In any case, it wouldn't have mattered to the cynical, flinty-hearted hacks of Fleet Street.

The precariously balanced equation worked out, for the first three years of the Stones affair, to mutual satisfaction: London's Press Row needed headlines, and the Stones wanted to be in them. "You soon get to know how to manipulate people," said Mick, the expert manipulator, about the Stones' collusion with the press. "This particular band is quite good at that. The

media are very easy to manipulate, especially in England. If you give them a tag, they'll just go for anything." He laughed. "Once it works, it all becomes routine, selling the media the same crap."

By early 1964 Andrew had begun planting stories in the press. He supplied journalists with contagious quotes and catchy captions. The provocative headline that appeared in *Melody Maker* in March had all the earmarks of a well-honed Oldham aphorism: "WOULD YOU LET YOUR SISTER GO WITH A ROLLING STONE?" It was just a variation on his slogan "The Stones are

the group parents love to hate."

Keith: "He had a genius for getting things through the media. Before people really knew what media was, to get messages through without people knowing . . ."

No country is so addicted to scandal sheets, muckracking dailies, and Sunday sensationals as England. "FILM STAR DIES UNDER MYSTERIOUS CIRCUMSTANCES"; "PEER CAUGHT IN ORGY"; "SHOCKING REVELATIONS"; "MAYFAIR

Andrew Loog Oldham.

DOPE RING CRACKDOWN." Ghoulish Moors murders and titillating "tits and arse" on page five.

Mick: "We thought it was hilarious. Civic dignitaries, justices of the peace denouncing us. It was just publicity and we didn't have to go along with it, it just sorta happened outside of us.

"When you get the ball rolling, they do it all for you, especially in this country. You don't have to do a thing, the media will pick up on it and exaggerate it beyond all recognition. If they get so much as a smell of a story they'll make it up or get a quote and turn it around to suit themselves.

"I don't have to tell you . . . the media need a story and the bands need to be publicized."

But the Stones generated publicity spontaneously. They "twitched" in Twickenham, caused a "ruckus" at Richmond and pandemonium at the Empire Pool, Wembley: "Jobsworths battle eight thousand fans at Mad Mod Ball. Outside police battled battalions of rockers. There were thirty arrests."

Mick calls the British press "pathetically amusing, but it's efficient at spreading news, wow, you can't beat it." The fastest way to get attention was through the press. "We'd do any stupid thing to get our picture in the paper. It meant record sales. The surest thing was to do something rude, shock people. We'd do something as a put-on, and they'd write about it for weeks."

The Stones were taking their love-us-hate-us attitude on their one-night stands across the land and onto the continent. There was a riot going on, and as Charlie told *Disc*, it all started in cold type. "Sure, there's a lot of screaming and that. They scream because we're popular, I think, and because they want to let us know it. They get excited, too, and so do we when we're playing to 'em. It's the atmosphere, you know. Gets all hot and sticky, and everybody's having a great time. Riot's the wrong word. Enthusiasm is more like it . . . the faints and the shovings only started happening regularly since the newspapers started writing about riots."

"Sipping a lager in the sun outside a London pub, Jones told me: 'I know the image of us is that we are hooligans and unwashed layabouts, but as a matter of fact, we're all very interested in clothes. I would love to be a fashion designer—but I never will be, of course. On stage we dress like we do, because we feel more comfortable that way. They say we've long hair. Short hair makes you clean, they say, but that doesn't follow at all.'" (Peter Dacre)

The press, confused by the twin threat of the Stones' Cro-Magnon image and Mick and Brian's androgyny, didn't know which way to turn. These two items appeared back to back in the humor column of a British weekly:

There's absolutely no truth in the rumor that Fred Flintstone was the first ever Rolling Stone!

Comedian's gag I liked: "The Rolling Stones? They're the ones who look like five shots of Hayley Mills!"

Their counteroffensive to personal attacks was "nankering." Jack Hutton reported on the Stones in the *Daily Mirror*: "As if by a prearranged signal, all five simultaneously pulled down the skin under their eyes and pushed up their noses. Believe me, it's frightening . . ."

By the fall the Stones' appearance had become a matter of national debate on the floor of the House of Commons. On September 16 Tom Driberg, MP, asked the House of Commons to "deplore" the action of a magistrate who called the Rolling Stones "complete morons" who wore "filthy clothes." And on November 21 the following letter appeared in the *Daily Mirror*: "Is there any MP with the courage to introduce a bill into the House of Commons compelling boys to have their hair cut?" It came from a Mrs. K. in Plymouth, Devon.

The Stones' very first mention in the press, Barry May's article in the *Richmond and Twickenham Times* (April 1963), was an encouraging if humid review ("A musical magnet is drawing the jazz beatniks . . . to a new Mecca in Richmond"). Their first mention in the national press, two months later on June 13, was a full-page article in the *Daily Mirror* that was so enthusiastic it resulted in the Stones being evicted from the Station Hotel bar by the conservative brewery chain which owned it.

For specific events we have drawn throughout the book on the English music papers, especially *Melody Maker* and the *New Musical Express*. *Melody Maker*, begun in the thirties, is the grand old lady of the English music press and, essentially, *the* musician's paper (where you'd look in the classifieds for a bass player or a drumkit). It remained the leader until the early seventies when the *New Musical Express* was completely revamped by the then revolutionary move of hiring ex-underground writers like Charles Shaar Murray, Nick Kent, and Mick Farren.

The English music weeklies—*Disc* and *Music Echo*, as well as the two just mentioned—are as far away from the English national press as they are from American rock publications. In the sixties they were halfway between a music trade paper like *Billboard* and the later rock magazines. They were almost entirely chart-oriented and, like the Queen, gave their support to the ruling faction or fashion in pop music.

"The whole thing then," Andrew Oldham says, "was to get in the *New Musical Express* and papers like that. You could just measure your success by how many inches you'd get a week."

The weeklies' attitude toward the wayward ways of the stars was, and continued until fairly recently to be, sympathetic, amused, ironically good-natured, playful. Their articles are the most accurate record of the progress of pop music in Britain beginning with the rise of the Beatles.

Always exhibiting camaraderie in the sixties, *Melody Maker* was delighted to find itself on the side of the *Times* during the drug trials of Keith and Mick. It sent the old dowager this bouquet.

MICK JAGGER

Because the case has aroused public interest to a large degree, many national newspapers have passed comment. The Melody Maker has read them all and we find ourselves, a little surprisingly, handing not one flower but a large bouquet to The Times. For last Saturday, The Times ran a leader on the Jagger case. It was objective, informed and fair. Thankfully it lacked hysteria . . . The Melody Maker, unasked by the Rolling Stones, thanks The Times. The Melody Maker bows to The Times. The Melody Maker has a message for The Times: KEEP SWINGING!

The pop seismograph reading in the English music weeklies could have an adverse effect too, as Mick explained in the *Rolling Stones Monthly*: "There are several differences between the United States and Britain, but the one that occurs most strongly to me is over the music-business newspaper side. We've got all these weekly newspapers, all filled with news, up-to-date news, about the scene. So that means everybody catches on fast—unlike America where they just don't have these papers. So, if somebody doesn't get a hit record, it is immediately pointed out in Britain. You get these headlines like: 'Beatles toppled from No. 1 spot,' or 'Rolling Stones only at top for two weeks' or something. It makes everyone react to what's going on so much quicker. Right . . . you can say that's a good thing for British fans. But it can also kill off an artist or a group very quickly indeed—have them written off as failures. And in many cases this is done undeservedly."

The mother lode of information for the classic period of the early Stones (plus many interviews and bits of information on their childhood, background and early history) is the *Rolling Stone Monthly* series as described by Tom Beach in the fanzine *Sounds Fine*:

STONES MONTHLIES

Published by Beat Publications (who also published the Beatles monthlies). There were 30 issues between June 1964 and November 1966. They contained information on upcoming tours, recording sessions, television appearances, release dates of records, and many great photographs, most of which were never reprinted anywhere else. Each month's issue was edited by a different Stone (according to the publisher). Though this is hard to believe due to the Stones' hectic schedule in those days. Easily

obtainable by fan club members and sold at newsstands in England, these magazines were hard to obtain in the U.S. without a subscription. Some news agents in major cities did import issues, but they were not always able to get back issues. Today these monthlies are getting harder and harder to find.

In this chapter we rely mostly on primary sources: first, the members of the band commenting in their own words on the first four years of the band (either from contemporary sources or in retrospective interviews); and second, clippings from the British music papers, items from the national press and excerpts from the *Rolling Stones Monthly*. These snapshot narratives keep a purer, more direct focus on how the Stones were perceived than later histories can give with the dubious benefits of hindsight.

DAVID DALTON

THE RITES OF PAN
AT RICHMOND, 1963

On a snowy Sunday in February the Rolling Stones began their residency at the Crawdaddy Club in Richmond, run by one Giorgio Gomelsky.

Q: How did you first meet them?

GOMELSKY: Well, by that time I was the man on the scene, everybody knew that Giorgio was like a sucker for rhythm and blues so we'll go talk to him about doing this doing that, but, in fact, there weren't that many people around. Brian used to come up to me and say . . . (*whispers*) "Giorgio, you must come and hear this band, best band in London, we play rhythm and blues." I went to see them in Sutton, at the Red Lion.

Q: What was your reaction the first time you saw them?

GOMELSKY: I liked what they were doing. I said, "Listen, I promised this guy I would give him a job but the first time he goofs, you're in." And then came that famous day. Dave Hunt had a terrible problem getting everybody together, he just wasn't together, and the next Sunday they didn't turn up. I was there, it was snowing and they didn't show up. So Monday I called Ian Stewart: "Tell everybody in the band you guys are on next Sunday. This was January/February, 1963, this was the whole band.

Q: By that time, was Charlie a permanent part of the band or was he just sitting in occasionally?

GOMELSKY: Oh yes, they were definitely five, they were definitely a group then, there was no doubt about it. Mick didn't have that much to say then, really, he was sort of quiet. Actually they were six, cause Ian [Stewart] used to play the piano. The Crawdaddy in Richmond was like twelve miles away on the outskirts of London. The ABC in Ealing was on the outskirts of London but farther up north. They weren't all down the street from each other.

Q: The Crawdaddy Club was in the Station Hotel in Richmond?

GOMELSKY: It was in a pub. You just had to walk out of the room and buy a drink at the bar in the front. What we used to call a club was really the back room of a pub. The same room would be on Tuesday night a jazz club, on Thursday night a rock 'n roll club and so on. I never saw one policeman in five years at the Crawdaddy. There was no alcohol served in rock 'n roll clubs. We went upstairs to the pub or around the corner for a pint, then back for the next set.

Q: What were the Stones getting paid for a night then?

GOMELSKY: Whoever I paid, Brian or Stu, we shared everything. If there was ten pounds at the door, I kept five, I gave them five. But since I guaranteed them one pound ten shillings each, if there was ten pounds, they would get 7½ cause there was Stu, there were six of them, and I would get 2½.

Q: Did they consider you their manager? Did you have a contract?

GOMELSKY: No, no, nothing signed! I didn't know anything about the music business. I wasn't interested in making any money through the business. The first time I made any money in the club it was like £100. I put it under my bed and said, "Jesus Christ that's for a rainy day," you know, and took it out to pay for things. I couldn't believe making money from something you liked. When we went from 4, really, to later 50, 60 people the atmosphere got really great. Art students from the Kingston College of Technology and Art. Eric Clapton. It was like really a scene. The thing I loved about that period more than anything else was that you had that feeling of being in a clan of people who were sharing information and musical abilities, who were into the blues, they were into the same thing. And that is what made the whole thing gel.

Q: How did the Stones manage to develop that tremendous following in Richmond in a matter of weeks, just coming virtually out of nowhere?

GOMELSKY: We started to teach people how to react to the Stones, 'cause at first they were all standing there like this . . . immobile. We said this is ridiculous, we've got to get something going. Hamish Grimes said "How about dancing?" I said, "Sure, but you've got to do it up on the table where people can see you." Mick Jagger and the others saw Hamish doing it and said yeah! So that was the beginning of that whole real Stones thing, that Crawdaddy thing was that audience participation, opening that scene between the band and the audience and that's where the audience sort of went, wow. And so that last 45 minutes used to be *the* ritual, tribal thing. They would do like the Pretty Thing or the Crawdad for twenty minutes, it would be hypnotic. "We've got this hypnotic thing going," I said to Brian. "That's it, that's the angle." The Stones are great, but that was a ritual thing, and the Stones were nothing but ritual, really. In the end people just went berserk. All the other clubs had their wars, mods and rockers. They come to my club. Once I said, "Hey, you guys come in there, just come in and then make up your minds if you want to destroy the place or no." Cause the place was eminently destroyable! It was all glass. Then they saw all this tribal ritual going on, they were a part of it and there was no time for confrontation, you know, it was bigger than individual groups of people. And that was the angle really. Cause the Stones, man, the great supporters of the Stones were guys, young guys.

Q: Did anyone ever get up and jam with the Stones at Richmond?

GOMELSKY: Oh no, nobody ever sat in at the Crawdaddy. It wasn't sort of necessary. They wouldn't dare come up, it was too good. I mean Eric [Clapton] used to be there, watching. And the Yardbirds and all those people, watching. Before even they became a band. I cannot tell you the excitement that place was in those months. It was like all of a sudden man you hit the fucking civilization a head right on the nail, WOK! The energy was incredible, it gave everybody courage for years and years and years.

Q: Was there a stage?

GOMELSKY: No, no chairs, nothing. Couple of tables. The light was one red and one blue spot, couldn't afford anything else.

Q: At Richmond, what were the

Stones playing?

GOMELSKY: They did Jimmy Reed really well, it's not so much that Jimmy Reed is difficult, it's the *timing*, the tempo, the beat is very important: it's got to be fast/slow, you know? (*Laughs*) A fast/slow thing . . . and to keep the tension is not easy and Keith knew that inside out . . . Keith is not a great guitar player by any . . . imagination, but he is a great rhythm guitar player because he always gets on the right feel. People will cry for days saying should we do it like this (da da da) or like this (da dada) or . . . etc. Like Paul McCartney was always walking around saying (bum bum) gotta find the right feel, the feel, the feel. And that's what it's all about, the magic of the song working or a piece of music working.

Q: Mick and Keith. What were they like then?

GOMELSKY: Listen . . . I don't know . . . Keith is . . . like a child, he's a baby! Keith has never grown up, in my opinion. He's always at war! He's too much! He's a rubbery kind of person, he bounces off anything, he comes back. Nobody knows how he does it, he's always there, he's great. He's a very great character, if you went to make circus characters out of the Stones he would be the clown who is always being beaten up but gets up again, Mick would be like the white clown. Keith was the rhythm guitar player, he was putting out the fucking energy.

Q: When the Stones started out playing at clubs like the Crawdaddy, who was responsible for the musical direction and the choice of material?

BILL: It was all pretty much down to Mick, Keith and Brian who were at school together and then sharing the same flat. They were listening to stuff all the time and trying to work out things like those intricate Jimmy Reed guitar runs that interlaced, while Brian was sounding really great on those Elmore James bottle-neck runs and those exciting Bo Diddley rhythms. So as you can see it was pretty much in the hands of the three of them. Charlie and I just slotted in.

Q: Around that time, it was accepted that most British R & B bands were just performing straight cover versions of American records. Can you recall, when as a group the Rolling Stones realised that they were formulating their own identity, as opposed to being just another live jukebox?

BILL: Oh, it was quite early on when things just started to change within the band. Speaking for myself, I wasn't sticking exactly to what Chuck Berry's bass player did anymore.

For instance, when we performed "Talkin' 'Bout You" and other Berry things the rhythms would change considerably. Instead of what was on the records, which was usually eight-in-the-bar, Charlie would lay down a shuffle beat over the band, while the rest of us would play eighths, which is a very weird thing to do.

In fact we were doing that kinda thing on our last tour of America and Europe . . . playing "Let It Rock" with a shuffle and eighths at the same time, which isn't the way it has been done before.

Q: On April 21 the Stones had some

unexpected visitors.

GOMELSKY: The Beatles came to see the Stones after *Thank Your Lucky Stars* in Twickenham and my club in Richmond was on the way back from Twickenham. *Thank Your Lucky Stars* was being recorded on a Sunday. It was after the first *Thank Your Lucky Stars* the Beatles did.

The Beatles hadn't yet hit it off big, they were just like talk of the town. So anyway we were in there and we had a really good contact with them and I said, "Hey you guys, you've got to listen to this band on the way home tonight." We went down at lunchtime Sunday to talk about making this film and making a promise to meet again and one thing and another. "You've got to come and see this band when you finish recording the show, it's on the way back, you've just got to

come." "Yeah, okay, we'll come." It was like 9 o'clock, they were supposed to finish at 8:30 or 9:00 so I thought twenty minutes, half an hour, they'll be here at nine-thirty at the latest. And I didn't tell the Stones until that night, until I knew, until I came back from that thing. And the Stones used to finish at Studio 51 about 5 and about six or six-thirty they would be at the Crawdaddy which was still at the Station Hotel; have a beer, do a sound-check, have a sandwich. That's when I told them, "Hey, something nice might happen today." "What?" "The Beatles might come to . . ." Brian: (*whisper*) "What? The Beatles? You're joking! What, wha?" This was the encouragement they needed.

Q: Did anyone tape it?

GOMELSKY: Nah, well somebody must have. But it happened so fast I wasn't even aware of selling the media or any of that shit. The idea came to actually if I can sell the Beatles coming down it's great, if not fuck it. And it just happened having lunch I just said, "By the way, come down, don't forget," and they came. The club used to open at seven, the Stones used to go on first time eight-fifteen to nine o'clock. Then a break, have to finish by ten-thirty, Sunday pubs close, and out of the place by eleven. So first set they didn't come. Brian came and said "They didn't come, they didn't come." I said "Brian I told you they're prob-

ably finishing now they'll be here nine-fifteen nine-thirty." He said all right, he was so nervous. When the Beatles came down we ended up at Edith Grove, spent the whole night, and four days later they were doing the Albert Hall and that's when Brian started having the whole idea. Mick was still at the London School of Economics, you know. Bill was still working in the brewery. And that's when Brian started having the whole idea of being a star. Brian didn't work, he had that girl working for him, for eight pounds a week, had a child from . . . the cross-eyed girl, ugly little thing from Cheltenham. Their apartment was a bit of a strange thing, Keith's mother used to come once a week with fresh shirts for Keith. When we used to go out fly posting we used to buy glue and often we ended up with more glue than we needed so all that glue was put in the bathtub in the bathroom of the apartment and after a while trees were coming out of that glue. Everything was thrown in there, this glue was kind of growing out of the bathroom into the kitchen and everywhere, it was crazy. Brian was very desperate, he really wanted to make it quickly, quick, quick, he was impatient. Just after I got him together with the Beatles, we ended up at the Albert Hall, invited by the Beatles to watch the concert. Later, we were carrying the equipment out and we came out of the stage door and the girls there mobbed Brian thinking he was one of the Beatles. And on the way out of the Albert Hall—down the stairs to the back was my apartment—Brian told me, "Giorgio, *that is what I want.*" He didn't enlighten the girls as to who he was, or wasn't!

Q: How did Mick go from this obsession for R & B to becoming almost detached from his "roots?"

GOMELSKY: Because the stage being such a tremendous altar, you know, of pleasure for Mick, he'd do anything to keep it that way. So, the press and everybody pick on him, and he finally had some power, and he found that he could invent for the world what . . . came to his mind to invent! And then he started conceptualizing him and the Stones and that's where the authenticity . . .

Q: So what was it in the Stones that created all that insanity? That first piece by Barry May, that piece in the *Twickenham Times* it makes the scene going on at the Station Hotel sound positively orgiastic!

GOMELSKY: It's blood, it's circulating, makes you want to circulate. That's it, that comes from the ritual thing, you know, and in my Diaghilevian underground manner that's what I've encouraged ever since I've been involved with musicians. That's what I think music will do, it's that catharsis, it's that purification, it's that participation, kind of participatory orgasm. I've seen people, I'm not lying, I wish I had photographic documentation, when we moved the Crawdaddy from the Station Hotel to the Richmond Athletic Association grounds, one wall grandstand like this, room for 500 to 1200, stage was beer cases with planks on them. And they usually had to bring the cases and planks in themselves, you go up and build the stage, you guys. The greatest pleasure when I see a musician carrying his amp, I say HEY! Nowadays . . .

Q: That kind of excitement, though, has to be connected to something other than twelve bar blues.

GOMELSKY: You're going back to being a macumba person, going back to being a shaman, going back to be a priest, going back to be a healer, which is what a musician should be, he should frighten you then he should heal you, in my opinion! That's the whole process of art: frighten you, dispossess you of your references and then give you new ones if you can look for long enough. See what there is to be seen. In a strange way that is what made the Stones and the whole blues movement in England then, for me; analyzing as a social psychologist. There was union between sensibilities and that created a strength, an affirmation which came totally naturally, which was not structured physically or educationally, it just came out of the visceral consciousness of the people at the time. And music should bring this out in people.

Andrew Loog Oldham tells how he first met the Stones, in an interview in the *New Musical Express*:

OLDHAM: I was working for Epstein at the time. I was handling the press side for him from the record after the Beatles' "Love Me Do" . . . "Please Please Me." Then I did the publicity for the Beatles' next single.

One evening I was drinking with an editor of one of the pop papers down in Shaftesbury Avenue and he told me I should go and see this group down in Richmond. It was as simple as that. I was probably 48 hours ahead of the rest of the business in getting there. But that's the way God planned it.

Q: Which club did you see the Stones in?

OLDHAM: The Station Hotel.

Q: And they made an immediate impact on you?

OLDHAM: Yeah.

Q: Can you pin down the things that excited you about them?

OLDHAM: Music. Sex. The fact that in just a few months the country would need an opposite to what the Beatles were doing.

I remember seeing the Beatles in Doncaster when they were about eighth on the bill to people like Helen Shapiro and Tommy Roe. I sat there with a lump in my throat. In just one night you know they were going to be very big. It was just an instinctive thing.

From that night on it registered subconsciously that when they made it, another section of the public were gonna want an opposite. The Stones were gonna be that opposite.

That's the way it worked out. In the early days, the way the media was running was that you could invite the Beatles in for tea, but you couldn't invite the Stones.

Oldham added, in the BBC's *Rolling Stone Story*: "It was very rigid, the setup the first time I saw them. They were very much into sort of a blues roots thing. There was no production to the act at all. Everyone sat on stools and played very comfortably and saying 'Just listen to what I'm playing,' and I went down there at a time when I was renting with an agent, Eric Easton, and I intimidated his interest in the group although he felt at the time that one of the members we should get rid of was Mick Jagger because technically 'Mick Jagger could not sing.' "

On May 3 Oldham and Easton made an exclusive management agreement with the Stones. Giorgio's father died in the middle of April and he flew to Switzerland to make arrangements for the funeral and be with his family. By the time he returned, the Stones had been signed to Impact Sound, the company Oldham and Easton had formed to supervise their recording sessions.

GOMELSKY: Brian would do anything. They wanted to get money for stage gear and shit like that and I was telling them, 'Don't wait for the money to come from outside. You're going to have to give things away, you know.

Let's earn it ourselves, let's be independent, let's keep out a bit, let's pull the belt another couple of months and we'll be our own bosses and we don't have to do deals with people' . . . Anyway, Brian wanted to be the star so badly, much worse than Mick or the others. Don't forget Brian was in London totally on his own, with Pat and his child, no money coming in 'cause he was incapable of working. The others all went to school, had parents and everything, jobs. Brian was very desperate, he really wanted to make it quickly, quick, quick; he was impatient. So he would do anything to make it.

I showed the Stones the rushes of movie I had made originally to get Peter Jones from the N.M.E. (*New Musical Express*) down to see them, and Andrew Oldham came. Brian said to me, "I want you to meet this friend of mine, I went to school with him, he wants to help us," blah blah blah. . . . So Andrew came and saw the

Photo Dick Bucans.

5 31/10   ↑ 531/9   5 31/12   ↑ 531/11

movie and we went to the pub and we talked. And it appeared a few weeks later that they had signed.

At the end of January and the beginning of February the Stones cut five sides at the IBC studios and before they could sign with Decca, Oldham had to buy them back.

GLOMELSKY: Brian came to me and said, "What are we going to do? IBC gave us the time, so they own those tapes." So I told him to go to IBC and tell them the group is splitting up and you just want to get the tapes back for your own collection."

Eventually the tapes were bought back for £90 put up by Eric Easton.

A week after signing, on May 10, the Stones cut their first single, Chuck Berry's "Come On," at Olympic Studios with Andrew as producer and Roger Savage as engineer.

OLDHAM: At the end of that first recording session I went, "Hmmm, right, let's go." And the engineer said to me, "What about mixing it?" I said, "What's that?" and he looked at me like "What the fuck is this?" I think he tried to be as nice about it as possible. The thing was that everybody in the group was just as interested to hear what mixing was. So he said, "Well, you know we have four tracks and in order for it to become a record we have to get it down to one." I said, "Oh, you do that, I'll come back in the morning," figuring that if I stay it will probably take longer.

After that experience we decided that was too complicated and we went to recording in mono.

One of the reasons "Come On" was chosen is that it hadn't been released in Britain, which virtually eliminated the possibility of it being covered by another group.

MICK: I don't think "Come On" was very good, in fact it was shit . . . God knows how it ever got in the charts, it was such a hype.

In fact we disliked it so much we didn't do it on any of our gigs.

The Stones, used to the atmosphere of clubs, did an accelerated "Come On" in barely 1¾ minutes. Decca pronounced the results of the first three-hour session "dreadful" and Dick Rowe suggested they try again at the Decca Studios in West Hampstead. At the next session they also cut the B side, Willie Dixon's "I Wanna Be Loved."

"Come On"/"I Wanna Be Loved" was released June 7 and got on *Disc*'s Top 30 the week it was released.

A week later *Disc* also predicted success, of a sort: "There's such a rush on for this sort of group noise that I believe this quintet will be making plenty of room for themselves . . . I

particularly like Brian Jones' work on mouth organ.

Record Minor was cautious: "A bluesy commercial group that should make the charts in a small way."

Ten years later, when "Come On" was finally released in the U.S., Robert Palmer gave a more sophisticated account:

"The Chuck Berry 'Come On' has a loping beat that curiously prefigures reggae. Jagger sounds timid in the studio and the key change bridge is as corny as they come but the tune really moves along." (*Rolling Stone*, February 1973)

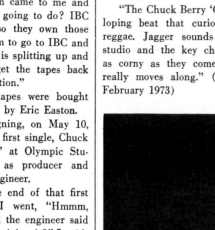

The day their first record was released the Stones appeared on *Thank Your Lucky Stars*. Oldham had tucked them into matching houndstooth jackets with velvet collars, a legendary incident that almost caused a rift between him and the Stones. Oldham felt he was on his own "dividing line between art and commerce." He added: "There were a couple of compromises that had to be made at first. Someone even said we would have to get rid of the lead singer because he would never pass a BBC audition . . . We compromised to the extent of wearing some sort of uniform. We knew we had to. 'Come

On' was no great melody, it was just a good riff.

"The TV people were used to dealing with groups like the Searchers and Swinging Blue Jeans. If the Stones had dressed the way they wanted, they wouldn't have been allowed inside the building. So they all wore those checked jackets. But we got rid of them as soon as we could."

This momentary appeasement was prematurely—and briefly—seen by the press as a sign of healthy conformity.

KEITH: It's funny . . . people think Oldham made the image, but he tried to tidy us up. He fought it. Absolutely.

There are photographs of us in suits he put us in, those dogtooth checked suits with the black velvet collars. Everybody's got black pants, and a tie and a shirt. For a month on the first tour, we said, "All right. We'll do it You know the game. We'll try it out." But then the Stones thing started taking over. Charlie'd leave his jacket in some dressing room and I'd pull mine out and there'd be whiskey stains all over it or chocolate pudding.

But tidying up the Stones was a fruitless task. It was also counterproductive to the Stones propaganda. Their image, as the "bad boy" foil to

the Beatles, was classically orchestrated by Oldham. He didn't need to custom-tailor it, it was readymade. If Andrew resisted at first, he soon got the picture. According to Keith, "Andrew wasn't ahead of us in that respect from the beginning—the press picked up on us only when we'd personally got rid of those dogtooth jackets and the Lord John shirts. It was only then that Andrew suddenly realized the full consequences of it all and got fully behind it. After that the press did all the work for us. We only needed to be refused admission in a hotel and that set the whole thing rolling."

By the end of July "Come On" reached Number 26 in the NME Charts, one peg below Freddie and the Dreamers' "If You've Got To Make A Fool Of Somebody" and one above the Beatles "From Me To You." "Da Doo-Ron Ron" was No. 5, the Searchers were No. 1 with "Sweets From My Sweets," the Beatles, 6th, with "Twist and Shout." Lesley Gore's "It's My Party" and Ray Charles' "Take These Chains From My Heart" tied for No. 10, The Surfaris No. 18 with "Wipe Out" and Buddy Holly's "Bo Diddley" was No. 20.

June 13th the Stones got their first mention in the national press.

If "Bad news is good news for the Stones" was soon to become Andrew's slogan, in this case good news was bad luck for Giorgio and the Stones.

GOMELSKY: Pat Doncaster from the *Daily Mirror* did an incredible article, a whole page on the Stones and the wild atmosphere at Richmond. Then the secretary of the Ind-Coope breweries saw the article, and said: "Is that OUR station hotel in Richmond?" Yes it was, so they said: "Close it down immediately." So I had to find another place.

As for "Come On," it never got above the lower levels on the charts. Also, the Stones were not recording the R & B they loved, but more commercial numbers.

Mick was already perfecting his Southern drawl here—"Come awn . . ." And the tone of the song, in the genre of "Too Much Monkey Business," is that of sheer frustration: "Couldn't get my car started/Laid off from my job and I can't afford to check it/I wish somebody'd come along and run into it and wreck it." Berry can barely conceal his fury, underlined by J.C. Davis' smouldering sax, but as in most frustration blues of the fifties, he has to console himself with "baby." Although the Stones' version, for the first and last time, is milder (for "some stupid jerk trying to reach another number," they substitute "some guy"), and Mick is not in control of the vocal as much as Berry. It's what the Stones did with

this kind of song that created political idiom in rock.

BILL: You only have to look at the stuff we had recorded at IBC to see the direction Andrew was nudging us. We had recorded mostly blues there: "Bright Lights, Big City," "Honey What's Wrong," "I Want To Be Loved" and two Bo Diddley numbers, you can find them floating around on a few bootlegs. But we couldn't get a record deal, so we had to do commercial songs and we did. We still wanted to play blues music and we did do it live. It really was our roots. It wasn't an endeavor to make everybody know

we were a blues band. We really wanted to play our songs on the original basis.

In mid-July Bo Diddley was added to the Stones' tour wtih the Everly Brothers:

BO DIDDLEY SIGNED FOR EVERLY BROTHERS TOUR

American singer-guitarist Bo Diddley will join the Everly Brothers on their autumn tour of Britain. New concert and television dates here are being

negotiated for Chubby Checker next month. Johnny Cash is confirmed for an Irish tour and two dates in England. These are the latest plans for American visitors.

The Everly Brothers' tour opens at the New Victoria on September 29 and continues for 30 dates, as previously reported. Bo Diddley is a leading rhythm-and-blues singer in the U.S., and wrote the song to which he gave his name. It has been recorded by many other artists, including Buddy Holly's current hit.

Diddley will be making his British debut.

On August 5 the Stones hit the ballroom circuit for the first time.

BILL: When we started, we were just playing blues and rhythm-and-blues because that's what we liked. We were playing it well and nobody else was doing it. We were doing up to three-hour sets.

When we went into the ballrooms in the autumn of '63 we soon found out that you couldn't play such things as those slow Jimmy Reed blues-type numbers. You were expected to play music for them to dance to, but they stood there in front of you and gaped.

So at that time, we started concentrating on much more up-tempo songs . . . fast rhythm things . . . hard rockers which seemed to work out quite well. (*Go-Set*)

A second feature on the "unique" Stones appeared in the *New Musical Express* on August 23 by Chris Williams:

ROLLING STONES R AND B CHAMPS

The Rolling Stones is a London group with the Liverpool sound, according to some.

Rhythm-and-blues fans say they are the only British combo which bears comparison with American R & B units.

Their own opinion is simply that they are unique! Spokesman Brian Jones, who sings and plays harmonica, says: "We believe that we sound like ourselves and no one else."

They are, they claim, first and foremost a rhythm-and-blues group. If you refer to them as a beat outfit, they frown. If you venture to suggest that they play rock 'n roll, they positively glower.

In appearances on stage they seem

to resemble long-haired dervishes. Why the haircuts? Again Brian Jones explains: "We've had it like this for ages," he says patting his own luxurious bob cut.

"Though we didn't grow it this way as a gimmick, we see no reason why we should cut it off to conform."

Their music reflects this freedom. All keen R & B fans, they started off playing solid, earthy Muddy Waters stuff. Lately, though, their repertoire has included more generally popular material, by people like Chuck Berry and the Drifters.

On September 29 the Stones began their first big tour, with the Everly Brothers. Bo Diddley, with "The Duchess" and Jerome, Julie Grant, the Flintstones and Bob Bain. On October 5 Little Richard was flown in from the States to boost box-office returns. In deference to the master the Stones dropped all Bo Diddley numbers from the set.

MICK: In the beginning, they [the Beatles] were so enormous, and we were just playing small clubs. It was weird because they came down to see us a couple of times and invited us to one of their gigs at the Albert Hall, which we went to. It was incredible for us to watch. I'd never seen hysteria on that level before, and I didn't know at the time that I was going to see it every night for the

next three years. We were so turned on by those riots. . . . well it was great that they were around because their presence took the edge off all the teen mania for us. It gave us exactly a reason not to get caught up in that whole "pre-packaged moptop" deal for which I'm very thankful. It must have been such a drag for them.

Afterward, that indelible image floated hypnotically in their Stony Skulls. From then on there was no turning back.

Q: Was there a problem with the Stones in the beginning because they were five guys who thought they were an R & B band, unlike the Beatles, who were into pop? They were very serious about the blues at that time, weren't they?

OLDHAM: Well, not *that* serious. In terms of me saying to them, "Well, we're going to make a single, play me the five things you think are most commercial"—they knew we were dealing with reality.

Before the Beatles showed up with "I Wanna Be Your Man," the Stones had considered releasing "Poison Ivy" as their next single with "Fortune Teller" as the B side. Decca gave it a catalog number but no discs were pressed and it was canceled. The sides would turn up four months later on the BBC's "Saturday Club" compilation album.

Andrew Oldham, suffering from psycholithic poisoning, left abruptly for France, leaving in Easton's hands the fate of the Stones' first hit single.

Q: How did you come to record "I Wanna Be Your Man," the Beatle's thing?

MICK: Well, we knew them by then and we were rehearsing and Andrew brought Paul and John down to the rehearsal. They said they had this tune, they were really hustlers then. I mean the way they used to hustle tunes was great: "Hey Mick, we've got this great song." (*done with a John Lennon accent*) So they played it and we thought it sounded pretty commercial, which is what we were looking for, so we did it like Elmore James or something. I haven't heard it for ages but it must be pretty freaky 'cause nobody really produced it. The guy who happened to be our manager at the time was a 50-year-old northern mill owner [Eric Easton]. It was completely crackers, but it was a hit and sounded great onstage.

Mick has a few friendly words for the Fab Four (it was they, after all, who first planted the pernicious notion that they could pen their *own* platters) : "Even though people don't like

giving them credit for it now, these days, because they're gone and they're passé almost, the Beatles told me we could write our own songs and I said 'Oh! You're right, that's a good idea.' Around that period, you remember, which I very rarely do. Everyone used to just do all those records, redo hits, even hits like standards which no one had heard except a few rock bands which was like for instance 'Money,' 'Some Other Guy,' 'Mashed Potatoes.' But then you got the feeling you had to write your own thing because you were running out of them. So we just started writing, but never really wrote any blues numbers to start off with; well, kind of, the things we wrote were more like ballads or like pop songs; more of the pop variety which came naturally to us . . . rather than writing the original blues which is very difficult to write, actually. It's very difficult to write good original blues even now. Ask any blues singer, whatever color. It just is. But I'm not writing pop songs which was really what we started writing. The

first song we ever wrote was called 'It Should Be You.' "

Q: So when did you start to incorporate original material into your programme?

KEITH: Oh, I don't know. Like a lot of things it just happened. For instance, our second single was the Beatles "I Wanna Be Your Man" and the B-side of that was something that the group put together called "Stoned." It was nothing more than just a nick off Booker T's "Green Onions." (*Go-Set*, August 3, 1972)

"STONED"

The famous Nanker-Phelge name only started when the Stones came to record the B side of their second single "I Wanna Be Your Man." This track was recorded in Kingsway Studios, opposite Holborn Tube Station in central London. The studio had only been booked for a few hours and when a good take of the A side had been put in the can there was very little time left to do a B side. Eric Easton recalls that he said to the Stones "Come on, we've only half-an-hour left so let's do a quick 12-bar Blues." Everyone duly punched straight into the usual chord sequence with Mick adding some words whenever he felt like it. That number, of course, was "Stoned."

All the Stones, plus Ian Stewart, who had also played on the take, were given an equal share in the song-writing royalties, and Brian Jones suggested that they call it a Nanker-Phelge composition. "As far as I can remember now," recalls Eric Easton, "there was some bloke the boys came across while they were living in Edith Grove, Chelsea, called Phelge who the boys thought was a bit of a 'name,' and this led to —in some people's opinion—that horrible face they used to pull for certain photographers and to the name Nanker-Phelge."

(*Beat Instrumental*)

"Stoned" (misspelt "Stones" on the first few hundred pressings) was originally planned as the Stones first U.S. single but "pressures were brought to bear to have it withdrawn instantly on moral grounds."

It was still being played on the radio in Denmark as late as November 1965, a Scandanavian Stones fan reported in issue 19 of the *Monthly*.

On November 6 "I Wanna Be Your Man" thrust itself into the *Disc* charts at number 30, getting a good review in *Disc* also.

On November 15 the Stones were banner headliners on the cover of the *New Musical Express* and there was a heartwarming story just in time for Christmas within.

STONE US! LIVERPOOL NODS TO LONDON!

The Iron Curtain has been breached, friendly relations have at last been established and representatives from London have succeeded in creating goodwill in the opposition's capital! Don't worry, this isn't a political commentary—and I'm not even discussing the Anglo-Russian situation.

I am referrng to the invisible barrier which has for so long divided London and Liverpool and which the Rolling Stones have finally penetrated.

Not only have the Londoners won the hearts of all northern fans following their two visits to the hub of the Liverpop entertainment scene, the Cavern Club, but they have also entered into a coalition with the Beatles, because the Rolling Stones' new chart entry was written by John Lennon and Paul McCartney!

DAVID DALTON

R & B Band Blitz Brit Music Biz

The English record industry has an almost Chinese predilection for naming years—not for mythological animals, but for pop stars. If 1963 had been the Year of the Beatles, 1964 would be the Year of the Stones.

The Stones had been playing as a unit for almost a year by January of 1964. Within a month they would have their first hit single, "Not Fade Away"; by the beginning of April their LP would knock the Beatles off the charts, break the Beatles' phenomenal record for first-day sales of an album and, during the year, "pip" the Beatles in all British popularity polls.

Brian and Dave Hassinger at the RCA Studios, Hollywood.

Not only were the Stones more prolific than they ever would be again, releasing some fifty *different* tracks (on two English EPs, three English and five U.S. singles, an English and two U.S. LPs), they broke the one-night-stand record for an English band (only 22 days off in the whole year!) and by the end of the year had established themselves in the Rock 'n Roll Hall of Fame.

On January 17 the Stones released their first EP, *The Rolling Stones*, containing four "cover" versions of American hits. Three of the tracks, "You Better Move On," "Money" and "Bye, Bye Johnny," had been cut at Kingsway Studios on September 14 and 15 of the previous year, before their first British tour, and were produced by their co-manager Eric Easton. The Stones had cut two versions of "Poison Ivy," twice each at Decca's West Hampstead Studios in late July and early August 1963 with Andrew Oldham as producer. Because of the delayed release of the EP, both versions were released in January. The first version appears on the LP of the BBC SATURDAY CLUB anthology, the second version on the EP.

Altogether, "Poison Ivy" had been cut four times by the Stones. For a while, before Lennon and McCartney had given them "I Wanna Be Your Man," they had considered "Poison Ivy" and "Fortune Teller" as a follow-up to their first single, "Come On," but they were never really satisfied with their takes. Even though Decca was also dissatisfied with the selection and sound quality, they got as far as giving it a catalogue number (F56117) but it was subsequently cancelled. "Poison Ivy" is easily the most (unintentionally) comical track on the EP as Mick, in a series of vocal contortions, tries to get a bite on the word "around" in the chorus, "sounding," wrote Robert Palmer, "like an amplified jew's-harp."

You can hear the Human Riff shifting gears expertly on Chuck Berry's "Bye, Bye Johnny," matching the master lick for lick. Keith and Brian's guitars mesh impeccably on this track in the dual guitar style that was to become the trademark of the Stones sound; "a definition-in-action of rock & roll" as Robert Palmer described it in his review of *More Hot Rocks*, the collection on which this song was first released in the States in 1972. "You Better Move On" could well have held its own as a single and many fans bought the EP for this track alone. It became one of the most requested (and crowd-inciting) numbers on their upcoming British tours. It has the classic Stones R & B treatment, tasty guitar/drum dialogues, Mick's plaintive/assertive vocal and roughly sketched-in harmonies. Ironically die-hard Stones R & B fans put it down as a concession to the pop market.

Perhaps the most requested number on the EP is the slowest—"You Better Move On." But a lot of people have been decrying it as not R & B.

Mike [sic] answered the critics: "It is an Arthur Alexander number, and as much R & B as 'Memphis' or 'Road Runner.' We have been using it in our act for ages and it has always gone down well; that's why we decided to record it." (New Musical Express)

However primitive the early Stones' productions were, the sound they put down in the studio was unique. Their recording procedure represented a radical departure. Control over production by the artist, as Keith explains, that was unheard of in the English music business, "because up until the Beatles and ourselves got into records, the cat who was singing had absolutely no control, man. None at all. He had no say in the studio. The backing track was laid down by session men, under the A and R man, artists and repertoire, whatever the fuck that means. He controlled the artist and the material. Bobby Vee or Billy Fury just laid down the vocal. They weren't allowed to go into the booth and say, 'I want my voice to sound like this or I want the guitar to sound like this.' The man from the record company decided what went where." (*Rolling Stone*)

In January the Stones got top billing for the first time on the *Group Scene 1964* tour of Britain (January

6–27) with the Ronettes, the Swinging Blue Jeans, Marty Wilde and the Wildcats, Dave Berry and the Cruisers, the Cheynes (a year later Bill Wyman produced their single "Down and Out" and wrote "Stop Running Round" for the B side) and Al Paige.

Ronnie Spector recalls Mick's effect on his audiences (girls) on that tour: "The Beatles were just four guys who stood there with their guitars. But the Stones were always different. They were more of a threat. They did gutsy things onstage. Mick was such a good mover. The girls took to Mick. He was so sexy, provocative and gorgeous onstage." (Barbara Charone, *Keith Richards*.)

THOSE RONETTES SET THE STONES ROLLING!

Three long-haired dusky girls (the Ronettes) and five mop-haired boys (the Rolling Stones) met each other for the first time but a short while ago—and suddenly, the Rolling Stones stopped rolling.

"Those Ronettes just stopped us dead in our tracks" smiles Stone No. 1, vocalist Mike [sic] Jagger. **"We were just knocked out—by their looks, their sense of humour, everything."**

How did this flourishing Mutual Admiration Society come about? Modestly, Stone Keith Richard gives most of the credit for this to the Ronettes.

"You couldn't really say the girls have different personalities. Ronnie and Estelle are just as friendly. In fact, they're all right little darlings!"

Fascinated by the smoochy Phil Spector sound on "Be My Baby" and "Baby I Love You," the Stones are looking forward to meeting Spector when he flies into Britain this week.

Big in States

Said Estelle, a quiet-spoken girl whose smile brought hard-bitten reporters flocking around in droves: "We just love that number, 'I Wanna Be Your Man.' It's got real go."

Said Nedra, smoothing down a crease in her tight-fitting dress: "We just never guessed they'd be so informal."

She beamed mischievously as the group's young co-manager (and, some say, the Phil Spector of British pop) Andrew Oldham—now making discs himself—came into the room.

". . . In fact, we like them almost as much as their manager. And he's not only a real nice person; he makes good records, too."

(New Musical Express)

Phil Spector, who's no fool, didn't want things to get *too* cozy on the road, and, according to Ronnie, sent a telegram before the Ronettes joined the tour, saying: "STAY AWAY FROM MY GIRLS." Predictably, this produced the opposite effect. "After we saw that," says Ronnie, "we became the best of friends."

Keith said: "There was no direct competition within the band for pulling chicks. The only time I remember Mick and I in any *slight* competition was with the Ronettes when Mick wanted to pull Ronnie and ended up with her sister Estelle." (Barbara Charone, *Keith Richards*.)

Spector flew to London at the end of January to attend the legendary sessions at Regent Sound where the Stones cut their first album. "Not Fade Away," as well as a number of as yet unreleased songs that have turned up on bootlegs over the years, were recorded at Regent in mid-February. (The most infamous of these is "Andrew's Blues," also known as "And the Rolling Stones Met Gene and Phil" or "Mr. Spector and Mr. Pitney Came Too.") Among those who attended these sessions were Phil Spector, Gene Pitney, and Graham Nash and other members of the Hollies. Spector magnificently mimics the marble-mouthed mutterings of Sir Edward Lewis (the head of Decca Records); he also sings the verses and does a takeoff on Andrew!

ANDREW'S BLUES

Well now Andrew Oldham
Sittin on a hill with Jack 'n' Jill
He fucked all night
'N' he sucked all night
'N' he taste that pussy
Till it taste just right

Whoa whoa Andrew
Oh oh Andrew
Come 'n' get it little Andrew
Before Sir Edward
Takes it away
From you

MICK:
    Come on get up front, Sir Edward,
    Come on now
SIR EDWARD VOICE (SPECTOR):
    Play the blues everybody
    Play the blues
PHIL SPECTOR:
    The Rolling Stones
    are a great fucking group
SIR EDWARD VOICE (MICK):
    What a load of balls
    Phil Spector is full of shit
PHIL SPECTOR:
    I thought the Rolling Stones were
    full of shit
    Then I heard the group
    Now I know
    They're full of shit

Ian "Stew" Stewart unloading the boys gear.

Got my Beatle shoes on
And I'm just raring to go
Oh Andrew (yes Andrew)
Oh Andrew yeah
Uh uh uhuh
Uh uh uh uhuh (etc.)

"Not Fade Away" was an obvious choice for the English market. Andrew could smell a hit:

ANDREW: Although it was a Buddy Holly song, I considered it to be like the first song Mick and Keith "wrote," in that they picked the concept of applying that Bo Diddley thing to it. The way they arranged it was the beginning of the shaping of them as songwriters. From then on they wrote.

At that time, Mick, Keith, and I were living together. They were into the last half bottle of wine and going through it—it was one of those magical moments. When Keith played that to me in the front room you could actually *hear* the record in the room.

What basically made the record was that whole Bo Diddley acoustic guitar crust. You *heard* the *whole* record in one room. "We gotta record it." But there's no way if someone had just said coldly "Right, let's do 'Not Fade Away'" that we would have wanted to do it without hearing the way that Keith was playing it on the guitar. Keith just *did* it. And *that* was that. To me, they wrote that song. It's a pity we couldn't have gotten the money. (*Trouser Press*)

But it may have been Andrew's almost total ignorance of R & B that led him to believe Keith's arrangement was so drastically different as to make it virtually his own song. As Bill Wyman points out, Holly borrowed that "guitar crust" from Bo Diddley in the first place. Keith, as was to be his manner of working from now on, had simply returned to the roots.

Bill: "Keith played guitar on that track, Brian the harmonica. The rhythm thing was formed basically around the Buddy Holly song. We brought the rhythm up and emphasized it. Holly had used that Bo Diddley trademark beat on his version, but because he was only using bass, drums and guitar, the rhythm element is sort of a throwaway. Holly played it very *lightly*. We just got into it more and put the Bo Diddley beat up front."

On the flip side was the Jimmy Reed influenced "Little By Little," co-written by the Stones (under the group name, Phelge) and Phil Spector. Spector also plays maracas on it and Ian Stewart "is heard on piano."

"The first takes of 'Not Fade Away' were too fast," said Oldham. "It's a common error among performing groups not familiar with recording in the studio. 'Come On' for instance, they took too much too fast. I insisted

on them slowing it down. This time it worked."

February 21: "Not Fade Away"/ "Little By Little" was released and for the first time music columnists predicted a hit. The new record was a marked improvement over their previous recordings, but the change in the columnists' attitude had come in part from the impact of the Stones' press. Because the Beatles were an already established group and the Stones, at the beginning of 1964, were virtually unknown, comparisons between the two could only work to the Stones' advantage. The press was programmed in a subtle, or often not so subtle manner, by Andrew's Law: for every star there is an anti-star. For every Elvis there is a Pat Boone, for every Cliff Richard there is a Billy Fury, for every Beatles there must be a Rolling Stones.

When "Not Fade Away" hit the charts the Top Ten was dominated by Merseybeat. Cilla Black had the No. 1 spot with "Anyone Who Had A Heart." Second were the Searchers. Gerry and the Pacemakers were fourth and the Merseybeats and the Swinging Blue Jeans were also in the Top Ten.

England had exchanged the syrupy American balladeers, the "Bobbys," for Liverpool Pollyannas. You *can* have too much of a good thing, especially the new mutant generation of mods and your "disaffected youth from the council houses." Yer mums and dads were becoming dangerously "comfy" with the Fab Four.

The group's press was already bearing out Oldham's self-fulfilling prophecy: "The Stones are the group parents love to hate."

Beatlemania was sweeping the States in February '64 as the Stones slipped noisily into the charts. The Stones' EP was still in the Top Twenty when they released their first single of the year.

The Stones method of recording tracks as raw and as close to live as possible was not exactly Phil Spector's idea of production. The Stones' sound came closer to a "wall of noise" than Spector's "wall of sound," which, as Keith was to discover sometime later was built of strings: "Spector was a big American record producer, kind of just another person that Andrew wanted you to meet. Although I really dug his sound, those records. Always wanted to know how he got such a big sound, and when I found out it was a 170-piece orchestra, OK."

While not denying Spector's influence on him, Oldham rightly points out their basic difference in attitude to production: "Well, Spector came in during the sessions of 'Not Fade Away.' His contribution was production, but it was also not production,

Giorgio Gomelsky emcees at the Richmond Jazz & Blues Festival.

in a sense. I'm not detracting from his influence on me—or on anybody—but his influence in that particular instance was more in spirit, because the reality of watching him work, apart from liking his records, had nothing to do with the way we worked just by virtue of the fact that the Rolling Stones were a band. When you walk into a studio and hear Bill Medley's part and then you hear this rather squeaking voice which was him because the two of them [The Righteous Brothers] wouldn't go into a studio at the same time, you know that his trip's got nothing to do with what you're doing. But his spirit was definitely a great asset to that session." (*Trouser Press*, June 1978)

Keith's relationship with Spector was colored by matters other than music: "Phil Spector is, was and always will be a complete weirdo. From 'To Know Him Is To Love Him' onwards. I mean, I used to hang around with Ronnie back then. She was really Phil's girl of course, he being that colossal Svengali-figure. But still, I mean, when Mick and I got to New York, first thing we'd do is get a cab down to Harlem—127th Street, it was, and . . . uh . . . 'get it on,' so to speak. But at the same time we'd be recording with Jack Nitzsche who we all know was Phil's arranger. And Phil would be there hiding somewhere in the studio just glowering at me. He's just a very, very jealous guy." (*Zigzag*)

Spector's major contribution to the Stones sound was his suggestion that they get into an American recording studio as soon as possible. Through his contacts he set up the Stones sessions at Chess that summer and at RCA in Hollywood in the Fall.

Nevertheless the Regent Sound tracks are considerably "brighter" than the Stones' previous releases. The guitars are crisper, the rhythm tracks have been brought up. The separation is better and there is a sophisticated use of echo as well as other techniques. Any or all of this could be ascribed to Spector's presence at the sessions, but it was his being there at all which helped draw press attention to the Stones' new single:

THE SPECTOR SOUND

The Rolling Stones' latest single "Not Fade Away" was originally recorded by the Crickets. But there is the world of difference between the two versions.

Keith Richard explained the situation: "We had been working on the number for about five minutes when two of the Hollies turned up, then Gene Pitney arrived. Phil Spector was already there, so everything came to a halt while everyone started talking.

"When we got around to recording again, Phil had grabbed hold of Mike's maracas and was shaking the daylights out of them. He really had a ball, and it's him you hear on the disc."

Tapes

If that sounds a remarkable way of conducting a recording session, listen to what Andrew says about the "B" side, "Little By Little."

"After we had done 'Not Fade Away,' Phil and Mike diappeared," he began. "Nobody noticed they had gone until about five minutes later when they returned, looking very pleased with themselves. They sat down, told me to listen, and played the number

they had just written in the outside corridor.

"It was very good, so we decided to use it as the 'B' side. Mike took hold of his harmonica, Phil found the maracas again, and Gene Pitney and the Stones' road manager, Ian Stewart, sat down at the same piano. It was a fantastic scene!"

All the early songs written by Mick and Keith were ballads, and gooey ones at that. Demos of some of these songs can be heard on the compilation album *Metamorphosis*, released by Abkco Records in 1975: "Each And Every Day Of The Year," "I'd Much Rather Be With The Boys" (written by Richards and Oldham), "(Walkin' Thru The) Sleepy City," and "Try A Little Harder." All were sung by Mick and "sweetened" with lush string arrangements and optimistic back-up vocals. Mick and Keith had no intention of recording these gelatinous compositions with the Stones. But Andrew, who had always been very much a "song" man in the Brill Building tradition, had a plan. Flog 'em to someone else!

Andrew had, by the beginning of 1964, managed to peddle two particularly insipid Jagger/Richards songs, "It Should Be You" (the first song Mick and Keith ever wrote) and "Will You Be My Lover Tonight," to the late George Bean, who released them with little chart action as the B and A sides respectively of a single in January.

The next songwriting effort by Mick and Keith, however, was to have spectacular results. Andrew was handling Gene Pitney's publicity in late 1963. A resourceful mod hustler, Oldham was ready to try anything. Here was Pop Hitmaker Pitney with a series of hit singles in the U.S. Top Ten! (two of his most recent sides, incidentally, had been produced by Spector). And weren't his apartment mates, Mick and Keith, budding songsmiths from Hammersmith? Sly old Andrew knew some good must come of it. Standing at this crossroads Andrew supposedly confided: "Before long, I reckon these two acts are going to be of real value to each other. Dunno how, right now. But I've got a feeling that they'll work closely together sometime, somehow."

Pitney said of his first encounter with the Stones: "When I met them I didn't know whether to shake hands or bark!" But then canine quips came easily to a man of whose piercing falsetto one journalist had written: "Pitney hits notes that only dogs and recording managers can hear."

Ten years later, on the BBC, Pitney described the session this way:

They had a song that I recorded and it was "That Girl Belongs To Yesterday," which they'd written but it's

funny because you know they wrote it their own way and it probably was a perfect opportunity to have a winner song and I changed the whole thing because the market hadn't changed yet and that song wasn't right for the market at the time, and I put it into more of a ballad type of thing. When I stopped off in from Paris one time and Phil Spector was in London and he called me from the hotel and told me he was having a terrible time because he was trying to do what was the follow-up to "I Wanna Be Your Man" and all the boys hated each other that day and he had them in a little dinky studio in Denmark Street and he couldn't get them to do anything, I had five fifths of cognac that I was bringing home, so I took one fifth over to the studio and I told him it was a custom in my family that when anybody had a birthday, and I told them it was my birthday, that everybody had a water glass of cognac until the bottle was empty. So, we ended up with a hell of a session and out of it came "Not Fade Away" and I played piano and Phil Spector played an empty cognac bottle with a half dollar, clickin' it and we played on the flip side which was "Little by Little."

By the beginning of February the Stones were wreaking havoc on their second British tour. Stonemania had been let loose on the land. On the first night of the tour the group played at the All-Night Rave in Tottenham. Earlier, a matinee at the Regal saw the first serious outbreak of Stonemania. It was, as Graeme Andrews reported, the beginning of a new Stone Age:

Welcomed by a tremendous barrage from boys and girls alike, the Stones opened with "Talkin' 'Bout You," but it was almost lost in the noise from the fans, who quieted down for Mick

Jagger's harmonica break in "Road Runner," which followed.

The screams did not let up for the slower "You Better Move On," or "I Wanna Be Your Man," with which the caveman-like quintet ended. (N.M.E.)

In Birmingham, three days later, their first "fan" letter was read aloud to the boys in the dressing room: "The whole lot of you should be given a good bath and then all that hair should be cut off. I'm not against pop music when it's performed by a nice clean boy like Cliff Richard, but you are a disgrace. Your filthy appearance is liable to corrupt teenagers all over the country . . ."

But it wasn't only parents who found the Stones . . . hair-raising. Professionals found them barbarous: "Mr. Wallace Scowcroft, President of the National Federation of Hairdressers, offered a free haircut to the next number one group or soloist in the pop chart, adding: 'The Rolling Stones are the worst. One of them looks as if he has got a feather duster on his head.' " (*Daily Mirror*)

Brian, who was so compulsive about his hair that "he washed it twice a day; we used to call him 'Mr. Shampoo,' " said Keith. "He was extremely sensitive about all that stuff about us having dirty hair. It upset him, it really did."

In March a famous headline appeared—so inspired, in fact, that it might have come straight from the fertile brain of Andrew Oldham—and, of all places, in that grand old lady of English music papers the *Melody Maker*: WOULD YOU LET YOUR DAUGHTER GO WITH A ROLLING STONE? This was only the beginning of Andrew's infamous dictum: "For the Stones bad news is good news." Clergymen denounced them as "long-haired morons," magistrates muttered about "blatant

exhibitionists," columists called them "the ugliest group in the world."

As Keith points out, the press and its hypocritical hacks were only playing into the hands of the basic Stones strategy as set forth by Andrew Oldham: "When people make these kind of irresponsible remarks it just draws the fans more firmly to our side . . . They are as aware as we are of the mentality which supposes anyone in a black leather jacket and riding a motorbike is a hooligan." (*Flip*)

While the rampant id of Rock's newest heroes raged at large through the ballrooms and cinemas of the Midlands and the south of England, to the principals it was just another moonlight mile down the M1 apiece.

Keith: "It happend so fast that one never had time to really get into that thing, 'Wow, I'm a Rolling Stone.' We were still sleeping in the back of this truck every night of the most hardhearted and callous roadie I've ever encountered, Stew. From one end of England to another in Stew's Volkswagen bus. With just an engine and a rear window and all the equipment and then you fit in. The gear first though." (*Rolling Stone* August 19, 1971)

The Stones' first English LP, released in April, had been recorded in ten days at the end of January and the beginning of February at Regent Sound.

BILL: "On the first album, we cut everything in mono; the band had to record more or less live in the studio so what was on the record was more or less our act, what we played on the ballroom and club circuits. It was really just the show you did on-stage recorded in one take—*as it should be!*

KEITH: "Many of the English punk records sound like our early records and that is very hard to achieve nowadays with sophisticated technology, 24-track studios. We did our early records on a two-track Revox in a room insulated with egg cartons at Regent Sound. It was a little demo studio in "Tin Pan Alley," as it used to be called. Denmark Street in Soho. It was all done on a two-track Revox that he had on the wall. We used to think, 'Oh, this is a recording studio, huh? This is what they're like?' A tiny little back room. Under those primitive conditions it was easy to make the kind of sound we got on our first album and the early singles, but hard to make a much better one."

R & B had never been done better by a white group; the Stones had an instinctive "feel" for it. Although other English blues singers like Eric Burdon and Stevie Winwood had voices closer to those of the black R & B singers, Jagger's nasal style of singing was more evocative: he was able to make it

personal and identifiable, instead of a facsimile. But the Stones' obsession with R & B presented some problems for their writing which had been mainly limited to uncanny re-creations of blues and soul songs.

Mick's vocal impersonations of soul and R & B singers on the first LP are especially uncanny. Oddly enough for England's premiere blues band, the Stones' version of Muddy Waters's "I Just Want To Make Love To You" is the least successful track on the English album.

By the time of *Beggars Banquet* in the late sixties the Stones had become masters of the ironic put-on, but here the sincerity of their interpretations is unquestioned, and devoid of any trace of self-consciousness. They bring an earnestness to "Walking The Dog," for example, that's completely missing on the original, a novelty song by DJ Rufus Thomas. Part of this is due to the way in which the guitar on the Stones version takes over some of the fat sound of the Mar-Keys horns which underline the jive nursery rhyme humor in the Rufus Thomas original. Much of the album is pure imitation: Jagger saying "buzz a while" on "King Bee," a direct lift from Slim Harpo's rendition, or Richards lifting Berry's guitar from "Carol," but they were being filtered through a new sensibility, peculiar to the Stones, which inevitably recast the originals in their own image. Chuck Berry's backbone beat has always been the pulse behind Keith's guitar style; but just as Chuck himself had lifted the riff from Carl Hogan, the Stones, in trying to duplicate Chuck's chops, unwittingly transformed it again.

It is *the* classic album of white rock, because, like Presley's *Sun Sessions*, it was the first of its kind and it has the startled, breathless intensity of doing it for the first time.

England's Newest Hitmakers, as their first album was called in the States, pointed pop music in a new direction. It wasn't poppy, it wasn't beaty, it wasn't rock 'n roll revisited. It was something completely different and its white funk R & B sound would define what shape rock would take. The very rawness of its production, recorded with equipment not far removed from that used on sessions in the mid-fifties, only added to its impact.

BILL: "Basically, we released everything in mono—up to *Aftermath*—because we always liked the mono sound on the original R & B records. You don't have that polarity you get with stereo, that spreads out the sound. With stereo you lose a lot of the guts of the sound. We liked the rawness of mono back then. On two tracks you couldn't do much anyway. For one thing, it couldn't be released in stereo. The band was on one track, the vocals on the other, and you couldn't mix stereo on two tracks. In any case, in '64 stereo was just coming into use, it wasn't in people's homes until '66. Also, you couldn't mix a single other than mono at that time because if it was mixed in stereo and you played it on a mono machine the sound was not balanced."

The album tracks were selected and assembled by Andrew while the group was doing one-nighters through February and March.

The LP contained the first Jagger/ Richards composition recorded by the Stones, "Tell Me." Keith claims this was "also a dub." The longest track on the album, it appeared, in a slightly shorter version, as a U.S. single in June. Jon Landau, in a retrospective review, referred to this first song-writing effort as "a wretched C-A minor-F-G tune that sounded like it belonged in the early '60s." Some reviewers found it reminiscent of Buddy Holly; others thought it "Spec-torish;" Bob Dawbarn in *Melody Maker*, made the unkindest cut of all: "A curious sidelight is shown by the one original tune on the album 'Tell Me.' The Negroid mask slips away and both tune and lyric are second-hand Liverpool."

The two most prestigious English music papers, perhaps overdosed on the Merseybeat sound, were openly enthusiastic. Norman Jopling and Peter Jones, for *Melody Maker*, wrote:

GREAT FIRST FROM STONES

It's out this week!—The long-awaited first LP by the Rolling Stones. No title on the sleeve, just a collection of twelve R & B-style numbers, in typical Stones tradition. And a racing certainty for the best-selling lists—it could even push the Beatles off the top.

A debut LP of guaranteed appeal. And the great thing is that the Stones themselves, normally very critical of their own work, are very pleased with the result. A final word of praise to Andrew Loog Oldham, who recorded the sessions—he's living up to his "boast" that he'd be the top independent recording manager in Britain— by November this year! (Melody Maker)

THE ROLLING STONES LP

I went along to Decca's offices on Monday for a preview of the disc that thousands of fans are screaming for. Believe me, it is fantastic! I will go as far as to say that if it doesn't take over from the Beatles at the top of the LP chart I will eat my chocolate flavored record player.

STONES' LP HITS 100,000 ON DAY OF RELEASE!

The Rolling Stones have struck a Beatle-type sales bonanza. with their first LP!—And they've crashed into the Disc Top Thirty with it at No. 22! Last Friday, its official release day, Decca reported sales had hit the staggering total of 100,000! No further statistics were available at press-time, but Decca are confidently predicting a score of a quarter million for the Stones' first album within a matter of days.

The Stones have trounced the initial sales figure of 6,000 recorded by the Beatles for their first LP Please Please Me in March of last year. But the fab four's second set With The Beatles notched a quarter million in advance orders by the time it was re-

leased. It climbed to No. eleven in Disc's Top Thirty on December 7.

Andrew gloated: "They've knocked off the Beatles in the long-playing charts." But in fairness to the Fab Four, the album in question, *With the Beatles* (released November 2, 1963), was getting to the end of its shelf life anyway, having stayed on the charts for almost five months. The next Beatles album, *A Hard Day's Night*, would not be released until July (to coincide with the premiere of the film).

The cover of the Stones' first English LP is a masterpiece of Andrew Oldham's "image tuning." It was revolutionary in concept because it was the first album ever without either a title or the name of the group on the cover; instead, just a shadow-drenched photograph of the group by David Bailey. Nothing but the DECCA logo in the upper right-hand corner distracted the eye from these five hypnotic heads staring with cool, penetrating glance. The absence of words created the effect of looking into an eerie charged space, not a flat surface, and the Stones, like the children from the *Village of the Damned*, look back dispassionately. They look with the curious expectation of mutants who already exist in a future that is about to adapt itself to them. Few albums have so successfully encoded their vinyl

content on their covers. "There seems not an iota of nostalgia in what that picture says," Greil Marcus wrote. "It does not provoke memories of Swinging London. The picture would be perfect, I imagine, if the world saw it for the first time ten years from now."

In May the Stones did a third English tour of one-nighters before leaving for their first U.S. tour. In 31 days they had three days off. Bill was home so seldom that his own dog failed to recognize him and attacked him as an intruder. As reported under the headline DOG BITES STONE: "We

had a dog once but we couldn't keep it because I was never at home and he tried to bite me when I turned up. That's rather sad really, isn't it?"

By the end of the month things had gotten so out of hand that reporters were driven to drastic measures:

LIP-READING THE TITLES!

Fifty police and a squad of first aid attendants were called in to deal with the crowds at East Ham Granada when the Rolling Stones appeared there on Monday. Many girls fainted and were treated. At the stage door over 300 fans gathered.

From my third row seat, I had to lip-read on many occasions to find out what song was being performed! The screams from the audience completely drowned the Stones.

Charlie sat amid a huge battery of amplifiers which, in normal circumstances, would have enabled people in the pub across the road to hear. But on Saturday, customers in the stalls strained to catch the music.

The long-haired ones began with "Beautiful Delilah" and were met with a torrent of gifts which plummeted on to the stage from all parts of the theater. To their credit the Stones carried on even though they were hit several times. Mick's dancing was grade one and served to incite fresh attacks of frenzy from the fans.

Even though "You Better Move On" is a slow number, the screams continued, but you should have heard what happened during "I'm Alright." From the moment Mick picked up his maracas and the Stones burst into action it was a battle between them and the teenagers as to who could make the most noise. The five lads built up such a wall of excitement that in the end they won.

Brian was scream-provoker-in-chief as he dashed backwards and forwards bashing a tambourine. He was aided by Keith, who can't stand still for more than two notes, and Mick, who kept creeping dangerously near to the edge of the stage.

After "Not Fade Away," Mick called Charlie to the front to announce the next number. It was almost two minutes before the drummer could say: "I Wanna Be Your Man" and it was over ten minutes after the act finished with that song before the fans stopped chanting "We want the Stones." (New Musical Express)

Brian ecstatically, even manically, here gives the Stones'-eye-view of hitting the stage at full tilt: "Standing in the wings, waiting for the curtains to part, you get your first real glimpse of all the excitement. Stage hands frantically beat off girls who are trying to wrench back the drapes.

"The atmosphere is more than electric by now—it's something tangible, like a vast elastic band, ready to snap at any moment!

"And then we're off. Keith roars into 'Talkin' About You.' The curtains slowly part. The Stones are rolling!

"As our music gains momentum, the kids sway like palm trees in a hurricane. A huge Hampden roar swamps our overworked amplifiers. We feel as if we're really in there with the fans.

"As the excitement mounts, the girls surge down to the footlights and start showering us with gifts—sweets, peanuts, cuddly toys. We're feeling very good.

"Suddenly it's all over. The curtains close quickly, shutting off the faces behind that ear-splitting roar.

"Back in the dressing room, we swallow cokes to get that sandpaper taste out of our throats. We start to unwind as we wait for the police to arrange our getaway.

"We always feel a little sad, driving away through the surging throng." (*Rave*, June, 1964)

The long-haired ones heard the chant "We want the Stones" that fused them with their fans (they would incorporate this anthem as a track on a live EP a year later) and they knew it announced the arrival of a new species; with this metamorphosis a new age had

begun with new creatures in it. Keith: "We'd walk into some of those places and it was like they had the Battle of the Crimea going on, people gasping, tits hanging out, chicks choking, nurses running around with ambulances.

"I know it was the same for the Beatles. One had been reading about that, 'Beatlemania.' 'Scream power' was the thing everything was judged by, as far as gigs were concerned. If Gerry and the Pacemakers were the top of the bill, incredible, man. You know that weird sound that thousands of chicks make when they're really lettin' it go. They couldn't hear the music. We couldn't hear ourselves, for years. Monitors were unheard of. It was impossible to play as a band on stage, and we forgot all about it." (*Rolling Stone*, August 19, 1971.)

Meanwhile, in the States the Stones were still an unknown quantity despite a single out in March ("Not Fade Away"/"I Wanna Be Your Man") which barely squeaked into the Top Hundred and an album in May (*England's Newest Hitmakers*). The press began to prepare the way for the visit by dragging out—yet again—the Stones' dirty laundry. In an item from the Associated Press these sharp dressers with expensive shopping habits seem more bored than wild, and with Mick actually shampooing his hair during the interview, it is hard to believe the American public needed to be warned about the Stones' personal hygene:

Beatles' Look-Alikes

BRITAIN'S ROLLING STONES ON THEIR WAY TO AMERICA

LONDON—(AP)—Americans—brace yourselves.

In the tracks of the Beatles, a second wave of sheepdoglooking, angry acting, guitar-playing Britons is on the way.

They call themselves the Rolling Stones and they're due in New York Tuesday.

Of the Rolling Stones, one detractor has said:

"They are dirtier, and are streakier and more disheveled than the Beatles and in some places they're more popular than the Beatles."

Says Mick Jagger:

"I hate to get up in the morning. I'm not over fond of being hungry either."

From Keith Richard:

"People think we're wild and unruly. But it isn't true, I would say that the most important thing about us is that we are our own best friends."

More than the others, perhaps, Brian Jones likes clothes. He put his

philosophy this way:

"It depends on what I feel like really. Sometimes I'll wear very flamboyant clothes like this frilly shirt. Other times I'll wear very casual stuff. I spend a lot of my free time buying stuff."

Then he adds:

"There's really not much else to do."

Unlike the Beatles, a genuinely proletarian pop group, the Stones from their beginnings as a cult group in Richmond were hip, fashionable and elite. As the Stones set out on their first American tour to become teeny-bopper chart toppers, Andrew, through David ("*Blow Up*") Bailey, *the* photographer of swinging London, was getting a more subtle message across to sophisticated tastemakers. In the May issue of American *Vogue*, facing Bailey's luminous portrait of Mick as an angelic, precocious and sexually disturbing child star, appeared this tantalizing comment:

MICK JAGGER, A BRITISH "ROLLING STONE" ROCKER

To the inner group in London, the new spectacular is a solemn young man, Mick Jagger, one of the five Rolling Stones, those singers who set out to cross America by bandwagon in June. For the British, the Stones have a perverse, unsettling sex appeal with Jagger out in front of his teammates who in turn are out in front of The Pacemakers, The Searchers, The Breakaways, and Freddie and the Dreamers. To women, Jagger looks fascinating, to men, a scare. (Most of the groups look pretty much alike, dressed in their own costume way, their hair banged to the eyebrows.) With, especially, "Not Fade Away," The Rolling Stones pushed ahead of the Beatles, perhaps because their message and their music is a shade more gutsy. They are quite

different from the Beatles, and more terrifying. "The effect is sex," wrote one observer, "that isn't sex, which is the end of the road."

This item, anticipating Mick's role as one of the BPs (beautiful people) is a far cry from the early Neanderthal image of the Stones being played up in the British press at the time. Less than four months earlier, a picture of the group looking like a bunch of local lads (only Brian, always "ahead of his time," suggests the future androgynous androids) appeared with the caption: "The Rolling Stones may be considered terrific musicians, great personalities, well behaved young men, etc. But one thing is certain—they will never be considered GOOD-LOOKING!"

It wasn't so much what the Stones did to America, as the British press pondered ("What sort of picture of British youth will they create across the Atlantic?" worried the *Daily Express*—with apparent apprehension) as what America did to the Stones. According to Bill Wyman: "Well, from the very start we always had a very good standard of morale, but it did almost collapse during the first American tour, which was like a disaster. When we arrived in the States we didn't have a hit record or anything really going for us, if I remember. I think 'Not Fade Away' was about number 82 on the charts the week we arrived. All the other English groups that had ever been to the States had at least a number 1 record, perhaps two to their credit. We had nothing except that we were English."

The London *Daily Mirror* reported (June 3):

U.S. publicity release sent out with the caption: "The Rolling Stones, who haven't bathed in a week, arrive here for their second U.S. tour yesterday."

STONES FLEE FROM FANS

Teenage girls armed with scissors are keeping the Rolling Stones prisoner in a Broadway hotel. For the fans have caught a "curl for a souvenir" fever . . . Now the Rolling Stones are busy dodging the scissors.

The initial reaction to the Stones on their first trip was tepid compared to the reception the Beatles got in February with ten thousand fans at Kennedy Airport, boys combing their pompadours into bangs and shaking their ducktails, DJs recording the temperature in "Beatle degrees" and the time in "Beatle seconds." But then, as Oldham testily pointed out, it had taken the Beatles two years to break into the American market.

Eric Easton had pondered the problem of "the boys" taking R & B to America, home of the blues. "I think the boys," he said in an unfortunate metaphor, "are carrying coals to Newcastle. If they accept them at all in the States it will be on 'face' value."

The image of these mannish boys with their Spanish heels and their mother's drugs singing the down-home "Delta Blues" might have seemed absurd if it weren't for the intensity with which the Stones identified with the blues. It was the eerie juxtaposition itself—the Stones' Blonde-on-Black effect—that gave them an almost mystical attraction and left a hypnotic, oscillating imprint on their audiences.

The Stones were, by embodying the blues, bringing back a lost American music; their younger fans weren't even born when Muddy Waters and Howlin' Wolf cut their classic sessions and were toddlers in the heyday of Chuck Berry and Bo Diddley, so the Stones' re-creations had the impact on teenagers of music being heard for the first time.

When the time came for the *Les Crane Show*, the Stones were in fine voice. Crane's TV show didn't go out until the early hours of the morning: "Hardly good for teen fans," noted the *Rolling Stones Monthly*. Crane made a few attempts to take the mickey out of the Stones, but the boys remained their droogishly droll selves.

Q: This is your—this is your first appearance on American television.

KEITH: Yeah!!

Q: Isn't it exciting?

KEITH: Yeah, knocks me out! (*laughter—Stones and camera crew*)

Q: You wouldn't be sending me up, would you?

KEITH: No, I wouldn't dare. (*more laughter*)

Q: You wouldn't dare. Brian Jones is the third and one of the loveliest members of your group. (*laughter*)

MICK (*sarcastically*): Oh, he's very lovely.

Q: Do you sing—what sort of stuff do you do. Do you do Bach and do you do, ah . . .

MICK: Yeah, Beethoven's Fifth Symphony occasionally, when the mood takes us.

Q: Oh, yeah, well of course, I understand. Where's, ah, Bill Wyman? Here he is. How are you, Bill? Welcome to the program. You guys all dress differently. How come?

MICK: 'Cause we're all different persons.

Q: You play guitar? How many guitars are there?

KEITH: There's—ah—three guitars; one bass guitar, drums.

Q: Three guitars—like a Fender bass. Is that what . . .

KEITH: Ah, yeah—we double it as a Fender.

MICK: Shall I pinch one of your fags?

Q: Can you do what?

MICK: Cigarettes, I mean, not fags.

Q: Shall you pinch one of our fags? Now you see . . . (*laughter*)

The next morning, June 3, they flew to L.A. to tape the *Hollywood Palace*, playing live versions of their first American single, "Not Fade Away" and the B side ("I Just Want To Make Love To You") of their next single, "Tell Me," released later that month. The Stones were unusually cooperative, letting themselves be photographed with clowns, cowboys, comedians, the King Sisters, cameramen and elephants—"We'll pose with anything, man!"—but it was Dean Martin, the show's host, who gave them their first sensational plug by playing up the "freak angle" and unwittingly feeding Andrew's publicity machine: "Their hair is not that long. It's just smaller foreheads and higher eyebrows. . . . Now don't go away, anybody. You wouldn't leave me with these Rolling Stones, would you?" That was just before a commercial break. He went on: "Actually the boys are soon back to England to have a hair-pulling contest with the Beatles." And of a trampoline-bouncer artist on the same production, he said: "That is the father of the Rolling Stones. He's been trying to kill himself ever since."

Aside from boosting their record sales, an urgent reason the Stones wanted to get to the States was that American sound. Keith: "On the records we were cutting in England all through that time . . . we all knew really, that the sound we were getting live and in the clubs was not what we were getting on record.

"Before we went to America it was very difficult to record in England. Nobody *could* record or *had* recorded the *sound* we were *tryin'* to get. People weren't used to *that* kind of roughness. Everyone in England at the time was incapable: engineers, equipment, producers and to a certain extent musicians. No one could get a *really* good funky American sound which is what *we* were after. The best move we could *possibly* do, was get to America as quickly as possible and record there.' " (Barbara Charone, *Keith Richards*.)

The highlight of the first American tour was a visit to the legendary Chess Studios in Chicago where Howlin' Wolf, Muddy Waters, Chuck Berry and Bo Diddley had recorded their classic R & B records. In one marathon session the Stones recorded their next single, "It's All Over Now," and eight more tracks that would show up on albums and singles over the next six months.

BILL: The methods of recording in England and America were completely different.

The only people you could use over here were Bill Fowley at Regent Sound and Glyn Johns, if you could get hold of him. The big trouble with recording in England was that for a rock group the studio acoustics were so bad because you couldn't play loud.

When we recorded at the Chess studios in Chicago, we had Ron, the guy who engineered all the Chuck Berry, Bo Diddley and Howlin' Wolf records. He knew exactly what we wanted and he got it almost instantly. (*Go-Set*, June 3, 1972.)

While the Stones were at Chess many of their blues idols dropped by the sessions. Bill chronicled the historic encounters: "Willie Dixon called in to see us and talked about the scene. So did Buddy Guy. We felt we were taking part in a little bit of history there—after all, those studios were used by Muddy Waters as well as Chuck Berry and Bo Diddley. We knew pretty well what numbers we wanted to get in the can . . . like 'It's All Over Now' . . . and the atmosphere was so marvelous that we got through them in double-quick time.

"Then, on the next day, both Chuck and Muddy came in to see us. Fantastic."

Muddy, after whose song "Rollin' Stone" the group was named, spoke of the Stones like a master passing on his mantle to his chosen disciples, saying: "They're my boys. I like their version of 'I Just Want To Make Love To You.' They fade it out just like we did. One more trip and they'll have it. Believe me, I'll come back one more time and then I won't need to. That guitar player ain't bad either."

After the session, Chuck Berry invited them all down to visit him at his very own amusement arcade, Berry Park (admission: $2.50).

BILL: Chuck Berry was the nicest I can remember him ever being but don't forget we were making *money* for him. We all stood around talking about guitars, amplifiers and all that. We played one of his songs, "Reelin' And Rockin'." He really liked it. Most of the cover versions of his songs didn't *swing*. Actually Chuck Berry walked in while we were recording "Down The Road Apiece," and he said to us, "Wow, you guys are really getting it on!"

On June 28 the Stones' fourth British single was released. The A side, "It's All Over Now," was recorded at Chess in Chicago and the B side, "Good Times, Bad Times," written by Mick and Keith, was recorded at Regent Sound in London before the group left for the States. With advance orders of over 150,000 copies it went straight into the British Top Ten the first week, dislodging the Animals' "House of the Rising Sun" from the top of the charts the following week to give the Stones their first number one single. Released in the States a week later it eventually made it to number 25 on the U.S. charts, while *England's Newest Hit Makers* was in the Top Ten American LPs.

In the singles race the *New Musical Express* put its money on the Stones:

EARTHY GOSPEL FEELING BEST STONES YET

What a tremendously vibrant and earthy sound the Rolling Stones have achieved in their American-recorded "It's All Over Now" (Decca)! Basically an R & B medium-pacer, it has a sort of jog-trotting pace which—combined with the rattling tambourine and pungent guitar work—gives it a distinct gospel flavor.

"It's All Over Now" shows a dramatic improvement in sound quality from previous cuts. Ron Malo, the engineer on the Stones' sessions at Chess, honed the Stones' sound into a finely tooled weapon by recording the songs raw, clean and razor sharp. The sound presence brings up the intent of the song from the first notes of the guitar intro, the momentum of the rhythm guitar mixed *up* out of the roar.

While this malignity has always been latent in the blues, for social reasons it was usually laid back in an ambivalent but suggestive language, leaving the guitar and harp to articulate its aggression. The Stones made it explicit. With "It's All Over Now" they began a new phase. They had been known through their singles as singers of R & B, rockers or bluesy ballads. To "It's All Over Now" the Stones brought a new menacing and petulant tone, underlined by Keith's ominous intro and stinging guitar breaks combined with a merciless rhythm section. The Stones inflection inverts the Valentinos' original. Where lead singer Bobby Womack seems relieved it's all over, endorsing the Valentinos' jaunty, New Orleans-flavored track, the Stones version, insinuatingly delivered by Mick, is pure invective and the first in a long line of Stones put-downs.

As the first street-fighters of a new sensibility, the Stones, through their songs, threatened and challenged. They sharpened the sting of the original versions by stepping up the aggression. Mod culture used the blues in its most ancient form "*in preparation* for war." In an article by Bob Palmer, Leon Thomas tells about the roots of the blues: "The Zulus would run to war and sing blues chants, that's why people become so spirited behind the blues, and sometimes become violent. The reason why *we* sing the blues is because we're praying. We're saying,

Keith: "The first gig was San Bernadino. It was a straight gas, man."

"I feel like this is my laaast recourse." In other words, the blues is a final statement, so the fact that the children sing the blues now means that they're telling their parents, "We've had it up to here!"

The Stones' affair with the U.S.A. had begun innocently enough with pages from Chuck Berry's Southern Book of Days, "Come On," "Bye, Bye, Johnny," "Around And Around," "Down The Road Apiece" (the adventures of Charlie McCoy—you all remember that rubber-legged boy) and the super rock highway "Route 66."

KEITH: "Actually, the first gig was in San Bernardino. It was a straight gas, man. They all knew the songs and they were all bopping. It was like being back home. 'Ah, love these American gigs,' and 'Route 66' mentioned San Bernardino, so everybody was into it." The Midwest proved problematical. If there were "bags of screams" in San Bernardino, the audience in Omaha was a bit spotty. It wasn't on Route 66.

KEITH: "Nebraska. We really felt like a sore pimple in Omaha. On top of that, the first time we arrived there, the only people to meet us off the plane were twelve motorcycle cops who insisted on doing this motorcade thing right through town, And nobody in Omaha had ever heard of us. We

thought, 'Wow, we've made it. We must be heavy.' And we get to the auditorium and there's 600 people there in a 15,000-seat hall. But we had a good time.

"That's what stopped us from turning into pop stars then, we were always having those continual complete somebody hittin' you in the face, 'Don't forget, boy.' Then we really had to work America and it really got the band together. We'd fallen off in playing in England 'cause nobody was listening, we'd do four numbers and be gone. Don't blink, you'll miss us.

"Some towns you went into on that first tour they'd look at you with a look that could kill. You could just tell they wanted to beat the shit out of you."

BILL: "We were always amazed that people hated us. I think they never realized that while they were afraid of us, we were just as afraid of them."

The Stones were cheered considerably during their American campaign by news that in the first *Record Mirror* poll ever the Stones "pipped" the Beatles as the most popular British vocal group and Mick had been voted England's most popular individual group member. "Not Fade Away" came in second to "She Loves You" as best disc, but since the Beatles single had been released in August

'63, the Stones could claim theirs top disc for the current year. The most galling was the award for best dressed artist category in which Mick placed sixth! This caused incredulous headlines in several national newspapers. One English daily printed Mick's picture and a caption listing his position in the best dressed with five exclamation points.

At the last two concerts of the tour, at Carnegie Hall, fans expressed their devotion in a manner dear to the hearts of Stones:

However, New York was particularly kind to the Stones on Saturday. There were RIOTS during their first house at the Carnegie Hall, which resulted in police insisting that the group should close the first half on the second house and be whipped away before the audience poured out! (NME)

But myths die slowly. Diehard Dick Frame, who apparently reviewed the concert from the safety of the press-room, wrote: "The boys appeared on stage last night in their dirty laundry."

They returned home to a triumphant welcome—a fan's sincerest form of affection—on June 23:

Tired, and "glad to be back" the Stones flew into London Airport on

Monday morning to a welcome by about a hundred screamers who lined the barricades . . . during the screaming and ensuing fights police helmets rolled on the floor. Whilst waiting for a convoy of five cars with a police escort to rush them to London, Mick Jagger told reporters he thought the trip had been "quite successful." Told he had been chosen 6th best dressed man in Britain in the RM Pop Poll, Mick said: "It's a joke." Brian Jones blew a raspberry and said: "No comment."

Keith Richard said he had cut two inches off Bill Wyman's hair in America "because it was so hot." Charlie Watts agreed: "You've got to

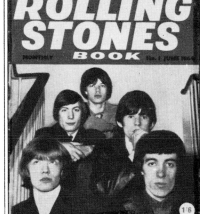

have a crew-cut out there," he said.

Mick's girlfriend Chrissie Shrimpton was waiting at the airport.

Mick's got Chrissie, Andrew's got answers, but Keith's got the gun:

Just for souvenir value most of the boys picked up guns on their travels. "You can buy them as easily as you can buy candy floss. Everybody has a gun," Keith told me, brandishing a small pistol.

Would the Stones' image change in view of the controversy about their appearance and manners?

"We've got a way with critics," he smiled, twirling the pistol.

In a quiet moment I asked Keith how long he felt the Stones could last: "Who's to say. On our present strength I think we can count on earning big money for at least another two years, even if something new comes in.

"But if there's nothing new on its way then we can literally go on indefinitely. One thing though, I wouldn't want to struggle along if the group

really lost popularity. There would be no point." (New Musical Express)

For the July 7 premiere of *"A Hard Day's Night"* Brian, Keith and Bill, "casually dressed and uninvited, barged in on the Beatles' bash at the Dorchester":

STONES GATECRASH BEATLES' PARTY

What a surprise! Just look who turned up at the Beatles exclusive party—shaggy haired Rolling Stones Bill Wyman, Keith Richard, and Brian Jones. They were not permitted to enter so they had to get a messenger to take a note to the Beatles. The message said they would like to see the Beatles if possible. The messenger who brought the note said, "I'm afraid they're dressed rather untidily." John Lennon overheard this and said, "What's the difference. They're friends of ours. Get them in."

July 5th was the date of what was then laughingly called the Stones' "controversial *Juke Box Jury* appearance" and what in retrospect seems little more than a Stone in a tea cup. Ridiculous precautions were taken to protect them including being driven on stage in an armoured car. "Disgusting exhibition" wrote an irate Channel

Islander.

The dailies slammed the Stones: "RUDE," "ANTHROPOID," "BOORISH," even "CHARMLESS." Bill retorts: "People shouldn't take these programs so seriously. And anyway they know where the 'off' switch on the television set is, so why torture themselves by sticking with the show?" Mick said earnestly: "If the producer had wanted a sophisticated panel, he could have got a bunch of West End actresses . . ."

The so-called Siege of Blackpool took place less than three weeks later (July 24), and was to be Britain's biggest rock riot ever.

A Steinway grand piano was pushed off the stage and pulverized. Several chandeliers were wrenched from the ceiling and shattered. The pandemonium got so out of control that it took seventy of Blackpool's bobbies and thirty attendants to quell the riot. Fifty injured rioters had to be taken to hospital and the Empress herself sustained some three thousand pounds' damage.

Mick was interviewed on BBC radio the following day.

Q: What happened? Was it something that developed quickly?

MICK: Well, it seemed it developed during the second half-hour show we did. It was building up tension to those blokes who seemed to be getting drunker and drunker, getting more and more violent at the time.

Q: How did it reach crisis point?

MICK: It wasn't more than twenty that really started it off. They sort of pushed their way to the front. I saw some girls being punched in the stomach and knee'd in the stomach and it was really violent and horrible. I had never seen anything like it. And then when we were pulled off, they just got madder and madder when we were pulled off.

The Stones sustained damage to their instruments, but because of the confusion on stage there hadn't been enough time between acts to switch equipment and they were mostly using amps owned by the Leroys, the previous group on the bill, when the rioters climbed onstage.

Bill: "Later that night, after the riot was over, Ian Stewart, our road manager, went back to get our equipment. He came into our hotel room with little pieces of wood and metal. 'Here's your amp,' he'd say, and gives us a chip. 'Here's your guitar . . .'"

The siege of Blackpool took place on the last night of the annual Glasgow holiday fortnight, and the seaside town had been full of Scots getting drunk. It was the most violent confrontation between Scots and Sassenachs since the battle of Culloden in 1745 and actually involved more

Chrissie Shrimpton.

"troops."

The Stones' tours of Britain and Europe in the fall of 1964 read like the campaigns of Napoleon, with their lightning victories, body counts, tactical maneuvers and liberating energy.

July 31, Belfast: Concert called off after twelve minutes due to riot. Hysterical girls carried off in strait-jackets.

August 8: Riots at The Hague, Holland. "Two girls had their clothes ripped off when the audience got out of hand during the performance." (A very graphic newsreel shot of this concert shows just how wild Stones audiences were during those early tours.)

August 9: Door torn off Stones car after their appearance on *Ready, Steady, Go!* That evening in Manchester:

WOMEN P.C.s FAINT AT "STONES" SHOW

Two policewomen fainted, another was taken to hospital with rib injuries and barmen helped more than 50 policemen control 3,000 screaming teenagers during a performance by the Rolling Stones at the New Elizabethan Ballroom, Bellevue, Manchester. (Daily Telegraph, August 10, 1964.)

August 21-22: Jersey, Channel Islands:

ENRAGED "INFORMAL" FANS IN FRACAS WITH JERSEY POLICE

Irate fans ran rampant after being refused admission to a Rolling Stone concert at the Springfield Ballroom, Jersey, because they were wearing "inappropriate attire" (blue jeans and no ties). During the last set a peach and four tomatoes hit Mick Jagger. On the balcony a scuffle broke out while a running fight raged on the floor of the ballroom among 4,000 teenagers at the concert last night. Girls were sent flying as burly chuckers-out—42 of them were hired for the evening—dragged leather jacketed troublemakers from the hall by their hair. One girl was seen with a flick knife. She struggled with officials before being overpowered. Then she was dragged down two flights of stairs to the exit. (Daily Mirror, August 23.)

Here is a rapturous first-person account, worthy of St. Theresa, of the ecstasies of fainting by one of the fallen at Longleat (August 3):

SQUEEZE TO REMEMBER

Thousands upon thousands of hot, sticky bodies pushing, shoving. Must get closer, closer. Near the front. By the wire. Hot, getting hotter. Can't see. Must get nearer.

Here they come! Here they are. They, my gods all five. Jumping, raving, seductive sounds.

Bodies hurt hurling over the wire. Big blue daddies of the law with strong arms carting off the empty beings. Empty of love, empty of words, empty of soul.

The noise. Can't hear: just noise. Brian must get to. . . . Oh, the heat. Can't get. . . . Can't see: can't breathe. The wire: up against the wire. Hurts, hurt all over. Got to get out. Get me out. Stop the noise. Turn off the sun!

Quiet. So quiet. Sleep. Can sleep. Gentle. Be gentle. Please, lovely cool quiet. Everything's beautiful. Far away music. So far away. Oh, poor creatures still high with hysteria, panic, love. I am away. Got away. I am lying still: lovely and still. Cool by trees. Soaked with exhaustion. Got cut: red blood. I'm human. Again back to earth.

Would I do it again? Of course I would. Why? Who knows why. I guess to flaunt authority. Yes, that's it! To be free, free to do as I please. Now let me rest. In the cool. Go away, far away.

October 14 Charlie Watts married Shirley Ann Shepherd in Bradford.

By the beginning of September the Stones had two EPs on the charts: *Five By Five* was number one and *The Rolling Stones* was number four. Their first LP was still at the top of the English album charts and "It's All Over Now" was into its third month in *Disc*'s Top Fifty.

On September 5 the Stones began their fifth British tour at the Finsbury Park Astoria with the Mojos and Charlie and Inez Foxx. During this tour Mick, the multiphrenic mimic, nicked his first stage moves from the

Bill and Charlie Foxx.

foxy Inez.

On the day the tour began the Stones were voted Britain's Most Popular Rock Group in the Melody Maker poll and in the same poll "Not Fade Away" was voted Best Song.

Following taping TV shows in Berlin, October 16–17th, the Stones fly to Brussels to tape more shows.

The Beatles had stormed Paris during a three-week engagement in January on a bill with Trini Lopez and Sylvie Vartan. The Stones were to do

Down the road apiece. Stones on a tour of the North.

as much damage in two days. Things started the night before the first concert with Brian disappearing drunk in the early hours of the morning attempting to climb the Eiffel Tower.

Following the Olympia concert, riots broke out in the streets. Gendarmes made 150 arrests, and damage to the theatre totalled some five thousand pounds.

ANGRY FANS RIOT AT 'STONES' SHOW. Hundreds of stampeding teen-

agers smashed seats and broke windows at a Paris theatre today at the end of a show given by Britain's Rolling Stones beat group. The police were called. They hustled the audience out of the theatre. As they went, some of the youths yelled insults at the police and smashed windows in the foyer. In the street, scores of youths were bundled into police vans. But many others dodged the police and went down the boulevard. They tore down posters, broke windows and slashed the fronts of newspaper kiosks. At a cafe, the youths overturned tables and threw customers on to the pavement (Daily Mirror, Oct. 22)

On August 24, Marianne Faithfull released "As Tears Go By," written by Jagger/Richards, their fourth song to come out as a single by another artist before appearing on a Stones record. The original version cut by the Stones, "As Time Goes By," was slightly faster than the single released (in the U.S. only) in December 1965.

Marianne Faithfull recounted her strategy to Andrew Taylor.

"When I was about sixteen, I wanted to be an actress and a scholar too. But whatever I wanted to be I wanted to be great at it. My first move was to get a Rolling Stone as a boy-

friend. I slept with three and then decided the lead singer was the best bet.

"I knew he wasn't the most important because I had always understood that, in the Stones, Keith was the most important—and, I think, in the beginning, I was always really in love with Keith much more than anyone else, as a fan. He's the epitome of the Romantic Hero and, if you're a middle-class girl and you've read your Byron, that's Keith Richard . . . even now. He's turned into Count Dracula now, but he's still an injured, tortured, damned youth which is really such fun, isn't it? I mean, he really is such fun.

"It isn't that Mick was *less* of a Rolling Stone. He's cleaner. I mean that's the thing about the Stones. That they're dirty and awful and arrogant, and Keith is still like that." (*Creem*)

The press were a little bemused that such a slow poignant ballad had been penned by the terrible twosome. "Just shows what I've believed all along," said one daily newspaper critic. "Those Stones can't be *all* bad —not if they can write material like that."

MICK: "We never dreamed of doing 'As Tears Go By' ourselves when we wrote it. We just gave it straight to

Marianne Faithfull. We wrote a lot of songs for other people, most of which were very unsuccessful."

When asked, "Did you write 'As Tears Go By' specifically for Marianne?" Mick answered, "Yeah, but I could never do it again. I keep trying, night after night."

On October 23 the Stones flew to New York to begin their second U.S. tour. By the time of this second tour of America, during October and November, they still hadn't had a number one hit. However, the climate had dramatically changed toward them. This was partly due to a fanatical following. Stones fan clubs had a colossal 80,000 members who functioned like a secret society, witnesses to the true faith.

The Stones were to remain a cult group in the States until "Satisfaction" in May of the following year. It was their sizable and fanatical core of fans who propelled the Stones when the hits came and sustained them in their absence. There are no more fanatical followers than Stones fans and there are no more fanatical Stones fans than American Stones fans. As early as 1964 this devoted flock searched for signs, symbols and crypto-clues, with cabalistic fervor. Mick looked on this new development with reserved curiosity: "They go into their reasons for liking a group in such detail that you feel you must have been put under a microscope. But it makes their letters specially interesting to read. And they seem to have got a really furious sense of fanaticism."

MICK'S NOTES ON THEIR AMERICAN TOUR

Friday, October 23rd:

Fantastic job getting out to first Ed Sullivan rehearsal. Everyone going mad crazy. Two hopeless attempts, then third successful.

After the rehearsal, which was just to work out positions and camera angles, we all went over to see our old mate, Murray the K, at WINS radio station.

Started broadcasting—then weirdest thing happened. It seemed that half the

Stones on the ubiquitous Ready Steady Go! *TV show.*

people listening decided to leave their radio sets and come over to the radio station. Result was, we couldn't get out when the program finished. (*Monthly*)

The Stones were becoming "people to be seen with," as London gossip columnist William Hickey noted earlier in the month, saying: "There is no harm these days in knowing a Rolling Stone. And pop people do not seem to mind who they mix with. Some of their best friends, in fact, are fledgelings from the upper classes." (*Daily Express*)

In the New York pop aristocracy Andy Warhol, Edie Sedgwick and Baby Jane Holzer turned out to see Mick prancing in his velvet suit at the Academy of Music.

Tom Wolfe: And, finally, the Stones, now—how can one express it? the Stones come on stage—

"Oh, God, Andy, aren't they *divine!*"

—and spread out over the stage, the five Rolling Stones, from England, who are modeled after the Beatles, only more lower-class-deformed. One, Brian Jones, has an enormous blonde Beatle bouffant.

"Oh, Andy, look at Mick! Isn't he *Beautiful!* Mick! Mick!"

In the center of the stage a short thin boy with a sweat shirt on, the neck of the sweat shirt almost falling over his shoulders, they are so narrow, all surmounted by this . . . enormous head . . . with the hair puffing down over the forehead and ears, this boy has exceptional lips. He has two peculiarly gross and extraordinary red lips. They hang off his face like giblets. Slowly his eyes pour over the flaming bud horde soft as Karo syrup and then close and then the lips start spreading into the most languid, most confidential, the wettest, most labial, most concupiscent grin imaginable. Nirvana! The buds start shrieking, pawing toward the stage.

The girls have Their Experience. They stand up on their seats. They begin to ululate, even between songs. The looks on their faces! Rapturous agony! There, right up there, under the sulphur? lights, that is *them*. God, they're right there! Mick Jagger takes the microphone with his tabescent hands and puts his huge head against it, opens his giblet lips and begins to sing . . . with the voice of a bull Negro. Bo Diddley. You movung boo meb bee-uhtul, bah-bee, oh vona breemb you' honey snurks oh crim pulzy yo' min down and, camping again, then turning toward the shrieking girls with his wet giblet lips dissolving . . . (*The Kandy Kolored Tangerine Flake Streamline Baby*)

Mick's diary continues:

Sunday, 25th:

Another rehearsal for the Ed Sullivan Show in first half of the day. Then did actual performance. Fantastic welcome.

Ed told us that it was the wildest, most enthusiastic audience he'd seen any artist get in the history of his show. Got a message from him a few days later saying: "Received hundreds of letters from parents complaining about you, but thousands from teenagers saying how much they enjoyed your performance." (Stones Monthly)

Most purists completely missed the point of the Stones. Nat Hentoff, a New York jazz critic, just didn't understand what the little girls all knew.

Perhaps fearing a backlash, Ed swore a solemn oath:

I promise you they'll never be back on our show. If things can't be handled we'll stop the whole business. We won't book any more rock and roll groups and we'll ban teenagers from the theater if we have to.

Frankly, I didn't see the Rolling Stones until the day before the broadcast. They were recommended by my scouts in England. I was shocked when I saw them.

Now the Dave Clark Five are nice fellows. They are gentlemen and they perform well. It took me seventeen years to build this show. I'm not going to have it destroyed in a matter of weeks.

Ed had to eat his words. The Stones reappeared on his show May 2, 1965, and again, and again, and again, and again.

The Stones' appearance on the *TAMI* [Teen Age Music International] *Show* at the end of October confirmed the success of their second U.S. tour. Even if they weren't chart toppers, they were the leaders of the pack. Their first album, *England's Newest Hitmakers*, had made the U.S. Top Ten, but their last single, "It's All Over Now," had only reached number 25 and their next release, "Time Is On My Side," was just entering the Top Hundred. Nevertheless, the Stones were the unquestioned stars of this star-spangled show. Rehearsed and recorded on October 28 and 29 at the Santa Monica Civic Auditorium, the *TAMI Show* is one of the best rock 'n roll movies ever made. It was an event that could only have happened in the sixties when the charts were enough to hold together its mix of pop stars. The cast consisted of surfers (the Beach Boys, and Jan and Dean, who arrived on skateboards), Motown (the Supremes, Marvin Gaye, Smokey Robinson and

the Miracles), Merseysiders (Gerry and the Pacemakers, Billy J. Kramer and the Dakotas) *plus* Chuck Berry, Leslie Gore and James Brown and the Famous Flames. And . . . topping the bill: "All the way from London, the Rolling Stones!" Bo Diddley was also on the show (you can see him in the concluding jam, but he) was censored out of the released version after repeated takes were considered too sexually explicit). James Brown got second billing. Mr. Dynamite, *the* ultimate funk, could outdance anything in the mid-sixties. Watching his stroboscopic splits and stop-time jerk from the wings, the Stones trembled. But Mick miraculously pulled it off doing a direct, if somewhat spastic, cop of James Brown's own faster-than-sound footwork. Admittedly this wasn't the Apollo. "Were we scared," Keith admitted. "But we managed to top James Brown 'cause the audience was *all* white chicks and fifteen years old."

Mick soon began to parody James Brown's funky footwork in his own performances. "He got off the plane doing the 'James Brown slide,' " says Giorgio Gomelsky, about Jagger's infatuation with Mr. Dynamite's dancing. Later that year he and Keith would write the Stone's first Jagger/Richards' hit, using James Brown's famous put-on, pleading routine with the Flames, "Please, Please, Please," as the basis for "The Last Time."

Chess had been the ideal recording studio for the Stones as an R & B band; but, as devoted as they were to their Richmond roots, they were not purists and, perhaps with a little nudge from Andrew, were in search of another kind of sound—the type of studio where the hits were made. While filming the *TAMI Show* they had run into Jack Nitzsche, the show's musical director and Phil Spector's arranger. Earlier that year they had met him for the first time when he attended the Stones' Regent Sound sessions with Spector. Nitzsche recommended RCA's Hollywood studios to the Stones and while in L.A. the Stones cut half a dozen tracks, including a version of "Heart of Stone" written by Mick and Keith which would be released as a U.S. single in December.

If the Stones had never seen anything quite the size of the RCA studios, Jack Nitzsche and David Hassinger, the studio's engineers had never ever seen anything remotely like the Stones before. In her authorized biography of Keith Richards, Barbara Charone recounts the event: "When they first breezed in, everybody in the studio stopped what they were doing and stared. Mick came in bobbing and weaving and snapping his fingers. Keith looked like he al-

ways looks—like a Gypsy criminal. I'm sure he would've become a convict if he hadn't made it as a musician. Brian was dressed ultra-mod, in a suit and vest. I mean it was all totally out of place—it just didn't fit. Nitzsche prefers to think of the early recording sessions as madcap exercises in music-making, where the finished tracks came together magically through sheer spontaneous energy."

DAVE HASSINGER: After a playback you had to get an OK from the Stones before mixing. And an OK from the Stones was Mick and Keith. Not even Andrew. That's why I liked Andrew. He never claimed or appeared to be *the* Rolling Stones. Mick, Keith and Andrew seemed to have that understanding. The determination and what was said musically was always Keith. If a *feel* wasn't right. Keith got it every time. You knew if it was a good take by Keith's smile. I always remember looking at Keith and if he was smiling we had a good take. Keith never said anything. He just smiled. And it would never be questioned, never a discussion.

Nitzsche, who played piano on three of the tracks cut in this marathon session, described the Stones' unorthodox manner of working in the studio: "There was no guidance at all on those records. And very little need for it. What the fuck, this was the first time a band got together and just *played*. They changed my whole idea of recording. Before I'd just been doing sessions, three hours to get the tunes down. Working with the Stones made sense right away. Booked studio time for twenty-four hours a day for two weeks and if ya didn't get it, fuck it. The great new thing about them was they'd record a song the way they had written it. If it didn't work nobody thought twice about making it a tango! They tried every way possible. Nobody had that big ego thing about keeping a song a certain way. That changed me. That was the first really free feeling I had in the studio."

Meanwhile, back in Britain Decca rush-released "Little Red Rooster"/ "Off The Hook" with advance orders of 200,000 copies. It entered the *New Musical Express* singles charts at number one, a feat previously achieved only by Elvis, the Beatles, Cliff Richard and "skiffle king" Lonnie Donnegan.

With "Little Red Rooster" their last British release of 1964, the Stones kissed the blues goodbye, at least on 45s. It was their last R & B single to be released in England. "Heart Of Stone," written by Mick and Keith (as was the B-side "What A Shame"), was released in the States (only) in December and on this blues-based song the Stones brought the same flinty metallic attitude as they had to their incursions into R & B.

Although Oldham had been totally against releasing "Little Red Rooster" as a single, the Stones defiantly insisted on it, it was the first of many examples of the Stones uncanny sense of timing and intuitive genius for succeeding by going against the grain.

Having lived with the Merseybeat sound for two years, the British fans at least had had too much of what had once been a good thing. The tide was turning away from Liverpool and the British charts in September were already registering it.

The Beatles were moving on themselves. Only Gerry and the Pacemakers and Cilla Black were now making chart appearances on behalf of the Liverpool Chamber of Commerce.

On November 13 Pete Goodman's *Our Own Story* by the Rolling Stones, selling at a modest five bob, was published. It contained a mine of myth and fact about the origins of the group that was to be the gospel of the Rolling Stones for almost a decade. A modest 50,000 words, written in a cheerful, jaunty and, needless to say totally uncritical style, it got onto the Top Ten Paperbacks list within five weeks of publication and was seriously reviewed by literary critics like Kenneth Alsop. The reviewer in the London *Observer* referred to it as "a saga of contemporary Rebels With A Cause."

In mid-December, *Ode to a High Flying Bird*, by Charlie Watts, was published by Beat Publications. Written in 1961, Charlie's book about Charlie "Yardbird" Parker is a little gem. Known throughout the world simply as "Bird," Parker is whimsically portrayed by Charlie as an actual bird, hunched over a saxophone so that body blends into head. Bird is born of a "spotty-shelled egg"; a typical Rolling Stone! He's even born wearing the sunglasses that were his trademark, shielding his eyes from the glare of the limelight. Charlie's drawings are tender and understated and so is his storytelling.

By December, in the U.S., "Time Is On My Side" had reached no. 5 in Billboard's Hot 100, making it the biggest hit "stateside" for the Stones to date. In Britain they had the most successful EP (*Five By Five*) of the year, the most successful LP and three No. 1 singles. In the *New Musical Express* year-end poll, the most comprehensive of its kind, the Stones came in second only to the Beatles in the World Vocal Department. Mick got highest placed *group member* in World Male Singer category, two notches up on John Lennon and five on Paul, and came in fourth in Vocal Personality. They also walked off with Best R & B Group of the year *and* Best New Group.

Mick sent the paper this telegram: WALKING ON AIR LOVE MICK

DAVID DALTON

SATISFACTION, 1965

"Satisfaction", the quintessential rock song by the quintessential rock band, flashes the five flinty facets of these crystal quints at their most ferocious and feline. Released (unleashed?) in the U.S. in May "Satisfaction" was the "sure-shot" heard around the world that propelled the Stones into myth history and . . . and megalomania. From now on these Princlings of Pop would be permanent residents at rocks' Valhalla Hotel.

If groups like the Kinks, the Yardbirds and the Who were breathing heavily on their heels, the Stones were still *the* oddity in the English music scene. Partly as a result of Keith's continuing obsession with Chuck Berry riffs and a general revival of R & B among English groups, Chuck was doing a series of successful one-nighters at the end of January.

Apart from this, the situation in pop music in England was still a mawkish wasteland. This month Cliff Richard and the Shadows were playing to sold out houses at the Palladium, Herman's Hermits were packing them in at the Royalty in Chester, Frankie Vaughan was doing a successful tour with Jimmy Tarbuck, the Bachelors were cleaning up the midlands and . . . the Black and White Minstrel Show was selling out at the Victoria Palace.

In the charts the Moody Blues hit the top spot with their "Go Now," followed by Georgie Fame and "Yeh Yeh," his big hit. Twinkle was singing "Terry" into the Top Twenty. But something new *was* happening and it was albums. Specifically Stones albums. They created a minor sensation by getting their new LP into the *singles* chart of *Disc* magazine. This was something else—it meant they were selling more albums than top stars like the Shadows, the Seekers, Chuck Berry, were selling singles.

The big event of January 1965: P. J. Proby splits his pants while performing at the ABC cinema and is subsequently banned from *Ready, Steady Go!* and all major theater circuits. The Stones had been offered an appearance on the show *Sun. Night at the London Palladium* a televised variety show. With conventional wisdom, their co-manager Eric Easton had turned down the invitation: "This is a family show, after all, and I sincerely don't think the country is quite ready to have the boys in their living rooms." *Melody Maker* printed an accompanying photo of the Stones' heads stuck on Beatles bodies (in their Nehru jackets as *they* had appeared on the program) just to underline the absurdity of the idea.

The year began with a short Irish tour. "What was it like?" Keith Altham asked. It was a bit peculiar: swarming with crazed car-crushing codgers, and green all over. The *New Musical Express* reported: "The recent Irish tour was a tonic," grinned Brian. "The Irish are such fantastic characters. We were travelling on the Cork-Dublin road one morning and I got out of the car to ask a couple of locals with a donkey if they would mind Keith filming them with his ciné.

"They thought I was going to attack them or something. Next moment they came at me with shovels! I just made it to the car."

Keith interrupted with another Irish tour story: "We stopped outside a fabulous old shop one morning to buy some gear. It was kind of an old Army surplus store right out in the sticks. There was an old fella behind the counter who screamed that we'd been sent by Oliver Cromwell.

"He chased us out of the shop and jumped on the hood of the car. Then he proceeded to try and boot the windshield to pieces. He must have been at least eighty!"

Rave girl Dawn Adams accompanied the Stones on the Irish tour:

The theatre was empty now. Earlier, through purple spotlights—moving in a frenzied circle—Brian, Mick, Keith, Bill and Charlie had played and sung their way into the hearts of the Irish audience. Screams had even swamped the Stones' noise and the purple lights had lost their colour to eyes dimmed by tears of ecstasy. An ashtray missed Bill's face by inches, an iron bolt hit Mick on the thigh. A mod patent shoe swirled towards Brian. He smiled, and ducked elegantly. A programme hissed past Charlie's ear, but he didn't even notice. These strange tokens of a strange love were hurled from the turbulent sea beyond the footlights.

On January 15th they release their second LP, simply titled *Rolling Stones No. 2* and, as on the first album, it has only a moody photograph of the Stones (and, naturally, the Decca logo) dramatically lit by David Bailey. The same cover photo appears on the *12X5* American LP. The

Stones heads are almost surrealistically stacked and shot with chiaroscuro lighting making them appear to be *lurking* in space like asteroids. The prominence of Keith's face only seems to exaggerate his unfortunate complexion. The fact that Keith's skin condition is here so blatantly put on display was seen as another of Oldham's coded messages. The generally wasted look of the group confirmed every parent's worst fear. Teenagers at least could identify with it. One fan wrote "I'm glad I'm not the only person in the whole world with pimples. Just goes to show I guess even stars get spots. So you're human after all!" As for Keef, as he was now (innocently) being called in the fan magazines, he was becoming more popular than ever.

The cover, nevertheless, is another of Andrew's "I'M LOOKING THROUGH YOU BUT WE'RE NOT THE SAME" telegrams. Really a sophisticated Mod message is being beamed here. Window display as propaganda. The Stones faces at first look menacing but on second glance dissolve into quizical, almost poignant expressions. Unlike other bouncy beat group covers, there is here both intimacy and distance as if we see them through a pane of glass.

But it wasn't the front of the album that caused as much of a commotion as the synthamesc soaked liner notes on the back. An admitted idolizer of Anthony Burgess' droogish novel *A Clockwork Orange* Andrew is at his "Loogish" best here, in his recollection of crystal nights in Richmond and the camraderie of the "six hip malchicks." He deserves a purple heart for this priceless piece of posey

Mod prose; at *least* one!

"It is the summer of the night. London's eyes be tight shut, all but twelve peepers and six hip malchicks who prance the street. Newspaper strewn and grey which waits another day to hide its dirgy countenance; the six have been sound ball journey made to another sphere which pays royalties in eight months or a year.

"Sound is over back eight visions clear and dear. Friends, here are your new groovies so please a-bound to the sound of THE ROLLING STONES. We walk past flat-blocks. 'There's a femme in a frock.'

"'Come on luv,' says Bill, 'Give us a kiss of Christmas.' 'For why I should,' says she, 'you bods ain't Mistahs, with hair like that. You should wear skirts, not shirts!' What abut Charles 1? says Mick. 'I am Charles 1' says she— 'Ah dear; foiled again,' said Keith, whose quite a wit, 'she'd have kissed you in Richmond.'

"Well, my groobies, what about Richmond? With its grass green and hippy scene from which the Stones untaned. The cry in those days of May was have you heard of STONES, a new groupie who look wild and good. Their music is Berry-chuck and all the Chicago hippies.

"Travel to Chicago and ask the malchek plebbies where is Howlin' Wolf? Be he be not the one with Cheyanie Bodie. Oh my groogie back to your window box. Meanwhile back in Richmond, the Stones have grown

and people come from far and wide to hear THE STONES.

"'Somewhat like the Pied Piper,' one mal observed. 'What a wit,' said Keith. A day in May at Richmond came to the treen, two showbiz genties with ideas plenty for the Stones, Easton and Oldham named they were. The rest is not history so I'll tell you bout it. Records followed so did fame, Beatles wrote a song for them that got to number ten. Tours of the country and fame at large the Stones were here, and we'll be back with you when break commercial is over. (This is the Stones new disc within. Cast deep in your pockets for loot to buy this disc of groovies and fancy words. If you don't have bread, see that blind man—knock him on the head, steal his wallet and low and behold you have the loot if you put in the boot, good, another one sold!)

"Back to the show, all was on the go, fame was having its toll of sweat and grime of a million dimes, ah! What a lovely war, Man, Easton called a meet one day; Stones arrived. 'Columbus went to America, so shall we!,' so we went, naturally. They want you in France, in Germany you can dance. No, Brian, no need to grow a moustache. That's all over. It's different now—come on, just you see.

"So see we did, all over the globe, here and there. I remember when we arrived one day at a town called Knokke-le-Zoute. Imagine my surprise and of the plane we got that Charlie

had on the same suit. 'Never mind,' said Mick, 'go to your analyst, he'll sort you out.'

"So off we went, Charlie and me. The doctor knew the score. 'Change your tailor,' said he, as he handed us a bill for 50 gins. 'Ah,' said Keith, who is quite a wit, 'such is fame.' So now it's time to ponder as my penmind can write no longer. What to say on the back of this bag of groovies. I could tell, tale of talent, fame and fortune and stories untold of how these teen peepers (eyes, that is, to you) have taken groupdom by storm, slur you with well-worn clichés compare them to Wagner, Stravinsky and Paramour. I could say more about talent that grows in many directions. To their glory and their story, let the trumpets play. Hold on there, what I say is from the core of this malchik. To this groupie that I have grown with and lived with . . . Dear Mick, Keith, Brian, Bill and Charlie—please autograph this leg I send you 'cause man, that's the sign of a real fan!"

In March, by which time Sir Edward Lewis had presumably had his pet gold bug and a consortium of cryptographers decipher Andrew's Loogese, Decca deleted the passage (in parenthesis) beginning: "This is THE STONES new disc within . . ." to . . . "if you put in the boot, good, another one sold!)" as "in very dubious taste, indeed!" on the second pressing of the LP.

These liner notes, with the offending passages intact, appeared on the jacket of *The Rolling Stones, Now!* in the U.S.

Within, lurked "twelve new black bands" as revolutionary in the Stones inflection of soul music as the first LP had been in their recreation of R & B.

Brian's masterpiece of slide playing, "I Can't Be Satisfied" was not to show up on an American album until the 1972 greatest hits collection *More Hot Rocks.* About this track Robert Palmer wrote:

[The Stones' version of] Muddy Waters' "I Can't Be Satisfied" is the funkiest blues in the Stones discography. Jones was playing excellent bottleneck as far back as 1964. His use of the slide's harmonic potential behind Jagger's unusually authoritarian vocal is worth hearing again and again. He underlines words with whooping washes of metallic sound while Richards plays a characteristically lean back up figure. (Rolling Stone).

Keith was still (and is still) copping Chuck Berry's chops ("You Can't Catch Me," "Down The Road Apiece) and Muddy Waters' "I Can't

Be Satisfied" is included on the album for sentimental reasons, but the Stones had come to the end of their first affair with Fifties rock, R & B and blues.

Keith tilted the licks into Stone hard rock riffs as Mick slyly slinked through the lyrics with a mix of macho and irony. "Jagger," said Robert Christgau, "equivocated around the usages of black singing and around the lyrics themselves, however, he rocked, and even when the Stones were as crude and out-of-tune as their detractors claimed, they made us shake our money-makers. Whatever nuance we thought we pinned down in Jagger's singing—lust or tease, self-confidence or self-mockery—he would most certainly baffle us one convolution later. Only the physical reality of the music was certain."

Recorded at three different locations, the album reflects the differences in the sound of the songs.

The English musical press, in their quaint and jaunty fashion, gave the album top marks.

Before flying off to begin their thirty-day tour of Australia, New Zealand and the Far East they stopped off in Los Angeles on January 17 to cut some tracks at RCA, including their next single, "The Last Time"/ "Play With Fire." The B side, as Andrew recalled it, originally had another title, and they weren't entirely satisfied with the vocals of "The Last Time."

The Stones landed at Sydney Airport at 8:15 a.m. on Thursday, January 21. Imperial Oldham, in mock newsreelese, announced their arrival like the Queen Mum on her Diamond Jubilee visit: "The boys and I were moved as we stood on the steps of the airliner which had brought us to this distant land, receiving a tremendous welcome from those warmhearted and wonderful colonials."

"Three thousand fans, most of them girls, rioted as the five Rolling Stones flew into Sydney airport yesterday to start an Australian tour . . . About three hundred of them tore through a chain wire fence . . . and then smashed into a quarantine area ripping a steel Customs Hall rail." (*Daily Mirror*)

With the Rolling Stones now out of sight inside the airport building, the crowd of three thousand became very restless, chanting "We want the Stones!" Angry teenagers wrenched the railings from the steel floor-bolts and smashed them down to the ground. In the riot twenty girls were crushed, two seriously, and in their scuffles with the police some had their clothing torn.

Horrified Australian papers responded with headlines: "SHOCKERS! UGLY LOOKS! UGLY SPEECH! UGLY MANNERS!"

"The newspapers, trying to dig up scandal stories, ran banner headlines about the Stones having wild all-night parties," Mick complained to the *New Musical Express.* "We wish we were."

But Brian was not to be distracted from the battle by kindness—he telephoned a radio station the same night and requested they play the Honeycombs' "Have I the Right" at 78 r.p.m. It was hysterical and the boys scratched another winning notch on their guitars.

Today the Stones will be entering Melbourne where they will be playing nine shows to houses already sold right out.

"I feel it is our city before we enter it," concluded Mr. Oldham, as confident as Caesar before the gates of Alexandria. (New Musical Express)

By the time the tour was over the Stones had four records in the Australian Top Ten. "Under The Boardwalk" jumped into the Top Hundred at number one, "The Last Time" was number two, "Walking The Dog" number three, and the *Around and Around* EP number six. Appropriately, their Australian fan club presented them with a solid gold map of Australia.

"Such a huge mob of fans pressed around the Chevron Hilton that the boys were forced to use the laundry entrance," John Drew reported from Christchurch, New Zealand. He headed his story "STONES UNWASHED," stating that the Stones "tonight complained that their hotel in Christchurch had too few bathrooms." Said leader Mick Jagger: "So you can't blame us if we smell." (Daily Express, February 1, 1965)

All five Stones took a dip today in Auckland's famous hot springs. "It's just like taking a bath out in the open!" commented lead singer Mick Jagger, after his unusual experience. (London Daily Mirror)

DOWN UNDER RIOTS

The Stones have caused major or minor riots almost everywhere they have appeared in Australia and New Zealand. From the moment they touched down at Kingsford Smith Airport near Sydney they have not had a quiet moment to themselves. But as Keith once said: "Once you've survived a Liverpool or London crowd you can take care of yourself anywhere in the world." (Rolling Stones Monthly, No. 9).

Meanwhile this article appeared in that bible of the well-dressed, *Tailor & Cutter*:

SAVE THE TIE MAKERS

This article is triggered by the sartorial discrepancies of Mr. Mick Jagger (lead singer of the Rolling Stones) but the trend toward disregard of proper clothes for proper occasions is one shared in its instigation by other celebrities of the show business world. The Stones are not the only pebbles on the beach, but an authoritative lead from the Number One spot on the Top 20 would be clearly welcome. It might do more for the necktie than all the tie weeks from here to forever. . . .

HEAD RAPS PARENTS AT SPEECH DAY

On April 9th, it was reported that the headmaster, Mr. E. H. Roberts, of the 1,000 pupil Grove Park Grammar School at Wrexham attacked those parents who allowed their children to wear Rolling Stones "corduroy" trousers. "It was a disservice to the young if adults interpreted freedom as a complete disregard of the rules . . ." (Daily Express).

In February the Stones' third U.S. LP, *The Rolling Stones Now!* (with tracks similar to those on the English *The Rolling Stones No. 2*) was released.

On February 17 they paid another visit to RCA to redo the vocals on "The Last Time," released with "Play With Fire" as the B side in the States and the U.K. during the same week. It entered the *New Musical Express* charts at number eight and *Melody Maker* at number seventeen.

A week after release "The Last Time" was number one. With two previous number one singles, both their EPs and LPs were still at the top of the charts.

At the beginning of March the Stones were a "triple chart threat" with the No. 1 single, No. 1 EP (*Five by Five*) and No. 1 LP (*The Rolling Stones No. 2*).

On the day of its release in England, February 25, the Stones performed "The Last Time" on *Ready, Steady, Go!* where Mick was attacked by "an avalanche of fans" and injured his ankle. "I thudded down on the floor," Mick recalled, "and a mass of girls buried me. I was stomped on by scores of stiletto heels."

Andrew obviously had songwriting in mind for Mick and Keith all along and when he moved into their flat in Hampstead he insisted: "Start writing your own material!" Keith was incredulous:

"This was the point where Andrew Oldham got hold of Mick and me and said: 'Start writing songs.' It was a shock to us. We'd never even thought of it. My first reaction was, Who do you think I am—John Lennon! But we were fortunate enough to have someone naive enough to think we could do it. Andrew's approach was simple: 'You play guitar, write a song.' That was how he was. So, like good little boys, we went back to our little rooms and started to try and do it. And after a few horrendous nights of getting everything off our chests and writing songs that sounded exactly like everybody else's, suddenly something clicked.

"'The Last Time' was the first of our own songs that we really liked. I suppose really the credit, as it happens, goes to Andrew because I never thought of writing; it never occurred to me."

MICK: I suppose we'd been writing for almost nine months to a year by then, just learning how to put songs together. And with "The Last Time," it became fun. After that, we were confident that we were on our way, that we'd just got started.

It's easiest to work together, but it's a lot more difficult to *get* together these days—that's the hassle. Before,

Andrew knows where the key-light is, at the Olympia Palace, Paris, 1965.

it was so easy because we were on the road all the time, and if you got an idea for a song, you just went two doors down the corridor and put it together. Nowadays, we're often 3000 miles apart, and it just doesn't sound as good over the phone. (*Rolling Stones Monthly* No. 14)

"The Last Time" has the distinction of being the first Jagger/Richards composition to to be deemed worthy enough to appear on the A side of an English single.

The B side has a distinction of its own. It is the only song that was not recorded by the band and released as such. At the end of a twenty hour session only Mick and Keith still remained awake. "It was a classic example," says Oldham "of the Stones ability to absorb different types of sound even when the whole band was not playing on the track. Brian, Bill and Charlie didn't play on "Play With Fire." They'd all dropped off to sleep. One could have got them up again but one didn't. So it was Phil Spector on tuned down guitar and Jack Nitzsche on harpsichord in addition to Richards and Jagger. It was at the end of the session with some old guy sweeping up."

In the U.S. the Stones had had two Jagger/Richards A sides previous to "The Last Time": "Tell Me" in June of 1964 and "Heart Of Stone" in December.

Abrasive and yet mesmerising, "The Last Time" is manic, hypnotic, obsessive and eccentric in a manner peculiar to the Stones. It's the first example of their perverse adaption of Phil Spector's "Wall of Sound" productions to their own "Ball of Noise" mixes where diverse frequencies of tone abrasively rub again each other to produce friction, tension and rejection.

Between 1962 and 1965, the Stones wrote some twenty songs in imitation of R & B, a phase of transition the Beatles never went through. Their recreations of R & B were so welded to the Chicago blues tradition that they were able to build on this rock hard sound as the basis for all their future styles. The success of "The Last Time" guaranteed that the Stones would never have to go back to doing other people's material again.

The flip side, "Play With Fire," was the first of the Stones socio-psycho-sexual submission songs in which a cool cruel eye is cast upon situations that in rock had previously been treated with pathetic pleading lyrics or, less frequently, with blunt "you'll get yours, little girl" vengeance. "Vengeance," says an old English

proverb, is a dish best served cold," an adage the Stones with their collective leathery eye took easily to their stony hearts.

Jonathan Cott, in a 1968 interview asked Mick: *I'd like to ask you a personal question about "Play With Fire." There are lines about getting your kicks in Knightsbridge and Stepney and a rich girl, and her father's away and there is a suggestion that the guy in the song is having an affair not only with the daughter but with the mother . . .*

MICK: *Ah, the imagination of teenagers! Well, one always wants to have an affair with one's mother. I mean it's a turn on.*

On March 5th the Stones set out for a two week British tour with the Hollies, Dave Berry, and Goldie and the Gingerbreads. They add four new numbers to their set on this tour. The reason: they are recording a live EP on this tour for release in England in the summer.

"NO TIES, NO MEALS" HOTEL BAN

LONDON, Tuesday.—The Rolling Stones were barred yesterday from having a celebration luncheon at the Midland Hotel, Manchester—because they were not wearing ties.

The ban happened on the day that teenagers swept the group to the top of the British hit parade for their number "The Last Time."

Long-haired singer Mick Jagger, wearing brown corduroy trousers and light grey sweater, went to the hotel to order the celebration lunch for the group.

Well-groomed, middle-aged head waiter Harold Sparrow, in tie and tails, told Jagger, "No ties, no meals."

BJ reads the NME on the Stones and R&B: "Not on your life."

On March 7 a fan defied gravity:

"STONES FAN FALLS FROM THE CIRCLE":

And what a Sunday night that was. The Manchester Palace Theatre jampacked to the back row of the top shelf with the faithful, Screamerama Unlimited. Call out the riot squad.

The Stones, in their best mood after an all-night party, were swinging crazily and raising a storm. Mick was up front astride the footlights stabbing a finger into the purple Bedlam . . . . . "I need you. You. You. You." It was too much.

Without warning, one hysterical girlie came soaring out of the circle and crunch into the stalls fifteen feet below. The stretcher gang moved in. Exit one way-out space-walking chick.

But five minutes later she was back. Minus three teeth. But she could still scream as good as the next. Out in the foyer the ambulance boys were looking for one lost patient.

Second house there was almost a repeat performance. The law pounced just in time. It needed three of them to smother the take-off of the real gone gal in blue. Good job. Yow. You lose more than any three teeth going over the top balcony rail at the Palace. (Ron Boyle, Daily Express.)

BILL: "In a place like Birkenhead, say, we'd go out and start, 'I'm gonna tell you how it's gonna be . . .' three bars and unnnnnh, they'd come sweepin' all over the stage . . . and we'd be back in the hotel with a thousand quid. Girls leapin' from balconies and arrows in the paper next day showin' where they jumped from . . .'"

THE STONES AND THE NORTH

Yes, friends, this is the way the Stones hit the North.

It all started up here and there's no audience in the world like them. South of Brum it's comparative Noddyland.

Admits Mick: "After that fantastic night in Manchester we were scared silly. You know how these things catch on. We could easily have ended up with an outbreak of swan-diving from the balconies and somebody killed.

Brian Jones agreed: "Give me the North for action. It's the craziest. They're not kidding when they tell you to check under the bed for fluff. One stop there were no less than four birds hiding under the bed. Don't ask me how they got past the police and hotel flunkies or found which was my room." (Daily Express.)

When asked why he hadn't let go of the mike while a dozen girls kissed and hugged him and tried to drag him from the stage at Manchester, Mick replied, "Well, I was recording, wasn't I?"

It was the night the Stones recorded the shortest-ever track to be given a label credit: "We Want the Stones." This ear-piercing chant from the audience backed by the tuning of guitars (writing credits to Nanker Phelge!) was to be the opening track of their EP *Got Live If You Want It*, released on June 11. Not to be confused with the LP of the same name recorded in September and October 1966 and released the following month (in the U.S. and Europe only).

Andrew Oldham had made an attempt to record on the first date of the tour in London but it wasn't until the next night at Liverpool that he and Glyn Johns got the balance down. The tracks on the finished EP were recorded at Manchester (March 7) and Greenford (March 16), as well as at Liverpool on the sixth.

On March 18, after their last gig of the tour at the Odeon Cinema, Romford, occurred the infamous incident at the filling station, a legendary event in the Stones' history, which has been engraved in the annals of rock 'n roll along with Mick's immortal words: "We piss anywhere, man!" The Stones on their way back to London stopped at the Francis Garage, Stratford, West Ham, and asked if they could use the toilet. When they were refused, Bill, Brian and Mick got out of their chauffeur-driven Daimler and urinated against the wall of the gas station. "A pleasure," Alexis Korner noted, "for which they were fined five pounds each and well worth it."

What happened that night on the Romford Road, according to Keith: "The funniest thing happened. It was just in that period, when the Rolling Stones were real big biggies. One night coming back from gig in North London, Bill Wyman, who has this prodigious bladder, decided he wanted to have a pee. So we told the driver to stop. The car is full up with people and a few other people say, 'Yeah, I could get into that. Let's take a pee.' So we leap out and we had chosen a gas station that looked closed but it wasn't. There we are, up against the wall, spraying away.

"And suddenly this guy steps out. And a cop flashes his torch on Bill's cock and says 'All right. What you up to then?' And that was it. The next day it was all in the papers. Bill was accused and Brian was accused of insulting language. Because what they did them for was not peeing but for trespassing.

"All these witnesses come up. 'There he was, your Honor, he was facing the wall, and well, he was, uh, urinating.'" (*Rolling Stone*, August 19, 1971).

From March 24 to April 5 the Stones did a brief Scandinavian tour. Something rotten happened to them in the state of Denmark that put the Stones in a state of shock and almost short-circuited their career.

STONES IN SHOCKING INCIDENT

During a sound check before their concert in Odense, Denmark last Friday the Rolling Stones received a nasty shock (of the electrical variety) when lead singer Mick Jagger came into contact with two live microphones at once. They short circuited, throwing him against Brian Jones who collided with Bill Wyman who was knocked unconscious by the 220-volt shock. The show's promoter, Knud Thorbjoersen, said, "Bill Wyman came to after a few minutes. The thing that saved them was that an electric plug was pulled out by Mick Jagger's fall." (London Daily Mirror, March 29, 1965)

On April 9 the Stones did their first live show on *Ready, Steady, Go!*

Up to this time on English TV, groups had mimed (lip-synched) their material. According to new regulations they now had to perform their songs "live," although the show itself was recorded.

At 9:00 a.m. on Thursday, April 22, the Stones flew out of London Airport en route to Montreal to begin their third American tour. They arrived ten hours later at 1:00 p.m. Canadian time on the afternoon of the 23d. They performed that night at the Maurice Richard Auditorium in Montreal.

The following day the Stones drove in three cars with their equipment to Ottawa. The show there, at the Y auditorium began at 8:30. Ten minutes later the stage was besieged. The

On Ready Steady Go!

noise from five thousand screaming fans was so loud that the fact that Brian's amp kept cutting out and the power turned off altogether a number of times wasn't even noticed. Finally, fifty local police formed a solid wall around the stage, making the Stones invisible, so that by the end of the show, they could neither be seen nor heard. The next day they drove to Toronto, photographing turnpikes, trees, truck stops and each other. On the way, the idea for what was to become "Satisfaction" came to Keith. After press conferences and radio shows they performed for their largest North American audience to date, 16,000, at the Maple Leaf Gardens. Police numbered over a hundred. The last Canadian concert was at the Treasure Island Gardens, London, Ontario. Although the audience was small, 3,500 fans had driven across the border from the U.S. to attend. Despite a six-foot fence in front of the stage and a large contingent of police, some fifty fans crashed through onto the stage. Halfway through the fifth number, "Off The Hook," police turned on the house lights and cut off the power to the amps and mikes. Charlie kept on drumming and Mick continued singing and playing maracas, with

Brian on tamborine and Keith and Bill clapping. When the police refused to switch the group's current on, Mick apologized to the audience, said a few parting nasties to the cops, and they left the stage after a show that had lasted barely fifteen minutes. Local radio stations the following day were bombarded with calls from irate fans blaming police for the disruption while the local papers gave the Stones their first sensational headlines of the tour: POLICE QUELL RIOT AT ROLLING STONES CONCERT; CRUDE AND RUDE ROLLING STONES HURL INSULTS AT POLICE; ROLLING STONES CREATE HAVOC AT GARDENS—DAMAGES IN THOUSANDS REPORTED.

Mick admitted: "We just felt sorry for the fans suddenly not having a show to watch. So we ganged up on the police." (*Rolling Stones Monthly*, no. 24.)

The first U.S. dates—Albany, New York, on April 29 and Worcester, Massachusetts, the following day—passed without serious incident. On May 1 the two afternoon concerts at the Academy of Music in Brooklyn were so successful that three more shows were added to the end of the tour.

During the Stones' stay in New York fans camped out on 55th Street in front of the Gotham Hotel. Outside suite number 709 armed security guards were posted day and night. Girls disguised as Chrissie Shrimpton, room service, Murray the K, and their mothers attempted to crash the Stones' camp.

Before their appearance on the *Ed Sullivan Show* on May 2, Ed sent a note to Andrew that he'd appreciate it if the boys would make some determined effort to smarten themselves up. The boys went shopping.

To avoid outbreaks of enthusiasm similar to those that had disrupted the rehearsals of the Stones' first appearance on the Sullivan show in October 1964, they were locked in the studio for twelve hours before air time. A minor disturbance occurred anyway when the Stones appeared on the first half of the show to perform only one song, "The Last Time," giving the impression that they were not the headliners. (Tom Jones appeared in the flesh and Dusty Springfield on a film strip.) Ed had to hurriedly explain that this was not "The Last Time" they would appear. In the second half they came back to do "Little Red Rooster" and an unprecedented two extra songs, "Everybody Needs Somebody To Love" and "2120 Michigan Avenue."

While in town the boys checked out the "brand-new beat" uptown. They stopped in to see Wilson Pickett backstage at the Apollo and were handed a note from James Brown, saying: "Missed you once again on this tour. Just wanted to pay my respects and say how much I like your new records."

During their stay in New York they appeared on an hour-long special TV show, *Beatles vs. Rolling Stones*, emceed by Clay Cole, who introduced the program with hype, hysteria and hokey homilies: "Beatlemania and the big shock wave of the Rolling Stones. Nobody said lightning couldn't strike twice, that there would ever be a group bigger or with better impact than the Beatles. The Rolling Stones are certainly gaining an edge on the Beatles. Their records are outselling the Beatles in England and reports from all over New York are that the Stones are outselling the Beatles three to one. The Stones have their cult of fans and the Beatles have their cult of fans. Two strong camps. We have both represented in the studio tonight. How many Beatles fans have we got? [*screams*] How many Rolling Stones fans? [*screams*] They're about equal. We have something for both of you. A whole show about the Beatles with exclusive films and interview and exclusive in-person performances by the Rolling Stones!"

The Stones' concerts were more successful than ever and "The Last Time" went gold, selling over a million copies worldwide. Released in the U.S. in March it became the Stones' biggest hit to date, getting to number eight in *Billboard*'s Hot Hundred on March 8. Yet inside room 709 apprehensions were building about the Next Big Thing in pop music.

The latest trend sweeping the land was folk rock. By the summer of 1965 the Animals were doing it ("We Gotta Get Out of This Place") the Byrds were doing it, the Turtles were doing it, even Sonny and Cher were doing it. Like psychedelic music two years later, protest music was something to which the Stones just could not relate. They did not want to duplicate, assimilate, prognosticate, repudiate, alien-

The Ed Sullivan show; with chandeliers yet!

ate or underrate.

Whatever these sweet young things who dig Dylan say, I bet they don't understand much of what he is doing. We play a lot of his LPs, Brian and I, and quite a lot of his lyrics don't mean anything to us.

I have nothing against Dylan or Donovan but I'm sick to the back teeth about the characters who are just climbing on a craze, that think they can make quite a fortune. (Rolling Stones Monthly, No. 21).

Keith, a year later, was a convert.

STONES STONED ON DYLAN

Dylan is a progressive writer. You only have to listen to "Blonde on Blonde" and compare it with his early albums to see how far he's gone. People aren't really sympathetic to Bob Dylan.

"What do you think about Dave Clark, then, Mick?" (Australia).

They said that "Rainy Day Woman" was rubbish, but if you'd been stoned and listened to the disc you would have understood.

On May 3 the Stones flew to Georgia to begin a short tour of the South, playing Statesboro the fourth, Atlanta the fifth. They played the Tampa, Florida, baseball stadium on a stage set up over home plate. Riots as fans swarmed over the diamond. Concert called after five songs.

That night, May 6, while staying at the Gulf Motel in Clearwater, Florida (where the cover photos for *Black and Blue* were shot ten years later), Keith first played Mick the riff and refrain of "Satisfaction."

May 7, Birmingham, Alabama ("Wham, bam, Birmingham, Alabam don't give a damn"), with the Beach Boys and the Righteous Brothers. "Their time off," reported the *Rolling Stones Monthly*, was spent "swimming and sunbathing round a plush hotel pool. As ever, they drew astonished gazes from the other guests, but the boys also won new admirers by their quick repartee and their so-English efforts to fit in the American Scene." Well, it wasn't *that* easy.

STONES EXPOSED

Yes, here they are, the Rolling Stones exposed to the elements as they don bathing suits and go for a dip in a swimming pool. But when the Stones go for a swim strange things happen. As Brian reported in New Musical Express last June: "We were laying by a swimming pool just sunbathing. After a couple of hours a speed cop came up to us and said the police had been swamped with complaints from passing motorists saying they had seen a group of women indecently exposing themselves! It could only happen in the States! As our exclusive photographs show, our boys are quite masculine—and their hair isn't THAT long."

On May 9 the Stones flew to Chicago for a concert that night at the Crown Aire Theater. The following morning they entered Chess Studios:

The Stones spent all day in the atmosphere packed studios and by evening had completed four tracks. Titles were: "Have Mercy" ["Mercy, Mercy"], "Try Me," "That's How Strong My Love Is" and—a number entitled "The Under-assistant West Coast Promotion Man." This was a Nanker-Phelge composition, which means that the entire group had a hand in writing it but there are no prizes for guessing the name of the bloke who thought up the title. (Pop Weekly)

"The Under Assistant West Coast Promotion *Man*" is a tongue-in-cheek tribute to George Sherlock from London Records, who had been the Stones' promo man on their first U.S. tour. They also cut a still unreleased version of James Brown's "Try Me" and the first attempt at "Satisfaction."

According to the *Rolling Stones Monthly* (no. 1) there had already been two abortive attempts to cut this track at studios in England:

From all accounts of how "Satisfaction" evolved, this seems unlikely. Whether or not it first came to Keith literally "while driving in my car" as he told Barbara Charone, it's a classic Holiday Inn song written on the road during the Stones' third American tour.

The night of May 11 the Stones flew to L.A. The next morning at ten they entered RCA Studios to cut more tracks and specifically to have another try at "Satisfaction."

KEITH: "A week later we recorded it again in Los Angeles. This time everything went right. Charlie put down a different tempo and with the addition of a fuzz box on my guitar which takes off all the treble we achieved a very interesting sound."

Although "Satisfaction" was released only in mono and simulated stereo, like all their records up to *Aftermath*, the Stones had been recording in stereo since mid-1964. On the stereo master tape of "Satisfaction" there are two distinct layers. On the reference track, possibly from the Chess sessions, Keith chops out the basic riff on acoustic guitar, backed by Charlie on drums, Bill on bass and Ian Stewart on piano. Except as harmonics and overtones this track is barely audible (you can hear it under the opening fuzz guitar and under Mick's vocal as he goes into the last chorus) on the released version. It is buried under the predominantly mixed "up" track containing the Gibson fuzzbox guitar, lead, vocals and more pronounced drums, percussion and a moody lurking bass line from Bill. The earlier reference track with its lighter acoustic sound is perhaps the folk-rock subtext (in the vein of "Play With Fire" and "The Spider And The Fly") that Mick and Keith allude to and perhaps explains Keith's reluctance to release it because it sounded like a folk song.

Another of Keith's objections, apart from the track, was that "it sounded like a protest song." If this seems hard to believe in retrospect, you have to bear in mind that this was the year of Barry "Eve of Destruction" McGuire and other folk-rock propagandist propounding songs of great sociopolitical import.

MICK: It sounded like a folk song when we first started working on it and Keith didn't like it much, he didn't want it to be a single, he didn't think it would do very well. That's the only time we have had a disagreement.

Q: Even when it was finished, he didn't like it?

MICK: I think Keith thought it was a bit basic. I don't think he really listened to it properly. He was too close to it and just felt it was a silly kind of riff. (*Rolling Stone*, October 12, 1968.)

Opening with Keith Richards' menacing fuzz-tone riff and sung with an insinuating, calculated slowness by Jagger, the smoldering sound of "Satisfaction" sums up the frustrations of the sixties in a new emotional language: an ironic blend of blues, R & B and rock that the Stones had been working on since 1962, now powered with the driving infusion of soul music. The synthesis combined the ecstatic momentum of Motown with the disdainful tone of the blues in a lethal brew that scathingly indicted the hypocrisy, corruption and folly of the society they lived in while simultaneously celebrating their release from it. The American *Out of Our Heads*, recorded at Chess and RCA (plus a track, "I'm Alright," from the English *Got Live* EP), came out the same year. Its white-funk R & B sound was the culmination of the first phase of the Stones' career.

"Satisfaction" is the greatest of the Stones' inner-city hymns—blues words with a soul sound in a rock song. Keith has said that "Satisfaction" is based loosely on Martha and the Vandellas' "Dancing in the Streets." While this may be true of the tone of "Satisfaction," its punch and drive are much closer to the Vandellas' "Nowhere To Run." "Satisfaction" is the first of Keith's monolithic riff transformations: the model, matrix and *master*-piece for all future Stones' gold from "Get Off Of My Cloud" to "Miss You." Giorgio Gomelsky comments: "The Stones will pinch any good riff, any good riff they hear they'll pinch it, and they'll transform it in such a way you don't know where they pinched it from. And the Beatles are the same thing . . . they finally told me, I said where are you getting your fucking ideas? That's what everybody does in art, you know?"

"Satisfaction" is a classic car radio song. Oldham: "Hitting the States and hearing radio opened everybody up as to how *much* of everything existed. Finally we were hearing *everything*, not just what got through to England. Also, it helped to realize that all the records they liked but never heard on English radio actually *were* radio records." (Barbara Charone, *Keith Richards*)

Andrew felt that if the Stones were going to escalate, especially in the U.S., they would have to not only write their own material but use current American music as a model. Spector was Oldham's model, but obviously the Stones could not and would not be the Ronettes! Bob Crewe, a mutual friend of Spector's and Oldham's, produced the Four Seasons—and odd as it may seem, they were temporarily not only a favorite of Keith's and Brian's but the Stones actually attempted a few Four Seasons harmonies.

More plausible was the integration of current soul sound—Otis Redding, James Brown, Wilson Pickett and Marvin Gaye, who were black mainstream contemporary equivalents of the Chicago blues idols. Once into the groove, Keith tracked the brand-new beat to its gospel source on "The Last Time" and extended it into the chicken-scratch guitar chopping in James Brown's sound and the laid-back economy of Steve Cropper's lick on Otis Redding's and Wilson Pickett's records. Mick immediately picked up on the flash, coordinating cool moves of soul acts, and as a master mimic "covered" the vocal styles of soul singers like Marvin Gaye. By the time of *Out of Our Heads* Mick had really got it down. For once Andrew's instigations meshed with the Stones' natural inclinations. Or at least with Mick and Keith's.

Bill: "Andrew wanted us to do some much more pop-oriented material. He was always pushing to get us to do Motown things like "Can I Get A Witness." And he was right as well; he was more right than we were. And, of course, when Mick and Keith got into writing, the songs came out more like he was looking for. Keith was always more into soul music than me or Charlie, and Mick loved soul performers like Wilson Pickett and James Brown."

In constructing his synthamesc soul sound on "Satisfaction," Keith heard horns. Horns, on Motown and Stax, *pushed* the sound out; they also gave soul records a communal voice, the gospel sound of Joshua's trumpet that could bring down the walls and prepare the way for dancing in the streets. Horns, in black music of the sixties, meant party time. They lifted the R & B rhythm section, spelled cel-eb-ra-tion and then reinforced the message. Despite the cynical, self-mocking frustration stated in the lyrics, "Satisfaction" is an *up* song, as much about getting it as being frustrated about not getting it. The fuzz guitar riff balances neatly on the borderline of menace, arrogance and incitement, but the drive and feel of the song are liberating. This is the way Otis heard it too.

KEITH: "I mean, that riff needed to sustain itself and Gibson had just brought out these little boxes so . . . But the riff itself was in essence not meant for the guitar. Otis Redding got it right when he recorded it because it's actually a horn riff. I never thought that song was commercial anyway. Shows how wrong you can be."

After straining to hear the buried lyrics on *Exile*, "Satisfaction" seems an elementary Stones decoding problem. But as Professor Meltzer pointed out there were many interpretations flying around at the time:

"The Rolling Stones' 'Satisfaction' is on first hearing utterly baffling, beyond interpretation with words intentionally elusive (they sound like 'flagellation' and words of that ilk) and music loud enough to further obscure them. This first 'Satisfaction' experience is one of ambiguous defiance. Eventually the words become audible and understandable, yielding a second-level (lewd) 'Satisfaction' (where the word turns out to be 'magination'). Finally, hearing the song with stereophonic earphones and attending to each (erotic) nuance is the third-level 'Satisfaction' encounter. From ambiguous vulgarity embodiment to lewdness to eroticism."

Said *Time* in their April 28, 1967 issue:

"[The Rolling Stones] write songs about 'trying to make some girl,' with supposedly coded allusions to menstruation, marijuana and birth control pills."

The lyrics to "Satisfaction" *were* in fact buried in the track.

Nitzsche remembers burying the vocals on the early records. A bit naive in those days, Hassinger never understood why. "I never heard the damn lyrics to "Satisfaction" for years. They kept telling me to bring the voice down more and more into the track. I thought they were crazy. I didn't know it had to do with the lyric and getting radio play. (Barbara Charone, 'Keith Richards').

In the middle of May the Stones played West Coast dates. On the evening of the 16th they shared the bill with Chuck Berry on the *Hollywood A Go Go* TV show. Earlier that day following a concert at Civic Hall, Long Beach, they came close to autodestruction.

Screaming, jumping, weeping and clawing, two thousand frenzied fans threw themselves at, and on top of the Stones' limo like Indian widows on a funeral pyre. Keith, with a shudder, remembers the horror of premature entombment to this day: "We tried to get out through a narrow passage. But the kids roared down on us. Without exaggeration there must have been a hundred piled on top of the car and we could hear the roof creaking and cracking. Inside, panicking like mad, we stood up and tried to hold up the roof. But the kids were everywhere. Outside, trying to force the door-handles, trying to smash in the windows. We couldn't get moving, otherwise someone would have been killed. It was definitely the most frightening thing of my whole life."

On June 4 "Satisfaction" entered *Billboard*'s Top Hundred at 64. Two weeks later it jumped a phenomenal sixty places to number four. In L.A. the Stones won an AM radio poll by 500 votes with the Beatles in second place, Herman third.

In England, after two postponements due to problems with sound quality, the *Got Live If You Want It* EP was released June 11 and entered the *New Musical Express* Top Thirty singles chart a week later at number thirteen. A good buy it contained five frenzied Stones tracks (six, if you count the twelve-second "We Want The Stones" intro). The *New Musical Express* gave it a rave:

NEW STONES EP!

Don't expect technical perfection from the Stones' forthcoming EP, "Got LIVE If You Want It." The balance is far from perfect, and the continuous deafening screams mean that Mick's vocals are largely incomprehensible.

But if you're looking for seething

tension, an electrifying atmosphere, and spine-tingling excitement—you'll find 'em all on this disc. . . .

What this lacks in polish it makes up for in raw, vital enthusiasm. (Derek Johnson)

The *Got Live* EP was the first and most frenzied record of the Stones' tribal events, where the audience became inseparable from the group and the performance. Unlike the *Got Live* album of a year later, or *Get Your*

Ya Yas Out in 1970, this was a live recording without later overdubs of vocal, guitars or audience. On the British tour in March, engineer Glyn Johns had dangled a mike from the balcony of theaters like the Empire (Liverpool), the Palace (Manchester) and the Granada (Greenford) to capture the audience "in the field," while taping the Stones through the stage mikes on another machine. The crudeness of the sound quality of the *Got Live* EP gives it the immediacy of a bootleg (without the problems with balance that plague bootlegs), and it freezes in time not a performance but an *event*. To the true fan it's immaterial whether a certain song here is a "walloping thumper," it's the fetishism of the moment that counts. Events, by their nature, penetrate the hubbub.

On June 15–18 the Stones did a brief tour of Scotland. Perhaps remembering the havoc Glaswegians wreaked on Blackpool the year before, a contingent of mounted police were stationed in a ring around the Glasgow Odeon on opening night to keep fans and foes at bay. This didn't prevent enthusiastic audiences from demolishing several Scottish cinemas from within. Some two hundred theater seats were smashed on the tour. Mick countered that perhaps the seats just weren't what they used to be.

Released in the U.S. in May, by June 18 "Satisfaction" was number five in *Billboard*'s Hot Hundred. The following week it made No. 1, where it stayed until July 31, when it dropped to twelve.

On July 22 Mick, Brian and Bill appeared in court at West Ham to be arraigned for the incident at the Francis Garage on March 18:

"SHAGGY-HAIRED MONSTERS" FINED FOR "PUBLIC INSULT"

Nearly three hundred women and teenaged girls waited outside a court yesterday for the arrival of the Rolling Stones pop group.

Three members of the group—singer Mick Jagger, 21, and guitar-players Bill Wyman, 23, and Brian Jones, 21—appeared in court at West Ham accused of using insulting behavior at a London garage.

Sixty teenagers packed the public gallery, on each side of which stood three policemen. Outside, fifty policemen were on duty controlling the crowd.

Charlie Watts, the group's drummer, listened to the case from the back of the court.

The fifth member of the group, lead guitarist Keith Richard gave evidence for the three accused.

Jagger, Wyman and Jones denied

Keith: *"Bill has the biggest bladder in the world".*

using insulting behavior by urinating against a wall at the Francis service station in Romford-road, Forest Gate.

They were found guilty and fined £5 each. All three gave notice of appeal.

"Whether it is the Rolling Stones, the Beatles or anyone else, we will not tolerate conduct of this character.

"Because you have reached exalted heights in your profession it does not mean you have to act like this. On the contrary, you should set a standard of behavior which should be a moral pattern for your large numbers of supporters."

Their lawyer, Mr. Dale Parkinson, said they would appeal.

The three, who were ordered to pay 15 guineas costs, were mobbed by about 300 fans as they drove away from the court after the hearing.

"Their ideas of what to call 'home' are getting grander," reported Maureen O'Grady in *Rave*. "All of them, literally, fight over copies of *Country Life* that they come across, looking for big country houses to buy themselves." Charlie purchased a sixteenth-century mansion in Sussex, once the home of the archbishop of Canterbury. "Commented Charlie's dad, a parcels truck driver at King's Cross Railway Station: 'We are proud of Charlie, but we can't understand why he prefers an old place like this to

something modern, which is what I would have liked myself.'" (*Evening News*, July 29, 1965)

Even in the bemused prose of the English musical press, Brian's life began to appear more and more manic:

SUE MAUTNER TAKES YOU ON A VISIT TO BRIAN JONES' NEW PAD

It was 3:30 p.m. when I arrived at Brian Jones' pad. Brian had just arrived back from New York, and had been home precisely three hours. But on entering the lounge it looked as though he'd been there three days.

To say it was in a mess would be an understatement, bedlam was more like it. Dozens of plates with the remains of curry stuck to them were piled high on a table, letters and magazines were littered about, suitcases and clothes in the most unobvious places, weird instruments in one corner, Spencer Davis, Stevie Winwood, their road manager Dave and driver Tom in the other corner amidst a pile of album sleeves and Brian standing in the midst of it all clad in a rather weird assortment of clothes—plaid trousers, a white shirt dotted with small black motives, a neckerchief and stetson hat, not to mention his pink tinted specs perched on the end of his nose.

No Sleep For Fifty Hours

"You'll have to excuse the mess, you'd never believe I came into a clean place at 10 o'clock would you?" I thought it would be more tactful if I ignored that question.

"I haven't slept for fifty hours. I was going to go straight to bed, but Spence and Stevie put a stop to that—I don't mind, it was a great coming home present seeing them here. Man you should see the stuff we've got through.

"Come on, I'll give you a guided tour," said my host, as we approached the kitchen. It was, as one would imagine, a bachelor's kitchen —washing-up already piled high in the sink, half-opened packages strewn across the table and, to make the place look even more like "home," there were empty cans of Coke and milk bottles everywhere! (New Musical Express, March 26, 1965)

On August 24, the Stones had their first meeting with Allen Klein at the Hilton Hotel in London. Oldham, peddling Jagger/Richards songs, had met Klein a few days before. Oldham describes the encounter. "It's a very incestuous world. Our habits then were that if we had recorded an outside tune I would go around knocking on the doors of the various publishers going, 'Could be a single but we want a piece'—'cause we were making money, but not that much. I arranged a meeting with this guy called J. W. Alexander, the administrator of Kags Music, but Klein really owned it. As a manager he represented Sam Cooke, though I never met him in the days that I worked for Sam Cooke. He handled the catalogue for Kags Music, which had 'It's All Over Now.' I rolled up for breakfast at the Hilton to ask him my percentage for the Stones for doing the song. Klein was sitting there asking all the right questions like: 'Do you want to be a millionaire?' and 'Do the Stones want to be famous?' Yes. About a day later I brought Mick and Keith around to see him and they were as enchanted as I was. It was all go. It was really as simple as that."

"Satisfaction," when released in the States, was number eight in Billboard's Top Hundred two weeks later. The following week it made No. 1, the first No. 1 single for the Stones in the States. By the time it was released in England on August 20 it had been No. 1 in the U.S. charts for five weeks. It established the Stones the American market, made them superstars and brought them their first big money.

OLDHAM: "There hadn't been that much cash around prior to 'Satisfaction.' Partly this was due to their recording deals and American sales figures" . . . and Allen Klein.

Klein was Uncle $am personified. His style was American flamboyant, part mobster, part eccentric millionaire. It proved irresistible to the Stones. "The Stones were very taken with the Klein image," Ian Stewart recalled. "They thought it was marvelous. Eric Easton got rubbed out. Everybody thought Klein was a great idea."

The Stones' recording contract with Decca had expired in February. They have always been lucky to have large hits when signing time comes around: "Brown Sugar" in 1971, "Hot Stuff" in 1976. "Satisfaction" in May of 1965 put them in a very strong position.

Klein promised to make the Stones rich beyond their wildest dreams.

Andrew's eyes were as big as saucers. Oldham: "Ya gotta remember, Klein was brought in for one thing: 'All right we're famous, now let's have some money.' No one can say he didn't do that. At the time my idea was 'John Lennon's got this black Rolls-Royce with black windows, can I get one?'

By the time they went to America again they made money. Klein got them better gigs. "We could actually go shopping then." (Barbara Charone, Keith Richards)

On August 27 the new management agreement was announced in the New Musical Express. The next day it was reported in the national press and a week later the New Musical Express added:

Andrew Oldham becomes sole manager for the group. Eric Easton, previously their co-manager, is no longer associated with them.

American producer Allen Klein will act as business manager for both the Stones and Oldham, and will commute regularly between America and Britain.

From his penthouse suite high above London's fashionable Mayfair district, Klein had shown them the world laid out before them. It was now within their grasp—it could be theirs for a song!

Six years later—a year after they

had severed their ties with Klein—Keith, in an interview with Robert Greenfield, still had great admiration for Klein's tactics.

KEITH: Andrew got Klein to meet us, to get us out of the original English scene. There was a new deal with Decca to be made and no one really knew, everyone wanted to know about it, in a business we'd never thought of. Who's actually making the money. He was managing financial advisor for Donovan and the Dave Clark Five, Herman's Hermits, who were all enormous then.

The first time we met was in London. The only thing that impressed me about him was that he said he could do it. Nobody else had said that.

Q: Did the Stones decide together to go with Klein?

KEITH: I really pushed them. I was saying, "Let's turn things around. Let's do something." Either we go down to Decca and tell them to do it with us . . . which is what we did that very day with Klein, just went down there and scared the shit out of them.

Q: You originally signed a two-year contract with them?

KEITH: Yeah, in '63. He did a good job, man. Andrew told us that Klein was a fantastic cat for dealing with those people, which we couldn't do. Andrew knew he didn't know enough about the legal side of it to be able to do it. So we had to get someone who knew how to do it or someone who'd fuck it up once and for all. Then it would be up to us to deal with him. (Rolling Stone)

On Friday, September 2, the Stones taped Ready Steady Goes Live, taking over the program as hosts.

The highlight of the show was Mick and Andrew's campy send-up of Sonny and Cher's "I Got You Babe," with Andrew miming Cher's "I don't care if your hair's too long" and stroking Mick's hair while Mick mimed Sonny's reply, "With you I can't go wrong."

On September 3 and 4 the Stones played Dublin and Belfast and made a documentary, "Charlie Is My Darling." Andrew intended it to be a sort of trial run for the indefinitely postponed Stones feature film and the first page of an ongoing cinematic diary of the Stones. "We were very hot on the idea," Oldham recalls. "So much so that we were actually rehearsing making movies. There's a film around that I did with them in Ireland —'Charlie Is My Darling'—that I think we almost spent more money on the credits than we did on the film. I think it was actually two grand on the credits, four grand on the film. Looking back, it seems like it was just an exercise in bullshitting ourselves. We just wanted to be able to see the credits. Then we said, 'We'll go on with this,' but we never did." (Trouser Press)

Considering how good the film was, it is a pity Andrew never carried his ambitious project any further. The Stones' early promo films were really an extension of this idea and were also brilliantly directed by Peter Whitehead. Shot in black and white, the film was an intimate record of the

Brian: "I wear a Nazi uniform to show I'm anti-nazi".

Stones on tour in Ireland.

On September 5, the Stones flew to L.A. to record their next single, "Get Off Of My Cloud" and several other tracks, most of which would appear on *December's Children*: "She Said Yeah," "Talkin' About You," "The Singer Not The Song," "I'm Free," "Gotta Get Away" and "As Tears Go By," which was rerecorded in London at the IBC Studios on October 26.

"Get Off Of My Cloud"/"I'm Free" was released in the States at the end of September. The multidimensional curse of "Get Off Of My Cloud" is considerably more ambivalent and exclusive: "'Cause two's a crowd on my cloud, baby.'

Despite Dylan's famous remark to Keith that Dylan could have written "Satisfaction" but would have liked to see the Stones write "Mr. Tambourine Man," Mick has never resisted the temptation to try. "Get Off Of My Cloud" is the first in a long sequence of Dylanesque attempts. But where there always appeared to be a (mislaid) cabalistic key to Dylan's "chains of flashing images," the Stones' lyrics, though more blatant on the surface, oscillated wildly like coke-crazed cartoons jumping out of their frames.

Wednesday, September 8, the Stones played the Palace Ballroom in Douglas, Isle of Man. Riots within and without. Fans surrounded the Palace, preventing Mick from getting into the theater. He was forced to make an undignified entrance through the bathroom window. They announced this was to be their last ballroom appearance . . . ever.

On the German tour, September 11–17, fans, predominantly male, were so violent that the federal government feared an eruption of neo-Nazism.

STYMIED GERMAN POLICE REFUSE ROLLING STONES PROTECTION

(DUSSELDORF)—Police used fire-hoses on several thousand screaming teenagers here yesterday as the mob broke through security cordons when the group's plane touched down. Police called Press Conference after 15 minutes to say they could not guarantee the safety of the British group. (Daily Mirror, September 12)

Even before their arrival, leading hotels in Düsseldorf canceled reservations for the group. At a press conference in the Düsseldorf airport, thousands of fans went berserk, hundreds of them breaking through police cordons, attacking police and smashing doors. At the concerts fans stomped their feet and chanted the

words to "The Last Time" and "Satisfaction" so enthusiastically that buildings shook. Germany hadn't seen such mass hysteria since the Hitler Youth movement.

There had been running riots at Stones concerts since Sunderland in early '64, but this was a bloody *Blitzkrieg!* It was mother's milk to the Twin Sons of the She-Wolf and they did their best to incite the pack. Oldham:

Like on one German tour someone said to Mick that it would be really hysterical if he did the goose-step during the instrumental break in "Satisfaction." Well, Jagger being Jagger not only does that, he goes on stage and does the whole Hitler routine.

The audience [was] going crazy anyway and that just drove them berserk. There were too many fuzz and dogs in the theater for them to do anything then, but when they got outside they overturned 130 cars and every train leaving the city for the suburbs was wrecked completely.

Well, at the time I thought that was a buzz. That was a good show. . . . (New Musical Express, June 17, 1972)

Before leaving the theater, German fans managed to rip out fifty rows of seats and reduce them to splinters.

Appropriately enough, the Stones were extracted from their fans through an underground tunnel left over from World War II: "The police led them through an old Nazi bunker—the Aryan inscriptions still on the walls—and up into some pinewoods a mile and a half from the theater. But still they had to run." (*Rolling Stones Monthly*)

Anita Pallenberg as a London fashion model in the mid-sixties, whips up her charisma in a crotcheted turtle neck sheath.

In September *Out of Our Heads* was released in Britain (the American album, with differing tracks, had been released in July and had already gone gold).

This was the last Stones album where tracks on the English and American LPs differed substantially. While the English release was in the commendable tradition of "giving our fans their money's worth," the American *Out of Our Heads*, because it included singles like "Satisfaction," "The Last Time," and "Play With Fire," had a more dramatic impact and unified style, and is still considered by many to be *the* classic Rolling Stones album. Because of the high quality of album material on Stones, Beatles and Dylan LPs especially, the market was shifting. American fans bought albums because they had the singles on them; the new FM rock stations were playing more album tracks, and, in the case of the Big Three, entire albums. Even when they were essentially collections of as yet unreleased material, like *December's Children*, fans saw themes in Stones LPs from the beginning. The Beatles (and Dylan) were more deliberate in giving their albums themes; *Something New* is generally thought to be the first example of a rock concept album, and, whether deliberately or not, the American *Out of Our Heads* projected a similar integration of sound and style. The English release (with the same black-and-white cover photo that appeared on *December's*

Children) had a more diffused effect and got a mixed reception from the generally supportive English music press:

STONES LP: WHAT'S IT ALL ABOUT THEN?

At the risk of riots in Fleet Street, all I can really say about the Rolling Stones' "Out of Our Heads" LP is:

what's it all about?

The Stones are well up to standard for hard, punchy instrumental noise and beat, and Mick Jagger is singing better than ever. But the overall sound is samey and, for me, boring after a few tracks. Why they traipse across the Atlantic to America for studio sound like this is beyond me.

The sales of the album will undoubtedly outnumber even the complaining letters I'll get for this Loogwarm review. It's not bad, and it's great for parties and the like. But I can't get switched on to all this raving about what the Stones are putting down, and Andrew Oldham's written another nonsense sleeve note which zoomed at least 1,000 feet above my head if it had any meaning. (Disc, October 2, 1965)

On September 24 the Stones began their fifth British tour in London at the Finsbury Park Astoria, with the Spencer Davis Group, Unit 4 Plus 2 (replaced by the Moody Blues on three dates), the Checkmates, Charles Dickens, the End, and Ray Cameron.

Like a four-star general reminiscing about past campaigns, Mick waxed wistful in a pre-tour chat:

DON'T MIND

This new British tour brings back nostalgic memories for Mick—even though he admits that a lot of things that happen to the group he simply forgets.

He told me: "All these tours and things get hard to remember. All the memories merge into a kind of fuzz. Sometimes you're hard put recalling something just last week.

"This is the . . . er . . . one, two . . . yes, fifth tour we've done. The first time we went out on the road we were fourth on the bill, and we had three numbers, and sometimes they'd cut it to two when the show was running short.

"In the middle of the performance we used to be able to amble out and have a drink in the pub across the road, them amble back. Nobody disturbed us.

"After a couple of hits it got a lot tougher, 'specially in the ballrooms. They're the worst, because often you have to go in at the front because they's no other way."

He grinned at the thought. "I used to think very seriously about disguises at that time. I had this idea of dressing up as an attendant, with a moustache and so on. Then I thought it would be great to go in flat out on a stretcher.

"Heh-heh! That would have been a good one. Gave the ideas up in the end, though. They'd never have worked.

"One tour we did, some girls had hidden in the toilets all day just so they could be near our dressing rooms. Some came in through the roof. Jeeze! That's determination for you. A lot of girls are sensible when they see you, but there's those that go a bit soft and faint and cry. We try to be nice to them all." (New Musical Express, September 24)

The British tour (September 24–October 17) was considerably calmer than the German tour. There was a handful of casualties—hardly worth mentioning by the standards of Berlin—at the first gig of the British tour: "Twenty girls were carried out unconscious after the rush in the first house; and the people queuing up for the second performance were amazed to see the foyer looking something like a first-aid centre with lines of girls being treated by the Red Cross." (Rolling Stones Monthly, no. 17)

Mick has never looked more punk than he did on the German and British tours in the fall of 1965, whether man-handling the mike in Munich, tossing his tousled mane in Tooting Bec, or sporting his Southside Chicago shades at Stockton-on-Tees.

The tour didn't pass entirely without incident, which would have been too eerie. At the ABC Cinema, Chester, where the Stones played October 1, fire engines were called out to cool down flammable fans. The two shows at Manchester on the third were as wild as it got. Fifty fans at the height of their fury only managed to destroy a dozen seats. Mick: "In some places the security is being overdone. At our first show in Manchester police and security men were throwing fans out of the theater *just because they stood up!* I do think that this is going a little bit *too* far." The second show was more like it. Keith was knocked out for five minutes by a flying soda bottle, and Charlie was almost bodily heaved off the stage

Brian does a half-Nanker.

when he refused to give up his drum kit to a gang of souvenir hunters. Throughout it all Charlie, cool as Krupa, just kept on drumming, smiling benignly.

On October 22 "Get Off Of My Cloud"/"The Singer Not The Song" was released in England, barely five weeks after "Satisfaction." The new single leaped into the Top Thirty. The *New Musical Express* reported: "The ROLLING STONES are cock-a-hoop over the No. 3 entry." However, there were a few churlish remarks about the Stones' "garbled lyrics" and "word salad singing." Perhaps it was just Mick's enunciation running away with him. *Juke Box Jury* Jacobs said they were Greek to him, but then he doesn't have Keith's ears, does he?

On October 29 "Get Off Of My

Cloud" was No. 1 in the *New Musical Express* Top Thirty and No. 1 in *Billbord*'s Hot Hundred too, toppling Paul McCartney's "Yesterday" from the charts after five weeks at the top and giving the Stones their first simultaneous British and American No. 1 single.

On Wednesday, October 27, the Stones flew to New York before beginning their fourth American tour. They booked two floors of the Warwick Hotel as their base of operations and hired a private plane to transport them to their concerts. Souvenir hunters nicked Keith's passport in New York. From Bill Wyman's diary in the *New Musical Express:*

On our first Friday here there was a panic aboard our private plane flying towards Montreal when it was discovered that Keith had lost his passport. We had to smuggle him into Canada and make frantic phone calls to trace the passport back to New York.

The concert in Montreal on the Friday was the wildest ever. The audience repeatedly broke through the security men and rushed us on stage. Charlie had a drum stolen and our road manager "Stu" was only just in time to retrieve Keith's guitar from a boy halfway out of the arena! Brian got a cut forehead and Charlie had a new jacket ripped.

At the end we all ran but Keith and I were trapped on the stage and were finally relieved after 20 frightening minutes and a drive to the airport.

Backstage, Bill eloquently explained the two predominant puzzles the perplexed press—with bemused condescension—continued to pose: Why do fans bother to go to these concerts only to drown out the very performers they have come to hear? Why, when they have the objects of their heart's desire within their grasp,

should they want to tear them limb from limb?

"They don't come to hear us in person," Bill says; "they come to see us. They don't feel they have to hear us because they know the records. The only way to hear is to put your fingers in your ears; that cuts out a lot of the screaming and you can catch the music. They just want to touch you, be near you, just have the feeling that they are part of it. You might have one hundred and eighty policemen guarding you onstage. It sounds like a lot but if you have six or eight thousands girls, it's not much." Mick says, "We're all small-boned. I'm the biggest and I'm only five ten. We don't eat much."

Mick and Keith head uptown after the shows at the Academy of Music to catch James Brown at the Apollo.

"He had this great tub, full of ice . . . and champagne bottles. You just helped yourself. And there were people combing his hair and handing him the telephone and rushing about and generally making it unnecessary for him to even lift a finger. He creates this tremendous atmosphere about him wherever he goes, but in Harlem it's just plain ridiculous." (Rolling Stones Monthly, no. 30.)

As for Mr. Dynamite, he wasn't so sure he still felt that imitation was the sincerest form of flattery, as this account of their reunion by Al Aronowitz (The Night I Dropped a Name) shows:

But Mick'd always been disillusioned meeting his idols. Your mind dreams up gods and they turn out to be men. Like when he'd gone to get introduced to James Brown backstage at the Apollo Theater up on 125th Street in Harlem, another overrated romance of a place. That'd been back in the '60s when Mick still had some innocence left to lose. James'd used the occasion to try to belittle Mick, to try to pry a bigger tribute than the simple homage of Mick's visit. James'd wanted Mick to confess the Stones were just a limp ofay cop. That historic meeting'd degenerated in a boasting match.

"We hotter, man!"

"No you ain't, man!"

"We badder!"

"No you ain't!"

In Times Square a hundred-foot-high billboard is erected to advertise the release of *December's Children,* featuring a sixty-by-forty-foot blowup of a David Bailey photo of the Stones (similar to the one that appears on the cover of the American *Out of Our Heads*), looking moody, menacing and at their most archetypal.

Although it is a compilation album of singles and unreleased tracks from English LPs and EPs (as was *Flowers*) Greil Marcus points out "*December's Children*, a rag-tag collection of early rejects and live cuts (Keith commented at the time the album was released that the Stones could never have gotten away with releasing such an atrocity in England) appears as one of the Stones' most elemental records." (*Creem*)

November 9th, the Famous Lost Jam occurs (or where was Brian when the lights went out?). On the night of the New York blackout Dylan, Robbie Robertson, and Bobby Neuwirth climb five flights to Brian's hotel room for a historic and, needless to say, unrecorded (acoustic) jam.

BLACKOUT PARTY

Shall I tell you about the time the Stones threw a party in the $500-a-day penthouse of the New York Hilton and Brian brought Bob Dylan along with Bob's guitarist, Robbie Robertson? Bob sat down at the piano, Robbie played guitar and Brian blew harp. He blew and blew until his lips were red. When he wiped his mouth, he found it was blood. It always made Brian nervous to play with Bob. "Don't be paranoid, Brian," Bob would smile. On the night of New York's great harvest moon blackout, Bob led a party of visitors up the five flights of stairs to Brian's room at the Lincoln Square Motor Inn. They played guitars and sang by candlelight. (Al Aronowitz, "Over His Dead Body")

On November 13 the Stones played Washington. Brian's dulcimer was stolen by a fan. Paul Richard filed a review of their concert at the Washington Coliseum in Sunday's *Washington Post* and in a story a week later

the editor appended a tongue-in-cheek disclaimer.

Editor's Note: The following article by staff reporter Paul Richard is printed solely in the interest of his personal safety and peace of mind. The opinions presented therein are his alone. The Washington Post has no policy concerning the Rolling Stones. None at all. None.

TOSSING ROCKS AT STONES PROVES RISKY BUSINESS

Knocking the Stones is a dangerous business. Like, if you went to see a Stones' concert at the Washington Coliseum last weekend and then wrote a story for a newspaper saying you didn't like the concert very much, by now you'd know that everybody hates you.

You'd know because they'd have called you on the telephone and sent you bags of letters and told you so. . . .

"The United States," writes Jacquie Swift, "has been faced with war, depression, racial discrimination, murders, disease, rapists, natural disasters —and if we fall apart just because five men from England perform in an unusual manner, then I feel this country is in great need of help." (Paul Richard, Washington Post)

Andrew, on the phone to *Disc*, was quite pleased with the way things were going. Perhaps this had something to do with co-manager Allen Klein: "This is the boys' fourth American tour, but the first one that is going to pay dividends. During this six-week period of concerts and TV appearances, we will gross an unprecedented $1,500,000." (November 20, 1965)

In less than two years the Stones had conquered the States. No longer considered scruffy specimens by the press, they were now subjects of serious scrutiny. Mick wasn't so sure he liked this new turn of events: "The whole attitude to British groups has changed. They [the press] don't like most of the groups anymore. They quite like us, I think, but they have this ridiculous attitude toward us—a sort of intellectual approach towards the group." (*Disc*)

CULT OF ROLLING STONES

Like the Beatles, the Rolling Stones have developed a hysterical following that has reached cult proportions. The mop haired group have challenged the greats in the Rock 'N Roll brigade and emerged not necessarily victorious, but with dignity and with a fantastical following that listens to every slurred word of their songs.

They are, in their own ways, iconoclasts and choose the individual road of freedom of expression, as witnessed

by this remark of Jagger: "Everybody has their own moral code. I conduct myself as I think fit." (Cincinnati Herald)

The new seriousness had come about partly from the recent crop of protest pop, pot, and emerging student radicalization and the fact that rock was slowly replacing folk music as the contemporary sound on American campuses.

It wasn't until the 1969 *Tour of the Americas* that audiences became yer actual reverent Stones disciples. But, according to Ian Stewart, things weren't quite that dismal . . . yet:

GIRLS!
THEY'RE OUR BIGGEST PROBLEM, SAY THE STONES

Our biggest problem when we are on tour is GIRLS. We just can't escape them.

These fans seem to have a built-in homing device enabling them to find out where we are.

Sometimes the Stones book in at a new hotel, go up to their rooms, only to find fans hiding in the wardrobes, under the beds or in the bathroom.

These girls will even clamber over fire escapes, up drain pipes and across glass roofs, taking incredible risks. There have been one or two serious accidents.

In Los Angeles, a girl tried to clamber over a roof towards Mick's bedroom and fell 30 feet to the ground, breaking her leg.

Other times, girls have fallen through glass roofs, down stairs, and been trampled in a rush to get at the Stones.

But their biggest handicap is me. My job is to ward them off. Sometimes I have to grab three or four by the hair at once and whisk them off towards the hotel door.

It may sound vicious, but it is the only way. Some girls are as savage as Amazons, punching, scratching and swearing worse than soldiers in the heat of battle.

The Stones are not safe even on stage. (Music Echo)

On November 29, after their sold-out concert in Denver, Colorado, Governor John A. Love officially declared November 30th Rolling Stones Day throughout the city. This was sup-

posed to be proof that adults were no longer anti-Stones. Keith told quite a different account of their reception in Denver: "The Mayor of Denver once sent us a letter asking us to come in quietly, do the show as quietly as possible, and split the same night, if possible. 'Thank you very much, we'll be very pleased to see you in the near future.' I've got that letter with the seal of Denver on it. That's what the mayors wanted to do with us. They might entertain the Beatles, but they wanted to kick us out of town." (*Rolling Stone*, August 19, 1971)

In *Newsweek* the Stones were treated more sympathetically than in their previous appearance.

Even *Time* noted the difference:

NO PROTESTS FROM STONES

They have retained the gutsy, sharp edge of the old blues, but their laments have become mating calls and their style is more and more the declamatory wail of Bob Dylan and folk-rock without the politics. "What does Vietnam have to do with me?" asked Richard. "They fight, they don't fight—I don't care. People come to watch something as well as listen."

In Sacramento, on December 4, Keith was dead to the world for seven minutes following a massive electric shock during their second-to-last number, when he attempted to move an ungrounded mike with the neck of his guitar. Doctors, in an unsolicited

promo for Hush Puppies, subsequently issued a statement that had Keith been wearing his Spanish heels, he would almost certainly have died with his boots on.

The following day in San Jose (forty miles south of San Francisco), Keith was up despite doctor's orders to play a gig at the Civic Auditorium. Brian and Keith got a taste of a different kind of shock (Electric Kool Aid) at the second Acid Test party thrown by Ken Kesey and the Merry Pranksters after the concert.

On December 6–10 the Stones entered the RCA Studios where they recorded their next two singles, "19th Nervous Breakdown" and "Mother's Little Helper," and seven other tracks:

"Think," "Doncha Bother Me," "Going Home" (which would appear on *Aftermath*), "Ride On Baby," "Sittin' On A Fence" (in the American collection *Flowers*), the unreleased "Looking Tired," and "Sad Day" (the flip side of the U.S. single "19th Nervous Breakdown"). This was the first marathon session where all the tracks were Jagger/Richards compositions—most of them written in the early hours of the morning in hotel rooms on the American tour.

In the year-end *New Musical Express* poll the Stones are voted Top R & B Group, come in second only to the Beatles as Top World Vocal Group. They score first and third place in Best Disc Of The Year with "Satisfaction" and "Get Off Of My Cloud" respectively. Mick, "Mr. Personality," came in third in British Vocal Personality and British Male Singer categories and only fifth in the World Personality sweepstakes.

THESE ARE THE STARS YOU VOTED FOR

The Rolling Stones
★ **No. 1 R & B group**
★ **No. 1 British Disc of 1965—"Satisfaction." (New Musical Express)**

Andrew's plans had succeeded—tomorrow the world!

"Satisfaction" had reached No. 1 not only in the U.S. and U.K. but it had topped the charts in Sweden, Australia, Canada, Germany, Switzerland, Turkey, Denmark, New Zealand, Netherlands, Norway, France, Ireland, Italy, Finland, South Africa, Poland, Luxembourg, Hungary, Belgium, Burma, Austria, Greece, Malaysia, Japan, Hong Kong, Spain, Czechoslovakia, Philippines, Lebanon, Yugoslavia, Israel, Argentina, Portugal, Brazil, Bulgaria, Singapore and Bermuda.

MAY BE THE LAST TIME, 1966

The Stones started the year by appearing on the TV special, *The New Year Starts Here*, in England on January 1. To start the New Year off in the States, baldy Orien "Eight Ball" Fifer revived an issue so ancient it had hair on it. What cheered Orien up, though, was yet another blow for androgyny: the Sassoon cut.

SHEEP-DOG HAIRCUTS BUG EX-COLUMNIST

I am sure nothing I could write or say would have the slightest influence in persuading any of these poodles to reform.

Parents who permit Rolling Stones haircuts are obviously suffering in their own guilt. They have to look at the freaks day and night, so I'll not go into that phase of it.

But I am happy to report that a ray of hope has penetrated my gloom. And where does this come from?

Jolly Old England!

For there, in the land that sent the scourge of the dishmop to our shores, young women have found the antidote. They're cutting their hair short. By such action they're saying:

If the boys are trying to look like girls, then we'll fool 'em and look like boys!

If this fails to halt the plague, then our cause is lost. (Arizona Republic)

Ironically, this canine cliché had been perpetrated by the Stones themselves as part of the promotion for their second U.S. tour in 1964 when —as the brain wave of arch publicist Jim Moran—the group had had themselves photographed with an English sheepdog as part of their press kit. In February there was a tragic consequence of the hair controversy:

FIFTEEN-YEAR-OLD BOY COMMITS SUICIDE OVER POP IDOLS' HAIRCUT

(AP)—A fifteen-year-old Cleveland youngster reportedly committed suicide on Friday when his guardian ordered him to cut off his long hair. Neighbors described him as a "quiet and studious type" and a fanatic follower of the Rolling Stones rock and roll group. (Sacramento Bee)

By December 18 of the previous year their American single "Time Is On My Side/Congratulations," re-

leased in September, had reached its highest position in the charts: No. 5. In December they released another single in the U.S., "As Tears Go By/ Gotta Get Away," that was high in the American charts by the beginning of 1966, peaking at No. 3 in *Billboard*'s Hot 100.

"AS TEARS GO BY" RELEASED IN THE STATES

Such a fantastic demand was created in America for "As Tears Go By" that the boys' U.S. Record Company had to release it as a single. It's one of the most unusual recordings that Mick has ever done. He was backed solely by Keith and strings.

The song was recorded at the IBC studios at Portland Place, London, and the arrangement was by Mike Leander.

Just to prove how right the fans were the disc shot into the American Top Ten within two weeks of its release. (Rolling Stones Monthly)

On February 4 "19th Nervous Breakdown" was released in Britain with the recent American hit, "As Tears Go By," as the B side. The title had come to Mick during the closing days of the last American tour:

LOWDOWN ON "BREAKDOWN"

"Nineteenth [sic] Nervous Breakdown"—which in February this year whooshed up the charts to number one —was recorded back in December of last year in the RCA Studios in Hollywood.

First part of it to arrive was the title. Recalls Mick, "We had just done five weeks' hectic work in the States and I said, 'Dunno about you blokes, but I feel about ready for my nineteenth nervous breakdown.' We seized on it at once as a likely song title. Then Keith and I worked on the number at intervals during the rest of the tour.

"Brian, Charlie and Bill egged us on—especially as they liked having the

first two words starting with the same letter."

"From what do you get your inspiration for the lyrics," Sue Mautner asked Mick, shortly after the release of "19th Nervous Breakdown."

MICK: Things that are happening around me—everyday life as I see it. People say I'm always singing about pills and breakdowns, therefore I must be an addict—this is ridiculous. Some people are so narrow-minded they won't admit to themselves that this really does happen to other people beside pop stars. (Rolling Stones Monthly)

Three days after release, "19th

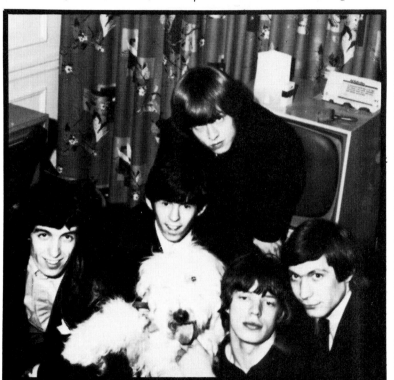

Nervous Breakdown" entered the *New Musical Express* chart at No. 2. By March 19, it had rapidly climbed to the No. 1 position in *Billboard*'s Hot 100, nudging the Beatles' "Nowhere Man" into third place.

AUNTIE BRIAN . . . HE ANSWERS YOUR PROBLEMS

"On the Stones new record, ["19th Nervous Breakdown"] Mick's voice is half hidden by the backing, which is getting much too loud. It's been getting this way for the last few records. Can anyone tell me why?" asks Pauline Phillips, Stonehouse Land, Dartmouth, Devon. Brian: "We're the Rolling Stones, not Mick Jagger. He has done 'As Tears Go By' on his own, but he doesn't set out to be the only one on records. Mick sings and we play instruments, it's us. It's an integrated group thing, no one's trying to drown Mick out."

On this single Keith moved from raiding Motown ("Satisfaction") and R & B ("Get Off Of My Cloud") riffs to a frantic rockabilly rhythm which he was to use on three of the four (U.S.) singles released this year: "Breakdown," "Mother's Little Helper," "Have You Seen Your Mother, Baby, Standing In The Shadows?"— not to mention many of the tracks on *Aftermath, Between The Buttons* and *Flowers*, all recorded in 1966. This was the most bleached-out, over-amped period in the Stones' career. Nothing on record is faster than the left channel instrumental track of "Nervous Breakdown" (the vocals were overdubbed on the right channel) of *Got Live If You Want It*.

From Keith's manic, almost Japanese opening guitar notes to Bill Wyman's vrooming bass in the fade-out on "Breakdown" this is the Stones at the beginning of their most eccentric, not to say, Kinky, period.

Bill told how he got the "dive-bombing" effect on his bass: "I played a small-bodied Framus on that one. Not the red Framus Star bass that I used a lot onstage around that time but the one with the brown and yellow stripes across it that looked like a humbug [type of English candy]. It was semi-acoustic. Andrew or Keith said something like "why don't you do something at the end there, some kind of a lick that will fill up the space between the vocals and the band." I came up with that Bo Diddley thing really, I just bounced the string with the top of my finger on the pickup, ran my finger down the string. That is what created that so-called 'dive-bombing' sound. Can't do it on guitars I use now."

A white line fever ran through 1966, accelerating until it shuddered to a vertiginous conclusion with "Have You Seen Your Mother." This breathless momentum (also used on the dehydrated "Let's Spend the Night Together," recorded in November and released January of 1967) was created by a sort of crazed country beat that hadn't been heard since Jerry Lee Lewis and wouldn't be heard again until punk reared its head in the seventies. "Country music," said Mick, "has always been Keith's thing." And Keith, chatting with John Carpenter in 1969, described his country connection in the hooded metaphor below:

Q: You dig country music, hey?

KEITH: Yeah. I've always been sort of into it. If you listen to a lot of the cuts on our albums you see that. I've never really sort of gotten into it but I've always been standing in the shadows of it. (*L.A. Free Press*)

Everybody wanted to know what it meant, or what it was meant to mean, from the mayor of Denver (who reportedly requested the lyrics to see if it was subversive enough to warrant banning) to Keith Altham, who had a go pulling teeth with the terrible twosome:

YOUR TURN AT THE DENTIST'S

An interview with the Rolling Stones is something to go to with mixed feelings. The prospect of being confined in a small office off Baker Street with what some have come to think of as that two-headed monster "Jaggerrichards" and arch-demon Andrew Loog Oldham could strike terror into the heart of even Bernard Levin . . .

We had now reached a time when I felt the subject of their recent hit, "19th Nervous Breakdown," might be introduced. Having just grasped the lyric of "Getofmyclow"—it may comfort others in similar difficulty to know that Bill Wyman still does not know the words—I now have to begin again.

What was "Breakdown" all about I ask?

"We're not Bob Dylan, y'know," said Mick. "It's not supposed to mean anything. It's just about a neurotic bird, that's all. I thought of the title first—it just sounded good."

"It's alliterative," offered Keith.

"Just before you, we had a journalist in here who seemed upset because he knew a girl called Jenny who actually had a nervous breakdown."

"So now we are going to get the disc played on 'Housewife's Choice,'" interrupted Andrew, announcing: **"And now for Jenny of Little Clumping we have '19th Nervous Breakdown' by the Rolling Stones."**

For those of you, like me, who would have liked a stronger vocal, I did discover that sound engineer Glyn Johns had prepared a tape bringing up the voice. But Andrew works on the principle that Mick's voice is just another instrument and the tape was discarded . . .

As I left, after an earnest enquiry from Mick and Keith as to whether "You've got what you wanted?" I met another journalist coming along the corridor to the office with the air of one who had been told: "The dentist will see you now."

Despite what he says above, the following exchange with Jonathan Cott suggests that Mick thought his current songwriting efforts quite Dylanesque:

Q: What other group ever wrote a song like "19th Nervous Breakdown," or "Mother's Little Helper"?

MICK: Well, Bob Dylan. (*Rolling Stone*)

Jon Landau, in a retrospective review in *Crawdaddy*, saw "Breakdown" as a sign of new humility and maturity in the Stones:

"Breakdown" is analytic. Not only is Jagger accusing and shouting, he's finally trying to explain his involvements and situation: 'On our first trip I tried so hard to rearrange your mind/ but after a while I realized you were disarranging mine.' The pure violence is gone. There's a little humility beginning to creep in: "Nothing I do don't seem to work/It only seems to make matters worse."

"Nervous Breakdown" contains the first overt, official mention of drugs in a Stones song ("On our first trip I tried so hard to rearrange your mind," etc.) although a case could be made for "Stoned," the B side of their second English single, with lines like "Stoned . . . Outta mah mind . . . here ah go (*sigh*) . . . where am ah at? . . ." Some saw drug references in "Satisfaction" (" 'Cause he doesn't smoke the same cigarettes as me") while others, like Bobby Abrams, saw drugs *everywhere* in "Get Off Of My Cloud": "It is the first brilliant drug song, containing references to all the well known drugs used in the Western World . . . Watts' heavy drumming effectively obscuring those words Jagger mistakenly allowed to be heard."

Surely, sir, you jest! (If not, put me down for a gram of that cloud.)

What Oscar Wilde said about Wordsworth ("he found in stones sermons he had hidden there himself") could be said of most exegetes of Stones lyrics. Before beginning to dissect "the text" one has—in the case of so cunning a linguist as Mick—to adjust for the ventriloquial factor. Who's talking? And to whom?

On February 12 the Stones flew to New York to tape the *Ed Sullivan Show*. A clash with paparazzi at the airport:

RELUCTANT STONES

The Rolling Stones refused to be photographed when they flew into New York last night. After one of the group shouted at photographers, a cameraman yelled "Say that again and we'll take your pictures lying down." (Daily Mail)

Brian and Anita at Heathrow fulfilling Andrew Oldham's maxim: "A celebrity is someone who gets photographed every time they walk through an airport."

On February 14 they flew to Sydney to begin a tour of Australia and New Zealand (February 18–March 1).

In Brisbane on the 21st the sun eventually came out and they made a short film of themselves on the beach, sunbathing and swimming, to be shown on *Top Of The Pops*. On the evening of the 22nd the usually placid Mr. Watts punched a native son in the nose. "Incredible! He just kept knocking on the door of my hotel room and every time I opened it he'd just stand there and insult me. So finally I just let him have it."

In Wellington, New Zealand, on the 28th there was a reassuring riot. A close shave this time for Brian and Charlie. Brian: "It was so frightening. The only thing we could do was throw our instruments to one side and hope for the best. The next day we had the coolest press reception ever, it was great. It took place round the swimming pool of our hotel, it was so relaxing, no shirt and tie performance, just a pair of swimming trunks—shame Bill wasn't around to enjoy it. We forgot to tell him, so he went shark fishing instead, but I don't think he caught anything except the sun." (*Rolling Stones Monthly*)

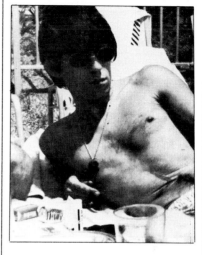

In February A NEW RELEASE FROM IMMEDIATE RECORDS!: The Aranbee Pop Symphony Orchestra (under the direction of Keith Richard), *Today's Pop Symphony*. This album with a cover illustration featuring the Beatles, Mozart, Sonny and Cher, Beethoven and Keith seemed an odd musical offering from Keith: ten pop songs (two by Lennon/McCartney, four by Jagger/Richards, Sonny and Cher's "I Got You Babe," Wilson Pickett's "In The Midnight Hour," the Four Seasons' hit "Rag Doll," etc.) done in a near classical style orchestration. "It's just something I've always wanted to do," Keith told Keith Altham in the *New Musical Express*. "He's just trying to prove he's a musician," added Mick, "not just a rock 'n roll guitarist."

In February Keith bought Redlands in West Wittering, a name to become infamous a year later, as the site of "NUDE GIRL AT DRUG ORGY."

KEITH BUYS A HOUSE:

Keith has recently bought himself a fifteenth-century house in Sussex. It is very olde-worlde with a thatched roof and is surrounded by a huge moat. Keith intends to keep some of the furniture that the previous owner left behind, as well as hunting for new pieces himself. He hopes to be able to move in about May and says—"I'll have to keep a large stock of bread as the moat has an added attraction—ducks." Incidentally, Brian and Mick are looking for country houses, but so

61

far have had no luck—but when they do find something to suit them, all three will still keep their London flats. (Rolling Stones Monthly, No. 23)

Sue Mautner paid a visit to the manse and its squire shortly after he moved in:

Fortunately it was a beautiful sunny day when I drove down to Keith's fifteenth-century house in Sussex, because "Mr. Richard hasn't arrived yet," said the old gardener as I approached the drive.

Much to my surprise (and only because I was being so nosy) I found the porch door open, so I took the liberty of entering. I was very interested and surprised to learn that his books consisted of "The Great War," "Dictionary of Slang," "Guns," "Great Sea Battles," "Drawings of Rembrandt," and books on England and even more surprised with his record collection. Among the Beatles, Otis Redding, Dylan, Simon and Garfunkel, the Everlys, the Temptations, and Elvis were albums of Chopin's Nineteen Waltzes, Rossini, and Segovia.

The upstairs consisted of five bedrooms and a bathroom. I knew which

Keith and friend at Redlands.

was Keith's room, because the bed was unmade, and there was a pair of shoes and a Dennis Wheatley book lying on the floor. All the rooms were unfurnished and, like the downstairs, it was all wooden beams and floors. One bedroom had half the floor missing so I could see immediately into the kitchen.

One side of an LP later I came downstairs through the large dining room and into the kitchen to find some dirty dishes, a burnt sausage in the frying pan on the cooker, a rifle on the wall,

a spur hanging on the other wall and a clock on the door, not to mention a truncheon hanging from the ceiling (Keith pinched it off a gendarme in Paris). Being a female, my immediate reaction was to put the kettle on for a cuppa.

As I was pouring out my tea, Keith drove up in his Bentley Continental plus L plates and Patrick.

"Sorry I'm late, how did you get in?" Keith was very annoyed with the builders for leaving the house unlocked, so it was just as well I arrived early.

"Who's boat is that?" I inquired. "Oh, that belonged to the owner, I bought it off him, you can paddle round the moat in it, but at the moment it's got a hole in the side!" (Rolling Stones Monthly, No. 25)

On March 3, the Stones went into RCA Studios to record the balance of the tracks for *Aftermath*: "Stupid Girl," "Lady Jane," "Under My Thumb," "Flight 505," "High And Dry," "It's Not Easy" and "I Am Waiting," as well as "Out Of Time" and "What To Do," which were on the English *Aftermath* and appeared on the American *Flowers* and *More Hot Rocks* respectively. "Long Long While" (*More Hot Rocks* and the B side of the British "Paint It Black") was also cut at this session, as was their next single, "Paint It Black."

In March the Stones' first collection of hit singles, *Big Hits (High Tide and Green Grass)* was released in the U.S. On March 26th, they began a two-week tour of five European countries. Pandemonium obligingly at-

tended most of their shows.

In Paris the ubiquitous Keith Altham met up with the boys and with his deft eye for droll detail described the following:

WHAT IT'S LIKE TO TRAVEL WITH THE ROLLING STONES!

The Cadillacs ordered for their tour of the Paris boutiques had arrived. "Thank heavens for that," said Bill Wyman dourly, "I could do with some good clothes. I couldn't get a thing in the States." Mike [sic] refused to rise to the bait because he knew Bill had run up an astronomical clothes bill while the group had been touring on the West Coast a few weeks previously.

Along the corridors of the hotel we were confronted at every turn by a waiter lying in wait with a camera to sneak a picture of the group. In France it appeared everyone had a camera.

Meanwhile Mick Jagger was having some difficulty with a little French girl. He finally shook her off, but not before she had left the imprint of her fingers on his neck. "I'm not sure whether she was an assassin or a fan," he choked as we drove off with one persistent fan still clinging to the fin of our car.

Once round the Eiffel Tower and through the Arc de Triomphe we finally lost our human barnacle. (Flip)

Hélas! the boutique she was closed! The boys settled for a beer in the rue St. Germain. They were immediately attacked by a French journalist who handed them forms to fill out. *Après tout, messieurs,* the Beatles filled out theirs when they were here.

"Where is John Lennon's questionnaire," asked Mick as he examined the forms.

"John Lennon was terrible," sighed the little man. "His answers were so bad that Monsieur Epstein threatened to sue me if I printed them." This amused Mick so much that he agreed to take the forms and fill them in.

Marcel Proust was the first to fill out this classic set of questions, hence the name, the Proust Questionnaire, by which this model for all fan magazine Faves and Fears lists is known. (See chapter 4 for answers.)

At the Olympia concert 3,000 fans went berserk (*toqués*). A dozen gendarmes were injured; one of them was hospitalized for bites! A smoke bomb thrown on stage was defused by ex-RAF officer Bill Wyman.

THE STONES SEND PARIS

Some 3,000 teenage fans howled, wept, wrecked fifty seats and fought the police last night during a performance here by the Rolling Stones. Police

took 85 fans into custody but released them all except one this morning—he had bitten a policeman. Said one of the Stones afterwards: "It's one of the best nights we've ever had." (Daily Worker, March 31, 1966)

"The highlight of the evening," Bill continues, "was when Brigitte Bardot came around to our hotel." A little more on this historic meeting, from Keith Altham, in *Flip*: "Bill Wyman and I got back to the hotel around 7:00 a.m., but we had to catch the plane for Marseille at 8:30! But back at the hotel Brigitte Bardot had turned up to see the Stones. She stayed for an hour and Mick promised to write a number for her next film—a spy thriller."

In September Brigitte Bardot asked the Stones to appear in this film, *"Two Weeks to September,"* in cameo roles. They turned down her offer: they had their own movie to make. "I know it's silly but we just did not know what to say to her," admitted Brian Jones afterwards. "I apologized to her for our apparent discourtesy . . . but it was just that she was Brigitte Bardot!" (*Flip*)

Fans went nuts (*frappaient de folie*) during the encore ("Satisfaction") of the second show at Marseilles and set out to wreck the Musicorama. Raging out of control (*hors de service*), the rioters smashed anything in their path. Gendarmes were hit with their own *bâtons*! An unidentified fan hurled an identifiable object at Mick:

BLACK LOOK FROM MICK

A two-inch scar above the right eye is Rolling Stone Mick Jagger's souvenir of a European tour.

He flew back to London last night with a black eye and the scar, and told what happened. "Somebody threw a chair at me while I was singing 'Satisfaction' in Marseilles.

"They do it when they get excited," he added. "It was just enthusiasm—they go a bit wild. It's stupid behavior but it's a risk we take. I did the whole British tour over here similarly plastered up. The only thing I was concerned about was that Chrissie shouldn't get some exaggerated newspaper report before I got back to show there was no real damage." (Daily Sketch)

Later that same night . . .

I shared a room with Mick that night and awoke feeling I'd had about five minutes sleep to the tune of what the Stones had come to call "The Mike Greuber Breakfast Show." A call from Mike went something like this—if you could get it straight through the haze:

"Good morning—wakyaselfupget-

LA CAVERNE
DES ROLLING STONES
CHAMBRES DU
GEORGE-V

Waiting for room service in the Oscar Wilde suite at the Georges Cinq Hotel, Paris.

yawbaggagetogether — carinthirtyminutesatthedouble—you in fifteen minutes —AWRIGHT?"

Mick had his own system for breaking in gently to the morning. He played a Beach Boys LP.

"It's wake up music," declared Mick viewing his face ruefully in a shaving mirror, "I made a study of it. Tamla Motown is impossible this early in the morning but the Beach Boys really set you up." (Flip)

In April "Paint It Black"/"Stupid Girl" was released as a single in the U.S. On April 15 *Aftermath*, the first Stones album of all Jagger/Richards songs, was released in England. The album's release was delayed over a month due to censorship of the original title and album cover (*Could You Walk On Water?* featuring a photograph of the group up to their necks in water) by Decca Records.

Mick, punk before his time, at the Royal Tennis Hall, Stockholm.

The English *Aftermath* differed from the American album (released in June) in that it included "Mother's Little Helper" in place of "Paint It Black" and contained an additional three tracks: "Out Of Time," "Take It Or Leave It" (on the U.S. album *Flowers*) and "What To Do" (*More Hot Rocks*).

Considering that most retrospective critics have focused on the "chauvinistic" lyrics, it is curious that at the time reviewers did not so much as allude to Mick's infamous misogyny.

In the *New Musical Express*, this is how Keith Altham summed up "Under My Thumb": "Another very commercial track which has Brian Jones on marimbas and Keith Richard dubbing over an extra bass with fuzz box. An hypnotic tempo sustains throughout."

Richard Green in *Melody Maker*: "Yet another belter. Clapping accentuates the pounding essence. Must be the dulcimer on this one. Mick is very decisive in his delivery. Compulsive listening."

BEATLES STONED

The Beatles, busy recording their next single, "Paperback Writer"/"Rain," were curious enough about the latest release of their arch-rivals, the Rolling Stones, to dispatch Mal Evans, their road manager, in mid-session at EMI Studios to buy a copy of the new Stones album. (Daily Express, April 18)

A photo in the *16* magazine annual for 1966 shows George and John in the studio wearing headphones and holding up copies of *Aftermath* and the 45 of "19th Nervous Breakdown" with the caption: "Wait a minute Paulie—George and I are coming up with a couple of really original ideas."

"You can hear Brian's colors all over those RCA sessions," said Andrew Oldham about the variety of styles and tonal inflections on *Aftermath*, where for the first time the Chicago blues sound the Stones had earlier aspired to was now contained within the scope of the Stones' own music. For the first time, too, the Stones released an album, *Aftermath*, not only entirely written by Jagger/Richards (and containing Keith's first solo vocals), but for which a wide variety of instrumental sounds (dulcimer, harpsichord, marimbas, sitar, six string guitars and zoom bass) and textures had been used. Unlike the Beatles, for whom exotic instruments and styles were their own reason for being there, the Stones needed the variety of voices projected on this album to express a wider range of disturbed, disturbing and ambivalent emotional states. *Aftermath* is also the

first Stones album released in stereo, (as opposed to the reprocessed mono of their earlier albums). With this album, the Stones had finally come to terms with the possibilities of the studio. Unlike earlier LPs recorded "on the run in great sprawling chunks," *Aftermath* has a cohesiveness and totality of effect that in part comes from recording it all at the same studio (RCA) and in two marathon sessions (December 1965 and May 1966).

Reviewers tended to make the easy assumption that the new, more complex Stones sound was simply a response to the Beatles' previous LP, *Rubber Soul*. But the moods of these two albums could hardly be further apart. (It is hard to imagine, for instance, any Rolling Stone having to "crawl off to sleep" in anybody's bath —on record, at least—as in "Norwegian Wood.") Blackness saturates *Aftermath*. While *Pepperland* is barely a year ahead for the Beatles, Stone City is fundamentally ominous and desolate, a metallic phantom fortress which sheltered its inhabitants from unknown terrors. Four gruelling rounds of one-nighters across the States in '64 and '65 had shifted the Stones' fantasy of America from the Delta to the flashing, futuristic city, a

chrome and amphetamine jungle, dangerous, seductive and conceived in the Deco style of Fritz Lang's *Metropolis*. The songs on *Aftermath* vibrate with the nervous system of the megalopolis and are the most eccentric in the Stones' career. Jagger's lyrics on these songs leap out of their personal cosmos, so flash and unpolished in their intensity they rival Little Richard in absurdity and sensuality.

The notorious "Under My Thumb" is so vituperative that it acquits itself through sheer bravura. Utterly brutal in such a sweet song are the chilling curselike whispers and crescendos of "I Am Waiting," with its ominous lines: "Like a withered stone/Fears will pierce your bones." "Going Home" broke the ten-minute time barrier (it runs 11 minutes, 45 seconds) for track length previously held by Dylan's "Like A Rolling Stone."

What has generally been stressed over the last decade about *Aftermath* (though barely mentioned by contemporary reviewers) is the unrepentent chauvinistic mysogyny of this album: "enough to make a feminist see purple . . ."

The songs on *Aftermath* and *Between The Buttons* are nothing, if not personal. The vindictive, retaliatory, gloating tone is, as Jagger said, not political, "just the Rolling Stones' sort of rambling on about what they feel." The Stones were merely rejecting one more of the consoling pieties of Pop: "nothing personal." Few bands have revealed their own emotional states and expressed them with such wayward precision as the Stones on *Aftermath*, *Buttons*, and *Majesties*.

In refusing to sentimentalize situations, the Stones were extending, as Robert Christgau continues to point out, the soul-searching irony and cynicism inherent in the blues:

All their realism stemmed from the anti-romanticism of rhythm-and-blues, which asserted that sex was good in itself ("I'm a king bee buzzin' 'round your hive" and "I just want to make

love to you") and connected to love ("we got a good thing goin'") and that love involved pain that was deeper and more complex than pop heartbreak. (Creem)

The women put down with such cool relish in the Stones' middle period songs are almost all from the English upper-middle class. The attacks on women are actually attacks on the mindless debutante who "purrs like a pussycat," the trendy "darling of the discotheque crowd" and neurotic daughters of the rich. The barely controlled fury of these songs is compounded of their undeniable ambivalence toward women and their rejection of middle-class values, a volatile mix that was the matrix for the "personna whose hostility toward women rose above and beyond the call of realism," wrote Robert Christgau, "almost as soon as Jagger and Richards began to compose."

The protagonist of "Heart of Stone" wasn't just a little red rooster strutting his stuff, or a heart-pained lover for whom blue had turned to gray, and he wasn't just tough, either. He was hard, bearing the same relationship to the blues stud that the metallic incursions of the Stones' music did to real rhythm-and-blues. It's almost as if women in their contradictory humanity symbolized the conditions of life that were the ultimate target of the Stones' anger. Or maybe it worked the other way 'round. (Creem)

Aftermath, reported the *Rolling Stones Monthly*, was doing a *Rubber Soul*. There were five cover versions of songs from the album in the first two weeks: Chris Farlowe with "Think" and "Out Of Time" (first single produced by Mick to get to number one in the charts). The Searchers did "Take It Or Leave It," the Zombies "Lady Jane," and Gene Latter "Mother's Little Helper."

On May 1 the Stones appeared at the *New Musical Express* Poll Winner's Concert with the Who, the Spencer Davis group, Herman's Hermits, the Walker Brothers, the Yardbirds and the Beatles.

Keith on sitars and commas:

NOT MEANT TO HAVE SITAR BACKING AT FIRST

"Most of them aren't made in India you know," he said. "We were in Fiji for about three days. There are more Indians there than Fijians. It's something to do with when we had the Empire, they didn't like us and all went there.

"They make sitars and all sorts of Indian stuff. Sitars are made out of watermelons or pumpkins or something

smashed so that they go hard. They're very brittle and you have to be careful how you handle them. Brian's cracked his already."

That Comma

Keith explained: "As we had the sitars, we thought we'd try them out in the studio. To get the right sound on "Paint It Black" we found the sitar fitted perfectly. We tried a guitar but you can't bend it enough. Don't ask me what the comma is in the title, that's Decca. I suppose they could have put 'black' in brackets." (Record Mirror)

The bizarre insertion of a comma ("Paint It, Black") by Decca caused allegations that the song was somehow racist.

The accepted version of how "Paint It Black" evolved, as described by Roy Carr: "In its formative structure, it was considerably more rhythmic and funky. What happened was that during a break in a session, Bill Wyman slid behind a Hammond organ and began vamping out a parody of their original manager Eric Easton—who had once been a professional organist. Charlie Watts quickly picked up the rhythm and thumped out the kind of stiff off-beat that accompanied harem dancing girls in Hollywood B movies, Brian twanged the melody line on sitar and from such bizarre beginnings the arrangement that appears on record was developed." (*The Rolling Stones: An Illustrated Record*)

What Keith, in his mammoth *Rolling Stone* interview, told Robert Greenfield confirms this: "Bill was playing an organ, doing a take-off of our first manager, Eric Easton, who started his career in show business as an organist in a cinema pit."

Bill recently told us that this story came about from a misunderstanding of his dry humor: "The organ-playing story is complete fiction, actually. What really happened was that I had put on a bass track and then another bass on top of that, but the sound still wasn't fat enough, it needed something on the bottom end. I wanted to play organ very loud on it to fill out the sound. I tried playing the organ pedals with my feet but the pedals kept sticking so I got down on the floor and hit them with my fists. I actually never touched the keyboard. If anything it was a bit of an in-joke because Eric Easton was a keyboard player and I was just playing the pedals."

So where did the "gypsy rhythm" come from?

The Stones asked him [Nitzsche] to play piano at their recording sessions. Nitzsche balked at first, explain- ing he wasn't an experienced studio musician. "That's all right," Jagger assured him, "neither are we." Nitzsche played on most of the Stones' early albums—Rolling Stones, Now!; Out of Our Heads; December's Children; Aftermath. Some rock writers credit him with having a heavy influence on the band's early sound. His deepest imprint, says Nitzsche, was on the frenzied "Paint It Black": "They didn't know what to play on the back-up and I started playing the piano gypsy style and they just picked it up. I thought it was just a joke." (Hit Parader)

The Beatles were first to use a sitar, on "Norwegian Wood" (*Rubber Soul*, released December 3, 1965), but its function was almost decorative; it was played as an acoustic instrument, like a harpsichord accompaniment. Brian's attack on the sitar was innovative. His playing was more percussive than melodic, sharper and more treble, exploiting its tonal range in a way George Harrison's respectful treatment did not begin to explore. Brian's innovation was to integrate the sitar in the total sound of "Paint It Black." He gave the sitar a rock inflection with a shrill, metallic twangy timbre that was closer to an electric guitar than to an exotic stringed instrument. There is nothing remotely quaint in Brian's exploitation of the sitar as a rock device; it fit naturally into the sound with the ease the Hawaiian guitar incorporated as pedal steel into country music or of eccentric Caribbean tunings adopted by Delta blues.

Although it must have been obvious that Brian's sitar playing was the antithesis of George's mellow accompaniments and transcendental interludes, John Lennon somewhat touchily cited "Paint It Black" as yet another example of the Stones' musical larceny ("Everything we do the Stones copy four months later"). This seems in retrospect gratuitously petty, but the Stones, once mock rivals of the Fab Four, were becoming a real challenge to the Beatles as cultural and musical tastemakers. The Stones were becoming quite sensitive on the subject of their alleged Beatle borrowings. Mick explained to Keith Altham why they had only released "As Tears Go By" in the States: "Because we'd have had to go through all that dreadful business about trying to copy the Beatles' 'Yesterday.'"

Brian commented on the Stones/ Beatles controversy: "I've no delusions about being bigger than the Beatles—you must understand that the Beatles are a phenomenon."

Perhaps he should have added: "We're only a way of life."

On May 20 "Paint It Black," with advance orders of 300,000 copies, entered the *New Musical Express* Top Thirty at No. 5. A week later it was No. 1—their seventh consecutive British No. 1 record. On the 27th the Stones appeared on *Ready, Steady, Go!* playing "Paint It Black," Brian looking hypnotic and hieratic, playing his sitar sitting cross-legged on a small round platform. Backstage, at the rehearsal, Keith was critical of the sound quality on the current hit: "It's overrecorded (too much volume) at the end. The electric guitar doesn't sound quite right to me, the one I play. I should have used a different guitar; at least, a different sound. And I think it sounds rushed. I think it sounds as if we've said, and that's why, I think, if we'd done a few more takes of it, to my mind it would have been a slightly better record. But that's very technical; probably what I would have liked to have heard on it wouldn't have sounded any different to thousands of other people." (Caroline Silver, *The Pop Makers*)

As always, the Stones were ambivalent about this new cultural interest. Earl McGrath once said that the Stones contributed as much to the English language as Gertrude Stein, and Mick, at least, has always been given to Steinian syllogisms. Backstage, again, at *Ready, Steady, Go!*:

Asked by one reporter for the meaning of the Stones' number, "Paint It Black," a sensitive lyric about a boy to whom everything looked black since his girl had left him, Mick Jagger replied in exasperation, "It means paint it black. 'I Can't Get No Satisfaction' means I can't get no satisfaction. The rest of the song is just expanding on that."

(Caroline Silver, The Pop Makers)

Distant Early Whispers. In January the *Rolling Stones Monthly* announced that the Stones' film (then titled "*Back, Behind, and in Front*") would begin production in April.

APRIL FILMING

It has already been announced that the Stones will start work on their first full-length movie on April 10th. The title at the moment is "Back, Behind, and in Front" but it is quite possible that this will be changed when the film is ready for release.

Andrew Oldham has written a basic original idea and at present film writers are busy turning it into a shooting script.

In May the subject of the Stones' unforthcoming feature film cropped up again:

Rolling Stones are to make their first film. Decca's are financing the film, based on a book by Dave Wallis called "Only Lovers Left Alive." In the novel, the grownups commit suicide, and teenagers turn Britain into a Fascist jungle. Stones manager Andrew Oldham said last night: "The book could have been written for the Stones." (Daily Mirror)

Earlier in the year Mick and Keith had claimed that they had already recorded the soundtrack for their Loogishly titled film, "*Back, Behind and in Front*." Perhaps *Aftermath* was originally thought of as the soundtrack album. In any case, this unscripted, almost unimaginable noirish epic was never made. Their new property, the novel *Only Lovers Left Alive*, was a bland substitute for Oldham's first choice, the synthamesc-spiked classic *A Clockwork Orange*.

A little *Clockwork Orange* had also slipped into the Stones' lives. Keith: "There was a time when Mick and I got on really well with Andrew. We went through the whole *Clockwork Orange* thing. We went through that whole trip together. Very sort of butch number. Riding around with that mad criminal chauffeur of his." (*Rolling Stone*)

Oldham: "We had our own little fantasies that we would run in-between each other—this or that shtick or the *Clockwork Orange* thing . . . those things were us hyping each other up."

Mick (or Keith for that matter), with his mixture of sensuality and violence, would have made an ideal choice for the novel's hero, a menacing, overamped sexual punk named Alex, but Stanley Kubrick unfortunately already owned the rights to *A Clockwork Orange*.

In *Trouser Press*, Andrew Oldham was interviewed by Dave Schulps:

OLDHAM: What happened was that Kubrick, without having finished "2001," already had the rights to the movie—he bought it for almost nothing off Anthony Burgess—something like one grand. The story is amazing.

Burgess had been told he was dying of cancer, so he began selling off everything he had cheap, to make some money to support his family. He started drinking more and taking benzedrine, because he didn't want to sleep away the last two years of his life, and he wrote four great books. Two years passed, though, and he was still there—the doctors had been wrong—but his writing has never been as good as when he thought he was dying.

Q: Didn't you at one point have the rights to *Clockwork Orange*, though?

OLDHAM: We never had the rights.

I believe if you lie enough it becomes a reality. In that instance, it didn't, but we had a great four or five months with it. I wouldn't have done all those great sleeve notes without Anthony Burgess.

That was all during the *Clockwork Orange* period. Eventually, though, we had to face the fact that we didn't have the rights to do it. It reached a point where I was reading the newspapers and believing the stories I'd planted in the first place, forgetting that it was me who told it to them.

Eventually we settled on another book called *Only Lovers Left Alive* to replace *Clockwork Orange*. It fitted the bill. It was no way as well written. It was written by a teacher from Yorkshire called Dave Wallis, but if you forgot that it wasn't as interestingly written, and you just reduced the plot to two pages, it ran fantastically. The mind just boggled. By that time Allen Klein was in the picture. (*Trouser Press*)

The Stones continued to mention "*Lovers*" in their interviews:

KEITH: Hmmm. Guess you've heard of the plans for our movie. We're all pretty excited about that, right now. It seems to be all we ever talk about. Mick's been running around seeing every movie he can. Trying to pick up some new ideas, or something, I guess. Mick will play a guy named Ernie, who is a kind of hero, you know what I mean, and I am sort of his right hand buddy.

Q: When will you start production?

KEITH: We hope to begin around October if we can. We're trying to get Nicholas Ray ("*Rebel Without a Cause*") to direct.

Q: I guess the question everybody's asking right now is whether the Stones are going to *play* in the movie. Will there be music, Keith?

KEITH (*smiles*): Oh yes! There most definitely will be. Mick and I are working on that right now! (*Hullabaloo*).

Nicholas Ray had directed James Dean in the archetypal teenage movie "*Rebel Without a Cause*" (released in 1955). It was considered so controversial at the time that the censors insisted on scissoring four major sequences from the film before allowing it to be released in England.

According to Oldham, however, the meeting with Ray was a disaster: "Getting back to the movie, our Decca deal had one of these great clauses in it—if they wanted a sound track album they would have to put up the money. So for a while it looked like the movie could actually happen. Then it got bogged down in detail. I bought the idea that we must be packaged

with what are now called 'bankable people.' I remember taking Mick to meet Nicholas Ray—he was sitting in a corner with a drink, going on and on about James Dean. Even to us it was apparent that the guy hadn't worked since he was called in to resurrect some Biblical film. I don't think Mick actually said it, but it was pretty apparent that he was thinking: 'Don't ever put me through that again,' because it was light years away from what we wanted. A few encounters like that with the 'establishment' end of film just got everybody a little sour on the whole thing. The fantasy was becoming too real. There was also too many other things to do. It was now getting a little harder to keep up with how many records you had to have out. The fun had already been had and if you can't keep the momentum going there are other things that you have to do. I don't think anybody ever completely forgot the importance of doing a film, but it was like, 'If we can't do it the way we want it—fuck it.'" (*Trouser Press*)

On May 26 the Stones performed their new single, "Paint It Black," on *Top of the Pops*, introduced in inimitable North Country hearty by DJ Jimmy Saville: "Top groups! . . . Top records! . . . Top everything! . . . So how's about a nice record now by one of the top groups . . . the Rolling Stones!"

Later that day they attended a command performance at the Albert Hall:

STONES ATTEND DYLAN CONCERT

All five Stones plus their respective wives and girlfriends attended Dylan's Royal Albert Hall concert on May 26th. Although many people will remember seeing them on Top of the Pops that evening, in actual fact they pre-recorded it the same afternoon, and dashed straight from the studios to the Royal Albert Hall, where they had a box. The boys hadn't seen Dylan for quite a while, so after the show they went backstage for a chat and general "get-together," which carried on into the wee small hours of the morning.

At the beginning of June "Paint It Black" was still at the top of the American charts; in England it was replaced by Sinatra's "Strangers in the Night":

SINATRA TOPPLES THE STONES

Well, old Frank Sinatra has shocked all the young'uns by reaching the top. Not even the raving Rolling Stones can top him—they have to be content with second place this week. (Daily Sketch)

At the beginning of June, Decca released the Andrew Oldham Orchestra versions of Stones' songs on *The Rolling Stones Songbook*, containing eight Jagger/Richards/Nanker Phelge compositions plus Arthur Alexander's "You Better Move On," Norman Meade's "Time Is On My Side" and one, "Theme For A Rolling Stone," attributed to Andrew, in syrupy arrangements loaded with Teen Angel back up singers. One of these cuts, "Heart Of Stone," was used on the sound track of the Irish tour film, "*Charlie Is My Darling*." The less said about *The Rolling Stones Songbook* the better. It's basically Stones muzak (and remarkably similar to Keith's *Aranbee Orchestra* LP earlier in the year).

On June 8 Mick collapsed from exhaustion.

MICK JAGGER RESTS

Rolling Stones singer Mick Jagger collapsed from overwork and exhaustion soon after moving into his new home near Regents Park. He has been ordered by his doctor to take two weeks rest as he is suffering from nervous stress. (Daily Express)

In June "Mother's Little Helper"/ "Lady Jane" was released as a single in the U.S. The American version of *Aftermath* was also released this month. In the first two days *Aftermath* sold 350,000 copies to become the Stones' fourth consecutive American gold album.

On June 21, two days before departing for their fifth American tour:

POP SINGERS SUE HOTELS FOR $5 MILLION

Rolling stones, as every schoolboy knows, gather no moss. Now it turns out they even have trouble finding a suitable place to bed down for the night.

That, at least, was the complaint Tuesday of the British rock 'n roll group known as the Rolling Stones. They sued 14 elite New York hotels for $5 million in damages because they were refused overnight lodging last week.

The shaggy-haired quintet, Britain's latest contribution to musical culture, contended their civil rights had been violated. They said the hotels told their agent they "did not desire to lodge the plaintiffs and that they must go elsewhere."

The five youths said this refusal discriminated against them on "account of their national origin." (Nyack, N.Y., Journal News)

On June 23 the Stones flew into

New York. Accounts of the next couple of days in New York are drawn from three contemporary accounts written from quite different journalistic perspectives. First, here's Richard Goldstein's account in the *Village Voice*. New Journalism Meets the Rolling Stones (again). Actually Tom Wolfe, the founding father of this subjective, novelistic style of journalism, had written an account of the Stones' first concert in New York (see June 1964) which focused as much on the audience as the Stones. The pop, almost cinematic style used by Goldstein at first seems a perfect fit for the rock life-style it examined, but New Journalism, actually a jazzy form of pop sociology, depended on aesthetic distance, irony and analysis of behavior entirely alien to rock 'n roll. The stress points were already visible:

SHANGO MICK ARRIVES

Shango, the African God of thunder, landed in New York City last Thursday afternoon.

He came wrapped in the steel body of a TWA jetliner, from the land of the new vinyl Shangos: London. At the airport that afternoon, worshipers stood tense and sweating along the open observation deck. Their hair lay plastered in streaks around their cheeks. Their binoculars were poised. Their Polaroid Swingers said "Yes!"

The jet landed amid a churning blast of mechanical thunder. A portable staircase was fixed in place. Stewardesses and health officials arrived and departed. Finally, the Godheads: Charlie first—in brown. Then Bill and Keith. Then Brian, who removed his purple glasses to survey the scene and wiped them on his candycane blazer. Finally, Mick, smiling lamely, supported by the brassbutton epaulets on his shoulder. The Gods descended and posed.

Their names are Bill Wyman, Charlie Watts, Keith Richard, Brian Jones, and Mick Jagger. All approximately twenty-one, and together the recipients of $8 million in hard popstar cash. Pete Hamill, a journalist who knows about such things, says they come on like an open switchblade. He means for real. We are not nice, but we are honest, says the image. We are not respectable, but we are genuine. We are evil, but cool.

Everybody here? Photographers, fashion models, lady editors, record executives, public-relations men, a few disheveled reporters, and a stray groupie who is hustled off the field screaming "Keith—Keeeyth?"

We pass customs easily with a TWA man easing us through the baggage and embracing relatives. Now, out on the field, we watch the plane circle

and descend. The party is small because King Faisal is landing today. The Stones may be rude but they don't insult Jews.

A PR man tells us what they're really like:

"Pigs. They're pigs."

A cop chimes in. "Last year a couple of girls broke through and touched them. We had to vaccinate them. You never saw so much smeared makeup. Jeezuz."

A free-lance photographer says he'd rather be up in Yankee Stadium with the baseball players. "They show you some respect; they ask about the family."

And an airport reporter advises: "They're down. Good luck. And remember the fifteen-foot business. Otherwise, you're contaminated."

JAN CREMER TELLS ALL ABOUT BRIAN JONES:

A large cardboard poster steals its way across the field. It's the cover of Town and Country—Stones meet society—blown up and transplanted to a 15-foot slab. Two fashion editors grasp the tribute and try to maneuver it into

the customs area, where the Stones are being processed. But the cops stop them, so they park it on the hood of a limousine, where the boys will be sure to see it. (Village Voice)

Allen Klein solved the accommodations problem by using his S.S. *Sea Panther*, a luxury yacht normally moored at the 79th Street Boat Basin, for their three-day stay. On the afternoon of the 24th Andrew threw a press party.

The motors churn and the yacht begins to move. Mick says: "It's 95 out and you'd never know it here." Charlie says: "Don't let those photographers make you nervous; ask your questions." Keith says efforts to censor rock songs because of their subject is: "Typical American prudery." Brian says: "The next thing in pop won't happen for another three years."

The press meets/versus the Rolling Stones. A starry-eyed reporter for the New York Post follows Oldham around, scrawling dutifully on a worn pad. Those ladies from Town and Country are back with their publicity blowup.

Meanwhile, Mick is responding to a question. "What's the difference between the Stones and the Beatles?"

"There are five of us and four of them."

Brian stares at the passing Statue of Liberty, pulls out a red handkerchief, and waves it in the general direction of the bronze lady.

"Who are more uncooperative,

Brian? British or American journalists?"

"We're the ones who are uncooperative, right mate?"

A pop writer compares the old and new Stones: "I think now there's a feeling of—don't touch me, I'm a Rolling Stone. Even their manager is so hung up on himself, it's unbelievable. And Mick is a hippy in the true sense of the word. When someone says something honest, he goes blank. He can't relate to honesty."

But Mick defies approach. The others are shorter, pudgier, softer than they sound on record. But Mick really looks like a Shango. A while ago, he was hospitalized suffering from a "nervous exhaustion." Now you observe him smiling, chatting, responding. You watch him "circulate." You notice his tired grin, his oval eyes and sagging lips; his yachtsman's jacket is an irony. You want to ask: "Mick, how the hell are you going to manage concerts in 29 cities in 27 days?" You want to say: "Mick, tell me about payola. About under-assistant West Coast promomen. How does $8 million feel? Does Ed Sullivan have bad breath?" But you can't do that at a press re-

ception, on a yacht circling Manhattan Island. You want to touch Mick Jagger? You can't even come close.

So, pen poised, eyes shining, you state lamely: "I want to do a piece about the reality of being a Rolling Stone." And Mick Jagger smiles. "The reality of being me? It's nasty today." (Village Voice)

As worldly-wise as the above account appears, it is almost completely lacking in context. Information is collected as if investigating some hermetic sect rather than "the hottest band in the world" who have had American hits for over two years. Goldstein, on the eve of this assignment, actually has to ask if the Stones are "queers!"

In comparison with the Mother Goose matter-of-factness of Lillian Roxon in the article below, Goldstein's auteur style seems unnecessarily contrived. Foxy Miss Roxon, incidently, was the only one to figure out that the $5 million hotel suit was one of Oldham's publicity stunts. No such damage claim was ever filed.

Also note that Lillian, as a veteran stringer, long time rock fan (Goldstein is a recently converted folkie) and fan-mag maven, does not accept the Stones' newly acquired aloofness as their normal behavior and proceeds to (silently) chide them for it:

FIASCO ABOARD THE SEA PANTHER!

Datebook Takes You Behind-the-Scenes at a Rolling Stones Press Party on Board a Yacht in the New York City Harbor. As Press Parties Go . . . It Went Badly.

It was a good idea—the floating lunch the Rolling Stones gave aboard the S.S. Sea Panther for the New York press. But, oh, the things that went wrong!

And did I say the New York press? Well, according to official Stones publicity people—the party was only for "important" press . . . and that definitely did not include the teen and fan mags which had always been giving the Stones an enormous amount of space. Well, maybe it did include a few who begged a little.

Once aboard, the atmosphere was one of intense suspicion. I had the distinct feeling that no one believed we were working journalists. I think they thought we were fans who'd somehow managed to get hold of invitations.

Only Brian Jones truly bubbled. He's articulate, curious, lively, intelligent. Some people might even call him obnoxious—like the Greenwich Village reporter who claimed to have seen Brian pin a button to the fly of his white corduroys. It said: "Sex is here to stay."

All of the Stones—especially Brian —use four-letter words like they're going out of business—openly, freely, blatantly, if you will. In fact it often seems that they go out of their way to substitute the words when other words would do just as well. And when I say four-letter words, I mean THE four-letter word!

I talked with Brian about the Andy Warhol pop cult in New York and found him willing to concede that some of it was sick but frankly admitting he found it fascinating as well.

I saw him put down a rather square reporter who asked "Which are you?" Brian simply turned his back. The poor bloke had a job to do and being squashed by Brian didn't help.

As I left the Sea Panther, I felt an urge to go over to the Stones and curt Andrew Oldham and to those publicity people in charge and say something like this:

"Come on, now, blokes—let's forget about the surly image. Perhaps it was necessary to hide behind that manufactured dirty image earlier in your careers—but it's later now. It's all right for you to emerge as human beings—especially when you're among the press. Honesty in performers is utterly refreshing and I wouldn't want you to

become something which you are not. But, the signs are that you're intelligent human beings, not sullen morons. How about easing up a little?

Of course, I didn't say a word of it, I just stepped down the gangplank and joined the mob of enthusiastic groupies and furious reporters waiting there.

"Aren't they adorable?" one of the groupies asked me. (Datebook)

It did seem a bit out of character for the Stones to appear on the cover of that dowdy relic of suburban snobbery, Town & Country, in June while almost all fan magazine writers were barred from the boat as déclassé.

The night of the S.S. Sea Panther press conference, June 24, the Stones gave their first concert at the Lynn Bowl in Lynn, Massachusetts, twenty miles north of Boston:

ROLLING STONES MOBBED: TEAR GAS STOPS TEENAGE STORM

Police used tear gas last night to turn back teen-agers who stormed an outdoor stage where Britain's Rolling Stones rock 'n roll group were performing. Five persons were arrested, and four others were injured, but re-

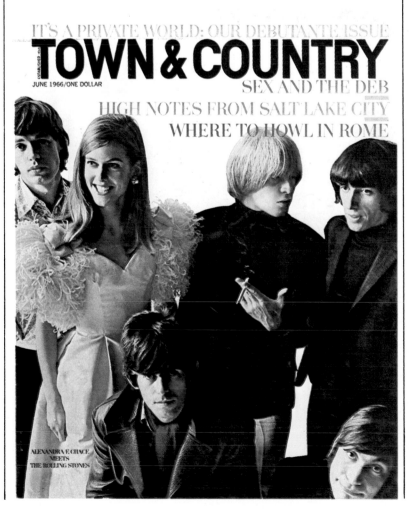

IT'S A PRIVATE WORLD: OUR DEBUTANTE ISSUE
TOWN & COUNTRY
JUNE 1966/ONE DOLLAR
SEX AND THE DEB
HIGH NOTES FROM SALT LAKE CITY
WHERE TO HOWL IN ROME

ALEXANDRA E. CHACE
MEETS
THE ROLLING STONES

leased after treatment.

Police ordered the show stopped when spectators broke through a police cordon of 75 men. Police said four tear gas grenades were used.

The singing group rushed to two automobiles parked behind the stage and left. Fans tried to reach them by breaking the cars' windows with planks torn from police barricades.

Caption for accompanying photo of riot: "THEY REALLY ROLLED. The scene is a familiar one. Was this picture snapped at a civil rights demonstration, an antiwar rally or a student protest meeting? Nope, it was just the expected reaction when the Rolling Stones did their stuff at the Lynn Bowl, in Lynn, Mass."

In Montreal, "STONES STOP CONCERT TO BOO BOUNCERS." Mick: "It was unbelievable. We've never seen anything like it before. I was disgusted.

"There were about thirty bouncers when we appeared—all of them huge blokes, wrestlers, I think. They were punching people up for no reason at all and then throwing them out. One fight broke out at the front of the theatre while we were playing and six of the chaps set on one kid. It was terrible. It was going on in front of twelve thousand people, too. In the end we stopped playing because the fans were booing and hissing and pointing at the bouncers. We joined in—and after the show, had to run for our lives because the wrestlers tried to get up on the stage after us. I was scared out of my life. I thought we were going to get it that time." (Disc)

On July 2 the Stones inaugurated the 1966 Music Festival at Forest Hills, New York. The temperature was in the nineties. Riots, tear gas, nightsticks.

And then, on July 6th, the Stones snubbed the stars and stripes:

ROLLING STONES IN U.S. FLAG INCIDENT

Police at Syracuse, New York, investigated today a report by a number of angry residents that a member of the Rolling Stones group, the British singers, dragged an American flag along the floor of the War Memorial Hall. The incident occurred when the singers were walking through the auditorium last night to the stage for a concert. One of the group, according to witnesses, snatched the flag from a chair where it had been spread to dry. During a brief scuffle it was grabbed by a member of the staff. Police said they wanted the flag as a souvenir, and had apologised for the incident. (Daily Telegraph)

Here's Brian's account, in a letter to Stones book readers: "You no doubt read about the U.S. flag incident in New York; I understand from our office in London that it was in all the papers, and I can imagine how bad they made it look. Actually it was one of those incidents where a 'mountain was made out of a molehill.' It happened when we were playing in Syracuse, New York, and as we were making our way to go on stage, one of the others—I can't really remember who it was, picked up the Stars and Stripes from a chair and asked if he could have it for a souvenir. All that happened was that one of the workers at the auditorium snatched it away, and, of course, this brought on a whole lot of other people who started arguing—so obviously we were involved in a controversy! Apparently they arrested a couple of people and accused them of disorderly conduct.

"Anyway, it's time for me to sign off, as we're due on stage in a couple of hours." *(Rolling Stones Monthly)*

On July 11 the Stones played the Coliseum in Houston, Texas. Mick proved to be as hard an interview in 1966 as he probably will be in 1986:

STONES FEEL FANS MISSING THEIR MESSAGE

"Where are we now?" asked one Stone, just off the plane from a gig in Chicago.

"We're in 'Hooston,'" said Mick Jagger, the Headstone. He then returned his attention to a reporter who was trying Jagger's patience with questions about the Stones' image.

"We don't create images," said Jagger. "We perform hoping everyone will enjoy themselves. You make your own opinion.

"I'm not trying to put you down, but you ask old-fashioned questions," he continued. "People were asking us that two years ago."

More up-to-date questions, Jagger continued, are those involving the change in the Stones' music which, he said, is becoming "more creative."

"When I write our songs," said Jagger, "I never think about boy-girl relationships."

The Stones' music also has become the subject for social investigation.

Is "Paint It Black" about blindness?

"No, it's about somebody dying, a funeral." said Jagger. "If you approach our music with one thing in mind, you'll see what you want to see."

"Satisfaction," say the observers, is about sexual frustration. Jagger says it merely concerns "frustration about everything." (Houston Chronicle, July 12)

Despite a special police documentary that had been shot in Vancouver, B.C., on their last visit in December 1965 to study how to control crowds at Stones concerts, one of the worst riots of the tour broke out in Vancouver on July 29:

STONES CONCERT CREATES BEDLAM

Thirty-six teenagers were carried from an auditorium here Tuesday after a disturbance broke out during a performance by the British rock 'n roll musical group the Rolling Stones.

Eleven youngsters were held in temporary custody in a detention room at the Pacific National Exhibition Forum during the show. Two were charged

"Then in flies a guy all dressed up just like a Union Jack. . ." (Shindig).

with being drunk.

Police said a policeman was kicked in the groin, an usher suffered concussion when hit by a youth, a policewoman collapsed from exhaustion and a youth suffered a broken ankle during the show.

Officers said a number of hysterical girls had to be carried over a riot fence between the audience and the performers. (Austin Statesman, July 21, 1966)

Let's hear a few words from Brian in L.A.: (July 25)—"I'm writing this letter to you, three days before the end of our tour, in our hotel suite in Los Angeles. Apart from our concert here tonight, we have only two more dates to play—San Francisco tomorrow night (Tuesday) and Hawaii on the 28th (Thursday). Speaking for myself, I probably won't return to England till the middle of August, because I'll more than likely hang around L.A. for an extended holiday; the others might stay on too, I don't know.

"I love Los Angeles, it means something special to me. I think about it a lot when I'm at home—about the sunshine, the Cadillacs down Sunset Boulevard, the big houses with their swimming pools and Beach Boy-type music. I often think how I'd like to live here in one of those big houses with its own pool, but it never comes to anything, it's probably because I like England too much."

Something rather drippy happened to Mick in Honolulu. Andrew told the anecdote on the BBC radio history of the Stones: "If it wasn't in Honolulu,

the gentleman who started it was from Honolulu because he had the Honolulu shirt and straw hat on, tapping Mick on the shoulder, a really grotesque big guy and says, 'Hey, are you Herman?'

"(*Mick Jagger voice*) 'Yeah, I'm Herman.'

"And Mick had no alternative but to sign autographs for Herman and the Hermits. It's like saying to Jackie Kennedy 'Have you crashed over a bridge lately?'"

On the evening of July 25, the Stones gave their last American concert . . . "ever." With Brian. Mick introduced the encore, "Satisfaction," in mock Yank emcee-ese with these auspicious words: "Well I can't tell you how wonderful it is to be here in Hawaii, everybody. It's really *wonderful*, the best audience we've ever 'ad . . . 'ere . . . and this is our last concert . . . ever. And we'd love to do for you now on our last concert . . . ever . . ."

On August 3 the Stones went into the RCA Studio to record their next single, "Have You Seen Your Mother, Baby, Standing In The Shadow?" and tracks for their next studio album, *Between the Buttons*.

After these sessions the boys went on vacation. Mick flew to Mexico, Keith to New York. Charlie Watts spent his holidays in the Greek islands with Shirley. Bill and Diane were in Palm Springs, Florida. Brian and Anita Pallenberg went to Tangier. Brian, while climbing in Morocco, had an accident. The Stones momentarily consider a "substitute guitarist."

INJURED BRIAN JONES "OUT OF ACTION TWO MONTHS"

Rolling Stones' lead guitarist Brian Jones has broken his left hand and will be unable to play for at least two months. This dramatic news was cabled to manager Andrew Oldham on Wednesday by Jones, who is on holiday in Tangier.

First engagement to be affected is a headlining appearance by the Rolling Stones on America's No. 1 TV showcase, the "Ed Sullivan Show," on Sunday week (11th).

"I am hoping that Brian will be able to go along with the rest of the group as planned" Oldham told the New Musical Express on Wednesday. But he did not say whether a substitute guitarist would travel with the group. (New Musical Express)

BRIAN WILL APPEAR

Brian's broken hand will probably not stop the Stones from appearing on the Ed Sullivan Show on September 11. He damaged his hand when he fell whilst climbing in Tangier. The result was two broken tendon bones in his

left hand.

He flew back to England on September 4 and saw a specialist on the following Monday. (Rolling Stones Monthly)

The day of "Mother"'s release, September 23, the Stones began their seventh British tour (with Ike and Tina Turner and the Yardbirds) at the Albert Hall. It was to be their last British tour for four years. Stones appearances in England were getting rare. Their last British tour had been a year ago and their last British public performance had been at the *New Musical Express* Poll Winners concert on May 1—which they had refused to allow to be filmed. At the Albert Hall a riot began almost as soon as the house lights were dimmed.

Brian with bandaged hand from his fall can be seen in the fish-eye photo on the back sleeve of the American "Mother" single and on the cover of the British *Big Hits* LP released in November. He did however appear on the *Ed Sullivan Show* on September 11.

On September 23 "Have You Seen Your Mother, Baby, Standing In The Shadow"/"Who's Driving Your Plane" was released simultaneously in Britain and the U.S. This was the first Stones single since "Not Fade Away," released in February 1964, not to make it to No. 1 in the British charts. The highest it got was number two; in the States it reached number five. This was the oddest single by a major group to have ever entered the Top Ten, even in a year of strange singles: Dylan's "Rainy Day Women," "Wild Thing" by the Troggs, "Over, Under, Sideways Down" by the Yardbirds, "Rain" on the flip side of "Paperback Writer." Andrew offered this sociopolitical interpretation in the *Rolling Stones Monthly*: "After playing the record at least a couple of dozen times I still cannot understand all the lyrics and am still uncertain of its meaning. Says manager Andrew Oldham: 'It is about the attitude that exists between parents and their children.' Apparently, The Shadow is the uncertainty of the future. The uncertainty is whether we slide into a vast depression or universal war."

However it wasn't the lyrics but Jerry Shatzberg's photo for the sleeve that got the most attention:

CRAZY PIX INTRODUCED "MOTHER" SINGLE!

The Stones have pulled all the stops out for their new single "Have You Seen Your Mother, Baby, Standing In The Shadow?"

No doubt, you all saw the photo that went out to coincide with their latest release, and whether you saw it at the breakfast table over your cornflakes or in the bus or train, you surely must have gasped, laughed or just stared with open mouth, for our dearly beloved Stones stood no longer resplendent in tight hipster trousers, decorative shirts with masses of shiny hair on top of their heads, but instead they were "dolled" up in clothes of yesteryear, which one could only associate with our grannies.

Why did Mick, Keith, Brian, Charlie and Bill attire themselves in wigs, hats, long skirts, furs and military uniforms? Though you must give Brian credit for looking like the East End's answer to Jean Harlow, Bill for looking like the "street's spinsters," Mick for portraying a Harlem granny and Charlie for a deadpan pose.

I don't think the Stones need worry about their new LP, they've still got a big following to keep them on top of the charts, but if the worst came to the worst, they could always become FEMALE IMPERSONATORS!!! (Rolling Stones Monthly)

HAVE THE ROLLING STONES GONE TOO FAR???

"We adopted the names of 'Molly' and 'Sarah' for fun," said Keith, continuing with: "I think Bill must be the 'king of the queens' award for his portrayal of the bird in the bathchair in the uniform. I mean just look at her." He indicated the picture in the New Musical Express, "I mean, that's the one who pressed the button, isn't it?"

"You must listen to it and place your own interpretation on the lyric. There is no attempt to present a con-

Backstage at the Royal Albert Hall, London.

troversial 'Mother' theme. 'Mother' is a word that is cropping up in a lot of numbers."

Keith informed me that the Stones are introducing a lot of instrumentally augmented tracks on their next LP and that they had chosen this particular track as their new single simply because they liked it.

"We don't ask ourselves what is most commercial," Keith explained. "We simply say—we like this one best. What we have liked over the past few years has proved to be what the young people like, so this is how to choose a single.

"This is probably the way that Mozart wrote. He wrote for himself. So do we. And it is a happy coincidence that what we like should also be what our public likes."

The Stones believe that this is, musically, the most progressive number they have recorded and they are already working on the next one, which will be technically even further forward.

"I'm not going to burst into tears if this doesn't go to number one," Mick commented.

A pop post mortem was conducted in *Disc* in April 1967 to find out why "Mother" never reached number one:

STONES—WHAT WENT WRONG?

That's the Big Question Over the Failure of "Mother, Baby" to Hit No. 1. Here's What Their Chart "Rivals" Think:

The most astounding shock of the financial year ending April 1967 is that the Rolling Stones failed to reach the No. 1 spot with "Have You Seen Your Mother, Baby, Standing In The Shadow!"

One of the most intriguing titles, backed up with some of the most stunning publicity films and posters, and one of the Stones' most vivid discs to date—already taken for granted to be a No. 1 record—before it was released—proved to be a relative loser.

The Rolling Stones, Britain's second biggest pop institution after the Beatles, didn't make the top!

The Stones' ladder of success, which seemed firmly planted and here to stay has had a little shake. The question now is this: Is it a shake big enough to have any serious repercussions on their career?

Here is the post mortem by others in the pop world:—

"Plonk" Lane from Small Faces didn't think "Mother" was up to usual Stones' standard:—

"Own up Stones, this just wasn't one of your best by any means! The days are gone when an artist gets to No. 1 on a name alone.

Eric Clapton of the Cream agrees: "Really, I just didn't think this was good enough a record to reach No. 1. It wasn't as well-constructed or as commercial as records they've made, but I really can't see this affecting them in any way at all. The Stones are big enough to cope."

Bobby Elliott of the Hollies: "The record was just basically above the fans' heads. It was too hippy and those photos showing the Stones in drag put the youngsters off a bit.

"The Stones need slowing down— I think they've been going too fast. Their future now lies in the hands of Jagger, Richard and Oldham."

Mike D'Abo has his own particular thoughtful philosophy on the Stones and the why's and wherefore's of "Mother's" failure.

"The thing is that the Beatles have an aura around them. They can be accepted for their music alone and don't have to rely on their image.

"And the image that has brought them to the top now looks a bit played out. I don't really think they have anything to worry about because they can be very shrewd and prove through LP's that they are musically worthy of staying at the top. Which they are."

BUT IT IS A SIGN OF THE TIMES THAT TODAY IT IS OFTEN ONLY THE SOUND ON A RECORD AND NOT THE ARTIST THAT WILL MAKE IT SELL. (Penny Valentine)

Despite Mick's protestation that "he wasn't going to burst into tears if it didn't get to number one," the poor showing that "Mother" made in the charts could have had something to do with the direction Stones' singles were to take from now on. "Mother" stayed a mere four weeks in the U.S. charts, barely reaching no. 8 in the Top Ten. It was not solely the ferocious phobicness of the lyrics which impeded "Mother"'s progress; there were words (almost) as weird on the airways. "Psychotic Reaction" by the Count Five, in the charts at the same time, hung around longer and reached a higher position.

Keith has always insisted that the wrong mix was accidentally released on this single (and this would not be the first time that happened to them) and that the original track was fat and fantastic as opposed to the wasted one that got out.

On the British tour, which continued till October 9, the Stones recorded the *Got Live If You Want It* LP, released in the U.S. in November. Although the liner notes indicated that the live tracks were taped at the Albert Hall, only two of the tracks, as Bill Wyman later explained to us, were actually recorded there, due to riots: "At Albert Hall we only played six songs before it turned into a bloody riot. So the only cuts we used from Albert Hall live were 'Under My Thumb' and 'The Last Time.' On the stereophonically reprocessed mono album, if you turn off the right channel you can hear screaming on one side and the studio on the other. We just didn't have enough live material, that was it. Andrew was the producer, a strange gentleman. The other live tracks were done either at City Hall, Newcastle, or at Colston Hall, Bristol, on the 7th. 'Get Off Of My Cloud' was Newcastle, I think. *Got Live* we recorded on four-track. Some of the vocals were overdubbed later and some of the guitars, too. I remember Mick and Keith going into the studio a few times on that one. Charlie and I didn't do any studio stuff so the rhythm section is pretty much from our concerts. Plus there are two studio cuts, of course, 'Fortune Teller' and 'I've Been Loving You Too Long' with audience tracks overdubbed onto them. Don't forget in those days we didn't do very long shows, we used to play 25 minutes at the most if you or we were lucky. Kids would get on stage, attack me, attack Brian, Charlie, Mick and Keith. So you would have the guitar go out for twenty seconds, drums, etc, half a minute where you would lose the bass or drums completely. Out of six shows you would be lucky to get together a full set LP. Most of the songs were being interrupted constantly . . . there was so much screaming we often had to overdub. Also, we couldn't hear what the others were playing so you couldn't help making mistakes or being out of tune. On a

record all those things become very apparent; they have to be rectified. I don't think it's cheating. In fact, you're spending more time and money making the record *better*, getting a good quality sound. It is still *live*. Look at Chuck Berry's . . . there isn't a live track on them."

At the beginning of October, the end of the British tour, dates for the start of production for "*Only Lovers Left Alive*" were again announced.

Mick had always been the Stone most interested in making films. Sue Mautner described a chat with Mick under the dryer!

When I last saw Mick Jagger he was standing stripped to the waist bending over a wash basin with shower in hand washing his hair in one of the BBC's make-up rooms. In between an eyeful of soap he managed

to say to the make-up girl that he could manage himself.

"You wouldn't believe it, but some people think just 'cos I'm a big pop star that I'm helpless and I have to have everything done for me. I was up at the office the other day, and I mentioned to one of the girls that I was going to use the phone, so she asked me if I could manage, if not she'd dial for me—honestly just 'cos I'm a big name doesn't mean I've got big fingers as well, they still fit in the telephone dial!"

Whilst Mick stood rubbing his hair with a towel he mumbled something about the sides always sticking out when he dries it with a hand drier—"but anything's better than sitting under the big drier with a hair-net on."

No sooner had Mick started to dry his hair, when the most petrifying noise came out of the drier. Mick got the horrors and thought the whole place was going to blow up—"quick, go and fetch the girl back in here."

It was decided that as something had got caught in the fan the best thing would be for Mick to sit under the big drier! Whilst she was tying the bright yellow hair-net under Mick's chin, he was doing an impersonation of a typical woman, talking to her neighbor whilst under the drier—"Oh my dear, I saw so-and-so the other day and she . . . !"

"You'll have to yell, Sue, 'cos I can't hear a thing," said Mick, shouting at me. I said that I wanted to compare his interests now to what they were three years ago.

"Actually I haven't changed much. I still want to act, produce records and write books. At the moment I have no time for acting, but when it's all over I think I'd like to go to drama school. I rather go for the contemporaries, like the John Cassavetes film "Shadows," there was no script, the whole thing was ad-libbed."

Throughout 1966 hopes ran high among fans and Stones that a Stones film would become a reality. Andrew felt film would be an ideal vehicle for the group at this point, as "*A Hard Day's Night*" and "*Help!*" had been for the Beatles.

Penny Valentine (a true fan) was driven to comic exasperation:

WILL THE STONES EVER ROLL ON FILM?

A CRY FROM THE WILDERNESS. NOT FROM A. FAN, CHIGWELL, ESSEX—BUT FROM AN INTERESTED PARTY, FLEET STREET, LONDON: WHAT HAS HAPPENED TO THE ROLLING STONES' FIRST FILM? (Disc)

The first mention of a forthcoming Stones feature film had appeared in the press just before their first American tour in June 1964.

The film, then titled simply "*Rolling Stones*," was scheduled to go into production on their return from the States in July 1964; Peter Sellers and Lionel Bart were to be the co-producers and the script, to be written by Lionel Bart "in association with Andrew Oldham," was reported to "deal with a group of drifters." The announcement added cryptically that "The Stones will actually meet in the film," which suggests it was to be about the band getting together in the early days in Richmond.

In the conclusion of her article, Penny Valentine wittily summarized the Stones' celluloid sagas from 1965 on:

The Strange Saga Of The Rolling Stones' First Film starts in July 1965.
● July 1965: A Rolling Stones' film

is planned and all the Stones are very happy.

• October, 23, 1965: The first official announcement. The Rolling Stones' film would go into production early 1966 and would be produced by a company formed by elegant Andrew Oldham. "We will be bringing in a director from outside but production will be done by our own company," said Andrew and then went to America for over two months to sort out the Rolling Stones' tour there.

• December 18, 1965: Elegant Andrew flies back to London and says that filming will definitely start in April 1966. The film, we are told, will be entitled "Back, Behind And In Front" and will cost over half-a-million to make. It will take eight to ten weeks filming and another month to write the musical score. It will be produced by Andrew and American Allen Klein and shot in four Iron Curtain countries. Mick and Keith will write eight songs for the film, "a projection of the Stones themselves." We are informed that a scriptwriter travelled all over America with the Stones to study them closely before writing the film script.

End of Part One

We open our second part with the news that David Bailey would like to make a film called "The Assassination of Mick Jagger" which would be all about a pop star but, obviously, not that straightforward.

And Mick says "I would love to be an actor and we're all really looking forward to starting work on the new film."

• February 5, 1966: The Rolling Stones are preparing for their tour of Australia and "The Assassination of Mick Jagger" has not been mentioned again.

• February 19, 1966: News comes that the Rolling Stones will record nine tracks for their new film in Los Angeles on the way back from Australia. Instead they cut tracks for their new LP.

• May 14, 1966: Enter Andrew, stepping lightly from his black windowed Rolls Royce, to stagger us all by announcing that the Rolling Stones will now film "Only Lovers Left Alive." What happened to the other idea? Who knows? The master of the art of surprise has struck again and left us dumbfounded. It will be based on the book by Dave Wallis about a country taken over by mass suicide and the only people left a gang of youths. Nasty ones at that. "The Stones will have starring roles in this film which will be a basic projection of themselves in the film situation," announces Andrew. (Which must have pleased their parents.)

• May 21, 1966: From out of the blue—and the "Daily Mail"—an attack on the poor old Stones by Mrs. Wallis, wife of Dave. The book, she says, will be ruined by the Stones doing it as a film. "I just don't see it being taken seriously," she says.

• May 21, 1966: Curiouser and curiouser. Dave Clark pops up and says that THEY were going to make "Only Lovers Left Alive" but thought the whole thing was too horrific!

From then until now nary a word. Little or no light relief except a strange quote from Keith Richard about how they were all going to have to take elocution lessons for the film.

Somewhere, in some darkened corner of a large studio lot, lies an acre or two of film simply aching to have a Rolling Stones imprinted onto her nice clean untainted surface.

Just how long is she—and us—going to wait? After all, it's getting cold out here . . . (Disc)

With the arrests of Mick and Keith in February 1967 and of Brian in May, the idea of a feature film starring all the Stones evaporated. Mick embarked on a solo film career at the end of 1968 with *Performance* and abruptly abandoned it a year later after the making of *Ned Kelly.* Mick explained his disenchantment with films variously. In March 1971 he told *Hit Parader*:

"I don't want to be an actor, I just want to do films. An actor does films all the time, but I just like to do them occasionally. It's the same as going on stage except it's a different character. You've got to study and do your homework to some extent. You've got to get into your character's mind, and take it very seriously and be involved with things that your character was into. Read the books that he did, do the things that he did . . . that's a very pretentious thing to try and do. To try to play someone else's life in a couple of weeks."

In 1976 he gave a more basic reason: "To me, going to a concert is actually *doing* something. Whereas acting is still playing charades. It is the same thing, admittedly, but I think the one thing is much more vital." The most successful fusions of the Stones' music have been in the promo films for their singles, and the most outrageous of these was the promo for "Have You Seen Your Mother, Baby, Standing In The Shadow?" where Peter Whitehead's manic fast-cutting perfectly paralleled the song's hyperventilated momentum. This is the way Tom Beach described it in his two part Stones filmography, *The Reel Stones*:

This is truly one of the Stones'

finest films. Made in 1966, the film begins with the Stones backstage at the Royal Albert Hall in London. While the recorded version of the song plays, we see the Stones readying themselves for their performance. Next, it's onstage with the Stones doing "Mother," still only the recorded version synched to the concert footage. The footage from that Sept. 23, 1966 concert shows fans rushing the stage, bounced back off into the crowd, only to climb back up again for another try. The whole time while singing, Mick is dancing away from a girl on the left, only to have two more come at him from the right. Then he's grabbed around the neck from behind by another. Wave after wave attack, only to be repelled. Most of the time, there are more fans and bouncers on the stage than there are Stones. Finally, the song ends and the Stones run off. Next the film cuts to New York City and the recorded version of "Mother" begins again as we see Jagger walking through the Village, being recognized by several people. Then we see the Stones putting make-up on and dressing up in drag for the infamous photograph which adorned the cover of the "Mother" single. The movie ends with them standing on a New York street corner posing for the photograph. (Trouser Press.)

At the beginning of 1967 the idea of a Stones feature film had been replaced by plans for a TV show:

"The next thing the Stones do in Britain will be a special show for young people—and not just a pop show," said Mick. "We want to include films, entertainers and comedians who will appeal to young people, and present our songs in a more original manner."

A happening perchance?

"Oh yus," retorted Mick, going into his moronic tones for replies to questions he finds ridiculous. "Yus—bigger and better things to smash up—we'll bring an elephant on stage and break that up while we're continually spinning on a roundabout to make up for the Palladium."

This was to be the *Rolling Stones Rock & Roll Circus*, which was not taped until December 1968 and has never been released.

Meanwhile, at the end of 1966 and the beginning of 1967, Brian was writing and producing the film score for Volker Schlondorff's *A Degree of Murder,* in which his fiancée, Anita Pallenberg, starred. Brian in his electronic lair:

Brian Jones was to be found in his South London flat with the enormous artificial sunflower wound around the banisters, the Moroccan tapestries slung

over the banisters of the minstrel gallery, the leather chair which collapses to suit your sitting position, the cine projector and screen, the giant tape recorder on the floor together with hundreds of LPs and the copy of a "Psychology Of Insanity" kept somewhat incongruously in the toilet.

Brian told me that he has been writing and producing the music for a short film starring girlfriend Anita.

STONE BRIAN'S FILM FOR CANNES FESTIVAL

Brian Jones' first feature film—for which he wrote and produced the music—has been selected as Germany's entry for the Cannes Film Festival

(from April 24 to May 11).

The film was made in Munich by 27-year-old Volker Schlondorff, who last year won the Cannes Critics Award.

"Brian's music has worked out marvellously . . . his special music fits the film wonderfully—and I do not think anyone but he could have done it. He visited Munich three times to see the film," said Schlondorff.

Brian explained that in writing the soundtrack he has used various styles and sizes of units—"ranging from one musician to ten."

He added: "I ran the gamut of line-ups—from the conventional brass combination to a country band with jew's harp, violin and banjo. In the main the musicians were established session men—though some of the boys from the groups also played."

Brian played a jazzy piano, sitar, sax, organ, dulcimer, autoharp and harmonica in the film. The faint vocals which appear at one point in the film seem to be Brian also. Dealing with guilt and responsibility in the face of accidental death, *A Degree of Murder* seems in retrospect to have been prophetic of Brian's fate, and the slogan used to promote the film—"MEN COULDN'T OWN HER!"—presaged what would happen to his relationship with Anita.

A Degree Of Murder might be described in a future TV guide listing: "Munich waitress accidentally shoots ex-boyfriend, after which she approaches a complete stranger who, with his friend, agrees to dispose of the corpse for a sum of money. A

ménage-à-trois develops before all go their separate ways."

In November the Stones recorded their double single "Ruby Tuesday"/ "Let's Spend The Night Together" at Regent Sound in London. Released in January 1967 simultaneously in Britain and the U.S. (but in flopped order, with "Night" as the English and "Ruby" as the American A side), it was a radical departure for the Stones. None of the Stones singles (with the exception of "I Wanna Be Your Man") had been love songs in the traditional sense. From "Come On" (Chuck Berry's variation on his own "Too Much Monkey Business") to "Have You Seen Your Mother, Baby" the principal subject of Stones 45s had been frustration. The Stones had never consoled their social frustration with romantic love. It was their total rejection of this cliché of the fifties that gave such an edge of menace

to their music, articulating their anger into a single focused instrument for prying themselves, and their subculture with them, away from existing moralities and conventions.

STARS TALK ABOUT STONES

Answering the following questions:

What do you think about the Stones musically?

Have they influenced the British scene?

How have they changed over the past two years?

ERIC CLAPTON: Technically the Stones haven't influenced the British scene, but otherwise they have opened a new field with R & B, and given everyone else an opportunity.

Their latest singles are excellent—they are a criterion of English pop music. There is a great cohesion with

their instruments and Mick has become more adult in his singing—more sophisticated.

At the beginning they didn't have that much of a bandwagon to jump on, but now they have because of Mick and Keith's songwriting. (Rolling Stones Monthly)

Beginning with "Satisfaction," the Stones exploited the smouldering resentment of the blues in a hard rock form and with a social protest quite unknown to blues singers and never before or since used so successfully in pop music. From "Get Off Of My Cloud" onward, their demonic, amphetamine-spiked negativity accelerates, pushed by a manic momentum that speeds up to a whirl of sound and fury until it seems to screw itself into the ground. For Phil Spector's Wall Of Sound they had substituted a dissonant Wail Of Noise. By the

end of 1966, it reached a critical mass with "Mother."

"'Have You Seen Your Mother?' was like the ultimate freakout," Mick told Jonathan Cott in 1968. "We came to a full stop after that. I just couldn't make it with that anymore; what more could we say? We couldn't possibly have kept it up like that. You just drain out totally. Because it's just the end of a certain period and we just had to stop. Because we'd done it, you know, there was nothing more we could do. And we just had to wait until we'd organized ourselves, and, you know, things have changed a little." (*Rolling Stone*, October 12, 1968)

In 1969 John Carpenter asked Keith why the Stones stopped rolling in 1966.

Q: Why did you stop touring in the first place? It's been three years, hasn't it?

KEITH: Yeah, something like that. One of the reasons we stopped is we just couldn't get back out there, on the road. There were a lot of people coming in '66 and '67 with a lot more energy than we had back then. Don't forget we'd been on the road, touring steadily since '63, so we were just really wasted you know.

Q: When did that start to be a drag?

KEITH: Oh wow man, hah! That's going back a long time. Because it was getting to the point that we had been playing for years and nobody knew we were playing. You know, on twenty minutes, go off, collect the forty grand, then before the coffee got cold we'd be back on the plane playing poker. It was a drag. (*Los Angeles Free Press*, November 14, 1969)

In January, 1967, the Stones released a single ("Ruby Tuesday"/ "Let's Spend The Night Together"), that was devoid of irony, arrogance and invective. For the first time they seem tender, almost vulnerable. Mick had replaced his alternating whispered threats/enraged shouts with a more suggestive and edgy vocal, which was underlined by a new subtlety in the group's sound. In the first truly insightful and musically articulated commentary on a Stones album, Jon Landau wrote this about these two singles which appeared on the American version of *Between The Buttons*:

"Let's Spend The Night Together" is classic. From the title, one expects a "Satisfaction" type job. Instead, it is a serious lyric comparatively deeper than Jagger has given us before on this subject. The leer is gone. It's been replaced by a modicum of sensitivity and lots of honesty. This is not a song of rage or frustration: it is a proposition in musical form.

The instrumental sound of "Night" is one of the best on the record. It introduces the new piano-organ thing that dominates the album spectacularly. Notice especially how the organ doesn't get into the picture until the break in the middle and how it proceeds to creep up on you for the rest of the cut. The vocal is Jagger at his tensest and best with fine backup from Richard and Wyman.

The flip of "Night" was of course "Ruby Tuesday." Here we have, lyrically, the new Jagger in full bloom. The hardness is completely gone. No arrogance, no egotism; rather a sense of estrangement and inadequacy. There is no precedent for this kind of thing in all the previous Stones recordings. Instrumentally there are strains of "Lady Jane" but the main point is that the instruments are exquisitely in tune with what Jagger is saying. Again, a nearly perfect cut. (Crawdaddy, 1967)

Mick, in an interview in *Creem*, associated their shift in style to geography: "The States give you a lot of energy. There's a propensity to make you very uptight in some cases and you start to write complaining songs, whereas like in some places in Europe I can't write complaining songs because it doesn't give you that effect, you know, it gives you a feeling of being happy and sort of in harmony. In America I rarely feel in harmony, so you write songs that are sort of like jangling."

Toward the end of 1966, Keith told Keith Altham about their visions of the future:

BRIAN JONES FORECASTS:

FREER OUTLOOK ON LIFE MUST FOLLOW NEW WAVE

NEW POP GENERATION'S REVOLUTION IS AT HAND

Very young girls have invaded our concerts—Keith Richards

In Flanagan's bar off Kensington High Street, Keith Richard, Brian Jones, and I were being watched—by two bartenders in Edwardian dress and grey top hats, and by a variety of stuffed animal heads—lion, bear and moose—which gazed glassy eyed down upon us from the surrounding walls.

Plaques beneath these trophies fatuously credited their deaths to "Harold Wilson, Barbara Castle and Adolph Hitler. Among this antique setting the Stones sat on high stools and as representatives of our modern age expounded upon the "New Generation" asserting "The Revolution Is At Hand!"

"A new Generation came to see us on tour with Ike and Tina Turner" proclaimed Brian Jones. "Youngsters who had never seen us before from the age of about 12 were turning up at the concerts." "It was like it was 3 years ago when the excitement was all new." Keith Richard was equally enthusiastic. "The tour has been an enormous success because it's brought the young people back again." "In the 'All Over Now' era we were getting adults filling up half the theater and it was getting all 'draggy' and quiet.

"We were in danger of becoming respectable!" But now the new wave has arrived, rushing the stage just like old times!"

Brian Jones took the statement a stage further and expressed the opinion that the new generation would be responsible for a cultural break-through in the arts, theater, film and music.

"Censorship is still with us in a number of ugly forms" Brian declared. "But the days of when men like Lenny Bruce and artist Jim Dine are persecuted is coming to an end. Young people are measuring opinion with new yardsticks and it must mean greater individual freedom of expression."

"Pop music will have its part to play in all of this. When certain American Folk artists with important messages to tell are no longer suppressed maybe we will arrive nearer to the truth.

more popular than Jesus] was the subject of the same bigoted thinking. But the new generation will do away with all this—I hope." (New Musical Express)

Brian, who could never resist prophesying, proseletizing or pontificating was, in less than four months, to set the stage for the infamous *News Of The World*'s allegations about the Stones' trendy drug habits by holding forth in a Kensington club, on the subject of LSD and uppers to two journalists who supposedly mistook him for Mick. The press headlines that this attracted were eventually crowned by the drug bust that would lead not only to the arrest of Mick and Keith, but his own subsequent arrests, hospitalization, decline and death and—with his drowning in the summer of 1969—the end of the original Stones as a band.

By the end of 1966, the Stones had come to the end of the first phase of their meteoric career, which had begun in Richmond four years earlier. It was only the *first* "last time" for the Stones, but it was the end of an era.

With the November issue (No. 30), *The Rolling Stones Monthly*, that had faithfully chronicled the Stones rise to fame since April of 1964, ceased publication.

"The lyrics of 'Satisfaction' were subjected to a form of critical censorship in America. This must go. Lennon's recent piece of free speech [Beatles

EDITORIAL

HI!

The "Rolling Stones Book" was first brought out in order to keep all Stones fans in close and regular touch with

Mick, Bill, Brian, Charlie and Keith. Over the past two and a half years it has brought you many exclusive and unusual features on the boys themselves, together with hundreds of photographs of the group many consider to be the world's top exponents of Rhythm & Blues.

Unfortunately, this must be our last issue and I hope you will be as sorry as we are. Much as we would like to continue to publish the Rolling Stones Book, it is just not possible to do so . . .

LONG LIVE THE ROLLING STONES!

Bye,

BEAT PUBLICATIONS LTD.

While the *Beatles Monthlys* continued to come out for another four years, matter-of-factly reporting John and Yoko's Bed-Ins, bare bottoms and busts, Stones fans were cult phenomenon. They were too sophisticated for fan fodder. Consider this poem from a fan which appears in the June issue of the *Monthly*:

MR. BLUE

in Jaggertown
mister blue blows up
a storm of serious fun
mixed with a measure
of flaring protest
because his sunlight
burns a hole in our blackness
and he collides head on
with high intensity
and a throbbing night
turned white with
each electric motion
and he yields his
tense-tight soul to
our greedy madness

The preteens, who were into Dino, Desi, and Billy, just didn't "dig those crazy Stones." They stopped being featured on the covers of *16*, despite *16* editor Gloria Stavers' messianic devotion to the band.

By the end of 1966, the Stones were no longer pop stars in the fan mag sense of the word. Their photos were more likely to appear on the cover of *The Police Gazette* than on *16*. As a sign of the times Bill was divorced from his wife of six years, Diane, and when the ultimate Mod couple, Mick and Chrissie, split, it was the end of the debutante affair with the Stones. Mick said at the time: "Three years is a long time to be with someone, but although we were unofficially engaged we hadn't set any date for the wedding." Chrissie commented: "We were very much in love but we argued all the time. As time goes on you begin to feel different about life and each other. There wasn't a row. We broke by mutual agreement."

It was the end of *something*, as Mick sang in the epilogue to *Between The Buttons*, even if he wasn't sure "just what it was":

He don't know just where it's
  gone
He don't really care at all
No one's sure just what it was
Or the meaning or the cause

"Something Happened To Me Yesterday"
© 1966 Jagger/Richards

Between the buttons, between the sheets, between the years. The boys in Hyde Park, 1966, and in Los Angeles, 1978.

Mick and Marianne Faithful.

4

TOP SECRET FAX & PIX OF THE FEARSOME FIVE

IN WHICH GLORIA STAVERS INVITES YOU INTO THE INNER SANCTUM OF FANDOM

Fan magazines were virtually the only printed record of the Stones' activities in the U.S. before the arrival of fanzines like *Crawdaddy* and *Mojo Navigator* in 1966, and *Rolling Stone*, which first appeared at the end of 1967.

Fan magazines supplied teens with all the *fax*: "Mick: Who he sees, What he thinks, Why he loves!" or "How My Twin and I Pretended We Were One Person, Lowered Ourselves Down Three Flights, and Met the Rolling Stones!" The Stones toured almost nonstop between 1964 and 1966. At home, Mick was going steady with Chrissie Shrimpton (Jean Shrimpton's younger sister) who wrote the "From London With Love" column in *Tiger Beat's* "Mod Magazine" feature —all supposedly jotted down within earshot of the man himself: "Speaking of new records, Mick just shouted to me that I ought to mention their new LP. What's the point of writing a column if you can't put your friends in it, he said."

Fan magazines were an extension of the fifties publicity machine in the manner of the old Hollywood movie magazines. Under the guidance of Gloria Stavers, *16* magazine was the masterpiece of teen fan magazines and the epitome of the Teen Dream genre. The magazine originated in the late fifties as an outgrowth of sensational "one shots" on Elvis and James Dean in the style of the outrageous scandal-mongering *Confidential* magazine: (JAMES DEAN RETURNS!!! READ HIS OWN WORDS FROM THE BEYOND!). These were so successful that the publisher decided to put out a biannual magazine directed toward the audience that bought the "one shots." They picked *16* as the title because it was an easy logo to recognize on the newsstands. All you see on the magazine racks is the upper left hand corner: "You could see the *16* logo glaring at you from mile away," says Ms. Stavers. "You couldn't miss it."

Downbeat, at the time Gloria Stavers took over *16* in the late fifties, was the only magazine kids could buy to get information about rock and roll music. "I was a retarded teenager," Gloria confesses "and I loved rock and roll music, so *16* and I were made for each other."

Yet, even now, "there's a tremendous gulf between teen magazines and rock magazines. Teen magazines used to be for girls ages eleven to thirteen; now the range is nine-to-twelve-year-olds, while 80 percent of rock magazines are read by males. This diversity in readership created a complete dichotomy."

"At *Circus* we would get piles of abusive mail if we'd featured anything that appeared in a teen magazine," Howard Bloom, former editor of *Circus*, explains. "Why? When you're thirteen years old and trying to establish an identity, everything that's identified, associated with the sissy stuff your little sister reads, you have to kick in the face. Now Gloria Stavers had this incredible ability to empathize with a twelve- or thirteen-year-old girl and, as a consequence, she structured a magazine that aimed almost directly at the unfullfilled sexual longings of the pubescent girl. She managed to take every page she wrote and turn it into 'Bobby Wants to Hold Your Hand,' 'What He, Desi, Sees In A Girl,' or something you could identify with if you were a thirteen-year-old girl sitting in your bedroom just having been hit by hormones for the first time. There were very few things you could relate to. One was love comics, the other was Gloria Stavers who was presenting you with all these fantasy males who wanted to take you out on a date, hold your hand. Offering you an opportunity to *win* a date!"

Gloria describes the teen trance she put herself into while dreaming up the articles in *16*:

"All my fantasies came out in that book. I would sit down at the typewriter and become a twelve-year-old girl and think, What did I want when I was a twelve-year-old? I'm not joking when I say *People* magazine is a grown-up's *16*. Mick knew girls were more interested in what you ate for breakfast than how many strings you had on your guitar. I had all the emotional stuff, like 'What Are You Scared Of?' and 'What Do You Do When You Kiss A Girl?' This is how *16* took off."

"It was very much fantasy fullfillment. It's like every girl's dream. She picks her hero and that's her greatest love until she becomes sixteen, then leaves daddy, to go looking for the prince on the white horse, to find a real boy. It's a transitional period, like rites of passage." Connie De Nave, the Stones' American publicist in the Sixties, elaborates further: "Your eyes have to be that of a twelve- or thirteen-year-old girl who is eager, almost slightly obsessed to get information on her favorite star. Therefore the object of the fan magazine is to give you Who, What, When and Where. Do you sleep in your pyjamas? What's your favorite color? We don't want to know about politics. I don't want to know that you killed your dog in your sleep when you were aged three. That's heavy. I have to know the most important things about you. What kind of girls do you like? What do you do on a first date? What's your favorite color? 'Cause then I can run out and buy my red sweater. I want to be *breathless* when I finish

(continued on page 81)

ALONE WITH THE STONES **24 PRIVATE HOURS!!!**

BATMAN vs. BEATLES! WHY?

WHY STONES SAY: TUFF PADDUCKY BIRDS ON BARBERS

AN/25¢

TEEN **fax** and PIX

EVILS or DARLINGS? AVE THEY GONE TOO FAR?

Mick "Lips" agger: VE HATE THOSE ASTY LIES!

SECRET PIX 00 ERY INTIMATE "?s"

PLUS

ILL Win A Date With Him

EITH'S Solid Body Love

HARLIE'S Dark Horse

ICK Me Sexy? Ha! Ha!

RIAN Goes S-O-T-E-R-I-C!

MAN THESE CATS ARE WILD!

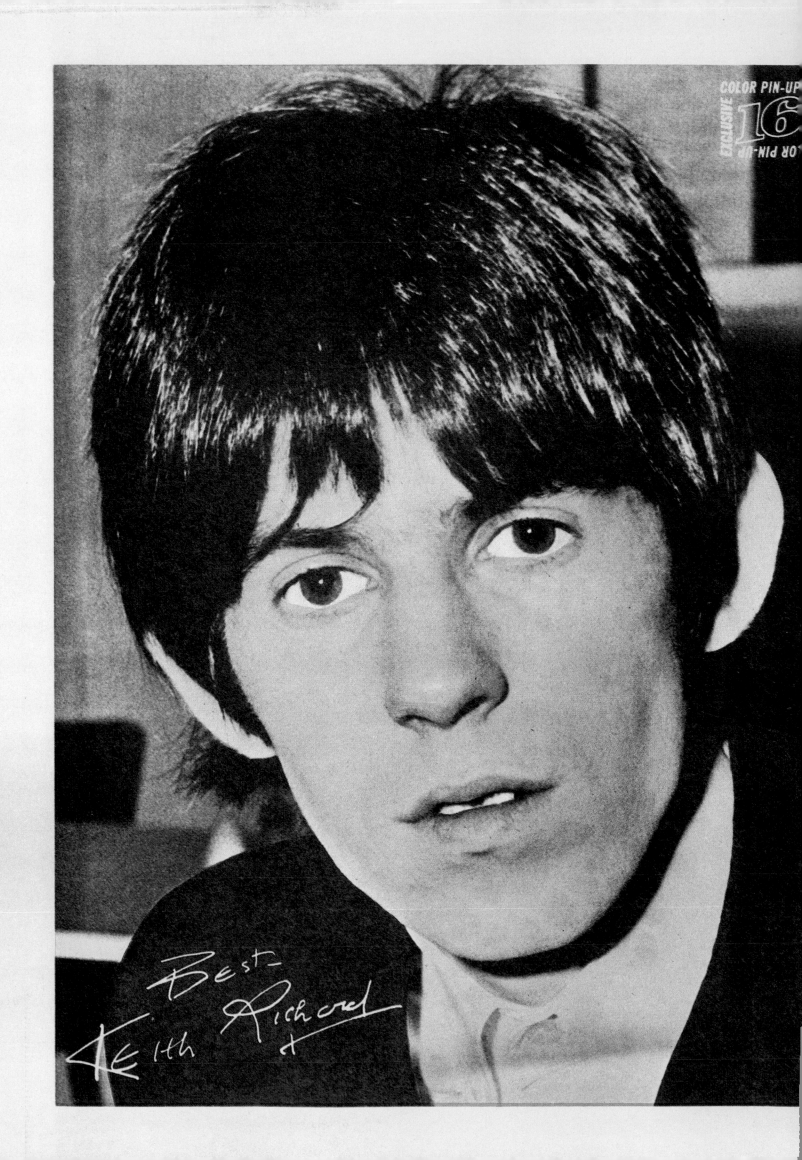

Best,
Keith Richard

Can YOU spot the 10 OMISSIONS?

The ROLLING STONES are always popular, so cartoonist Cunnington turned his talented attention on them. The result is seen above. This picture is exactly as he drew it.

Left, however, something went wrong and there are TEN omissions from the original drawing. Two from each Stone. How keen sighted are you? Can you spot them?

Take a good look at one cartoon, then the other, and you'll see what's missing. And if you can't the answer is on page 75.

In case you don't know the Stones by name, they are (clockwise from the left) Bill Wyman, Keith Richard, Mick Jagger, Brian Jones and Charlie Watts.

As the cartoonist sees the Stones and the camera

Left to right: Bill Wyman, Mick Jagger, Keith Richard, Brian Jones and Charlie Watts.

this magazine. Wow! I didn't *know* about *this*! I've got a chance with him, now. The whole object of the fan magazine is to tell me, the fat little girl with pimples, when I'm reading this sucker, that I've got a chance to hold hands with Mick Jagger or kiss him. Remember I'm also asexual; he's androgynous to me in that sense. When I look at a picture of dreamy Mick I don't want to sleep with him 'cause that's a dirty thought. What I really want is to hold hands with him, to go out on a DATE with him and he's going to dance with me, he's gonna kiss me goodnight in front of all my girlfriends.

"I don't want to hear about anything like divorce because it would shatter my dreams. I'm in a rose-colored garden and I want to know so much about YOU! I don't want to get upset by hearing you're getting married. I want to know that's your *latest* girlfriend. All the FAX. Mick likes . . . it's so intimate. So when I go to a restaurant I say: can I have a steak well done. If I'm a guy I'd paint my car royal blue like Mick. That's our sign. Teen idols were trend setters. We could copy what they did and nobody would know . . . except THEM."

One of the things that made *16* the fan magazine is that Gloria did her homework: "The Stones were really outrageous in the context of those times. You had Herman, the Dave Clark Five, Paul Revere and the Raiders. The Stones were dangerous. I went to their first press conference at the old Hotel Astor at Fortyfifth Street and Broadway. I knew their background, I'd sent away to the editor of the *New Musical Express* for all the clippings on them; I was Brenda Starr and so when Connie De Nave, who was their publicist, gave me the floor I knew what to mention, their playing in Richmond, all those things. Mick got up on the podium a little surprised and said, 'Cor, she really know wot she's talkin' abawt.' We were fast friends from then on."

Many fan magazines, especially in the pieces the Stones allegedly wrote themselves ("Bill this week—And don't say ungghh . . .") were obviously fabricated. This is even true of the *Rolling Stones Monthly* in which each Stone would "write" an editorial, in rotating sequence. Much of the material was taken straight from press kits, reprinted from English music papers or simply fabricated. Everything quoted or written about the Stones in *16* rings true, given the necessary naive point of view. The Stones were difficult to represent in this manner, to say the least.

"I had a very difficult time with the Stones," Gloria revealed during our very exclusive interview! "Even though the big play went to the pretty boys, I knew that what would now be called the 'subculture' would love them. And the Stones just kept on building.

slowly at first, making their big impact when other 'British Invasion' groups began to wane. The Stones fans were a different breed. At the tapings of the *Hullabaloo* TV shows I could tell the Beatles fans from the Stones fans easily because the Beatle teenyboppers would all have long silky beautiful hair like Jane Asher and the Stones fans were wearing their hair teased and too much make-up and chewing gum and they were *mean*. Whenever I had a piece on the Stones in *16* I would get letters from parents calling them 'communists,' 'degenerates' and 'anti-christs corrupting our children.' I would consistently print only positive things. I could never, for instance, write for *Rolling Stone* because Jann Wenner always wanted me to spice up my material. This is how I would handle the Stones: What would you do if you were walking down the street and saw a guy with long hair and a striped T-shirt and a surly look on his face? I bet you'd think 'Boy he's bad!' But that just shows how little you know about Mick Jagger!"

At Home with th

WELCOME to the super-private world of the Rolling Stones — where never an "outsider" has been allowed to tread! Since the Stones don't consider you **16**-ers outsiders (but rather the "in"-est of the "ins"), they are cordially opening the doors to their very own homes and inviting you in for a visit, a look and a chat.

The first Stone place we stop by is Mick Jagger's secret hideaway in the heart of London. He has just moved there and is already getting complaints from his neighbors about the frequent and rather noisy visits he gets from screaming fans!

Mick's living room is quite simple. He has black and white "op" draperies lined with red, oak woodwork and parquet, a white rug and white walls.

"How's for a spot of tea?" Actually, Mick digs into grapefruit while he shows you his over-sized tea cups of Canton design.

Furniture collector Jagger poses by his favorite possession — a huge gilt-framed mirror. On his left is his portable stereo set, and his bed and end tables are reflected in the mirror.

Rolling Stones

C'mon along and drop in on
Mick and Brian
at their London hideaways.

STONE "sitarist" and guitarist (also has been known to sing harmony and even lead!), bouncy Brian Jones lives in an adorable cottage in a mews street in the Chelsea section of London. Brian's "pad" is world-famous among the pop stars as the place where there's always a groovey party going on. Many is the night when such notables as John Lennon, Bob Dylan, the Spoonful and the other Stones are seen coming and going from Brian's friendly little white house.

This is what Brian's home looks like from the outside. He says, "I keep planning to plant something in those window boxes — but, then, I'm actually too lazy!"

How's this? A personal serenade just for you from Brian Jones himself! This is where Brian spends most of his spare time — on the floor in front of his hi-fi.

Or — wait a min! — flopped on his bed making phone calls. (Brian's bedroom is done all in white, except for the heavy orange drapes.) Looks like we caught him in the middle of calling up some bird!

Be sure to get the November issue of 16 Magazine — it goes on sale September 20th — and continue 16's exclusive visit to the homes of the Rolling Stones.

Fax were of vital importance to teenyboppers. They gave all the inside scoop. They were intimate. For a date with one of the Stones here's *all that's necessary to know to please Him*: Charlie collects antique guns and soldiers. Brian, in pink sunglasses, coordinated casuals and "way out" Western clothes, collects cuspidors. Keith has had his dog Bumble christened. Bill is interested in gardening and photography; Mick's Chrissie shares a kitten called Sydney. His latest and most favorite buy is a pair of white suede lace-up shoes. Historical encounters were thrown in as "tantalizing tidbits" about what the stars have in common: "Every chance he gets Brian visits Bob Dylan because they share the same sense of humor and both are deep thinkers!" Or: "Brian glows in the cameras," Cathy McGowan, emcee of *Ready, Steady, Go!*, exposed. "He can chat a lot and has a heap of ideas about life, himself and the group." You said it, sister!

Keith: "I remember once in Philadelphia some kids had picked up on an interview Brian had done with somebody; he'd used one of those intellectual words like 'esoteric.' And so, right in the front, these kids had big signs that said, 'Brian, you're so esoteric.' It had that aura. It was down to *16* magazine. Everything you did in America then, it could be in *16* magazine."

But the Stones weren't exactly unwilling! According to Gloria: "Mick loved me and he loved the magazine. He used to say 'OK, if you don't sit down and cooperate with Gloria we're not leaving this room."

**FAN CLUB SERIES NO. 2
THE ROLLING STONES**

THE OFFICIAL ROLLING STONES' FAN CLUB

Address: 10 Blenheim Street, New Bond Street, London, W.1.

Secretary: Miss Annabelle Smith.
Founded: 1963.
Current membership: 17,000.
Subscription rates: 5/- per year.

REMARKS: Upon joining the Club, each member receives an initiatory package containing membership card, badge, set of portrait-style stamps, group biography (generously laced with the Stones' own distinctive brand of humour) and the latest edition of the quarterly newsletter. This is followed during the subsequent twelve months by three further newsletters and various other items of interest, the most notable of these being copies of the extremely handsome pictorial sleeves in which the group's US singles are issued. Additional facilities provide for the availability of Stones T-shirts and photographs, and a query answering service.

Being a member of the Club means to me, and to most of the members, more than just a number on a membership card. It is in fact a way of life, as much a part of life as living and eating. Most of the members are not new to the Club but have been members for at least three years. Of course, the Club does have a few fickle members who join for a year then drop out, but mainly Stones' fans are amongst the most loyal to be found anywhere.

Through the Club I have found it possible to make many new friends amongst Stones' fans. Any girl or boy who wears the attractive Stones' Club badge can easily be recognized by fellow members, and there is also an efficient pen-pal service through which friendships may be formed.

I feel very honoured to belong to such a flourishing group, and as far as I am concerned the Stones can keep rolling forever and I shall still be paying my usual subscription because for each 5/-. I am sure I receive pounds' worth of pleasure.

ALAN STINTON

ARE YOU FOR OR AGAINST?

Mick Jagger took the magazine and threw it against the wall. Keith Richard looked on with surprise. "Those bloody reporters," he sneered, "When are they going to run out of things to say about us!"

"Never," chortled Andrew Loog Oldham, smiling in the background. "You're stars now. You've got to take the bad with the good."

The good up to now has been the success the Stones have received internationally for their unbeatable talents in the record world.

The bad has been the unfair way the Stones have sometimes been treated by the press and outraged adults who insist on labeling these English wonders as the 'Bad Boys of the Music Business.'

It all started years ago when someone picked up the phrase, "Would you let your daughter go out with a Rolling Stone?" Since this time the Stones have not been regarded in the best circles as "those most likely to be honored by the Queen." And this is a far different case than their famous friends, The Beatles.

Nevertheless, The Stones have managed to gain the friendship of Ed Sullivan, who's notoriously hard on misbehaved singers. Their last concert tour in the United States was a smashing success. And according to a few hotels where the Stones stayed on their tour, their after hours performances were also smashing successes with hundreds of dollars in bills to be paid for property breakage.

Whether or not any of the stories told about the Stones' misbehavior is true, the boys still manage to have more Pro and Con statements hurled their way than any other group.

Here at TiGER BEAT, our daily mail is always flooded with them. Reprinted, without the names of course, are some of the more candid comments from our readers.

THOSE FOR THEM:

1. "The Stones are the one group in England with the true Soul Sound. They, alone, have captured the magic of the old-time Southern rhythm."

2. "I met Mick Jagger only once. He was as interested in me as I was in him. He took the time to not only sign my autograph book, but also he asked me questions about myself and what I was like as a person. At all times he was polite and a gentleman. His clothes were off-beat, but very neat and clean."

3. "If you've ever seen the Stones in person, you'll never forget them. They don't just come out and sing a few songs and then go back behind the curtains. They put on a real show. Each and everyone of them is a true professional. To see them is even better than to hear them, and you can't say that about most of the other groups who just come out and sing for 20 minutes and don't even move around."

4. "Keith Richard and Mick Jagger are as talented a songwriting team as Lennon and McCartney. This year will prove that they have a talent that is unbeatable in every respect. Just listen to their new recordings and you'll discover what I mean."

5. "The Stones are current. They're up-to-date about every subject. When they're questioned on anything from religion to music, they have a good answer. They are informed."

6. "They don't brag about it, but the Stones are very good to their parents. I know for a fact that each of them conducts themselves in a well-behaved way toward adults."

7. "Mick Jagger gives pleasure to so many people by really giving everything he has to a song. True, he's sexy, but that's just Mick putting his all into his work so that audiences will enjoy themselves and for a little while forget the troubles of the world."

8. "This isn't something that the Stones brag about, but I happen to know that the last time they were here in town, Keith personally phoned an invalid girl who had been sick for years. After she heard his voice, the girl began to improve. Now, she's almost well. Don't tell me the Stones are Godless boys."

9. "Someone who's gifted with rhythm like Mick just can't help himself. Anyone who has natural rhythm like this is fortunate. There's nothing wrong with his movements."

10. "Charlie Watts doesn't brag about it, but he's a wonderful husband. I know a girl who is friends with his wife and she tells me about all the sweet things Charlie does for his wife while he's on tour. He calls her every day without fail no matter where they are and talks for as long as he wants. When he gets home he always brings the most beautiful gifts. I wonder how many girls have husbands as thoughtful as Charlie."

11. "At a concert in California, I saw a fan throw a medal that hit Brian in the face. Though it cut him, Brian simply laughed this off and picked the medal up and put it in his pocket saying 'thank you.' I've seen this happen to other groups and they aren't nearly as polite about it. Some, whom I could mention by name, get furious and throw things back at the fans. I say, hooray, for the Stones."

12. "My girlfriend and I were in Florida when the Stones were there and we went to their hotel to try to meet them. We met Andrew Loog Oldham in the lobby and we asked him if we could see the Stones. He was wonderful to us and said they were up in their room. He not only told us we could meet them, but he took us up to the room and personally introduced us. They were all charming to us and I can truthfully say I've never had a better time."

Well, that's just a sampling of controversy over the Stones. As far as we're concerned, any group which stirs up this much comment must have talent and a lot to offer. Otherwise, they'd be totally overlooked. What's your opinion of the Stones? Are you For or Against?

The fan clubs were secret societies in that one could both belong and be "special" at the same time. Note the initiatory package; "the attractive Stones' club badge can be easily recognized by fellow members" for whom devotion to the Stones literally became a way of life approaching transubstantiation. Perhaps the most interesting thing about this letter is that it was written by a boy. Mentioning this to Gloria, she points out that, "the Stones had a small but vociferous subculture following. It was the first group following teen idols that included guys openly. The guys loved the Beatles but they wouldn't let on. If you were fifteen and you loved a girl who had a crush on Paul McCartney you weren't going to be too crazy about Paul McCartney. But somehow the Stones weren't that kind of a threat. You wanted as a guy to hang out in their gang. We had only about ten per cent male readership. Guys got into 16 to look at the clothes the guys wore. So I began running more three-quarter- and full-length pix. I used to use most of my own photos in the magazine; that was what was different about 16 from other fan books. I hated those 'embalmers pictures,' as I used to call them, that you'd get in press kits. Mick was a fabulous model. A photographer's delight. You could put him in anything and he looked *great!* There was this rough core to the Stones but that slowly amalgamated to form a mainstream. They used that image of dirty, nasty guys to get publicity, but as they became more accepted they did clean themselves up a bit."

For the Stones, it was "bad news, good news." They were the first group to experience press backlash and, true to form, they made the most of it. Connie De Nave, sent the "straight" press a photo of the Stones on a rooftop with the caption: "The Rolling Stones Who Do Not Believe In Bathing Arrive In The United States." While this got them tremendous publicity in the newspapers, it provided a perfect foil for fan magazines, to whom Connie cannily supplied press kits and press conferences. After they hooked you with a hairy headline, they'd let you in on the inside dope. "Has Success Spoiled The Rolling Stones?"— with a "Yes" (from Bob Hope and friends) and a "No" (from Goldie and the Gingerbreads on tour with the boys). Other threats to be resisted righteously included "The Rolling Stones vs. The Barbers." The fan magazines had a cause!

In another *exclusive*, Connie explained to us that the kids' backlash to the press backlash "began when they said, 'You Can't Love The Rolling Stones.' Then the kids started putting up signs during Beatles concerts at the Stadium, Forest Hills: WE LOVE YOU ROLLING STONES. When the *New York Times* did a negative piece on the Stones, an editor called me up. 'Connie, please remove your children. You set this thing up, now get 'em out of here.' I said, 'How many kids are there?' and he said, 'oh, about three thousand.' I said, 'Are you out of your *mind*?' Fifty kids maybe you could do but not hundreds, never mind thousands."

MICK: "ME SEXY? HA!HA!"

WHEN the ROLLING STONES first burst on the recording scene teens went WILD over their WOW sound. Their London hotcakes smashed records. As a matter of fact, saleswise, they were in the BEATLE-DC5 class. And that's a lot of class. Teens loved 'em sight unseen.

Then the Rolling Stones came to our shores, and the ruckus their wayout appearance caused spread throughout the land. It was awful. The boys tried to laugh it off; they said they didn't care what people—grownup people—thought about their looks and the way they dressed. But believe me, they did care. They were hurt. Deeply hurt. "We're non-conformists," MICK JAGGER said. "We dress as we please. We're not dirty. We're not going to cut our hair or wear conventional clothes because parents object to our casual style," Mick said.

The horrible headlines started in their native England; parents tried to keep their kids from attending their concerts. It didn't work. The Rolling Stones became more popular with each passing day. Especially Mick.

Mick, with his sandy-silken hair, is a teenage idol. He laughed like crazy when he was told that girls consider him the sexiest Stone. "Me, sexy!" he howled. "Ha! Ha!" He dates the most beautiful birds, and do they coo over him!

THE TOP SECRET LOVE LIVES OF THE ROLLING STONES!!!

FOR THE FIRST TIME—PIX AND FAX ON THE GIRLS IN THE LIVES OF MICK, KEITH, CHARLIE, BILL AND BRIAN!

UNTIL Charlie Watts' recent marriage, the love life of the Rolling Stones was "non-existent," except for happily married Bill Wyman. Charlie's wedding set off a series of explosions in the Stone-age, and fans began to clamor for the truth about the biggest and best kept secret in English show-biz — the love lives of the Rolling Stones.

It may be heart-breaking, but it *does* exist, and *16*, as usual, has scooped all the other magazines and come up with the first pictures and the first stories about the secret girls behind-the-scenes in the lives of the Rolling Stones.

Mick Jagger's steady girl for over a year is lovely Christine Shrimpton (he calls her "Chrissie"). Chrissie is the sister of England's top model, Jean Shrimpton (who happens to be Terence Stamp's steady girl). Christine, who is a secretary, says this about Mick: "When I first

met him, I thought he was very weird and needed a head-doctor. I had seen Mick on TV and thought he looked thin and pathetic. Anyway, when I finally met him at a party, I completely changed my mind about him. I fell for him right off.

"When we first started dating, there were times when I wanted to scream. Mick wouldn't eat for days — not because he couldn't afford it, but because his life was so disorganized. He'd turn up for dates at least two hours late and then just sit and not say anything, with this little smile on his lips. It took me about three months to discover what was ailing Mick — he was completely wrapped up in the Stones! The group was just getting started and they were all very deeply involved with one another and very concerned about each other. If one got a cold, they all suffered — literally. What happened to one, happened to all.

"Mick would call at my flat to take me out to the pictures and stand in the doorway, smiling shyly and looking for all the world like a little boy lost. Often I'd ask him if he'd eaten, and he'd airily reel off a list of meals he'd had in the last 24 hours. But I soon learned to catch him out. He's the sort of person who can't lie. When this happened, I'd tell him off and fling on my apron and start to cook. I can't tell you how many of our dates have been spent in the kitchen.

"I know that I have influenced Mick's way of dressing. He used to wear anything, provided it *wasn't* smart. He'd buy ludicrous things and then wear them till they fell off, practically. I encouraged him to spend a little more on clothes and, if he found something he really liked, to buy two or three of the same. Slowly, he changed, and now I think he is one of the best dressers in the business."

In spite of Chrissie's influence, however, Mick has re-

It was hard to make the Stones look "adorable" like Mark Lindsay or Dino, Desi and Billy—but where there's a fan there's a way. Chrissie describes Mick "looking for all the world like a little boy lost." He never remembers to eat and she's influencing his choice of clothes. Keith's living room is revealed as "tidy and well-furnished." Brian is shy but a "doll" once you get to know him. In a ludicrous oxymoron, *Tiger Beat* once described Keith as "sexy and in a spotless sports coat." Adding, "they're the cleanest boys you've ever seen. Everybody comments on their immaculate appearance. Mick's grooming is especially impeccable."

Gloria invented the ultimate teen fantasy—YOU ARE THERE—and she did it better than anyone else, because she really was there, both in body and spirit: "Teen idols were fantasy vehicles. You would take your readers into their world, literally carry them away into this beautiful, magical dreamspace. When I was writing the magazine it was like transference. What would I want if I was a twelve-year-old girl and in love with Mick Jagger? You become that girl. I could be a country girl, an urban girl, a California girl, a mid-Western girl, a Florida girl. You try to write so you give it to her in such a way that you don't stand between her and him. That's where you get the YOU ARE THERE feeling. It wasn't me taking her there, like a reporter turning in a story. It was a fantasy for the reader. You *transported* them to these PRIVATE and SECRET places. Although occasionally I did the Auntie Mame routine. Auntie Gloria takes you off to meet the Stones. Or, BACKSTAGE WITH THE STONES. Or, WE VISIT MICK'S FLAT. BEHIND THE CLOSED DOOR!!! That you *were* there is obvious from the articles. We used to go to L.A. and be right there in the bedroom, or in Mick's kitchen."

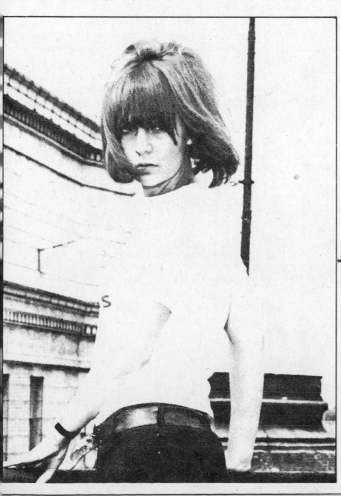

"Chrissie" Shrimpton, a secretary, is Mick Jagger's steady girl.

Often the raptures summoned up by the FAX and PIX created suspension of disbelief when your living, breathing, Stone materialized: "Mick," I said, not believing my eyes, "it's you, not a picture, it's you!"

Encounters with their teen dreams often proved almost indescribable, as in this account, which seems to have been influenced by Andrew Loog Oldham's liner-note Loogese. "Life begins at fourteen. That's Fourteenth Street, that's where I found the little ole movie house (the Academy of Music) that had the LURE. The Lure within a Lure—Mick Jagger. Oh, I like all the Stones and I keep pinching myself it's true that all those really INDIVIDUAL and SPECIAL persons are actually ONE group. No, I mean any one of them would make it on his own, would make all the gals' hearts flutter da-bum-da-bum, but yiccks there's that GROUP. It would be about like having one group made up of five Elvises.

"All right, if you have to pick one, I guess I'll pick *The Mick*. I mean, they are all slim and all the gone-most, but Mick is the rebel of rebels. You have to give him just a shade on the others and I guess I'll get some argument on THAT. But you can't argue that he has the sexiest stare of all . . . of anyone, in fact. Some of the others make you go jelly, but Mick is for jell-jell . . . It scares you a little, thinking of all those thousands going out of that Academy taking a little of the Stones with them . . . Mick Jagger, most of all, has made me different . . . Let him sulk, let him be the rebel, I dig that boy. I know exactly what he is getting at and if he could see exactly the way I am on that same wave length with him I'm sure . . ."

Keith Richard's steady girl is Linda Keith, a model.

mained a bachelor and shares a flat in Hampstead with co-songwriter and fellow-Stone, Keith Richard. Here they occasionally have small parties, where you'd be very likely to meet model Linda Keith — Keith's steady girl friend.

Both Keith and Mick try to encourage their girl friends not to ". . . get too wrapped up in us, as we are away on tour so much."

When Mick was recently asked about this, he explained, "If Chrissie and Linda didn't have outside interests, they'd start moping about when we were away.

After all, it's hard enough on them (and us), so it's best they have something to keep occupied with."

"I don't know how they stand us, anyhow," Keith chimed in. "We can't really take them out, as too many people stop us in the street. Once in a while we make it out for a good Continental meal."

Apart from Keith, Mick's closest friend is drummer Charlie Watts, of the Stones. Charlie, who is soft-spoken, with a taste for Mod clothes and a leaning toward jazz — was secretly married to Shirley Ann Shepherd in Bradford, England, on October 14th last. Charlie, who is three years young than his bride, met her three years ago when he was playing with the guitarist who is widely credited with starting the resurgence of rhythm and blues in England, Alexis Korner.

At that time, Charlie was training to be a commercial artist, and he saw Shirley later at the Royal College of Art, where she was studying to be a sculptress. Charlie and Shirley still go to college dances, especially if Georgia Fame or Long John Baldry are performing. At college, Shirley wears jeans and jumpers like all the rest, but at night she is always very well-dressed. Charlie still refuses to discuss his marriage, saying, "This is something very precious to us — not something we want to share with others. I hope everyone understands."

The other married Stone is bass guitarist Bill Wyman, whose home is in a $15,000 flat over a petrol station in Penge, South London — with his wife, Diane, and their young son, Stephen. Says Diane of Bill, "He's such a

Charlie Watts was secretly married to Shirley Ann Shepherd a few months ago.

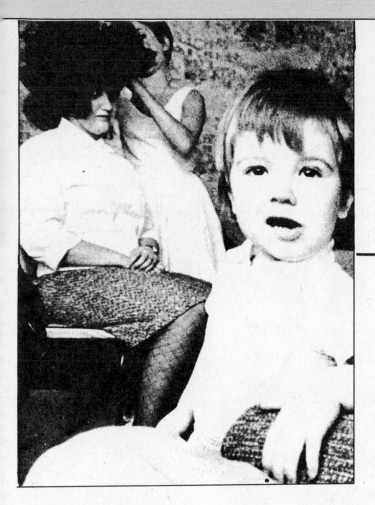

Bill Wyman's wife is named Diane — shown here getting her hair done. In the foreground is the Wyman's young son, Stephen.

quiet, easygoing person that you'd never think he keeps an eye on tiny little details that needn't bother him. Sometimes he even asks me the price of things like butter, or the roast for the weekend. And he can store all the information he gathers. Right off, he can tell you the difference between the price of steak per pound in England and in America."

Of Diane, Bill says, "She is a born manager and housekeeper — and loves kids. That's why we had Stephen the first year we were married. We hadn't much money then, but we managed. We never dreamed we'd ever have as much money as we do now."

Most secretive of all about his girl friend is Brian Jones, who has been secretly dating model Linda Lawrence for about two and a half years now.

"We first met when Brian was still unknown," Linda says. "He was playing at the Ricky Tick Club in London. I thought the group was fabulous, and made a real effort to get to meet them. Brian and I hit it off immediately, but he was very shy and it was all he could do to pluck

up enough courage to ask me to come back and hear them play the next night.

"After that," recalls Linda, who lives with her mom and dad in a bungalow near Reading, Berkshire, England, "he started taking me out regularly, and I asked him back home to meet my folks. They took to him at once, and he's become like a part of the family. Dad is always lending Brian his car to drive out to see his own family, who live over a 100 miles outside of London. He used to stay at different flats with friends all over London. Mum took pity on him and asked him to stay at our house with us (that's Mum, Dad and my sisters, Sharon and Carol, and me), whenever he's in town.

"Brian is a very quiet person who is always trying to hide his shyness. In spite of his long hair, we look very smart when we go out together. At first, he used to take me to all the Stones shows, but" — and Linda looks a little sad when she says this — "now that they are famous, there's such a crush backstage that it's dangerous — so I rarely go to their shows at all now."

Linda Lawrence, a model, has been dating Brian Jones for about two and a half years.

'Yer actual ruthless rampaging fan would as soon *take* your leg as have you write on theirs. The combination of unfulfilled longing and unfocused sexuality with the fanaticism of a devotee to a religious cult turned their idols (like Ringo in *Help!*) into objects of worship and subjects for sacrifice. In the presence of the Stones, fans became as predatory as piranhas in a feeding frenzy. It was an awesome sight to behold.

Connie: "At Carneigie Hall I got knocked down a flight of stairs, Mick had to help me across Fifty-seventh Street. A week later I was covered with broken glass from kids breaking a window and at another concert a guy, trying to stop some fan, put his fist out, missed, and knocked me out cold. Fun days."

Gloria: "We had the first genuine out-of-control riots with the Stones' concerts. They closed Carnegie Hall for rock 'n roll. The Beatles had played there, Herman's Hermits, but there had been nothing like *this*! Mick called me to say that they'd be going on at 9:30 and I said I'd see him there backstage. It was a riot, my dear. You could hear the screaming going on inside from the street. It just got so out of hand that the police forced the management to put the Stones on an hour earlier. By the time I got there they'd already gone. They'd been rushed to the Park Sheraton with a police escort, my dear."

Inveterate fetishists, fans go to incredible lengths just to touch an object once held by the object of their heart's desire. The *Daily Express* reported: "A youth sold two empty pop bottles for five pounds today to fans of the Rolling Stones who were watching the group's plane arrive at Sydney. He said the Stones' leader, Mick Jagger, had touched them."

Some other fans made contact with their idols by proxy—after the Stones vacated their hotel rooms. "Pat took a picture of Keith's room and I took one of Brian's . . . they were as messy as magazines say, with things draped everywhere, including the floor. (It reminded me greatly of my own room!) . . . Anyway, we sorted out a few souvenirs . . . we split up a box of rum-filled candy found in Brian's room. There were some sketches by fans, sent up to them, that we found . . . I also found a guitar pick on the nightstand in Brian's room which I slipped into my wallet, next to a picture of the Stones." True to teen magazine morality, "we didn't stoop to lifting the usual items, sheets, pillowcases, towels and the like, however, Pat did find a pair of swim trunks in the suite where Keith's room was and I did find a pair of socks under the bed of one Mr. Jones, sooo!"

These same fans would and did, however, literally stoop to anything: "One girl told me how she would go up to the door, lay down and place a small mirror under the door, tilting it so that she could see the room inside. I didn't believe her until she showed me, by looking under Keith's door, and I looked too just to see and, sure enough, parts of the room, fragments of furniture, all upside-down, not much, but something."

KEITH Richard's dark eyes shot fire when the inquiring reporter asked: "Is it true Mick is leaving the Stones?"

"That's a stupid question," Keith spit out. "I won't answer it."

Keith, noted for his bad manners and explosive temper, was only repeating what every member of the **Rolling Stones** has said before. **Mick Jagger** won't leave the group.

Brian Jones insists **Mick** will never leave. But **Bill Wyman** and **Charlie Watts,** the two most reliable members of the **Stones,** aren't so positive. **Bill** admits that if **Mick** ever should decide to leave, then they'd worry about that when it happened. **Charlie Watts** says, "It wouldn't be the same if anyone of us left. Right now, no one is planning such a move and we're not so clever that we can read the future anyway!"

Mick Jagger can afford to leave the **Stones** if he wants to. He's got it made as a single singer and has had several acting bids in the last few years. **Mick** says he won't leave because there's no reason to. But what happens if the boys have trouble amongst themselves. They've been known to battle before and this could happen again.

Right now **Mick** doesn't want any more responsibility than he already has. Marriage, he says, would be too much for him because he doesn't want the responsibility of taking care of anyone but himself. So it makes good sense that he wouldn't want to start off on establishing a single career for himself right now. The **Stones** are booked up for years in advance and **Mick Jagger** as a single has no set bookings. It would take a fantastic event to make **Mick** cut out on the other **Stones** right now and sing a lifelong solo.

It's been said that the **Stones** wouldn't ever break up because of their strong attachment for each other. True, they're friends, but it's actually only **Keith** and **Mick** who are especially close. The other **Stones** are mainly business associates who work and travel together.

Friendship won't keep the **Stones** together. Business will. And whatever else **Mick** might be, he's not one to ruin a good business deal. The **Stones** have it made. Without **Mick,** all might be lost for everyone concerned.

The big question of group friend-

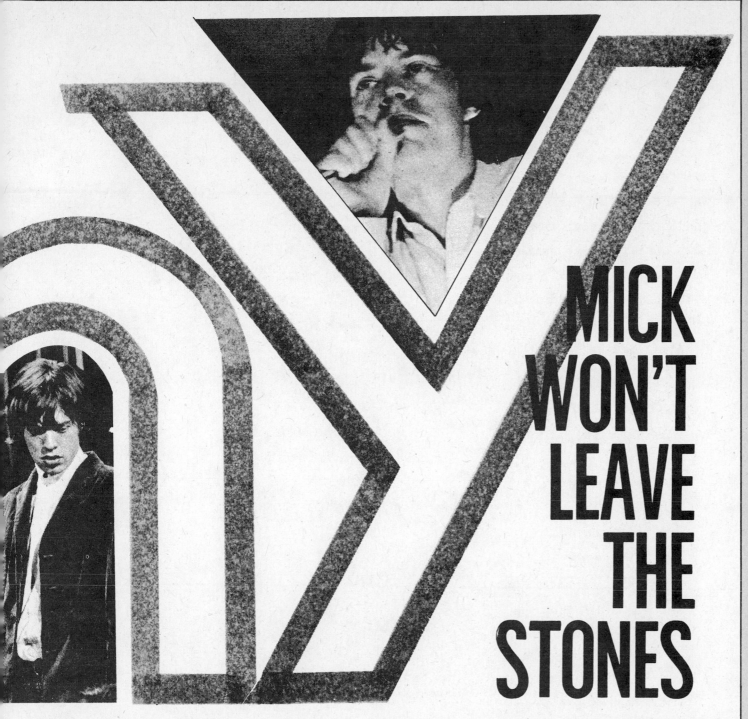

You weren't safe on stage either, even then. At the Academy of Music, one teen reporter saw "jelly beans, gumdrops, marshmallows, paper pie plates with messages written on them, lipstick, sneakers, fuzzy pink stuffed bunny rabbits, pencils, erasers, paper clips, wrappers with and without candy bars inside, a fat toy penguin, combs, wallets stuffed with notes, various coins and other assorted garbage, junk and trash rained onto the stage."

Some pieces of intended humor, especially concerning Brian, appear ominously prophetic in retrospect. Photo caption: "Brian is asking 'Are you *sure* we're headed for the stage and *not* the jailhouse?'" Or, "Anita Tallenburg (sic) with her modern casual looks is a bit tough on Brian, arguing with him if she does not agree with him and never afraid of offending him just because he's a Stone. In fact, she is unlike any other girl in his life."

A staple of the fan magazine format is the Marcel Proust questionnaire (What is your favorite color? What is the height of misery for you?). An additional probe into the Stones' psyches was provided by a handwriting analyst! Brian's responses are left unreported because his answers, we're told, were unprintable . . .

David Dalton

MICK WON'T LEAVE THE STONES

ship often comes up when discussing various lead singers who could make or break a group by leaving. **Paul McCartney** and **John Lennon** are known throughout the world as the closest of buddies and this is true. **Paul** respects **John** above all other people and their relationship has given us some of our greatest music today. **George** and **Ringo**, however, are not the close friends that **John** and **Paul** are. They're friends and that's it. **Keith Hopwood** and **Peter Noone** are close friends because their personal interest jibe more than the other **Hermits**. If **Herman** were to leave the **Hermits**, he'd think twice about cutting his friendship with **Keith**.

One thing many forget when considering the stars like **Mick Jagger** who might leave their groups is that most of these English boys did not come from great wealth. The **Beatles** are always quick to admit that they love being rich. So do the **Stones**. **Mick** wants to lead an unconventional life allowing him to do and say all kinds of things that aren't generally acceptable under ordinary conditions. Having money gives him the security he needs to continue doing this.

Another factor in **Mick** staying with the **Stones** is the fact that their success has been due largely to their combined talents. True, **Mick's** fantastic movements and high and low singing interpretations usually steal the show, but the **Stone's** sound couldn't be easily duplicated and **Mick** knows this. With some of the

elements missing, **Mick** might not be the star he is today.

Ask yourself this question: Would you like **Mick** as well away from the **Stones**? Chances are you'd say 'No.'

Mick supposedly told **Chrissie** that he'd rather retire than do a solo. Those who know him best say this is true, but it's also true that **Mick's** stubborn enough to up and retire if the mood hit him. He likes being alone and not having to be at a certain place at a certain time. Total retirement would give him this opportunity.

Taking everything into account, it's very unlikely that **Mick** will leave the **Stones**. He is the **Stones** and they are **Mick Jagger** . . . and they're all sitting way up there on that cloud together.

THE ROLLING STONES ANSWER
THE PROUST QUESTIONNAIRE IN
THEIR OWN WRITING

When in France the Stones agreed to fill in the famous Marcel Proust questionnaire for Rave. A questionnaire aimed at revealing your true character through your answers! All five Stones answered, though unfortunately we couldn't print Brian's replies. They were unprintable. However, we have given you the analysis of his answers . . .

Brian Jones

ANALYSIS: He is subtle, hypersensitive and the intellectual of the group. He has great artistic talent and is capable of creation on a highly original and personal level. Loves to shock, lives at a very fast pace, almost as though he doesn't want time to think. He has an aggressive quality, is inwardly anxious and a little vulnerable—slightly afraid of life. But he has a tremendous charm, a great deal of personal magnetism, and a devilish streak which is unconsciously revealed in his answers.

HANDWRITING REPORT: An explosive personality that he cultivates with great care. Beneath the surface there is the soul of a real poet with great sensitivity.

STRONG POINTS: A vivid imagination, authority, abundant energy and a very good memory. He has initiative, ambition and loves independence, is a persuasive talker, frank and strongly sensual.

WEAK POINTS: He's overskeptical and stubborn. A pessimist, never fully satisfied with life, proud, impulsive and slightly distrustful.

Mick Jagger

ANALYSIS: He's got loads of personality, but isn't as free as he'd like to be in expressing it. Plenty of creative talent, spontaneous kindness and an easy-going nature. He has an amazing talent for communicating with people. Mick is the soul of the Rolling Stones.

HANDWRITING REPORT: He has a sensitivity which he exploits to good effect. He's not anxious to reveal himself as he really is, changes his mind.

STRONG POINTS: Natural intelligence, imagination and artistic ability. He is frank, idealistic and sentimental.

WEAK POINTS: Lacks a sense of reality and has a tendency to exaggerate.

CHARLIE WATTS

1 What is, for you, the height of misery? NO PAPER IN THE LAVORTRY.
2 Where would you like to live? HOME.
3 What is your idea of happiness? HOME.
4 What mistake do you disregard most frequently? MINE.
5 Who is your favourite personality in history? NONE.
6 Who are your favourite heroines in real life? NONE.
7 Who is your favourite musician? STRAVINSKY.
8 What quality do you like most in a woman? THEIR GREAT BIG-ARMS.
9 What quality do you prefer in a man? THEIR GREAT BIG-EARS.
10 What is your most admirable virtue? MY ~~SPELL SPELL SPELL~~ PLAYING WITH MY EARS.

MICK JAGGER

1 What is, for you, the height of misery? NOT HAVING A MATCH
2 Where would you like to live? AT MY HOUSE
3 What is your idea of happiness? GROVELLING IN WEEDS
4 What mistake do you disregard most frequently? CHILDREN
5 Who is your favourite personality in history? QUEEN HAROLD
6 Who are your favourite heroines in real life? PRINCESS ANNE
7 Who is your favourite musician? TOMMY STEELE
8 What quality do you like most in a woman? MASCULINITY
9 What quality do you prefer in a man? TROUSERS
10 What is your most admirable virtue? PRODDING
11 What is your favourite occupation? EPILEPTIC FITS
12 Who would you like to have been? ALBERT
13 What is the main feature of your character? CONSTIPATION
14 What qualities do you appreciate most in a friend? SINCERITY, AND KINDNESS
15 What is the main fault in your character? CONCEITED ANKLE
What is the greatest misfortune that could happen to you? TO LOSE PEOPLE I LOVE
What would you like to be? BEATLE
What is your favourite colour? NNCCP S BSC.
What is your favourite flower? HAYSEED
What is your favourite bird? WOODCOCK
Who are your favourite heroes in real life? DUKES
What are your favourite names? MICHAEL PHILIP
Who do you hate most? ASH ON MY SHOES
What historical character do you despise most? ISAAC II
What military event do you admire most? CHANGING OF THE GUARD
What reform do you admire most? BORSTAL
What natural gift would you like to have? BRYLCREEM DISPENSER
How would you like to die? QUICKLY
What is the present state of your . . .

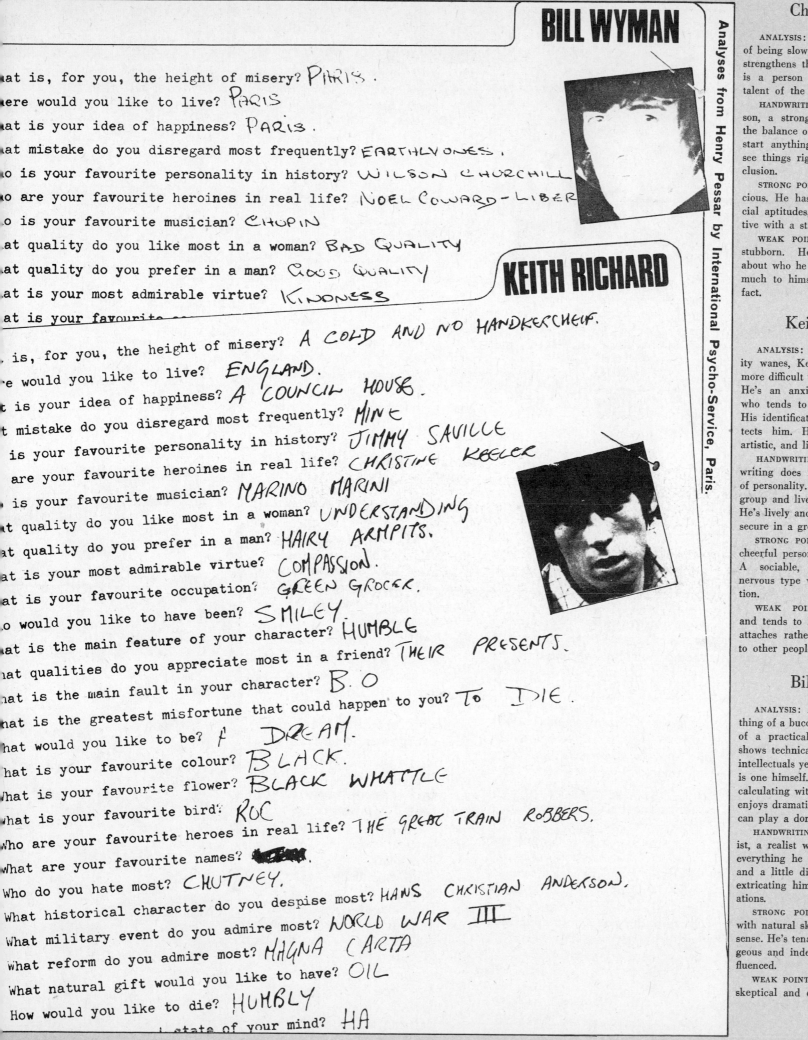

BILL WYMAN

Analyses from Henry Pessar by International Psycho-Service, Paris.

at is, for you, the height of misery? PARIS.

ere would you like to live? PARIS

at is your idea of happiness? PARIS.

at mistake do you disregard most frequently? EARTHLY ONES.

o is your favourite personality in history? WILSON CHURCHILL

o are your favourite heroines in real life? NOEL COWARD - LIBER

o is your favourite musician? CHOPIN

at quality do you like most in a woman? BAD QUALITY

at quality do you prefer in a man? GOOD QUALITY

at is your most admirable virtue? KINDNESS

at is your favourite

KEITH RICHARD

is, for you, the height of misery? A COLD AND NO HANDKERCHEIF.

e would you like to live? ENGLAND.

t is your idea of happiness? A COUNCIL HOUSE.

t mistake do you disregard most frequently? MINE

is your favourite personality in history? JIMMY SAVILLE

are your favourite heroines in real life? CHRISTINE KEELER

is your favourite musician? MARINO MARINI

t quality do you like most in a woman? UNDERSTANDING

t quality do you prefer in a man? HAIRY ARMPITS.

t is your most admirable virtue? COMPASSION.

t is your favourite occupation? GREEN GROCER.

o would you like to have been? SMILEY

at is the main feature of your character? HUMBLE

at qualities do you appreciate most in a friend? THEIR PRESENTS.

at is the main fault in your character? B.O

at is the greatest misfortune that could happen to you? TO DIE.

hat would you like to be? A DREAM.

hat is your favourite colour? BLACK.

What is your favourite flower? BLACK WHATTLE

What is your favourite bird? ROC

Who are your favourite heroes in real life? THE GREAT TRAIN ROBBERS.

What are your favourite names? ~~crossed out~~.

Who do you hate most? CHUTNEY.

What historical character do you despise most? HANS CHRISTIAN ANDERSON.

What military event do you admire most? WORLD WAR III

What reform do you admire most? MAGNA CARTA

What natural gift would you like to have? OIL

How would you like to die? HUMBLY

state of your mind? HA

Charlie Watts

ANALYSIS: He gives the impression of being slow, but his presence visibly strengthens the rest of the group. He is a person who lacks the creative talent of the others.

HANDWRITING REPORT: A good person, a strong-silent type essential to the balance of the group. He's slow to start anything, but once started will see things right through to their conclusion.

STRONG POINTS: Practical and tenacious. He has technical and commercial aptitudes, is ambitious and sensitive with a strong vitality.

WEAK POINTS: A tendency to be stubborn. He's extremely reserved about who he trusts, keeps himself too much to himself. Strong introvert, in fact.

Keith Richard

ANALYSIS: If the Stones' popularity wanes, Keith will find it a little more difficult to adjust than the others. He's an anxious, affectionate person who tends to shy away from reality. His identification with the group protects him. He's very sensitive and artistic, and lives spontaneously.

HANDWRITING REPORT: His handwriting does not reveal a great deal of personality. He's borne along by the group and lives in a world of fantasy. He's lively and nonconformist, he feels secure in a group.

STRONG POINTS: He is a practical, cheerful person with artistic aptitudes. A sociable, strongly sensual and nervous type with a fanciful imagination.

WEAK POINTS: Lacks confidence and tends to be easily influenced. He attaches rather too much importance to other people's opinions.

Bill Wyman

ANALYSIS: A craftsman and something of a buccaneer. He has the hands of a practical man and his writing shows technical aptitudes. He dislikes intellectuals yet, to a certain extent, he is one himself. He's rational, cool and calculating with a very strong will. He enjoys dramatic situations in which he can play a dominating role.

HANDWRITING REPORT: A materialist, a realist who carefully weighs up everything he does. He's authoritative and a little distant, but an expert at extricating himself from difficult situations.

STRONG POINTS: A practical man with natural skills and sound common sense. He's tenacious, ambitious, courageous and independent—not easily influenced.

WEAK POINTS: Argumentative, over-skeptical and distrustful.

from London with Luv

by Chrissie Shrimpton

Mick and I went down to visit George and Patti Harrison recently. They were just about ready to go out to a Saturday night movie when we arrived and so they asked us to go with them. The film happened to be at John Lennon's private home cinema. What a great way to see a movie. We saw a film called "Citizen Kane" with Orson Welles surrounded by Bourneville chocolate and cups of coffee!

I think **Stevie Winwood** with the **Spencer Davis Group** is a fantastic singer. In fact the best singer we have. (ouch! **Mick** just hit me!) He showed up one day wearing some terrific clothes. Turned out he'd bought them in Paris. I like crepe shirts and **Steve** had a beautiful one in blue and green stripes. He's bought a blue-green corduroy jacket to go with it. It is comforting to know that it isn't only me who likes to spend money in Paris!

Recently I had my 21st birth-day. It wasn't too painful, as these things go, I guess. **Mick** gave me a huge rocking horse on big rockers which I named Petunia. Also a bird cage with a Victorian brass bird in it. The bird sings. That is, it does if you put money into it. And my mother gave me some gypsy gold hoop earrings, which I had been eyeing for ages.

I've been taking a look at some of the terrific groups that are around. **The Who,** for example, really are quite incredible. Their stage act may be a trifle unexpected, but it certainly is alive. On a recent appearance with the **Beatles** and **Stones,** they outdid themselves. By the end of their act, drummer **Keith Moon** was left with one cymbal. He had thrown the rest of his drum kit, piece by piece, to the audience.

Keith wore a beautiful red shirt that evening. It was all sort of silky with red roses on it. He said it had been made for him at a boutique called "Granny Takes a Trip." This is hidden away in the depths of darkest Chelsea. But it's worth looking for. It is crammed full of old-fashioned Victoriana.

Charlie Watts bought a four-bedroomed 16th Century house in Sussex and is furnishing it with a mixture of modern contemporary-styled furniture along with antiques and paintings.

About **Charlie:** "He is so modest he never thinks of himself as a famous person. And he's kind to everybody. He never tries to interfere in what people are doing. Actually, I'd say **Dave Clark** is very much the same kind of person—in fact, I could say quite a lot about him, too. But back to Charlie, he is mad keen on modern jazz and, unlike some people who enthuse over this sort of thing, he doesn't try to ram his opinions down anyone's throat. But if you catch Charlie with a modern jazz man . . . well the talk is all sewn up

for the whole evening."

Bill Wyman moved to a newish house further out in Kent. He used to live in Penge. His new home has four bedrooms.

Tara Brown, 21 year old heir to the Guinness family fortune, gave a coming-of-age party recently. In Ireland. He invited friends to the family house. Or, rather, I should say, castle, because that's what it looks like. It is about 30 miles from Dublin and the nearest village is called Bray. There was quite a collection of people who had come over from London — from the pop scene to debs to —well, I'll just say that Tara has a lot of friends. **Brian Jones** was there with **Anita Pallenberg.**

MICK AND I IN NEW YORK

THE ROLLING STONES

as I know Them!

By RODNEY DICKINSON

Being close to the Rolling Stones is probably the best life a person can have. I've been fortunate enough to be in at the beginning of their career and watch them closely over the years. They've always been the same fair boys as they are today. Though it's been said many times before, success hasn't spoilt them.

Here in England we are proud of the **Rolling Stones.** Every month in TIGER BEAT's **Mod Magazine,** I'll try to keep you well in touch with what's happening in each of their lives. This is quite a job as the **Stones** are forever on the move in both their professional as well as personal lives.

Brian Jones was telling me the other day that the thing he is happiest about in his life is the fact that the Stones are no long-er treated as "freaks." Brian, as you know, loves America and wants very much to buy a house in Hollywood. He says the American attitude has greatly changed toward the group and this makes him happy.

Nowadays, they know most of the topographical pitfalls of badly-placed theaters, theaters with stagedoors on the main road or fire-escapes and other means of access by which fans could almost reach their idols while endangering their own lives.

"The Stones are best-known by their hair," reasons Oldham. "If we hide their hair, we have a fighting chance."

There is the "twin" bit, too.

You may have noticed that road managers, drivers, and backstage workers who travel with Brian, Mick, Charlie, Keith and Bill bear an uncanny resemblance from certain angles.

If no other measure is possible, the "twins" are sent out to lay a false trail.

MY BROTHER MICK
BY CHRIS JAGGER

IT's already been a wonderful experience for me, just sitting here and seeing how Mick and The Stones have become gradually but surely popular, from the day Mick first started singing R and B, and The Rolling Stones clicked.

Mick first took me to see The Stones at the Piccadilly Club (now The Scene) where about twenty people turned up to twist and listen to the little-known R and B. It was a time when Trad was just dying out. But the people in the club didn't really know what they liked or wanted.

The Stones did such numbers as *Tiger In Your Tank*, *Blues Before Sunrise* and *Hoochie Coochie Man*, of which the last number has become quite a blues standard over here.

In those days there was no Bill Wyman or Charlie Watts and "Stu" (now road manager) would bang it out on the piano. But he was barely audible.

Frankly the sound they made was good and loud but not really great. However it didn't take them long to develop their own particular sound.

At first, just after The Stones had formed, I used to keep newspaper and magazine snippets on them. I gave that up ages ago. But I've still got the first one from Jazz News when Mick was quoted as saying: "I hope they don't think we're a rock and roll outfit." They're still having the same argument now!

The R and B thing probably started when Mick bought his first Chuck Berry record at the age of thirteen, though he didn't realise what it would lead to at the time. I lent that record out to a friend who took it to Australia with him and you can imagine how pleased Mick was with me. I had to pay him the grand sum of 4s. 3d. for that 78.

Mick went on collecting R and B records and I went on hearing them until I just had to like them. At first, though I liked Muddy Waters and Howlin' Wolf, it took me a bit longer to get to know Chuck Berry and Bo Diddley.

I think that R and B is more lasting than rock and roll. My taste seems to improve as I listen to it.

But I expect you'd like to know how it feels being Mick's brother. In many ways it's rather peculiar going into a news-agent's and seeing a dozen pictures of your brother frowning at you. When I hear people talking about The Stones I always feel like chipping in—but I seldom do.

Chances are anyway that people won't believe you. People get quite suspicious when I say I *actually know* The Stones!

Still, I suppose it's hardly surprising. Half my friends go around saying they are Mick's brother.

On one occasion when I told the stage door man that Mick was expecting me and I was his brother he just bawled at me to go away as Mick had had seven sisters call already that evening!

It isn't always easy getting into a Stones' show—especially if you're like myself and inclined to arrive late. After having fought through about 20 fans to reach the stage door you might be lucky and talk to a sympathetic doorman who'll go and tell Mick—and you're in.

On the other hand if The Stones are playing at a vast place like the Empire Pool or the Albert Hall it's a mighty hard job to get in. The main problem is contacting somebody inside and this may be through an ice-cream seller, a Merseybeat, or who-ever's going in.

Once you do manage to get inside the theatre there's usually Keith strumming away at one of his many guitars, Fab's June Southworth hastily scribbling down what Mick and Brian are saying and Charlie gone off to look for Bill who's looking for somebody to do something.

After the show it's a mad rush for any sort of transport—Mick's car, Brian's car, a taxi that Bill has hired or the group van, you just jump in and get off as quickly as you can.

Of course, I don't see Mick that much nowadays. Perhaps once in a fortnight during term time and once a week in the holidays. But he does try hard to get home every now and then. Although I see Mick more often now than when he was at the London School of Economics and didn't have much money, or a car to come home in. I think I can safely say that Mick in all his hectic and busy life doesn't forget about his "little brother."

Bo Diddley once called me that, though I hastened to remind him that I'm only two inches shorter than Mick—and still growing!

It's great to be with the Stones and to meet all their friends. They all ask me the obvious question. "Are you going to follow in your brother's footsteps?" Although my interests are similar to Mick's I would hate to be thought of as a second Mick. Perhaps I can keep my own interests and at the same time develop my own life.

5

I GOT NASTY HABITS

Rock 'n roll adolescents storm into the streets of all nations. They rush into the Louvre and throw acid in the Mona Lisa's face. They open zoos, insane asylums, prisons, burst water mains with air hammers, chop the floor out of passenger plane lavatories, shoot out lighthouses . . . turn sewers into the water supply . . . administer injections with bicycle pumps, disconnect artificial kidneys . . . they shit on the floor of the United Nations, and wipe their ass with treaties, pacts, alliances. (William Burroughs, The Wild Boys)

The events of the first seven months of 1967, wherein her Britanic Majesty's government, custodian of an eroding empire, and her attendant ministers, judges, constables and clerks and Members of Parliament were pitted against a rock 'n roll group, could well have provided the scenario for the Stones long-awaited first feature film.

Both the dailies with their reactionary ravings and the Underground press with its self-serving revolutionary rhetoric did their best to encourage inflammatory visions of the Stones as the ringleaders of an international conspiracy of rock 'n roll punks to Undermine Western Civilization with drugs, polymorphous sexuality, violence and over-amped anti-social anthems. Opposing sides had worked themselves up into such a pitch of pieties that following their sentencing in June, Mick and Keith were considered so dangerous they were actually banned from entering Scotland!

"For the Stones, bad news is good news." This was one of Andrew's infamous axioms, but by the beginning of 1967 it had started to backfire. In the end, they were to collide with their own self-perpetuating publicity.

For more than two years the Stones had been symbols of new and dangerous attitudes that were particularly attractive to their teenage fans. They had participated in and provoked the transformation of the morals and manners of their generation so effectively that the Stones were now actually being made out by the press to be sinister "corrupters of Britain's youth." Mick, the Pied Piper of this revolution, protested "all this stuff about me leading them and perverting them . . . we just sort of went along together, didn't we?" But the combination of pop stars and drugs was like a red rag to a raging bull. If the Stones' Bad Boy image sold papers, the newly pressed stereotype of them as degenerates and drug fiends saw flaming front page headlines.

From Mick and Keith's bust in February 1967 until Brian's acquittal in September scarcely a week went by in Britain that the Stones were not in the headlines—the whole campaign could well have been masterminded by Andrew Oldham. But it was Oldham's conspicuous absence during the busts and trials that in part led to the split with the group later that year.

Nothing could have done more to consolidate the Stones' already fanatical following than their "drug martydrom"—the outrageous sentences imposed on them by the court at their trial—which enlisted the sympathy of the general public and raised the Stones case to the level of national debate in the houses of Parliament.

Mick and Keith were charged with offenses contrary to drug laws barely three years old at the time of their arrest, Mick for having pep pills without a prescription under Section 1 of the Drugs Prevention and Misuse Act (1964) and Keith for permitting his house to be used for the smoking of hashish under Section 5(A) of the Dangerous Drug Act (1965). The pills for which Mick was prosecuted were actually found in the pocket of Marianne Faithfull's green velvet jacket and it was a sign of the times that when one of the arresting officers asked, "Who does this coat belong to?" Mick claimed it as his.

Pep pills (methamphetamines), known on the street as leapers or purple hearts, were the drug of choice of London's mods and were immortalized in the speed-induced stutter of the Who's "My G-g-g-generation." The influence of methamphetamines on the works of the Rolling Stones is too vast a subject to deal with here without adequate medication. Some claim "Jumping Jack Flash" as the ultimate hymn to crank, (Keith: "It was about my gardener, actually") and allusions to speed can be found sprinkled throughout the albums of the 70s. At the time, drug exegetes ingeniously interpreted "Lady Jane" as a resolution to abandon speed—Lady Ann (phetamine)—for marijuana, Lady (Mary) Jane. Leaving aside the chemical analysis of the Stone's lyrics for the moment it should be mentioned that the so-called cult of the purple heart was seen as a very real threat.

Before 1964 possession of pep pills was not illegal; a new bill was passed because the police were having trouble catching dealers in the act. The new bill was passed to make mere possession without a perscription illegal. This bill was disengenuously presented to the House of Commons by the Home Secretary, Mr. Henry Brooke, as an expedient measure to aid the police in arresting traffickers.

What was especially insidious about the new law was that no distinction was drawn between trafficker and user or public and private places.

Like all possession bills, the 1964 act invited discriminatory application. Housewives were not being carted off for their "mother's little helpers," while members of unpopular groups were prosecuted in cases that allowed more than a suspicion of police "planting."

Mick was prosecuted on a technicality and Keith on the most tenuous circumstantial evidence. For a band once described as "rattling drugs like maracas," it seems incredible that the police could only present such flimsy evidence.

Following their trial in June public sympathy changed in their favor. A combination of the insufficiency of evidence with the ferocious sentences handed down by Judge Block made the case against Mick and Keith seem particularly illogical and illegal and this eventually led to their successful appeal.

BRIAN BLOWS IT AT BLASES

Brian could barely resist the temptation to hold forth *ex cathedra* to the press. One of these occasions in May of 1966 was to lead to the notorious *The News of the World* article which (mistakenly) reported Mick's (actually Brian's) opinions and adventures on acid which led to Mick's libel suit against *The News of the World* which in turn led to the raid on Redlands which led to the trials of Mick and Keith.

On the morning of Sunday, February 5, 1967, the British Isles awoke to these headlines in *The News of the World*:

POP STARS AND DRUGS— FACTS THAT WILL SHOCK YOU.

Untold thousands of citizens recoiled in semi-detached horror as visions of the unmentionable drugs hashish, heroin, cannabis, LSD-teenage orgies, etc. sexploded in large-than-life stroboscopic detail.

While the article focused on the Moody Blues so called "Roehampton Raves" LSD parties also attended by Peter Townshend, Ginger Baker and others, the paper contained the following erroneous statements about and from Mick (actually Brian): "He told us: 'I don't go much on it (LSD) now the cats (fans) have taken it up. It'll just get a dirty name. I remember the first time I took It. It was on our tour with Bo Diddley and Little Richard.'

"During the time we were at the Blases Club, in Kensington, London, Jagger took about six benzedrine full tablets. 'I just would not keep awake in places like this if I didn't have them,' . . . Later at Blases, Jagger showed a companion and two girls a small piece of hash (marijuana) and invited them to his flat for 'a smoke.'"

The person speaking, was of course not Mick at all, who was and is scrupulously careful about exposing his drug habits in public.

But the confusion of Brian for Mick was-to have disastrous consequences for Mick and the Stones in general.

As chance would have it, Mick was to appear on the telly the afternoon the article appeared! When the host, Eammon Andrews, asked him if all those horrible things they'd been saying about him in the morning's paper was true, Mick promptly told the audience that his solicitors has issued a writ of libel against *The News of the World*.

Like Wilde, with whose aristocratic "decadent" style he has often been associated, and whom he would portray in a promo film parody for "We Love You," Mick underestimated the tide of resentment that was lying in wait for him and the Stones.

According to Jagger's version in the court proceedings, *The News of the World* stationed a van outside Mick's house on Cheyne Walk to keep him under constant surveillance. In the remaining five days before the bust at Redlands, Keith's country home in West Wittering, Mick was subjected to being followed and watched wherever he went and whatever he said or did. At the trial, Mick's solicitor, Mr. Havers commented dryly: "I can think of no better way [for *The News of the World*] to kill off the ensuing libel action."

Retribution came swiftly. According to Keith: "*The News of the World* got hold of someone who was working for us. I think it was the cat who was driving me at the time. They knew we were going to be down there at a party. Really, just something I'd done a million times before and I've done a million times since. I simply said, 'Let's go down to my place for the weekend.'"

Whoever the "Mr. X" was who tipped off *The News of the World*, it was *The News of the World* who tipped off the police. With the appropriate smugness of an organization that has always profited from the misfortunes of others, *The News of the World* later called the suggestion that they had dispatched a spy "A Monstrous Charge," adding with apparent contradiction "that where a crime is suspected it is a public duty to assist the authorities." Widely criticized for 'blowing the whistle,' *The News of the World*'s responded: "There was never the slightest doubt that it was our duty to tell the police. We had been given information and if we had suppressed it we would have become accessories—morally and actually—to acts that were criminal under the existing laws of the land." Coming from a newspaper that had made its fortune from the scandals and deviations of a society, this struck many as a crushingly pretentious statement.

Whatever story they alleged, on the night of February 11th, while the following week's issue of *The News of the World* was rolling off the presses, containing still more revelations about drugs and pop stars, a call came from a dutiful member of the public to the city desk informing the editor that some "nasty business" was afoot at Redlands.

The Raid on Redlands

KEITH: There's a big knock at the door. Eight o'clock. Everybody is just sort of gliding down slowly from the whole day of sort of freaking about. Everyone has managed to find their way back to the house. TV is on with the sound off and the record player is on. Strobe lights are flickering. Marianne Faithfull has just decided that she wanted a bath and has wrapped herself up in a rug and is watching the box.

"Bang, bang, bang," this big knock at the door and I go to answer it. "Oh look, there's lots of little ladies and gentlemen outside." He says, "Read this," and I'm going, "Wha, wha? All right."

We were just gliding off from a twelve-hour trip. You know how that freaks people out when they walk in on you. The vibes were so funny for them. I told one of the women with them they'd brought to search the ladies, "Would you mind stepping off that Moroccan cushion? Because you're ruining the tapestries." We were playing it like that. They tried to get us to turn the record player off but we said, "No. We won't turn it off but we'll turn it down." As they went, as they started going out the door, somebody put on "Rainy Day Women" really loud.

"Everybody must get stoned." And that was it.

On February 19th, a week after the raid, *The News of the World*'s front-page headline was: "DRUG SQUAD RAIDS POP STARS' PARTY." For a paper so intimately involved with the goings on at Redlands, *The News of the World* report was curiously vague. "Several stars, at least three of them nationally known names, were present at the party. It was held at a secluded country house near the South Coast." The three were Mick, Keith and Marianne Faithfull (whose name was omitted from all reports, and the subsequent court transcripts, wherein she was discretely referred to as "Miss X," "a nymphomaniac," or "NUDE GIRL IN MERRY MOOD AT DRUG PARTY"). George Harrison had been at Redlands earlier in the day but got bored and left. If a Beatle had been involved in the "drug raid," subsequent events would have taken a quite different turn.

KEITH: The heavy trial came in June, about five months after. It was really starting to wear us out by then. The lawyers were saying, "It seems really weird, they want to really do it to you."

The trials of Mick and Keith took place on July 27-29 at the West Sussex Quarter Sessions before two juries under the wrathful and vindictive eye of Judge Block.

Mick's counsel took the line that Mick had obtained the pep pills legally in Italy for "airsickness" (on his way back from the San Remo Song Festival with Marianne Faithfull) from an airport vending machine. Curiously, no one questioned this, although Italian law for over five years had been particularly ferocious in prosecuting possession of methamphetamines.

Second, it was claimed that when Mick's personal physician told Mick over the phone that it was all right for him to pop a few leapers now and again, this amounted to a prescription.

STONES: 'A STRONG, SWEET SMELL OF INCENSE'

Robert Fraser and Mick Jagger try to shield their faces from photographers on their way to court today.

ROLLING STONE Mick Jagger—on right in picture—and Mayfair art gallery director Robert Fraser were handcuffed yesterday during journeys between Lewes Prison and the Chichester court.

A Home Office spokesman explained last night that the two men travelled with other prisoners to the court and all were handcuffed for security reasons. Although they made the return journey on their own, Jagger and Fraser were still handcuffed because prison officers had not received further instructions.

THE RATHER grim scenes of Mick Jagger and Robert Fraser appearing handcuffed together at the Chichester court this morning are surely an unnecessary humiliation. Are the two really considered dangerous criminals liable to make trouble unless they are manacled? The Governor of Lewes prison and the police, who are jointly responsible for security arrangements in the movement of prisoners, apparently think so. The Home Office explanation is that when a number of prisoners who are security risks are being moved together it is "desirable for them all to be handcuffed." To the public, however, it must seem in this case an act of unnecessary harshness.

At this stage Mr. Havers, helped by his junior, produced a large fawn and white fur rug with orange lining. Holding it up between them, Mr. Havers said: "It is an enormous thing. It is a bed cover."

Robert Fraser's gallery is currently In enough to draw Lady Jane Ormsby-Go... (*left*), seen chatting with Michael Rainey, owner of a Chelsea men's shop he calls Hung on You.

and gay." Says Robert Fraser, owner of London's most pioneering art gallery: "Right now, London has something that New York used to have: everybody wants to be there. There's no

Incense found

Mr. McCowan said that when he officers arrived at Richard's nouse they noticed a very strong, sweet and unusual smell.

Police found sticks of incense and a tin which appeared to contain incense

Story of girl in a fur-skin rug

BY A SPECIAL CORRESPONDENT
Chichester, Sussex, Wednesday

ONE of the party guests at Rolling Stone Keith Richard's house, when it was raided by police one night last February was a young woman wearing only a fur-skin rug, the West Sussex Quarter Sessions jury heard today.

Mr Malcolm Morris, QC, prosecuting, said there was a strong, sweet smell in the house. He suggested that it was incense, being burned to hide the smell of cannabis resin, traces of which were found in ash deposits.

Detective Inspector Lynch, Scotland Yard's Drug Squad, said Mr Morris, would tell the court what effect cannabis resin (Indian hemp) had on people.

"It produces an effect of tranquillity and happiness and tends to dispel inhibitions," said Mr Morris.

"All she wore"

"It seems to have had exactly that effect upon one of the guests. This was the young lady who was sitting on the sofa.

"**All that she was wearing was a light-coloured fur-skin rug which, from time to time, she let fall, disclosing her nude body.**

"How people behave in their own houses is usually no concern of anybody else. The only significance of that young lady is that when the police arrived in force she remained unperturbed and apparently enjoying the situation.

"Indeed, although she was taken upstairs to be searched and into a bedroom where her clothes were, she returned downstairs afterwards where, apart from Mr Richard and his guests there was a large number of plain-clothes policemen, still only wearing that fur rug."

No alcohol

There were no glasses containing alcohol in the drawing-room, said Mr Morris.

He submitted that the reason why Richard was not surprised at the young lady's behaviour was because he knew cannabis resin was being smoked on the premises.

Richard, aged 23, of Redlands Lane, West Wittering, Sussex, is accused under his full name, Keith Richards, that, as the occupier of "Redlands," Redlands Lane, West Wittering, he permitted the premises to be used for the smoking of cannabis resin on February 12 this year. He was pleading not guilty.

The group's lead singer Mick Jagger, and London art gallery director, Robert Hugh Fraser, appeared on different charges yesterday relating to the same date and were remanded in custody for sentence at the end of the hearing.

Jagger, aged 23, was found guilty of being in possession of four tablets containing amphetamine sulphate and methylamphetamine hydrochloride on February 12. He had denied the charge. He spent last night in Lewes prison.

Fraser had pleaded guilty to being in unlawful possession of 24 heroin tablets.

Jagger and Fraser were in handcuffs when they arrived at the court from jail in a police van.

Black suit

Remanded on bail yesterday.

KEITH RICHARD—he wore a black four-button Regency style suit, trimmed with black braid. With it he had a white high-necked shirt.

MICK JAGGER

ROBERT FRASER

Keith Richards, more soberly dressed in pale-pink T-shirt and jeans, rushed to the court with it in his blue Bentley just before the court adjourned.

KEITH RICHARD
"Party guests"

A crowd of about 50 waited at the rear exit of the court in the hope of seeing Jagger—dressed in an eggshell-green jacket with dark green trousers—leave.

They rushed forward [redacted] blue police van drove out, but it was a false alarm. Only policemen were inside.

Fans of the Rolling Stones at Chichester today before the hearing.

The agony of seeing your idols jailed . . .

Tudor-style farmhouse in West Wittering.

REDLANDS, THE HOUSE IN WHICH POLICE SAID THEY FOUND DRUGS

Redlands is a beautiful old thatched farmhouse partly surrounded by a moat. It is in a secluded position at the end of a lane in West Wittering, Sussex, and is owned by Keith Richards of the Rolling Stones.

Proper course

The Editor of the News of the World was made aware of the information. He decided that since there was no doubt of the informant's sincerity,

Keith Richard.

A third man, Robert Hugh Fraser, aged 29, art gallery

Thirty-year-old Fraser runs a fashionable gallery in Mount - street Mayfair London.

He specialises in "pop" paintings and sculptures.

on Robert Hugh Fraser, aged 39, London art gallery director, for possessing 24

Mr. Fraser runs an avant-garde gallery where works by contemporary and pop-type artists are often on view.

ROBERT HUGH FRASER

Art man's sentence to stand

REGINA v. FRASER
Before the LORD CHIEF JUSTICE, LORD JUSTICE WINN *and* MR. JUSTICE CUSACK

ROBERT FRASER
Runs a gallery

Lord Parker said that Fraser, of Mayfair, the son of a merchant banker, was educated at a famous public school and had served in two renowned regiments.

"Those privileges, if anything, raise greater responsibilities and would tempt the court to give more rather than less by way of sentence than to a person whom I will deem the man in the street."

ROBERT FRASER IN HIS GALLERY

Fraser (29), of Mount Street, Mayfair,

Rolling Stone Brian remanded

Keith Richard . . . after being remanded on bail

In London today . . . Brian Jones.

Brian Jones, 25-year-old Rolling Stones guitarist, and Prince Stanislas Klossowski de Rola were remanded on £250 bail at West London today on a drugs charge.

The two, who wore "mod" gear and arrived in a Rolls-Royce, were accused of the unauthorised possession of cannabis resin (Indian hemp).

Prince Stanislas is known to his friends as "Stash." His father is a director of the Villa de Medici in Rome and he played several small roles in Hollywood before joining the pop world.

The two, who live in Courtfield Road, South Kensington, were remanded for three weeks.

Fuller report—PAGE 17.

Jones appeared in court wearing a blue lounge suit, a white shirt with lace cuffs and a large blue and white polka-dot tie. Prince Stanislas wore a brown fur-type coat over a blue suit.

When the two men left the court after the two-minute hearing, a crowd of about 80 people was waiting, many of them young girls, some of whom screamed: "They're gorgeous."

They drove away in a silver Rolls Royce.

with lace cuffs and a large blue and white polka-dot tie. Prince Stanislas wore a brown fur-type coat over a blue suit.

Pop idol Mick Jagger of the Rolling Stones went to court today in a lime green jacket, dark green trousers, a green and black tie and a floral-pattern white shirt to answer drug accusations.

Jagger, pale and trembling slightly, wore tight trousers, a yellow flounced shirt with a large green tie. On his trouser-belt was a button badge: "*Mick is sex.*"

Granting Mr. Jagger an appeal certificate, Judge Block told Mr Havers: "I wish you the best of luck."

MOD-STYLE SUIT AND STRIPED SHIRT

lilac green jacket with white buttons, a fancy floral shirt, loud black-and-green striped tie, olive-green pin-stripe trousers.

Keith Richard stood in the dock wearing a four-button Mod-style black suit and a Regency-striped, high-necked shirt.

jacket and pink tie, and Fraser a light grey suit. All three stood in

A green jacket

"Name blackened"

roBert Fraser GaLlery 69 DuKe street, grosVENor Square, lonDon w1,

The Swinging City

GREEN JACKET

CHANGE OVER

Jagger wore a double-breasted green jacket, cream silk shirt and fancy grey tie in court and Richard had a black coat and orange tie.

After lunch they appeared wearing each other's jackets.

MICK JAGGER, in frilly orange shirt and embroidered tie, celebrating his freedom in a Fleet Street public-house last night. At his elbow—a glass of vodka and lime.

wore a lime green [redacted]

WHITE TABLETS

On the case against Fraser, Mr. McCowan said a police officer found a dark coloured jacket behind the drawing room door. From inside the right-hand pocket he took out eight green capsules and handed them to a detective constable.

SPECIAL JASMINE

Jagger, wearing a yellow frilly shirt and black tie with a light green jacket mopped his brow after hearing his sentence and was led away into the cells holding his head and whistling softly.

Jagger, 23, had earlier been found guilty of possessing Italian pep pills.

'TABLETS WERE FOUND IN A GREEN JACKET'

Green capsules

BROWN SUBSTANCE

like a James Cagney film except everything went black.

"My clothes were taken away and I was dressed in blue prison uniform, but you don't care what you look like in a place like that."

Richards's Regency-style suit and silk choker contrasted with the blue denims he wore in the Scrubs.

MICK JAGGER, lead singer in the Rolling Stones pop group, arrived at a court yesterday in a blue Bentley. He left last night in a grey van—bound with other men on remand to spend a night in Lewes Jail, Sussex.

MICK JAGGER
Eggshell-green jacket

In pipe

Also on the table was a briar pipe-bowl. This was taken away and on analysis its contents were found to contain traces of cannabis resin.

The constable was not satisfied and searched him. The constable took from a pocket a tin containing pieces of a brown substance and a decorated wooden pipe

Shown the briar pipe bowl the police found in the house, Mr. Richard said it originally came from Los Angeles, where it was given to him by an American road manager.

contain 66 grains of cannabis resin.

There was also an envelope containing herbal cannabis—untreated hemp—and a substantial ball of brown substance which, when analysed, turned out to be 150 grains of cannabis resin.

Detective Inspector John Lynch, of the Drug Squad at New Scotland Yard, said it was normal practice fo joss sticks or incense to be burned to nullify the smell of cannabis resin.

Det Sgt Cudmore said a well-known national newspaper gave him the information which led to the visit to Richards's house.

Sgt Cudmore also named Mr X as David Henry Schneiderman, alias Britton, a Canadian who left the country two days after the raid.

Jagger was wearing a green jacket, white shirt and dark grey floral tie, Richard a navy-blue jacket and pink tie, and Fraser a light grey suit.

coat.

At this stage Mr Havers, helped by his junior, produced a large fawn and white fur rug with orange lining, holding it up between them. Mr Havers said: "It is an enormous thing. It is a bed cover."

(Proceeding)

WOODEN PIPE

Plastic

Phial

Italian writing

The phial containing the tablets had Italian writing on it.

From Milan

NEWS SUMMARY

Jones (of the Stones) on drug charge

One of the Rolling Stones pop group, (Lewis) Brian Jones (25), was charged in Kensington last night with unlawful possession of a dangerous drug—cannabis resin. He is to appear in West London court to-day.

Charged with him—and also to be in court to-day: Stanislas Klossowski de Rowla, Baron de Witteville (24), Swiss born entertainer. Both were bailed.

The charges followed a Yard drug squad raid yesterday.

2 Stones for trial

Mick Jagger (23), lead singer of the Rolling Stones, Stones' guitarist Keith Richard (23) and art gallery director Robert Hugh Fraser (29),

MICK JAGGER

KEITH RICHARD

KEITH RICHARD

Stones: switch on way to court

Evening Standard Reporter

CHICHESTER, Wednesday.—Police were on duty ready to stop any fan scenes when the Rolling Stones Mick Jagger and Keith Richard appeared on drug summonses at Chichester today.

They were accused together with West End art gallery director Robert Hugh Fraser, of Mount Street, Mayfair, of offences under the Dangerous Drugs Act alleged to have occurred at Richard's home at West Wittering.

After lunch, Mr. Jagger had changed his bright green jacket to one of charcoal grey and Mr. Richard had changed out of a jacket with thick black and white stripes into green.

overnight at Redlands, West Wittering, Richard's country home, a few miles from Chichester. They left for the court in a Daimler but changed to another car on the way, to a Minor 1000.

It drove into car park by mista yards along th through blue gat immediately shut guard inside.

Marianne Faithfull, 20-year-old pop singer and girl friend of Mick Jagger—she is seen here signing autographs in Chichester today—was hoping to visit Jagger in the Sessions cells this evening.

Earlier Marianne had failed to see Jagger but sent in a draughts board and 60 cigarettes.

She wore a two-tone brown trouser suit and a green scarf and had large cuff links in her shirt.

Jagger and Fraser had lunch sent into the cells from a local hotel.

JAGGER APPEAL

"Wish you luck"

When the case against Jagger ended, Mr. MICHAEL HAVERS, Q.C., defending, intimated there would be an appeal on a point of law.

Judge BLOCK, who tried the case agreed, adding: "I wish you luck."

JAGGER, 23, wore a pale green double-breasted jacket with white buttons, olive green trousers a floral shirt and green and black striped tie. He sat in the dock beside Richard, who pleads not guilty.

Richard, with hair down the back of his neck like Jagger, wore a navy blue frock coat, black military-style trousers, a lace collar and maroon and black shoes.

Marianne Faithfull, Mick Jagger's girl friend, lunched today at the same hotel in Chichester as Keith Richards.

Mr. Jagger appeared dazed after the Judge had passed sentence.

About 20 minutes after the sentences had been passed a blue Bentley with darkened windows drove out of the back entrance of the court and sped off in the direction of West Wittering. It returned about 20 minutes later and drove straight into the rear entrance again.

Miss Marianne Faithfull, the singer, got out and went up the steps into the court building. She was crying.

The main group of the party had arrived at Redlands at 11 and 12 midnight on Saturday night, followed by the married couple. "Everyone was a little hungry so I cooked some eggs and bacon.

Richards said some of the guests might have been drinking Coca-Cola but not alcohol. There was a smell of incense pervading the house because he had dropped it in the grate.

This aroma was mixed with that of the highly-spiced Moroccan meal guests had eaten.

KEITH RICHARD
Screaming girls

ROLLING STONE Mick Jagger is driven to jail in a police van last night after being found guilty on a drug charge.

With him he took three books—one about art, another about Tibet—40 tipped cigarettes, a bar of chocolate and a jigsaw puzzle.

A suitcase full of clothing was brought for him.

Moroccan cooking

Describing the day's events before the raid Richard said that they had been to the beach and on a mystery tour. In the evening a Moroccan servant of one of the guests cooked a Moroccan dish, highly spiced, for a buffet dinner.

Afterwards they switched on the television without the sound and played records. Asked about using incense, Richard said he had used it for some time. "I picked it up from fans who used to send me joss sticks." It was not done to cover up the smell of hemp.

Meal in a cell for Mick Jagger

HOTELIER Arthur Collings carries meals to the court yesterday for Mick Jagger and Robert Fraser.

The two men, found guilty of drug offences on Tuesday, ate in cells below the court, where they waited all day.

For Jagger there was prawn cocktail, roast lamb and mint sauce, fresh strawberries and cream, and two half-bottles of Beaujolais.

Fraser had iced melon, fresh salmon salad and strawberries and cream.

SWINGEING LONDON 1967

After five minutes of deliberation the jury returned with a guilty verdict. As Mick drove from the court a dozen schoolgirls banged their fists on the close yard gate and tried to climb over it, screaming "We want Mick." In Lewes jail Mick, in a reflective mood, requested books about Tibet and modern art, and two packs of Benson and Hedges.

On the first day of Keith's trial Mr. Morris opened the case for the prosecution by telling the jury: "That there was a strong, sweet, unusual smell in these premises will be clear from the evidence, and you may well come to the conclusion that that smell could not fail to have been noticed by Keith Richard."

Keith contended that "Mr. X" (Mr. Sneiderman) was an agent of *The News of the World* and that he had been planted at Redlands not only to spy on the Rolling Stones but also to smuggle drugs into the house and thus implicate the Stones.

The jury, out for five minutes, came back with a verdict of guilty. A horrified chorus of "noes" came from the public gallery. Mick and Robert Frazer were brought into the court to join Keith in the dock for the sentencing. Judge Block began by saying: "The offence of which you have been properly convicted by the jury carries with it a maximum sentence of as much as ten years, which is a view of the seriousness of this offense which is taken by Parliament." Then he sentenced Keith to one year and Mick to six months.

Prurience and Prejudice

The business of "Miss X's" behavior was the most scandalous feature of Keith's trial. Wrapped in a skimpy fur rug and wreathed in clouds of strong sweet smoke she is presented, or rather conjured up, like some apparition from pulp fiction—as "evidence."

Opening the case for the prosecution, on the first day of Keith's trial, Mr. Morris devotes a good half of his address to the jury to the wanton ways of "Miss X".

Terse, surreal and suggestive, police Sgt. John Challen's description was worthy of Mickey Spillane: "I saw the young lady come upstairs with a policewoman. She allowed the fur rug to fall down. She had her back to me; she was naked. I heard a man in the bedroom, using the telephone, laugh." A less stylish peak is provided by Detective Sgt. Cudmore who managed to sustain voyeuristic interest while shamelessly exposing "Miss X" to the cruel light of middle class morality.

With guileful innuendo the prosecution shamelessly played on the pru-

rient prejudices of the jury. This exchange about "Miss X's" modesty provoked Keith's classic retort:

MORRIS: There was, as we know, a young woman sitting on a settee wearing only a rug. Would you agree, in the ordinary course of events, you would expect a young woman to be embarrassed if she had nothing on but a rug in the presence of eight men, two of whom were hangers-on and the third a Moroccan servant?

KEITH: Not at all.

MORRIS: You regard that, do you, as quite normal?

KEITH: We are not old men. We are not worried about petty morals.

"Miss X" was in fact, Marianne Faithfull, not a well kept secret. Mick and Keith had asked their lawyers to keep Marianne's name out of the case. "We thrive on publicity like this," Mick is said to have told her, "but it could kill your career stone dead."

The anonimity of "Miss X" unquestionably worked in the favor of the prosecution at Keith's trial, though it was not from the courtroom they wished to protect her but the notoriously predatory English press. This proved to be quite futile. Even the *Times* was not above common prurience, as this broadside from the underground paper *OZ*, points out:

HOW I JAILED JAGGER

Just as the Stones symbolize the new permissiveness—hence the vicious

exemplary punishments—this man's [Mr. Stafford Somerfield, editor of The News of the World] rag epitomizes the money–grubbing–witch–hunting, God–playing fascism of a decaying hypocrisy.

Yet, this paper's amorality has proved typical of all press ethics. Though the court guaranteed the anonymity of the female guest, almost every paper juxtaposed Nude Girl headlines with irrelevant pictures of Marianne Faithfull. This cruel innuendo was basic press strategy—too ungenerous to protect her completely, they were too gutless to name her outright. The Times, the so-called newspaper of record, was the worst offender, with a fuzzy head shot directly beneath "Young Woman Wearing Only Fur Rug."

The national press have been quick to cash in on the colourful antics of the Stones in the past, chronicling and approving. Now Richards and Jagger are in the dock, the boot is on the other foot, the Youth Kick is aimed to the groin.

Journalists have always defended their axe-jobs by claiming the public has "a right to know."

So that's why McCartney's LSD statements were lifted from the relative obscurity of Life and blasted across the nation by the Sundays? Who's kidding who?

McCartney told one man; News of the World told its 16,000,000 readers. Now who would you say is responsible for the spread of LSD?

The public does have a right to know—the right to know the truth; the right to know to just what lengths the self-appointed protectors of a questionable moral position are prepared to go, to perpetuate their pretence at piety.
—OZ, Sheet No. 1

Police testifying at Mick and Keith's trial added more malicious porno fiction to the gossip mills by spreading the story that on their arrival at Redlands Mick was retrieving a Mars bar with his tongue from Marianne Faithfull's ass.

On July 29, they were sentenced, Keith to one year and Mick six months. "Jagger almost broke down and put his head in his hands as he was sentenced," wrote The Daily Telegraph; "He stumbled out of the dock almost in tears."

Public opinion was divided:

"These heavy sentences will only serve to turn young people against the police, make them anti-law."

"Good stiff sentences will deter others and we know that youngsters copy the Rolling Stones."

"The sentences were too lenient. It is time drug taking was stamped out."

"I feel sorry for them . . . And this damn example the police want to set just won't work at all." (Evening Standard)

What turned public opinion in favor of the Stones was William Rees-Mogg's editorial in the London Times headed "WHO BREAKS A BUTTERFLY ON A WHEEL?" He concluded:

"If after his visit to the Pope, the Archbishop of Canterbury had bought proprietary airsickness pills on Rome airport, and imported the unused tablets into Britain on his return, he would have risked committing precisely the same offence. No one who has ever travelled and bought proprietary drugs abroad can be sure that he has not broken the law.

"Judge Block directed the jury that the approval of a doctor was not a defence in law to the charge of possessing drugs without a prescription, and the jury convicted. Mr. Jagger was not charged with complicity in any other drug offence that occurred in the same house.

"We have, therefore, a conviction against Mr. Jagger purely on the ground that he possessed four Italian pep pills, quite legally bought but not legally imported without a prescription. Four is not a large number. This is not the quantity which a pusher of drugs would have on him, nor even the quantity one would expect in an addict.

"In any case Mr. Jagger's career is obviously one that does involve great personal strain and exhaustion; his doctor says that he approved the occasional use of these drugs, and it seems likely that similar drugs would have been prescribed if there was a need for them. Millions of similar drugs are prescribed in Britain every year, and for a variety of conditions.

"One has to ask, therefore, how it is that this technical offence, divorced as it must be from other people's offences, was thought to deserve the penalty of imprisonment. In the courts at large it is most uncommon for imprisonment to be imposed on first offenders where the drugs are not major drugs of addiction and there is no question of drug traffic. . . .

"It should be the particular quality of British justice to ensure that Mr. Jagger is treated exactly the same as anyone else, no better and no worse.

"There must remain a suspicion in this case that Mr. Jagger received a more severe sentence than would have been thought proper for any purely anonymous young man."

Mick and Keith's appeals were fixed for July 31. Keith's guilty verdict was quashed. Lord Chief Justice Parker ruled that the evidence given to show that "Miss X" (Marianne Faithfull) had been smoking cannabis and that Keith knew it, was tenuous and prejudicial, and that the trial judge should have so warned the jury.

Ironically it was the role of the notorious "Miss X" so shamelessly exploited by the prosecution that led to Keith's sentence being quashed in appeal. While judge, jury, police, press and public found this brazenness quite irresistible it apparently slipped most people's minds that her state of undress was not grounds for prosecution.

Mick's sentence was commuted to a conditional discharge.

Following a press conference at Grenada TV Mick boarded a helicopter for an "undisclosed location" to tape an ITV panel discussion, World in Action. In the garden of an Essex country house there awaited him with almost apostolic respect the editor of the Times (William Rees-Mogg); Lord Stowhill, a former attorney general; the hip Bishop of Woolich; and a leading British Jesuit, Father Corbishley.

Mick held forth incoherently on a number of weighty subjects. As he confided later, he was "filled with tranquilizers."

Nothing Happened to Me Yesterday

The effects of Mick and Keith's busts, trial and acquittal hit trendy London instantaneously. Handcuffs and other prison paraphernalia were a hot item on Carnaby Street within hours of the sentencing.

That corruption was rampant among the London Drug Squad became evident about two years later after one notorious member was thrown off the force for soliciting bribes from pop stars.

Judge Block showed his feelings in a speech in the fall of '67 to the Horsham Plowing and Agricultural Society: "We did our best, your fellow countrymen, I, and my fellow magistrates, to cut those Stones down to size, but alas, it was not to be because the Court of Criminal Appeal let them roll free."

One effect of the trial was to make the Stones "drug martyrs" to the underground press and further bond them to the goals of the counterculture. But not only did Mick decline his role as revolutionary leader, the court experience, more shattering to him than it was to Keith, apparently extended his schizophrenic attitude toward the world. He began to see everything as theater, as pure (and corrupt) games.

"That was a brick wall for Mick," Richards says of the Redlands bust.

"Mick came up against the brick wall of reality."

Jagger agrees that this brush with the law scared him. "I hated the bust because I felt it stopped the band and slowed it down. I think being busted still *does* slow the band down. And I'm trying to kick the habit," he suddenly jokes. "That's why I turned bourgeois."

Richards can be equally sarcastic. He sternly believes Jagger was never anything *but* bourgeois. "Mick *might* think there was something different about him *before* the bust but in actual *fact* there's *no* difference at all. He *hates* that part of himself."

Q: The trial must have really worn you out.

MICK: Ha! It wore me out. It wore my bank balance out. Cost a fortune. And those horrible gray people that get you off! You see, the whole thing is sort of a game between different lawyers. They set the whole thing up. They don't do any of this consciously . . . it's like two lots of people; the police and their lawyers, and us and our lawyers.

But they are all the same, the lawyers, they're all the same! You know, "Hello, Harry, how are you?" "Hi, Charlie. Groovy! Yeah great! Have a brandy." That's the game, but they play it to the extreme, you see, to the ultimate, "To the Highest Court in the Land we will . . ."—they play this whole game, and you're just sitting there, watching them like tennis, you know. Like you're gonna go to prison. You say, "OK, four days in prison." You're out again. "Oh great." Eventually they come and say, "You can go now, it's all over." and you think, "Nothing happened. It didn't really mean anything. It's got nothing to do with *me* anyway. I didn't do anything. Nothing happened. I was just there." [*Laughs*] I mean they put us through a lot of hassle and took a lot of bread off of us. It's very weird . . . it's just a lot of games they play. We were just there. You know, nothing *real* happened.
DAVID DALTON

THE STONES FILE: DRUG BUSTS 1967-1980

1967

February 12th
Sussex police raid Redlands, Keith's house in West Wittering and find "various substances of a suspicious nature."

May 10th
Mick and Keith in court for hearings on drug charges. Allowed bail of £100. To be tried at West Sussex Quarter Sessions. On the same day Brian is arrested in his London flat and charged with unlawful possession of drugs. He was remanded on £250 bail. He appeared at the Magistrates Court on May 11th.

June 27th-29th
Chichester. Mick and Keith tried on drug charges. Mick found guilty of illegal possession of pep pills found in his jacket at the houseparty at Redlands. He is fined £100 and sentenced to 6 months in jail. Keith is found guilty of permitting his house to be used for the smoking of Indian Hemp, fined £500 and sentenced to one year in jail.

July 31st
London Appeal Court. Keith Richards' conviction for permitting his house to be used for the purpose of smoking cannabis resin quashed. Mick Jagger given conditional discharge and Lord Parker, Lord Chief Justice, warns him of the responsibilities of being a pop idol.

October 30th
Brian is remanded to Wormwood Scrubs prison.

October 31st
Brian sentenced to 9 months on possession of cannabis charge.

December 12th
Brian's sentence set aside.

1968

May 21st
Brian arrested and charged with possessing cannabis. Appeared at Marlborough Street Magistrates Court. Bailed for £2,000.

June 11th
Brian committed for trial at Inner

Court Sessions.

September 26th
Brian fined £50 with £105 costs at Inner Court Sessions, after being found guilty of unauthorized possession of cannabis.

1969

May 28th
Mick and Marianne Faithfull busted for possession of hashish.

July 8th
Marianne found in coma.

July 10th
Marianne Faithfull enters Bexley Hospital for her heroin treatment.

December 19th
Mick fined £200 plus costs at Marlborough Street Magistrates Court, for being found in possession of cannabis resin. Marianne acquitted.

1970

August 30th
In Rome a judge orders Mick to pay a £1200 fine for allegedly punching a photographer.

1972

May 18th
Warwick Airport incident involving Jagger and Richards accused of assaulting photographer.

July 19th
Stones chauffeur arrested on U.S. tour for drug possession.

December 14th
French police search Nellcote, Keith's home in the south of France, finding large quantities of heroin, cocaine and hashish.

"'Thank Christ that's over,' he said when the lawyers told him the outcome of the case. 'Now, at last, I can stop paying that $2,400 a week rent for that bloody house. It's cost me more than a hundred grand already ($240,000) just to keep it going so the cops wouldn't try to extradite me.' He earned something like $25,000 a week. Using the rule-of-thumb that rent shouldn't exceed a quarter of your salary, I guess Keith could afford Nellcote."

(Tony Sanchez, *Up and Down with the Rolling Stones*)

December 28th
Anita arrested in Jamaica for possession of marijauna. Keith received a phone call from Jamaica to say that Anita had been arrested on a drug charge and was being held in prison. Keith wanted to fly out immediately, but he was worried the Jamaicans might be holding on to Anita as a trap for him.

"Much better," counseled his aristocratic friend Count X, "to let me sort it all out for you."

Count X contacted one of the island's most influential businessmen, a man who'd had many dealings with the Stones. He revealed that it would be possible for Anita's freedom to be purchased for a bribe of $12,000. "Tell him to pay straightaway," said Keith. "I'll give him the money back in any country he likes." (Tony Sanchez, *Up and Down with the Rolling Stones*)

1973

January 9th

Japanese Consulate refuses Mick a visa to enter Japan on account of past drug arrests. "You are too famous," explained the Consul.

June 26th

Guns, Chinese heroin, and Mandrax found in raid at Keith's house in Cheyne Walk.

"A chauffeur was dispatched to Switzerland to bring in a .38 snubnosed Smith & Wesson revolver that Leroy, one of the security men on the American tour, had given to Keith as a souvenir. Unfortunately, there was no ammunition for the gun, so Keith asked me if I could buy some for him from my contacts in Soho.

"A week later I picked up a box of .38 bullets for $60 from a contact in a bar on Wardour Street.

"Keith slid one of the heavy bullets into the chamber, but it slid straight through and fell to the ground. Each time he tried, the same thing happened. 'I don't understand it,' I said. 'They're definitely the same size—thirty-eights.'

"'Yeah, well,' said Keith. 'I understand it. The bullets for this gun should have a kind of rim around the back. You've got me thirty-eight sten gun bullets.'

"We laughed it off, but three days later, on June 26, 1973, we weren't laughing at all. There was a ring at the bell on Cheyne Walk. Luigi, the caretaker, opened the door, and ten narcs led by Detective Inspector Charles O'Hanlon burst in. They charged straight into the master bedroom where Keith and Anita were sleeping and zeroed in on the gun and ammo with uncanny speed. They found a tiny scrap of hash, a few Mandrax sleeping tablets, and they took away Keith's water pipes and his beautiful brass pharmaceutical scales. They also managed to find an antique shotgun that had been left in the house by the late Johnny Braces. They appeared delighted with their haul, and after the customary cautions to Keith, Anita and a friend, Prince Stanislaus, who had the misfortune to be staying at the house that night, they were on their way.

"'Phewee,' breathed Keith. 'Thank Christ they didn't really start taking the place apart. God knows what they would have found.'"

(Tony Sanchez, *Up and Down with the Rolling Stones*)

October 24th

Keith fined £205.

1975

July 5th

Keith busted for illegal possession of knife in Fordyce, Arkansas (case later dismissed). Freddie Sessler takes the rap.

1976

May 19th

Keith crashes his car on the M1 in England. An unidentified substance is found on him.

At the trial Keith arrives two hours late explaining that he was waiting for his trousers to come out of the dryer. "I find it extraordinary, Mr. Richards," the Judge commented, "that a man of your stature has only one pair of pants."

1977

January 12th

Keith fined £750 plus £250 costs for possessing cocaine; cleared of possessing LSD.

March 2nd

Keith arrested in Toronto for drug trafficking. Anita charged with possession of hashish and heroin in a separate incident.

March 15th

Anita Pallenberg fined for possession of marijuana and hashish.

October 2nd

Keith loses his motion to be charged with possession and have heroin trafficking charge dropped.

October 6th

Keith elects trial by judge and jury.

October 24th

Keith given suspended sentence. Judge orders him to perform a concert on behalf of the blind within six months and to continue his treatment in New York to cure his heroin addiction.

1980

February 23rd

Ron Wood and companion, Josephine Karlslake, are arrested with 260 grams of cocaine at their rented house in Phillipsburg on the Carribean island of St. Maarten. Police said they were tipped off by the two local dealers who had sold them the nine ounces. "We came down here for a complete rest to get away from drugs and all that stuff," Mr. Wood was quoted as saying. "We never bought any drugs." After spending five days in jail, they were deported, leaving for Los Angeles by private plane.

TOM BEACH

6
THROUGH EYES NOT USED YET

PICTURES OF US THROUGH THE STEAMY HAZE

Millennial delusions were rampant in the rarefied atmosphere of London's psychedelic district in 1967, with its jaded foppishness of the Antique Market, the stylish degeneracy of young nobility, and an often shallow occultism stemming from an English sensibility. London was second only to San Francisco as a proper breeding ground for psychedelic monsters. Flirtation and rumors flew everywhere on lysergic wings: the alchemist Fulcanelli had been seen in Paris; an oracular child was rewriting a history of the tenth century as she remembered it from a former life; the mammoth zodiac engraved in the land at Glastonbury was a guide for flying saucers; the rusty keys, unused since the Flood, that would unlock the mysteries of the world were being rediscovered. The singing head of the god Bran buried under the Tower Hill was about to wake from a thousand-year sleep.

Acid storm troopers, ye old whimsical English Loones, floated down the King's Road as if it were the Milky Way. Not surprisingly, the Stones—and especially Mick, who had an ear for the frequencies of fashion—weren't any more immune to the psychedelic bug than anyone else. "What effect did acid have on your personality?" Roy Carr asked Mick ten years later. "(*Laughs*) It drove me completely insane. No—I'm joking." Carr: "You know what I mean, some took the trip like Eric Burdon and . . ." Mick: ". . . and never came back. We came back in 1968. It didn't give me per-manent brain damage or anything at all like that. I shouldn't really own up to it even now. I took it before it was made illegal . . . well, isn't that what people used to say? Actually, speaking of Burdon, the last time I saw him he kept yelling 'Beer and Acid' at me, which was very peculiar at the time as well. However, I quite enjoyed it . . . I thought it was lovely."

Nearby, at the Middle Earth, the hippie grotto in Covent Garden, acid dancers levitated as liquid light shows sprinkled iridescent dust while the participants pranced into fourth, fifth, . . . *n*th dimensions and "looned about" in spaces previously known only to shamans, madmen, mystics and spirits.

"I went to one of those 'smashing happenings' at the London Roundhouse," said Mick at the time. "I thought everyone would be freaking out and wearing weird clothes but they were all wandering around in dirty macs—it was the most boring thing I've ever seen. Paul McCartney thought everyone would be wearing weird clothes and he went as an Arab, which must have been very lonely for him, because when I went there wasn't another Arab in sight."

On May 27 Pink Floyd performed at their most delirious peak, at the staid Queen Elizabeth Hall of London's Festival Gardens. The poster read: "Games for May—Space-Age Relaxation for the Climax of Spring." Their hallucinated "music in colors" and enchantments in technology aimed at disorganizing all the senses, using multi-dimensional protoplasmic projections, black light, flashing strobes, ear-splitting volume laced with echo, and at the center of this psychotropic maelstrom the group's lead singer, Syd Barnett, "the madcap" himself in a fringed cape, his hair matted with crushed Mandrax pills (Lemmons), a disquieting magnetic shadow against the melting images of the liquid light show.

It was the day after the release of *Sgt. Pepper*, and as the purple haze hung in the air to the pulsing of a billion synapses, Mick knew something was happening. Not to be outdone, and as a man who prides himself on being on time and in tune, Mick conceived the idea of a psychedelic satire on the Queen to be called *Her Satanic Majesties Request* (from the first line in the front of British passports—"Her Britannic Majesty's . . . Requests and requires . . .") The Stones, because of drug busts, were no longer able to "travel freely," as promised on the inside of their passports.

"*Satanic Majesties* was the mood of the times," Mick pointed out to Roy Carr. "You can't play or write outside the mood of the times, unless you live on a mountain—and even in the south of France I wasn't that out of it I couldn't get the *Melody Maker* . . . In those times it was flowers, beads and stars on yer face, that's what it was. In fact, I'm rather fond of that album, and I wouldn't mind doing something like that again."

Brian apparently resisted the move. This seems odd, considering Brian's obsession with electronic music; his track on the mellotron for "2,000 Light Years from Home" is drenched in an eerie extraterrestial light that should

have permeated the whole album.

Some of the components of *Satanic Majesties* come from Mick's reading at the time: a Tao classic, *The Secret of the Golden Flower*, the cranky percep-tion of a Bronx hermit Charles Hay Fort, author of *The Book of the Damned* (sometimes referred to as "the crackpot's *Golden Bough*"), who col-lected mountains of bizarre trivia in shoe boxes: rains of frogs and sulfur, green suns, flying disks, fiery oceans and argosies of celestial travelers. Some

ideas from the bubble-gum psychic classic *The Morning of the Magicians* peek out of the album, and inevitably Arthur Machen, cloven-hoofed messen-ger of the satanic, turns up too. All of this was filtered no doubt through friends like John Mitchell (*A View over Atlantis*) who were beginning to uncover substrata of the supernatural.

Mick had been reading *The Secret of the Golden Flower* during the mak-ing of the album, and while it's highly unlikely that he took any pains to program its message (the "circulation of the light" through action brought about by nonaction), major themes and ideas are echoed often enough that it's possible to assume that he found in the Chinese classic an appropriate set of symbols. To begin with, the book's title alone makes it the perfect guidebook for tripping. The Golden Flower is generally referred to as "the

Elixir of Life," literally, "the golden pill."

Even taking into account that it was a year in the making, and re-corded under very trying conditions—four busts (Brian was busted twice that year) and two trials—some found it hard to believe that the Stones were serious. Was it really a parody of *Sgt. Pepper* like the ironic single, "We Love You," that they put out earlier that year?

Less electric and flexible than the Beatles, the Stones seemed ill at ease with random experimentation and ex-ploration of other musical forms, and they lacked the production polish of George Martin that had made the freakier parts of *Sgt. Pepper* stand up.

The shadowy presences of *Satanic Majesties* seem first to have been ad-mitted in their single "Have You Seen Your Mother, Baby, Standing In The Shadow?" with *its* hooded imagery: "Tell me a story about . . . How we live in the shadow, how we glimpse in the shadow, how we tear at the shadow . . . and love in your shadowy life." These malign specters seem to finally be set to rest in "Jigsaw Puzzle" on *Beggars Banquet*, with Mick "waiting so patiently, lying on the floor" sur-rounded by Dylanesque fractions of his life, the tension of apathy finally con-juring up Her Britannic Majesty, who rides madly out of a hunting print.

DAVID DALTON

MICK ON MEDITATION, MUTATION AND THE MILLENIUM

This interview with Mick Jagger was done in May 1968 for the London underground newspaper *International Times,* at the time of the anti-Vietnam War demonstrations outside the American embassy in Grosvenor Square and just before the events of May in Paris. It seems natural, therefore, that the conversation drifted in the direction of political speculation. It reveals Jagger's thinking at the time of "Jumpin' Jack Flash," which had been recorded but not yet released at the time. It could only have been conducted in the sixties.

Q: Do you like working in London or would you rather live somewhere else?

MICK: London doesn't make me uptight enough to get into those uptight scenes which are very good for creation. 'Cause it's much easier to express a very uptight mood than it is my very relaxed and happy mood.

Q: This is writing, not the music?

MICK: Just the writing. It does relate to the music but as far as I'm involved in it . . . it's more obvious in the words than it is in the music though they both fit together . . . Yeah . . . They're all great to write when you're in New York you know. You can knock off for a day in a hotel room in New York . . . London doesn't give me that feeling.

Q: Is the quieter, happy music what your're trying to get at?

MICK: No. I'm not trying to get AT anything! I would like to be able to express everything equally as well. To be able to express *every* varying mood. I know what I'm good at, and I know what I really can't do.

Q: As a response to an environment?

MICK: Yes. To environment. To people . . . people influence me more than what you call environment, which is a totality . . . but . . . It's always the SAME PEOPLE! and you have to put them down. To get into women, to different kinds of them, they're all *such* a groove! But when there's no songs it nearly always means I'm very contented and I can't be bothered to write about it! I'm too busy to be worried about writing about it. Don't want to work, don't want to do anything, just want to . . . just carry on. But then someone phones up and says . . . "Mmmmm, got to make a record."

But it's good that they're there because otherwise we might not ever do anything . . . But then suddenly you get thrown back into it and you think: "Wow!" I just found that my ego and everything was just being totally submerged. But I think it was in the wrong way.

Q: Submerged rather than rid of?

MICK: Yeah.

Q: I'm interested in the idea of an alternative society growing out of what's been happening in the last few years. Not a specific drugs thing or hippie thing, but just a general re-evaluation of things that a lot of people are getting into, which is beginning to threaten a lot of the barriers which the old-style society has put up. I think it will mean the ending of one society and the starting of another rather than a natural flow of change from one to the other.

MICK: I think that about most cyclic changes. There's no doubt that there's a cyclic change, a VAST cyclic change, on top of a lot of smaller ones. I can imagine America becoming just ablaze, just being ruined . . . but this country, it's very weird you know, it always does things slightly differently. Always more moderately, and always very boringly, most of it, the changes are so suppressed. There definitely is this fantastic split, and it even cuts across class which shows how strong it is because there's very few things in England that do transcend class. All extremes meet at the other end but that's not the point in this one, it isn't one of those.

Q: The backlash has shown a lot of people that the left-wing wasn't left-wing for humanitarian reasons but for self-interest reasons. Everyone was relying on the dockers as the great communists who fought fascism.

MICK: Of course they're not, you know. Of course they're not! They're just totally self-interested. They can't see further than their noses. AND WHO CAN BLAME THEM? Why can't they see further than their noses? Part of the reason: they were very strictly brought up.

Q: The communication barrier is the armoring they've built around themselves . . . but that occurs in everybody.

MICK: Yes, well that's supposedly the thing which keeps you on the side of some sort of sanity. Your logic system is the thing which keeps your mind together because when you start destroying it, if you're not ready for it to be destroyed, you don't know what follows. All your life is built up on a logic system.

Q: Do you think you have it inherently?

MICK: Oh yes!

Q: You don't think it's part of the society and your reactions to it? Because you can bring up children in a different way so that they have no character armoring?

MICK: Oh yes, he'll have a totally different logic system, but he'll still have one. He's got to. I mean, there's probably so many variations on it as there are brain cells but still you've got to have it. I think there's many reasons underneath that aren't understood by Western man, or by Eastern society. I think some people know, why, as a global thing, man behaves in these ways and there are so many different ways out of it, so many explanations, because you don't know.

Q: How do you feel when students riot when you're on stage? Do you pick up on any energy?

MICK: Yes! Wow! Tingle with it! The energy's great. I mean, they give you so much energy. I never went on stage with the idea of keeping everything cool. I never wanted it to be peaceful, even if I did before I went on stage, soon as I got on there and felt what they felt, I've wanted to make, I mean, they were totally in control, as much as I was. I mean I was in control but they were also.

Q: So it becomes a dialogue?

MICK: Yeah. And if you've got nobody in between, that's when it becomes funny. Because it can turn on you, see, if you haven't got any policemen it's weird, because then they don't know what to do. I mean, I'm not talking about girls and that sort of scene, I'm talking about what you're talking about, like these students. 'Cause then they don't know what to do, but then there's very rarely no police. That's a mistake the authorities make, they never ought to have any police there at all! They're the only symbol there, the only outlet you can get, especially in the Western world, you can't really

A wary Leo and a weary tiger at the Rolling Stones Rock and Roll Circus, 1968.

touch anything can you? What can you touch? You can only touch the police!

Q: I felt very frustrated by that demonstration.*

MICK: But that's what it should have been!

Q: An expression of frustration?

MICK: But that's just fun you see! Because that's your own inherent violence. That's our way out. 'Cause we love it! And it's our excuse, see? We can't be guerrillas. We're so violent, we're violently frustrated. There's nothing. It's a whole drag, the army's all over, the *army!* There's no guerrillas, there's no, well there's Welsh Nationalists. You can go and join them, but what a joke! I mean there's nothing in this country, it's all . . . and there's all this violence. If you want to talk about it, it's here, it's there, you know. It's not a question of having to meet people, it's fun. You can push, you can push everyone into a situation.

Q: I wonder?

MICK: You can! You see the last war: that was a situation, you could get nearly all the youth of this country,

* *A reference to a huge anti-Vietnam war rally held in front of the U.S. Embassy. Jagger was in the front line.*

with very few exceptions, into a situation where they will defend their country. Maybe they were not defending their country, maybe they thought they were defending their families. And they were. Maybe they were defending their, whatever they were, they were defending something. And not only that, they were defending lots of other peoples, like America. They had this weird sort of illusion . . . But you can always get people into a situation where they can do it. It's rubbish to say that you can't because it's so obvious!

I can't see an alternative society, the only thing I can see, looking at it a lot, is that you're in a fantastic change period though. Everyone keeps saying so, and probably we are. And like you're just the first changed-off, so that, you know, it just happens.

Q: The first change-off is usually put down by a war. Like Paris between the wars, and before the First World War there were the pre-Raphaelites.

MICK: Oh yes, you can be sure. And that will be the biggest change. That's the mutation of the race. The combined students and hippies and everything amount to millions of people really, who are all re-evaluating society.

MICK: Yes, well they haven't got an alternative, and they've still got all the things of the other society, in other words, *their* society. The other society's veneer. They'll degenerate to the same thing. They'll degenerate to putting helmets on and fighting each other and when they come out they won't know who the fuck they are! Anybody's always known.

Q: I think people are breaking through.

MICK: Like what?

Q: Like you! When you have an audience you're able to break through all the veneer and they really start releasing energy.

MICK: There's a lot of energy, true, but it's so violent! That's what I mean about a veneer, it's total violence, that's the result! You can make total violence from vibration, that's all. For what? But I mean, I don't really put it down. I think that all the things we've said are wrong about it, but when it really comes down to it, to get people out of their seats is like difficult enough in this country.

Q: To see everyone so messed up makes people want to help each other solve their problems to some extent.

MICK: Yes but you must be careful of messing with people until you're sure of yourself. It's difficult to be constructive. Because to be constructive in a political manner is just a farce, because you know it's all the same.

Q: How about other ways? Artists have a huge effect . . .

MICK: Yes, they don't know what it is though, because they don't understand their audience, because you can't, you can't. How can you understand a worldwide audience? Of God knows how many million? How can you expect a pop singer to analyze his audience or his effect or anything? I mean, you can generalize vaguely.

Q: Not the audience but the effect?

MICK: You don't know what the effect is: the effect on stage is different from the effect on record. You can see what the effects on stage are, but that's all . . . I always think that's more superficial than the effect you have when somebody plays it at home. Because you get more into their head, because it's a different scene. There's no censorship involved with it. I mean, you can say anything you want.

Q: What about commercial considerations? Do you consider whether it will sell or not?

MICK: Long pause! The only time I think whether it will sell or not is when we make a single. Then you don't actually make a single, you make six or seven records, or we do, and somebody says: "That's good for a single." They mean, "If you put that out more people will like it than any of the others." You haven't recorded it for them, you've just done it. It's one of those things that you've done and yet you think it's easily understandable. You might say: "The lyrics are simple" or "It's good to dance to" but it's still same as the others, it's still one of them.

Q: Which direction d'you think you're going in?

MICK: I dunno!

Q: Are you aiming at technical improvement?

MICK: Yes, but I don't really think I will. Brian will get into electronics, I'm more interested in writing. I'd like to be a very good writer, of songs. It's a very weird medium actually, because it's so incredibly compressed.

Q: A lot of people think that modern pop lyrics are the only valid form of poetry these days.

MICK: But that's not true, you know a lot of it's very good verse, and is easily as good as popular verse in the last century. And more people will hear it. Some of it is probably very very good but it's not the best verse that's being written or the best poetry.

Q: Dylan stands up very well.

MICK: Oh yeah, Dylan stands up. There are very few modern poets I like that I've read, that I've picked up at Indica Bookshop that have been anywhere near as good. I mean, most of them aren't even as good as the Byrds' ones.

When the Stones stumbled into my pad in Tangier in 1886-87, wasn't it? . . . anyway, a long time ago, they were led in by Robert Fraser, the London art dealer and co-inventor of the Swinging Sixties. I had never heard a record of theirs and barely even heard of them. In my house, you heard only live Moroccan music or my tapes of it. Since 1950, I listened to very little else. That year, Paul Bowles, writer and composer friend of many years standing, persuaded me to come to Morocco for the summer. I went and I stayed some 23 years. One night he took me to a pre-Islamic festival in a sacred grove not far from the Caves of Hercules. There, I heard my music . . . MY music. When you hear your music like that, I guess you gotta pay the piper. I said to Paul: "I want to hear that music every day for the rest of my life." I still hear it.

My music turned out to be the piping of the Master Musicians of Jajouka in the foothills of the Rif. When I got to them in their mountain village, I told them what I had said. "*Glis ma rasek,*" they replied in Arabic, "Stay as long as you want." I laughed. They laughed: "If it's money you're laugh-

ing about, go back down to Tangier and take a cafe as big as a grass mat. Two grass mats. We'll come down and make music. Every night, we'll split the take. How about that?"

The Thousand and One Nights, as I called it, ran for just about exactly that number of nights. The Master Musicians of Jajouka opened it, followed by only slightly less magical Moroccan groups with their dancing boys, acrobats, fire-eaters, jugglers and snake charmers. The place was packed every night until Independa, as I call it, when the international city of Tangier lost its own free-wheeling independence and became part of Morocco again. Alas, the new Nationalists despised and persecuted their own "native" music, as in all the puritanical Third World. They were tough on us. By the time the Stones got to Tangier all that was in the past, but the music still goes on for a while longer up in Jajouka, a hard day's trip up into the Little Hills.

And Robert wants me to take these Stones up there: Mick and quietly saturnine Keith Richard with his eye on miniskirted Anita Pallenberg and Brian Jones with his fringe of frizzy pink hair almost hiding his beady little red rabbit eyes. Piled up on my bed with them are, also, the Stoned: Tom the egregious chauffeur who deliberately gives me the impression he is Charlie Watts. Robert Fraser the Razor snickers: "Charlie Wattsisname and the Other One . . . and the *Wives!*" In a chorus, everyone echoes: "The Wives, the Wives!" Michael Cooper, Robert's protégé and their official photographer

at the time, is taking pictures of the Stones and the Stoned, all curled up together on my big bed like a gaggle of iguanas. Paul Bowles pops in for a second to be introduced but splits in a state of shock at the sight. Can we really be taking this gang up to Jajouka? My two faithful old soldiers, Targuisti and Salah, can take care of the campaign. We'll need another car and horses will have to be found for the last lap up the mountain.

We take over the top floor of this hotel for a playpen hanging ten stories over the swimming pool. The action starts almost at once. Brian and I drop acid. Anita sulks and drops sleepers. Goes off to sleep in the suite she shares with Brian. Keith has plugged in and is sending some great throbbing sounds winging after her and on out into the moonlight over the desert. Robert puts on a great old Elmore James record out of his collection. Gets Mick doing little magic dances for him. For the first time, I see Mick really *is* magic. So. As the acid comes up on me, Brian recedes into Big Picture. Looks like a tiny celluloid kewpie doll, banked all around by choirs of identical little girl dolls looking just like him, chanting his hymns. Tom the sinister chauffeur shows up, rolling his eyes, hovering over Brian, whispering in his ear like a procurer. Brian wants me to translate something for Tom. With a finger I wigwag: I can't make it. No! Room Service arrives with great trays of food in which we toboggan around on the floor, I am sorry to say. Food? Who wants it? Who needs it? How very gross.

Say, let's get the cars out and shoot up into the Atlas, the moon. We can look out across the desert to see a range of snow-capped mountains looming so high up in the moonlight they look like a cloud bank.

We shoot across the desert with the sunrise, scaring up flocks of white marabout birds. There are flashes of lightning in which I try to take snaps of Mick with Michael Cooper's super camera. Then we are zigzagging up into the foothills with Keith's narrow face hanging heavy over the wheel like a meat chopper. Chrissy Gibbs has a house somewhere up there but we can't find it. We stop at a colonial French inn for breakfast, but on the terrace under a pergola the vines overhead turn into boa constrictors and we flee back to Marrakesh. Someone in the car says: "I wonder how Brian is making out with that tattooed Berber bitch. Is it true they tattoo their pussies and titties?" Yes, they do. It looks like blue basket work. Expensive ladies. This one cost Brian a packet, the

whole packet: Anita and the Stones. His life as a musician: eventually, his life.

The next day dawned late and lazy around the swimming pool. And there I saw something I can only call mythological. Mick is screaming about his bill, getting ready for takeoff. Now they are fluttering about in the bushes beyond the swimming pool with a camera. The cynics amongst us are snickering, it looks like love at first sight. At the deep end, Anita is swinging on a canvas seat. Keith is in the pool, dunking up and down in the

water, looming up at her. When I go to pass between them, I see that I can't. I can't make it. There is something there, a barrier, I can see it. What I see looks like a glass rod, a twisted glass rod, revolving rapidly. Between Keith's eyes and Anita's eyes, it shoots back and forth at the speed of light. Interesting. Tristan and Isolde stuff, eh? As bad as a laser beam. I don't like the looks of that one bit so I check out of the hotel immediately.

I go stay with an old school chum of mine who has an only slightly sinister house in the sleazy Arab quarter. It seems safer. Leaving the house next day, I run into Tom with a message for me. Tom comes on strong like a Stone: "The whole lot of them, they're after us! The Police. The Press. The People. The *News of the World*. The Establishment. All them 'Erdies. 'Erds of them. Terrible. Right now a small

plane has just landed in Marrakesh, chockablock full of reporters come down to persecute us. The Stones are strong. The Stones will win but we do have one weak link. You know who it is, Brian. Brian talks 'is bloody 'ead off to reporters. Tells 'em everything. Brian must be kept away from them for his own good. And ours. You know how he is. He thinks the world of you, too. You both have the same brand of tape recorder, your Uhers. Why don't you take him out recording live music on this great public square like you said you would. Bring him back about

six or a bit after, there's a good chap."

So I do. I take Brian to the Djemaa el Fna. No place like it. You can hear every kind of music in Morocco there. What I think Brian needs is a meet with the hash-head Mejdoubi brothers.

Crisp as corn flakes, cool as mint, the Mejdoubi, holy madmen to whom all is forgiven, wear live pigeons perched on top of their tipsy turbans as they sail over the ocean of madness and music in a cloud of cannabis smoke. They ride a rug like a raft loaded with a collection of kitsch that has Brian's eyes out on stalks like a stoned snail. They smoke fistfuls of great grass in a fantastic pipe at whose sight Brian forces his way into their circle, eyes glistening with greed. The Mejdoubi dig Brian for what he is and go into their long-drawn-out mint tea routine which can take a whole afternoon. I am tired. They make a little music. Fuck with their junk, fixing plastic flowers into plastic bottles. Boiling water over charcoal. Passing a pipe out to Brian. Brian grabs it and moves in onto the carpet, the magic carpet. Sails away, almost blowing out a lung on the first pipeful he takes from their super-sebsi hung with garlands of amulets, crackerjax, ancient beads, rotten teeth, coins and junk jewelry, etc. Brian wants it. Brian must have it. At once. I wigwag back at him, cool it. Tell you later. I refuse to translate.

Dragging Brian off that rug and on to my friend's house, not far from there, is a chore. Brian is furious. Sulks. He tells me exactly how much he would have been willing to pay for that pipe. A fortune. No bargain at half the price. On the way back, he gets it. On the way back through Cus-

toms at Heathrow, he loses it. That ain't all he loses. He finds out when he gets back to the hotel.

Less than half an hour later, Brian is on the blower to me, sobbing: "Come! Come quickly! They've all gone and left me. Cleared out. I don't know where they've gone. No message. The hotel won't tell me. I'm here all alone, help me. Come at once!"

I go over there. Get him into bed. Call a doctor to give him a shot and stick around long enough to see it take hold on him. Don't want him jumping down those ten stories into the swimming pool. Looking down into that time-pool, I see where it all got set up only yesterday. Now, looking back, there is another ghostly swimming pool. Those whom the gods love, die young. So, goodnight, sad prince, sleep tight.

BRION GYSIN

SATANISM AND THE STONES

A Conversation with Kenneth Anger

Q: How did Mick come to be involved with the sound track for your film *"Invocation of My Demon Brother"*?

ANGER: I was living in London, and was friendly with Marianne Faithfull, Robert Frazer and Christopher Gibbs. Through them I met the Stones and became friendly with Mick. I was cutting that film, and showed it to Mick. He volunteered to do the soundtrack with his new toy, which was a Moog synthesizer. He did it in the house on Cheyne Walk, in his sound house in the back garden. He knew the length of the film, and did this improvisation. The sound track was in stereo; I've always hoped to put it on 35-mm film. I broadly hinted to Mick that I wanted to put the stereo track on a 35-mm version of the film, but the hint was just one of those balloons which floats off into the air and never lands anywhere.

Q: A record was never made? It should have been.

ANGER: It would have been nice. This siren's sound he created performs a sort of call-and-response from one channel to the other in the original stereo version.

Q: There's footage of the Stones at Hyde Park [the Brian Jones memorial concert]. Had you been invited by the Stones to shoot the concert?

ANGER: Yes. I shot the footage the previous summer.

Q: What was the Stones' connec-

tion with magic? They were interested in the occult.

ANGER: In a dilettante's way.

Q: Anita still seems quite interested.

ANGER: I believe that Anita is, for want of a better word, a witch.

Q: There's a quote from Robert Greenfield's *Rolling Stone* magazine interview with Keith Richards in which Keith says, "Kenneth Anger calls me his [Lucifer's] right-hand man." How did you intend that?

ANGER: I was going to film a ver-

sion of *"Lucifer Rising"* [a film that Anger has attempted in at least three versions, on as many continents] with the Stones. All the roles were to be carefully cast, with Mick being Lucifer and Keith as Beelzebub. Beelzebub is really the Lord of the Flies, and is like the crown prince next to the King in the complicated hierarchy of demons. Beelzebub is like a henchman for Lucifer . . . The occult unit within the Stones was Keith and Anita . . . and Brian. You see, Brian was a witch, too. I'm convinced. He showed me his witch's tit. He had a supernu-

mary tit in a very sexy place on his inner thigh. He said: "In another time they would have burned me." He was very happy about that. Mick backed away from being identified with Lucifer. He thought that it was too heavy. When he married Bianca, he was wearing a rather prominent gold cross around his neck.

Q: Much as their lyrics have been concerned with freedom, there seem to be facist overtones in the Stones' music as well.

ANGER: The Stones are too anarchic to ever really be a menace. I was with Keith at one of the anti-American riots in front of the Amer-

ican embassy. He came as a spectator, watching English kids get clobbered by the cops.

Q: What is the active magical element in the Stones' music?

ANGER: It has such strong sexual connotations. It's basically music to fuck to.

Q: Which is where rock 'n roll came from.

ANGER: Sure . . . I was at their farewell party, when the Stones decided to leave England and move to the Riviera. They would, of course, prove to be far too notorious for the French police to ever accept. The party was given in an inn decorated with huge flowering trees. At about 2:00 A.M. the sound system went dead. Mick asked why this had happened, and was told that a village ordinance forbade music after 2:00 A.M. Mick promptly picked up the table and threw it through an enormous plate-glass window that overlooked the Thames. The piece of glass must of cost $20,000. That was *his* gesture toward having the music turned off.

DAVID DALTON, RICHARD HENDERSON

STRIKING WITH A SPIRIT'S KNIFE

A SHADE OF BLONDE

By the end of 1967 Brian, at the eye of psychotropic maelstroms, would awaken in trendy living rooms and, as in Wyman's "Another Land," find himself going into another dream. Miles described one such afternoon at David "Monster" Milnaric's house: "An advance pressing of *Their Satanic Majesties Request* played endlessly from the speakers, brought along by Brian Jones who was flopped out fast asleep on a huge settee in the middle of the room, a large straw hat on his flaxen head and a relaxed innocent face of sleep, a bit puffy, as he breathed noisily through open lips. His clothes were a harlequin of velvet and psychedelic patterns. A long scarf trailed from his neck across the lap of the Alice in Wonderland girl who sat next to him, holding his hand, her eyes wide and bright and her hair the same fine natural blond as Brian's. She wore a tiny dress of tatty lace, and scarves. An antique lace shawl was draped half over them and half in the large woven straw shopping basket they'd brought with them. They were the centerpiece of the party, like an eighteenth-century tableau.

"The record kept playing and Brian Jones awoke. In a stoned daze he kept repeating: 'It's too much man. Far out. Really far out!' He focused on Robert Fraser. 'Hey, Robert, that's you there, man. Banging that pot! This album's gonna knock everybody out. How can anyone *not* be knocked out *completely*?' He flopped back and closed his eyes, his straw hat slipped over his face and he slept."

Brian, always ahead of his time, was slowly getting out of his head on any number of "substances." To match his jaded need for astonishment, his Chelsea lair dripped with North African fetishes, hookahs, scarves and rugs. Decorated in Moroccan "mix-and-match," looking like a B movie set for a whorehouse in Tangier (or the set of *"Performance,"* for that matter), it was the ultimate psychedelic pad.

In the studio Brian manically mastered the Moroccan "interplanetary after-dinner music" Brion Gysin had recorded for him, a 21st-century hybrid of "funky hill music and sophisticated studio techniques." The result, *Brian Jones Presents the Pipes of Pan in Jajouka*, is the closest we will ever come to the sounds that danced in the back of Brian's mind. Bob Palmer wrote in *Rolling Stone* (October 14, 1971): "Whatever vibrations Brian Jones may have felt his one night in Jajouka, we know that he spent the next few weeks in Tangier, listening and relistening to his tapes, finding his way in the music. He heard it running forward, he heard it running backward, he heard it overlaid upon itself, and he recreated his multidirectional hearing with considerable expertise in a London studio."

Brian had not attended the week-long ceremonies of the Rites of Spring at Jajouka, a pre-Islamic Theater of Otherness so intense that, as he confessed in the liner notes to the album, "I don't know if I possess the stamina to endure the incredible constant strain of the festival, such psychic weaklings has Western Civilization made of us."

As the most complicated, prolix and subtle of the Stones musically, Brian had already brilliantly integrated the dulcimer ("Lady Jane") and the flute ("Ruby Tuesday") into the Stones' monolithic sound and introduced the only really effective use of a sitar in hard rock on "Paint It Black." What Brian did with the raw tapes was to feed the ancient ceremony through his own highly attuned nervous system. What is spine-chilling in the tapes of the ceremony is transposed on *Jajouka* to our own sensibilities. The music takes on an eeriness that is not remote and tribal but spooky in a disturbing, almost intimate way; it is the otherwordly, apocalyptic timbre that the Stones were able to exploit brillantly, though without Brian, on "Let It Bleed" and "Midnight Rambler." *Jajouka*, as Robert Palmer so evocatively put it, "suggests the menace of darkness outside the circle of firelight."

Later that year, Brian appeared at the Monterey Pop Festival, pale, swathed in the filigree lace of his Chinese robes. In spite of his glittering garb he seemed almost invisible, an iridescent ghost barely present on the threshold of the drugs that sustained him.

Keith: "It didn't hit me for months because I hadn't seen him a lot. The only time we'd seen him was down at the courthouse, at one of his trials. They really roughed him up, man. He wasn't a cat that could stand that kind of thing and they really went for him like when hunting dogs smell blood. 'There's one that'll break, so keep on.' And they busted him and busted him. That cat got so paranoid at the end like unto Lenny Bruce, the same tactics. Break him down. Maybe with Mick and me they felt they're just old lads."

One of the problems was disconnection. Keith's compass had always been magnetically aligned to the roots, the mother lode of rock ("You Got The Silver"): blues, C & W, gospel and R & B, building his monster sound out of simple, often spare patterns, while psychedelic music was trying to cut itself off from the sources and create a totally new source.

Brian may have thought he had found the connection for himself in the music of Jajouka. He was looking for the square root of the blues themselves. Ironically, the climate of *Satanic Majesties* is perversely summoned up by Jagger in *"Performance,"* where Mick seems to have absorbed Brian's persona.

Brian's personal implosion was a symptom of what happened to the whole psychedelic experience. It ultimately short-circuited its cosmic project from lack of energy. Self-conscious posturing, paranoia and, in its wake, a whole train of pieties disguised as revelations allowed people to betray themselves as if the demon of self-reflection, like the Ouroboros, had bitten its own tail before its spirit body had a chance to encircle the universe, so that in the end even the attempt seemed pretentious.

Only four Stones passed through the region where reason totters and came through intact. Tottering on the brink of psychic and psychotic thresholds, Brian went through chronic changes. At the time of the First Great Psychedelic Age few boundaries were acknowledged demarcating "freak-outs" from impinging insanity. Brian, in the uncharted space between, slowly became unhinged. As Keith once said of him, "Brian burnt out all his fuses a long time ago. He'd lived 26 years too fast. A whole lifetime in 26 years!"

Twice in the hospital that year for nervous breakdowns and in the following year subject to more harassment and brutality from the police, he completely disintegrated. When he found his paranoid delusions coming true (there actually *was* a police conspiracy against him), he simply gave up the ghost.

In his eulogy "Brian Jones: Sympathy for the Devil," Greil Marcus aptly quotes H. P. Lovecraft in *The Case of Charles Dexter Ward*: "I say to you againe, do not call up Any that you cannot put downe; by the which I meane, Any that can in turn call up somewhat against you, whereby your powerfullest devices may not be of use."

KEITH: "Brian got very fragile. As he went along, he got more and more fragile and delicate. His personality and physically. I think all that touring did a lot to break him. We worked our asses off from '63 to '66, right through those three years, nonstop. I believe we had two weeks off. That's nothing, I mean I tell that to B. B. King and he'll say, 'I been doing it for years.' But for cats like Brian . . . He was tough but one thing and another he slowly became more

fragile. When I first met Brian he was like a little Welsh bull . . . I don't think it was a sexual thing. He was always so open with his chicks . . . It was something else I've never been able to figure out. You can read Jung. I still can't figure it out. Maybe it was in the stars."

As early as 1966 Brian was visibly fading. Photographs of him on the cover of *Between the Buttons* and later are actually painful to look at. On the early LPs, especially the first one, Brian's glare was more than menace; he was looking through you.

In his last years Brian seemed like someone already living among the shadows. Even fan magazines, to which the physical disintegration of a star was almost inconceivable, became alarmed:

"Brian was the most psychic of the Stones; he *saw* the spirit world," says Kenneth Anger. "For the others it was just the climate of the times. One gets the impression he just dissolved into it."

AL ARONOWITZ: "'I don't just play rhythm guitar,' he would say. Once he stayed up all night writing a treatise on his paranoia. One of his greatest fears was that he had made it on his good looks and really had no talent."

By the end of 1967 Brian was living in the invisible world. He heard voices, otherworldly sounds pulsed through his synapses and he played instruments only he could hear.

After his first drug conviction in 1967, "he celebrated his release by pouring bottles full of pills into his mouth. He didn't care what the hell they were: acid, coke, speed—anything that would make the world go away. Then, after a day and a night of being totally strung-out, he went to a club in Covent Garden with one of his many women. The people in the club cheered him when he arrived and congratulated him on his success at the appeals court. The resident band invited him to play with them, and he did. He picked up a big double bass and started to play it fluidly, though as he played, he kicked

it with his Cuban-heeled boots until it was smashed to matchwood. Brian was so far gone that he carried on playing an invisible instrument, pumping out beautiful music only he could hear.

"The crowd cheered, believing that Brian knew what he was doing, that the whole thing was intentional. But then he started to weep uncontrollably, and his girl was forced to shove him into a cab and take him home. Once there he couldn't speak, and the tears were running down his face, pouring out the misery within. The girl, frightened, di-

aled 999 and asked for an ambulance. At St. George's Hospital he came to and told the doctor he had been under a great deal of pressure. Within an hour he was allowed to go home." (Sanchez, *Up and Down with the Rolling Stones*)

Brian, who had once described his treatment in a Chicago hospital (following an overdose of pills) with "I had so many tests I felt like a human sacrifice," seems to have had a premonition—in the following story by Brion Gysin—that he was to become the scapegoat, whose sacrifice would not renew the world but bring down with him a whole era:

"We were sitting on the ground with Brian, under the very low eaves of this thatched farm house, and the musicians were working just four or five feet away, ahead of us in the courtyard where the animals usually are. It was getting to be time to eat, and suddenly two of the musicians came along with a snow-white goat. The goat disappeared off into the shadows with the two musicians, one of whom was holding a long knife which Brian suddenly caught the glitter of, and he started to get up, making sort of funny noise, and he said, 'That's me!' And everybody picked up on it right at once and said, yeah right, it looks just like you. It was perfectly true, he had his fringe of blond hair hanging right down in front of his eyes, and we said, of course that's you. Then about twenty minutes later we were eating this goat's liver on shish-kebab sticks."

Brian was a dare-devil who liked to toy with the satanic: his insatiable appetite for drugs, Nazi uniforms, his unexpected outbursts of cruelty, all cast itself in his satyr-like grin. Perhaps in his flirtation with the dark powers, he let them sink their talons too deeply.

"Forces of Evil, in the magic sense of the word," Arthur Machen wrote in *The Great God Pan*, "are always lying in wait for certain individuals, ready to spirit them away to the other side of the world."

DAVID DALTON

ANITA ON BRIAN

Q: When did you first meet Brian?

ANITA: Brian is dead and gone. Next question.

Q: Come on, Anita . . . was it on the second German tour in '65?

ANITA: I met him on the Mount Everest and he was crying for Susquatch and Big Foot.

Q: You're intimidating me, Anita.

ANITA: I'm not. I'm being—you're too fucking—I'm having a hard time remembering.

Q: Was it you who egged Mick on to do the goosestep on that tour?

ANITA: Goosestep? Maybe he had a rip in his shirt or something. Everybody goosesteps or goose walks or whatever. That was Mick. Maybe it was that Brian was upstaging him and like, you know, he'd better do something. They were doing it to each other. Mick shit in his pants when James Brown went on before him on the TAMI show. He said "How I'm gonna go on after that"? Brian studied the way James Brown was moving and when they came on stage Brian leaps in the air, but Mick having flat feet, pink skin, sausage fingers, rolling eyes, rubber lips . . . get off of my cloud, why not?

Q: How did you meet Brian?

ANITA: Well, I was hired by the CIA and they told me, "Go stick around him and you get free tickets and make sure you keep on his back and make him freak out."

Q: But how did you come to be at a Stones concert in the first place? I mean, how did you first come to see them?

ANITA: I decided to kidnap Brian. It sounds ridiculous . . . But they even made a movie about it, about kidnapping a pop star . . . "*Privilege*." That was the original story. It was supposed to be Brian. Brian seemed sexually the most flexible. Guys or girls? It didn't matter. The others all seemed to have a chick on their side with a toupée, false eyelashes and all that. You know what I mean? And foam for the fanny and stuff for not getting pregnant and all that shit. Brian I knew I could just talk to him. As a matter of fact when I met him I was his groupie, really.

Q: So when did you first see him?

ANITA: Yeah, I met him first in the Oktoberfest circus. I got backstage with a photographer. I told him I just wanna meet them. I tell you I had a piece of hash and amyl nitrates. There were the Troggs, Spencer Davis, Stevie Winwood. They were the opening act. Backstage, it was like where the horses walk, it was a beerhall atmosphere... I asked him if he wanted to smoke a joint and Brian says, "Yeah, let's smoke a joint." So he says, "Come back to the hotel." Then he sat and cried there all night long. He was my groupie, I had a fling. But it wasn't American-style "Let's go and have a good time." Brian was a pain in the ass, you know. He was so vulnerable, he was so upset about Mick and Keith. They had teamed up on him and I really felt sorry for him. Brian had everything going for him. Brian was FAN-TAS-TIC! He was a very complicated person, like he used to dye his hair, blond it, and I used to cut it and he had like four mirrors all around him.

Q: He dyed his hair? He wasn't blond?

ANITA: Yeah, he was blond. I used to dye it blonder, he was really into chicks. He was quite a bully, you know? Like small guys are. He's a small guy, like when he got drunk, like what he would do if he felt threatened—that's when I knew trouble was coming—break a bottle on the table edge and put the glass in his pocket. I think he got away with slashing someone's face in a New York club. I think you see he was quite vicious on that end.

Q: Do you think that that stemmed from the insecurity within the group at the time, the thing that was going on with Mick and Keith?

ANITA: I think literally Mick and Keith thought it out and decided to do him in because they resented him. He had a suit when they were all still in school. He was a real fashionable punk rocker, Quadraphenia type. Black and white suit, thin tie and he had a car on top of it. He had chicks. All the chicks. And he used to fuck everybody else's chick. I mean he knew it, he really had it down and they didn't. Can you imagine having a car in England, at that time?

Q: Having everything too soon was to his disadvantage?

ANITA: He was so talented and he had that kind of pretty face, that jive talk. Brian was really dedicated. He'd get stoned and frustrated . . .

Q: Do you think it was the drug busts that finally put Brian over the edge?

ANITA: He was a total burnout before the busts. He took acid. Everyone said he took a lot of drugs. He never took heroin in his life. He took acid, of course. So no one believes that Brian didn't do any drugs? That's a misquote.

Q: Didn't do *any*?

ANITA: STP, which is a three day trip on acid, mandrax (English Quaaludes), desbutal, amphetamine, barbituates, and no heroin, none of that shit. All legal fucking shit, prescriptions. Prescription death. You go to a doctor and get a script because you don't want to be illegal, that's one way of doing it. He didn't have anything (illegal) at the second bust. Just, you know, desbutals, dexedrines . . . a long list.

Q: How did taking acid affect Brian, though?

ANITA: The first time he took acid he saw creatures coming out of the ground, the walls, the floors. He was looking in all the cupboards for people, "Where are they"? That's when he said to me, "Dress me up like Francoise Hardy." I powder him and all that shit. So I dress him up like a chick, you know? It's like he came out of it a haunted man.

Q: Was that the effeminate side of him that he couldn't handle?

ANITA: He obviously appealed to everybody . . . I mean there was a fling between him and Mick for a period. Brian *used* that . . . Brian could look really marvelous on stage, the way he moved. But Brian could get caught in his manners. He was very self-conscious. Also all his other hang-ups—his asthma, his constant little pump for asthma—basically it was opiates and he couldn't live without that, he'd go crazy. He was like a nervous wretch, you know.

Q: He always seemed a bit pedantic when he spoke . . .

ANITA: Yeah, but that was because he was always a perfectionist in the way he was talking, choosing his words. He did want to catch your attention when he was speaking, to captivate you. Then he had the way he moved and his hair which were captivating and I'm sure that all the Stones fell for it. Keith in a cynical way, maybe. Mick, he fell for it. Brian broke that barrier and Mick never really forgave him for it. Brian was so far ahead of them you wouldn't believe it. Here are Mick and Keith up on stage trying to learn how to be sex objects and Brian already having two illegitimate children. Brian was acting on it faster than anybody else, he knew his stuff very well. They were still schoolboys. Also Brian was the one who did the hustling, getting people together and believing it, I mean really knowing it, unlike Mick who couldn't make up his mind whether he wanted to be an account-

ant. Brian was saying in the early days, "Look, it's going to happen!" At the same time he had it in his hand so he could control it, so he used to control it. And when they found out he was right, that they did make it, instead of appreciating what he did they resented it. And that's when Brian's doom really started. They had a vendetta, Mick and Keith, a real vendetta.

Q: Do you think Mick absorbed Brian's persona?

ANITA: Yeah, I would say it's obvious.

Q: Do you think there was a conspiracy, then, to phase Brian out?

ANITA: I think there is a conspiracy right now too.

Q: Conspiracy? Towards whom?

ANITA: What I think is that the two of them, Mick and Keith, are going to have to face each other eventually. They should get married. Mayor Koch should marry them.

Q: Did Brian ever sit down and play a song for you that he had written?

ANITA: Yeah, he'd do all the parts himself.

Q: He did the music for *Mort und Totschlag* . . .

ANITA: Him and Jimmy Page. Then the drivers started to move in on Brian, the taxi drivers. Tom Keelock, the chauffeur. All that psychedelic stuff in England, honestly, it was disgusting. The maharishi was a dyke from Yorkshire.

Q: This is a hard idea for my mind to absorb . . . but wasn't Brian really into electronic music?

ANITA: Of course he was, but it was not Sgt. Pepper. Find out who has the

tapes and you can hear it for yourself.

Q: But I would have thought Brian would have been more into the psychedelic thing, like in *Satanic Majesties*, the mellotron track for "2,000 Light Years From Home."

ANITA: That's a misprint by Mick's paranoia who always blames it on somebody else. That's why I'd like to clear that up.

Q: You mean it was easy to blame it on Brian because he was so fucked up on drugs?

ANITA: No, he was fucked up because he didn't want to know what they were doing. In the studio he played all those different instruments. When he was in the studio during that period he was trying to hook up with someone else . . . Brian didn't like the whole London trend in music and so he just got more fucked up. He couldn't play with anyone anymore.

Q: What kind of relationship did Brian have with Dylan?

ANITA: Well, the one who was really hung up on Dylan was Jagger, you know. Brian was very interesting socially, though. He dealt with the percussions of fame and all that. He picked out the best, the cream of it. Dylan, Terry Southern, Warhol . . . Dylan is a teaser all the time cause he was acting like a rich guy with chick and all that. Brian used to go back to him all the time. Even Keith wouldn't dare meet Dylan. When Keith first met Dylan for the first time he was like, speechless. Brian set the pace. Afterwards it gave Keith the space to come in and be accepted in Dylan's camp. There are things about Brian that are like Cocteau.

— DAVID DALTON

CHELTENHAM 1969–1970

"**W**hile we were driving down to the cemetery—at the cemetery gates there was a policeman," Shirley Arnold is saying. "He saluted as Brian went past, and Charlie laughed. I was so tearful, and I said, 'What you laughin' at?' and he said, 'The policeman saluted. Brian's curlin' up somewhere, lookin' on and lovin' it.' "

I want to walk past the fine shops of the Promenade and the neat houses under the manicured trees. Cheltenham was designed to be a nice place, and it is a nice place, up to the point where they decide you are not so nice. Some of Cheltenham's nicest people have not spoken to Brian Jones's mother and father in years, while others have stopped speaking to them only

since Brian was buried in consecrated ground, his final outrage. You can listen close and hear the clippers clipping the hedges of Cheltenham.

Before I can look over my notes the taxi pulls into the parking lane to let me out. The mustard-colored semi-detached houses with tiny squares of grass behind brick fences, perched uneasily on the rim of the middle class,

look so small and regular that I think I must be at the wrong place. But I enter at the gate and go up to the front door, where a glowing plastic bell-ringer bears the name L.B. Jones. I ring the bell and wait, trying to smile. It is night now and I am standing in a pool of yellow light under the porch lantern, cars racing past on the dark road, flashing in each other's headlights.

The little man who opens the door has receding gray hair and a rather broad but sharp-nosed face, red under the pale, lined skin. As I begin talking to him I can't stop thinking that he is the same size as Brian, they must have identical skeletons. He has Brian's, or Brian had his, way of walking almost on tiptoe, holding his hands back beside his hips. He has the same short arms and small, strong hands, and though Mr. Jones's eyes, behind glasses framed with gilt metal and gray plastic, do not have the quality

Brian's eyes had of being lit from within, he has Brian's funny one-eyed way of looking at things. He stands before me, one foot forward, hands down by his pockets almost in fists, peering with one eye.

I say who I am, Mr. Jones says he's glad to see me and leads me into the living room, where I sit on a couch, my back to the front wall, and he sits in a stuffed chair printed with ugly flowers before the unlit electric fireplace. He tells me that I'm the fourth of my countrymen who have come to discuss writing about Brian. People come with letters from publishers, then they go away and one hears nothing more. "I don't know what to make of it. I think they're pulling my leg," he says, turning one eye on me again.

I start to answer him, getting as far as, "Er, ah," when Brian's mother comes in. I struggle to my feet and say hello. She looks gentler than Mr. Jones. She calls him Lewis and he calls her Louie, short for Louisa. Her eyes are a normal, pretty blue. Her hair is as yellow as Brian's, a shade that appears to age well if given the chance.

Brian was born on the last day of February 1942. The Jones's second child, a daughter, died at about the age of two.

"How did she die?" I ask as gently as possible.

"She died, and that's all I'll say about it," Mr. Jones says. I try again to explain why I am asking questions, but Mr. Jones has been hurt too many times by lies and by the truth in print, and he is nowhere near ready to trust a writer. He tells me that their other child, Barbara, born in 1946, now a physical education teacher, wants no part of anything to do with Brian, and he asks me to leave her alone. He grinds his teeth again. But he can't stop himself from talking and bringing out family photograph albums.

Mrs. Jones started giving Brian piano lessons when he was six. He studied piano until he was fourteen. "But he wasn't terribly interested," she says. "Then he started playing the clarinet."

"Which didn't help his asthma any," Mr. Jones says. "Brian had croup when he was four, and it left him with asthma. He had terrible asthma attacks. It was always bad when he went to the beach on holiday, and he'd been having bad attacks down at Cotchford, very bad attacks down there just before his death."

Cotchford Farm was once the home of A.A. Milne; the Hefalump Wood where Pooh Bear lived is there. It seemed right that Brian should have the place. There he soon died, less than a year after he bought it. Many things had hurt him by then, and Mr. Jones can not stop going over them, trying to find where things went wrong, where to place the blame. "I was down there with him, in a sort of junk room there at Cotchford, not long before he died. He came across a photograph of Anita and just stood for a moment looking at it. He said, 'Anita,' almost as if he were talking to himself, as if he'd forgotten I was there. Then he put the photograph down and we went on talking, doing what we'd been doing. The loss of Anita upset him terribly. Nothing was the same for Brian after that. Then the drug charges, all that trouble. I didn't know how to help him. We were close when he was young, but later we had . . . differences of opinion."

I hardly knew how to deal with him. The headmaster would complain about him, and I'd become very serious and sit Brian down for a talk. 'Why is the headmaster always writing us with complaints? Why do you disobey them?' And Brian would say, 'Look, Dad, they're only teachers. They've never done anything. You want me to do the things you did, but I can't be like you. I have to live my own life.' He was terribly logical about it all. I could hardly get anywhere trying to argue with him.

"Brian was obsessed with music. He used to play these, what are they, Modern Jazz Quartet records—"

"The reverberations used to drive me crazy," says Mrs. Jones.

"These records were playing morning, noon, and night," Mr. Jones says. "I saw it as a positive evil in his life, undermining a quite good career. Maybe music was his eventual downfall, but at the time I saw it as an evil because he was so obsessed. Music had driven out all thoughts of a conventional career. His involvement with music and London life, the life of the night clubs, all that, ruined his career at the opthalmic firm and school. He threw school and his job over and came back home. He had odd jobs, played with a band, worked in a music shop in Cheltenham, selling sheet music, records. He was becoming totally absorbed in a musical atmosphere. I knew Brian had musical ability, but I was very chary that he could achieve success. To me the most important thing was his security. I was unsatisfied to see him just drifting, and I saw no security or success likely to come from jazz. But to him—a religion it was, he was a fanatic. He went back to London for good when he was about twenty."

I don't want to outstay my small welcome at the Joneses, but Mrs. Jones sits with me and the cat as Mr. Jones talks, rambling from one time of Brian's life to another, putting together clues. "Very soon," he says, "the two together, Jagger-Richard, were getting very uptown. Louie and I went to Colston Hall, Bristol, in the fall of '66 to see Brian, when he and the group were playing there, and Brian seemed very different. All of his spark seemed to be gone. He was very unhappy. We didn't stay. Brian was not friendly. An indefinable change had come over him.

"It was typical of Brian that he called later, after the tour was over, and apologized. He said, 'I wasn't very nice.' I said, 'That's all right.' He said he had been upset about Anita—who I understand said after his death that she did him wrong.

"Brian played their last hit, 'Honky Tonk Women,' for me down at Cotchford Farm. It was his arrangement—but I believe it was re-recorded without him. We were with Brian about five weeks before he left the Rolling Stones—and I'm convinced that he had no notion of leaving the Rolling Stones then—but there were moves afoot to get him out.

"When Brian became a Rolling Stone it seemed that he had found his soul, he had achieved what he wanted. The criticism troubled him very much for our sake—when there'd be an attack in the newspapers he'd call. Especially later with the drugs, he'd say he was 'very upset because he knew it would react on you.' I told him it didn't, of course it did.

"After he was arrested the second time he called us—he was in tears. 'I've been fixed,' he said. 'I give you my word, Dad, I had no idea that blasted stuff was there.' I said, 'I believe you, Son,' and I did. He never told me a lie.

"And he'd call other times, fairly regularly—every month or so. When he felt happy and secure and strong he didn't. And sometimes he'd come to see us, thought nothing of time, he'd blow in at 4:00 A.M. He's rung me at all hours of the night, from Hollywood, Vienna, Paris, Melbourne. He called from Melbourne once and we talked for the best part of an hour. He was homesick. He'd been listening to Winston Churchill's funeral on the radio.

"I was very foolish once. I talked to the chauffeur about the family. He came here after having taken Brian to the Priory Nursing Home. I told him people had been rude to Brian's mother—he told Brian and Brian was terribly upset. He called up, all in

tears. The whole experience at the Priory was very bad for Brian, a lot of psychological rubbish which made him feel a freak.

"Down at Cotchford Farm that night, Brian had gone to bed with his sleeping tablet, a 'sleeper' as he called them. He knew this Frank Thorogood, who'd been down there working on the place, and this nurse were up in his flat—a flat in the garage, away from the house. Brian had said that Frank could stay in the flat. Then when Frank brought the nurse out Brian was not happy with that. It was a small town, and Brian knew it might cause trouble. He got up from bed and tried, so Anna told us later, to get Frank to leave, couldn't, then they had what was referred to as a 'party,' which I interpret to mean that they had a few drinks together, and Brian was sleepy, he'd taken a sleeping pill after all. He got up, tried to get them to leave, and then after a few drinks decided to have a swim. With the pills and the drink and the warmth of the pool—Brian kept it at about 90° or better—he simply went to sleep in the bath.

"I could never understand that statement the papers supposedly got from Anna about a 'party.' If one were planning to have a party, would he take sleeping pills first? Why? At the inquest, Anna never got to testify—she was so upset. I was horrified by people's knowing a physician had prescribed the drugs Brian had taken and their saying nothing at all about it. Nobody asked any questions. I wrote the police a letter telling them the drugs were prescribed by this man, so they could investigate and have that cleared up, at any rate, that the drugs were in fact prescribed for Brian by a doctor. I sent the letter on Friday, by Monday the doctor was out of the country. I have no idea what it means."

Jaws clenched, Mr. Jones peers at at the cold fire, unable, though Brian is buried in Cheltenham Cemetery, to stop wanting to make things right. "I think," he says, "that when Brian was in the sixth form the school made a mistake. They wanted him to study science and technology. I said, 'The boy has an artistic temperament—shouldn't that be taken into account?' The school said, 'No, that's not practical. Science, technology's where it's at today.' Brian wasn't interested in that sort of thing at all. I remember buying him a hammer when he was just a little chap. He wasn't interested in it at all. Most boys love hammers—not Brian."

Soon it is late, and I call a taxi. Mr. Jones, shaking my hand, says, "We've had no cards at Christmas, nothing

from the boys. If you see them, remember me to them—tell them that if they want to write or call, I'd be happy to hear from them."

Next morning I check out of the hotel, leaving my bags at the desk, and take a taxi to the cemetery, on Priory Road. It had been cloudy, then raining, then the sun started to shine, bright and warm, and now as we come to the cemetery it is starting to rain again, a few drops falling. We drive part way in, but a man trimming the flowers beside the motorpath stops us, and I tell the driver to wait. Down a path to the left, turn right, and there, on a corner south of the church, is Brian's grave, with its little metal marker. No stone yet; it takes at least a year for the earth to settle after being disturbed by gravediggers.

It looks so small, like Brian's old house, that once again I have the feeling this must be wrong—but it is right; this small man, never more than a boy really, from that small house, now in this small grave.

Standing before the grave, in the little cemetery on the edge of Cheltenham, you could see the Cotswolds in the distance, not too far away, not too tall, perfectly decent green English hills. The graveyard church is nearby, a small medieval building of dun and grey stones, decorated and protected by snarling, scaly gryphons, its spire reaching up into the grey sky. The rain is steady now, though lacy fir trees shelter the graves. The number of Brian's grave is V11393, a single plot on a little turning of a lane in the cemetery, next to Albert "Bert" Trigg, beloved husband of Ethel.

Three sprays of flowers are on the grave, and a poem written in a schoolgirl's insecure tiny round hand on a white sheet of paper, folded and wrapped round with cellophone to protect it from the rain, but already fading with each day's condensation of dew.

*Only the living die
By the hand of life
Privileged, Branded
Spoken to when alone
By the voice of earth—
Marked through multiplying nights
Of sorrow and defeat, eaten by
Victory.*

And then, at the bottom of the page, in the same hand: "But it will never be the same without the boy we used to adore."

STANLEY BOOTH

EULOGIES

Jim Morrison: Ode to L.A. While Thinking of Brian Jones, Deceased

I'm a resident of a city
They've just picked me to
    play
the Prince of Denmark

Poor Ophelia

All the ghosts he never
    saw
floating to doom
on an iron candle

Come back, brave warrior
Do the dive
On another channel

Hot buttered pool
Where's Marrakesh
under the Falls
the wild storm
where savages fell out
in late afternoon
monsters of rhythm

You've left your
Nothing
to compete with
Silence
I hope you went out
Smiling
Like a child
Into the cool remnant
of a dream

The angel man
with Serpents competing
for his palms
and fingers
Finally claimed

This benevolent
Soul

Ophelia

Leaves, sodden
in silk

Chlorine
dream
mad stifled
Witness

The diving board, the plunge
The pool

You were a fighter
a damask musky muse

You were the bleached
Sun
for TV afternoon

horned-toads
maverick of a yellow spot

Look now to where it's got
You

in meat heaven
w/ the cannibals
& jews

The gardener
Found
The body, rampant, floating

Lucky Stiff
What is this green pale stuff
You've made of

poke holes in the goddess
Skin

Will he Stink
Carried heavenward
Thru the halls
of music

No chance

Requiem for a heavy

That smile
That porky satyr's
leer
has leaped upward

into the loam

Pete Townshend

When Pete Townshend was asked to comment on Brian's death he said: "Oh, it's a normal day for Brian, like he died every day, you know.

"I used to know him quite well. Fairly well. I know a lot about the vibes that were about. The Stones have

always been a group that I really dug very much. Dug all the dodgy aspects of them as well, and Brian Jones has always been what I've regarded as one of the dodgy aspects. The way he fitted in there and the way he didn't fit in, I always felt was one of the strong dynamics of the group. And I felt that when he stopped playing with them that dynamic was going to be missing, but somehow it seems to be still there. I credited him with a lot. I think the thing is that the Stones have just managed by some miracle to kind of replace him somehow. Not with Mick Taylor, I mean, he's like a musician, but they've kind of filled the hole. Either that or the fact that he's dead has made that dynamic that was there when he was alive, kind of permanent, I don't know."

The day Brian died, Pete wrote and recorded this:

I used to play my guitar as a kid
    wishing that I could be like him
But today I changed my mind I
    decided that I don't want to die
But it was a normal day for Brian
Rock and Roll's that way
It was a normal day for Brian
A man who died every day

George Harrison

George Harrison, Brian's closest friend, says: "When I met him I liked him quite a lot. He was a good fellow, you know. I got to know him very well, I think, and I felt very close to him; you know how it is with some people, you feel for them, feel near to them.

"He was born on February 28, 1943, and I was born on February 25, 1943, and he was with Mick and Keith and I was with John and Paul in the groups, so there was a sort of understanding between the two of us.

"The positions were similar, and I often seemed to meet him in his times of trouble. There was nothing the matter with him that a little extra love wouldn't have cured.

"I don't think he had enough love or understanding. He was very nice and sincere and sensitive, and we must remember that's what he was."

Charlie Watts

"I can't really say anything about Brian—it's such a personal thing and it's impossible to sum up a friend cold-bloodedly.

"It's a great personal loss that leaves me at a loss for words.

"No matter what I were to say, it would not be enough."

PART II

t's hardly surprising that three of the songs on *Beggars Banquet* should project the radical climate of "sleepy London town" in 1968—Mick had taken part in the storming of the American embassy—but its politics are more symbolic and confounding than literal. "Street Fighting Man" is one more Stones acrostic on "Dancing In The Streets," this time picking up on the lyric as well: "Summer's here and the time is right for dancing/fighting in the street."

The words are evasive, but the Stones' politics have always been the politics of delinquency in the tradition of Eddie Cochran's "Summertime Blues." As twin sons of the she-wolf, they are leaders of its pack, and they have no need to indulge in justifying lyrics. The aggression is in the music. And the way in which the notes and words pile up against each other at the end of each verse is like a crowd rushing to break through a police barrier. The long open notes combined with the repeated menacing descent of the bass line, marching alongside it. This rhythm, first used by the Beatles on "I Am A Walrus" and subsequently by the Who ("I'm Free") is based on the oscillations of English police sirens.

Subtle, defensive and theatrical, the Stones' attitude to politics has always been more anarchist than socialist, manifesting an indifference to specific events, while offsetting it with massive assaults on all forms of bourgeois quackery. Their revolution has never concerned itself with details. Smash down *all* the doors and plate-glass windows—rape, murder, total penetration!

TOWNSEND: [Rock] is the single force which threatens a lot of the crap which is around at the moment in the middle class and in the middle-aged politics or philosophy . . . it blasts it out of sheer realisticness. It's like suddenly everybody getting hung up on bad trips: mother has just fallen downstairs, dad's lost all his money at the dog track, the baby's got TB. In comes the kid, man, with his transistor radio, grooving to Chuck Berry. He doesn't give a shit about mom falling down the stairs. He's with rock 'n roll. (*Rolling Stone*)

By the time of the Stones' 1969 tour, the political climate had totally changed.

KEITH: Before, America was a real fantasy land. It was still Walt Disney and hamburger dates and when you came back in 1969 it wasn't anymore. Kids were really into what was going on in their country. I remember watching Goldwater-Johnson in '64 and it was a complete little shame. But by the time it came Nixon's turn in 1968, people were concerned in a really different way. (*Rolling Stone*, August 19, 1971)

At many of their concerts on that tour Mick did not know whether to give the peace sign or the power salute. In Berkeley he was booed for doing both. What began as a hip stance became a deadly serious pantomime of values.

The Politics of Delinquency

"Violence. The Rolling Stones are violence," wrote Jon Landau in a review of *Beggars Banquet*. "Their music penetrates the raw nerve endings of their listeners and finds its way into the groove marked· 'release of frustration.' Their violence has always been a surrogate for the larger violence their audience is so obviously capable of.

"On *Beggars Banquet* the Stones try to come to terms with violence more explicitly than before and in so doing are forced to take up the subject of politics. The result is the most sophisticated and meaningful statement we can expect to hear concerning the two themes—violence and politics—that will probably dominate the rock of 1969." (*Rolling Stone*)

In the militant atmosphere of 1969 there was confusion about the riots that had always been an integral part of rock 'n roll concerts and "violent revolution." The violence in rock is an elemental, instinctive force; as Mick understood as far back as 1968, it could never be harnessed for social change, because it is undirected, primordial.

Arrogance, pansexuality, energy, noise, violence, sensuality, flash and fantasy are the essence of the Stones' stage magnetism.

"People come to Stones concerts to work it out," said Robert Greenfield.

Keith answered: "Yeah, which in turn has been interpreted as violence or 'a goddamn riot' when it's just people letting it out. Not against anybody but with each other." (*Rolling Stone*, August 19, 1971)

MICK: "I don't understand the connection between music and violence. People are always trying to explain it to me and I just blindly carry on. I just know that I get very aroused by music, but it doesn't arouse me violently. I never went to a rock 'n roll show and wanted to smash the windows or beat up anybody afterward. I feel more sexual than actually physically violent."

Initially, the Underground movement saw the Stones as psychotropic emblems and catalysts for the almost imminent violent revolution: the Acid Apocalypse. When they first played San Francisco in 1965, the Diggers put out a proclamation calling the Stones "the embodiment of what *we* represent, a psychic evolution . . . the breaking up of all the old values."

On the 1969 tour of the States, members of the Stones cult came to watch their Messiahs. "Their attraction for audiences so far transcends 'mere' entertainment," wrote Michael Lydon in *Ramparts*, "that it is tempting to suggest that they are not entertainers at all. Their importance is symbolic. They don't exist on a literal level."

This (intense) psychic bonding to the Stones continued well into the Seventies. Lenny Kaye: "Through a special community alchemy, we've chosen the Stones to bring our darkness into the light, in each case via a construct that fits the time and prevailing mood perfectly. And as a result, they have become the great white hopes. If you can't bleed on the Stones, who *can* you bleed on?"

But in 1969, when all the millennial aspirations of the Sixties seemed to totter on the brink of an unknowable abyss, the cult of the Stones had reached an alarming level of mass hysteria; their fans awaited their arrival like anemic vampires.

"Somehow," said Keith, "in America in '69—I don't know about now, and I never got it before—one got the feeling they really wanted to suck you out."

"I Hope We're Not Too Messianic or a Trifle Too Satanic . . ."

Q: What is evil?
Mick: Evil is putting bombs in people's shops.

Kenneth Anger thought it was Mick's androgyny that brought out the beast in the audience; Ed McCormack (in *Circus*) connected the androgyny to Satan and the superstud:

SEX SYMBOLS IN THE AGE OF UNISEX

Mick Jagger, bossman of the Rolling Stones, started out posing as a tough punk and evolved into rock's foremost hermaphrodite—ambiguous enough to appeal to all the newly created sexes, he has recently taken to wearing lipstick and fluffy dresslike frockcoats on stage. The new Mick is Satan, superstud and drag queen rolled into one ball of incredible quirks unbelievable to behold.

This combination of androgyny and violence suggested the next incarnation of the Stones, which in retrospect seems even more improbable than the image of the Stones as rock 'n roll storm troopers: Mick as Lucifer. (Altamont has frequently been cited as an example of the Stones' complicity with the dark powers.)

"*Sirs,* To those who know, it's been obvious that the Stones, or at least some of them, have been involved in the practice of Magick ever since the *Satanic Majesties' Request* album. But there at least the color was more white than black. Since then the hue has gone steadily darker and darker.

"At Altamont he appeared in his full Majesty with his full consort of demons, the Hell's Angels. It was just a few days before the Winter Solstice when the forces of darkness are at their most powerful. The moon was in Scorpio, which is the time of the month when the Universal vibration is at its most unstable. It was held in a place dedicated to destruction through motion. Then Mick comes on only after it is dark enough for the red lights to work their magick.

"I don't know if they were truly aware of what they were doing or not. I feel they are sadder and wiser from the experience. But an agonizing price was paid for the lesson. And we were all guilty because we have all eaten of the cake the Stones baked."
—Lee H., Los Angeles.

The press found this pantomime of the Satanic Stones as irresistible as they had previously found the Stones involvement with sex and drugs. Accounts of the '69 tour are spiced with melodramatic allusions to the Dark Powers such as this one: "Unisex. Zombies. Satanists. Kenneth Anger calls Keith Richard his 'right hand man.'"

Flirtation with demonic powers has a long history in England; Blake,

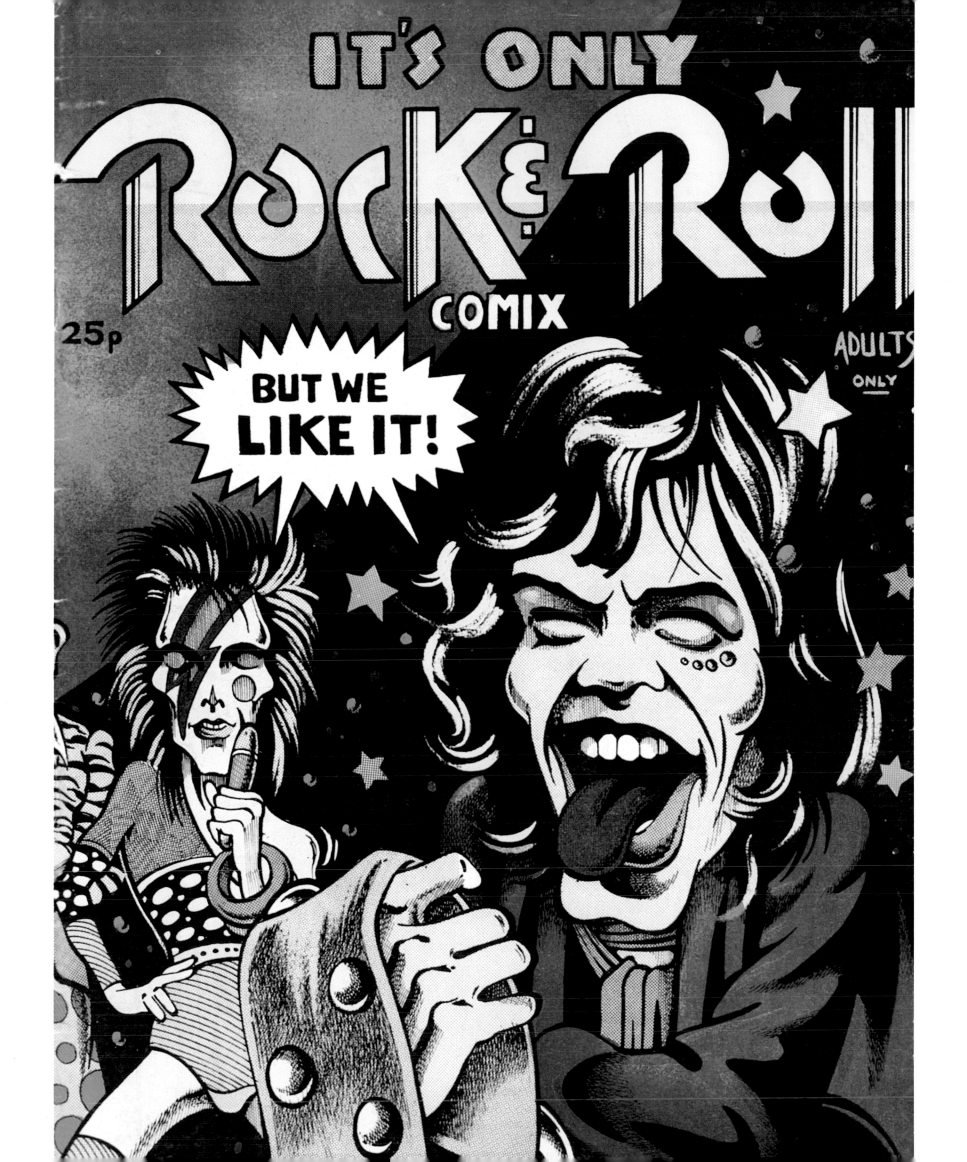

Byron, Oscar Wilde, Yeats and De Quincey were all sometime-servants of Satan.

While a tradition of demon worship in Europe had taken the form of decadent flirtation, the blues in the American South were a more violent and immediate occupation. Almost all blues singers, being drifters, were outcasts from the gospel-centered communities. Son House, Leadbelly and Bukka White served time for murder. An example of how seriously the playing of the blues was taken is exemplified in "Prodigal Son" on *Beggars Banquet*, written by the Rev. Robert Wilkins, originally a blues singer who reformed his ways and refused to sing anything but religious subjects, hence this blues parable.

The Stones welded the two traditions by *putting on* the Devil and becoming outlaws themselves, projecting a dazzling presence which is as compelling as it is deliberately contemptuous, theatrical and exhibitionist.

For many who have stepped into the Satanic circle, the proximity of the demonic has proved fatal. But the Stones are always at one remove—"what's puzzling you is the nature of my game"—and this theatricality has preserved them from being consumed.

Another journalistic obsession (not to say cliché) in '69 was the comparison of the fanatical responses of the audiences at Stones concerts to Nazi rallies. Richard Elman: "The constantly made analogy to Albert Speer's Nuremberg rallies of the Thirties is accurate in one sense; it's not so much a question of ideology as of stagecraft, of someone seeming to be leading an avant-garde for millions; yet there are moments when ideology and stagecraft seem to be but different facets of the same glittery gimmick." (*Uptight With The Rolling Stones*)

"The Fire Is Sweeping My Very Street Today . . ."

"They are still the *rank assimilators and disseminators of rock 'n roll streetnoize*, and they are not bothered at all by age or lifestyle" wrote Arthur Levy in *Zoo World*. "After all, the Rolling Stones' own lifestyles have been altered drastically since Altamont when they obsoleted any poses at the savagery of rock before that day.

"*Gimme Shelter* teaches you one important thing about the band—their inability to separate musical conscience from reality. Altamont changed the outlook of the Rolling Stones individually/collectively when it neatly pointed out their catalyzing potential in real, physical terms.

"While the Rolling Stones could make it easy to embrace *any* deteriorating set of lifestyles with rancorous glee just by being a part of their musical web over the years, they still *seemed to be moving away from their own storm center.*

"But Altamont was an accident! An accident of reality that was shaped into frozen fact by film and legend, turned back in on itself—a *mobius* strip that started with the impotent grace of Woodstock 3000 miles away on one end and mirror-imaged a negative, a reversal of Woodstock with Altamont, where even the Grateful Dead changed from the Rose unto the Skull. Accidentally, the Stones ferried the 60's into the 70's as Altamont became a standard of rock 'n roll meaning, insulated from reality, though, because just as *Gimme Shelter* had unleashed an apocalypse onto those who wanted to live with nothing less than apocalypse, so had the contemptuous politics of *Beggars Banquet* and *Let It Bleed* been realized at Altamont. (*Zoo World*, November 8th, 1973)

The Stones had been preternaturally aligned to the psychic climate of the sixties, their antennas sensitive to the least changes in the air. In 1969 there was a real fear that their immense power over their audiences had reached critical mass and was becoming personally dangerous. It was not improbable, given the intense feelings of desperation generated by the dissolution of the counterculture, that the Stones would literally become scapegoats.

During the 1972 U.S. tour Mick was reportedly plagued by fears of on-stage assassination attempts leading to "excessive" security precautions which combined with jet-set ambience only served to further isolate the Stones from their audience.

In many accounts of Altamont and reviews of *Gimme Shelter* there was the implication that the Stones' music and their satanic poses had somehow caused the violence at Altamont.

Pauline Kael wrote: Mick Jagger's performing style is a form of aggression not just against the straight world but against his own young audience, and this appeals to them, because it proves he hasn't sold out and gone soft. But when all this aggression is released, who can handle it?

The violence he provokes is well known: fans have pulled him off a platform, thrown a chair at him. He's greeted with a punch in the face when he arrives at Altamont. What the film doesn't deal with is the fact that Jagger attracts this volatile audience, that he magnetizes disintegrating people. This is, of course, an ingredient of the whole scene, but it is seen at its most extreme in the San Francisco-Berkeley audience that gathered for the Rolling Stones at Altamont. Everyone—the people who came and the people who planned it—must have wanted a big Dionysian freak-out. (*Deeper into the Movies*)

Not surprisingly, the Grateful Dead subscribed to this theory. Jerry Garcia: "Gaskin said that Altamont was the price everybody paid for having that little bit of sadism to color their sexual scene. The Rolling Stones put out that little bit of leather. Obviously there's a lot more to it than that, but I prefer that view. It's because the environment I live in is a high-energy one, and everyone is really conscious of this shift—we've all had the experience, of saying the wrong thing (or the right thing as the case may be) and all of a sudden . . . bam, it's a whole different situation."

Altamont remains a serial enigma of what became of the aspirations of the "mass bohemia" of the sixties, "a chilling fragment of our collective bad dream." By touching instinctively on the undercurrents and pressure points of American life the Stones' projections and fantasies were becoming frighteningly real. "Gimme Shelter" uncannily prefigured the apocalyptic climate of Altamont.

On *Let It Bleed* their sophisticated manipulation of sound shapes had gone far beyond anything R & B had (or could) ever have dreamed of. To deny that the Stones' music is *capable* of materializing or inciting anything is to deny that their music has had any effect on us at all. In any case the Stones, in some way or other cannot avoid expressing and thus anticipating the health *and* decadence working their way through the circuits of the whole culture.

"My Dreams Is Fading Down the Railway Lines . . ."

Like most artists the Stones are a combination of the prophetic and the reactionary. Their albums never make statements; they project psychic states of often conflicting and disturbing emotions. On *Let It Bleed* they invite us into the fantasy of the title song and conclude the album with "You Can't Always Get What You Want" where there is a lot of blood, drugs, and desolation but very little sympathy. The Stones rarely worry about contradicting themselves. Mick: "We wouldn't want to be a band people think they can rely on."

"Jagger is a great example of a

confusing myth: He can destroy what you want, what you thought of him, but on the other hand, the next time you meet him he can make up for it." (*Melody Maker*, December 30th 1972)

"Of course, some people wanted to say that Altamont was the end of an era," Mick said at the time. "People like that are fashion writers. Perhaps it was the end of *their* era, the end of their naivete. I would have thought that it would have ended long before Altamont."

The Stones had already crossed over into the savvy seventies. They'd sensed the end earlier, almost three years earlier, beginning with the drug busts in 1967 and ending with the death of Brian in 1969.

Ralph Gleason wrote: "At Altamont, only four months after the pastoral high of Woodstock, some beast was out in the open. Many of the most committed and intelligent people in the rock culture thought that something dismaying and irrevocable happened at Altamont. It was, perhaps, the end of rock's innocence, a warning that the vast amount of energy contained in the music and its immense worldwide audience had elements of danger that would have to be faced up to. And it seemed significant that all of this was presided over by the greatest live entertainer in rock history, Mick Jagger." (*Esquire*)

In *Ramparts*, Michael Lydon suggested that the feeling that this might be the last time permeated the crowd long before the murder of Meredith Hunter gave Altamont that finality and sense of loss: "The fans didn't come out to say farewell to the Rolling Stones, they came out to say farewell to their past, to the excitement and ferment of an epoch. Thus the performance became a sort of maturation ritual, even though for the most part the celebrants may have participated without being conscious of its resonance.

"I spoke with many fans before,

during and after the Stones' visit, and a remarkable number of them made comments to the effect that they wanted to see the Stones as a kind of farewell meeting, a farewell not necessarily to the Stones (although it is widely rumored that this is their last tour) but to the era of which they are possibly a living fossil."

By the end of the sixties the Stones had not even left us the illusion that they were revolutionaries. For the Stones it was always "The play's the thing." As Stanley Booth wrote a year before Altamont: "Few of the fans realize, as the Stones always have, that their revolutionary heroism is a pose, that it changes nothing, that rock 'n roll is only a little paprika on the nuclear television dinner."

Mick stated his case in a lengthy dialogue with Alan Corey in *Playboy*:

"Look, that's their bag." A dissociative shrug. "Like I said before, I'm sympathetic. I'm just not a barricade stormer. If you, or the mothers of America, or anyone else, are trying to hang it on me, well, it's just the same as their lousy sexual and drug fantasies, isn't it? They give the kids a society which they themselves have buggered up out of all sanity, and when the kids don't buy the package deal, the decent, sensible people turn around and drop the bundle on my doorstep. You know, like, I invented germ warfare. Like, I have this hot line to Mao Tse-tung." (*Playboy*, November 1969)

Unlike the Utopian visions of the hippie state, Mick was realistic enough to see the absurdity of applying the lessons of the Sierra Maestra to the Thames basin.

If the drug busts and Brian's death had disabused the Stones of any faith in the fairness of English justice, Altamont forced them to take an absurdist stance toward *any* social change. Robert Christgau (in *Creem*):

"In the end, in fact, their anger was

directed not at the cruelties of politics and economics so much as at a metaphysical joke."

On *Beggars Banquet* three years earlier, the Stones had made their skepticism about revolutions violent or vinyl quite explicit in "Street Fighting Man."

"Sympathy For The Devil," which has been naively interpreted in its most superficial sense as a satanic pact between the Stones and the powers of darkness, actually contained a coded message for the more cynical: new boss same as old boss. It's based on Mikhail Bulgakov's novel "The Master and Margarita," which describes Satan's scathing survey of the predictable results of the Communist revolution. The oppressed have overthrown a corrupt establishment and taken power into their own hands only to become as corrupt themselves as those they have displaced. The cycle repeats itself mechanically, over and over, like the flip of a coin. This is at the core of the Stones' fatalistic "heads is tails" philosophy. In both the novel and the song Satan is the *observer*, and it is this same ability to cast a cool eye on claptrap that has always made the Stones great.

Without even mentioning the paraphernalia of Satanism, we know that Satan is the rebel who promises freedom. He's always been the patron saint of blues and rock, the enemy of hypocrisy and complacency. He has nothing to live up to, and his honesty is never questioned.

The irony of history repeating itself must have appealed to Mick, the former L.S.E. student. It unwittingly predicted the future entente the Stones were to make with the Establishment. Their pact was not to be that of Romantic myth, an allegiance with the dark powers, but a far more diabolical contract between the band of former rock 'n roll delinquents and society.

The Elegant Defensive

In matters of politics, the Stones continue to exercise what John Kreidl has described as the "elegant defensive." Their aloofness is at the core of rock sentiment:

"Jagger never forces you to drink acid in water—like California—like most hip philosophers. He just leads you to water. He is the modern Pontius Pilate. He says we are innocent even if we are formally guilty. By going on record that we are innocent, we can fight bureaucracy even if bureaucracy behaves against our will to become cretins. Christ didn't believe in this way of doing it, but then Christ didn't survive."

In one of the rare interviews in which Mick confronted the issue of politics and the Stones' music directly, the reporter from West Germany's *Der Spiegel* begins by asking—

Q: Mr. Jagger, when the Rolling Stones play, hundreds of thousands of people come to your concerts. With your records you reach millions of people in the entire world. You sing of politics, protest and revolution.

MICK: Oh no, I don't sing of revolution.

Q: In your song "Street Fighting Man," it says: "The time is ripe for fighting in the street . . ."

MICK: But it then says: "But what can a poor boy do, except sing in a rock 'n roll band"—what else can I do besides sing? The song itself is the only thing that has to do with street fighting.

Q: Do you really think it's appropriate not to sing about the revolution?

MICK: We don't do that. In America, the rock 'n roll bands have gotten very political. They express themselves very directly about the Vietnam war. But when I come home to England, everything is completely different, so quiet and peaceful. If one lives in such an atmosphere, one has a great detachment from politics and writes completely differently about them.

Q: In the meantime, the Beatles, through their song "Revolution" seemed to have found harmony with middle-class society. Dylan, who once sang: "The times they are a-changin'," today says: "My songs have no political meaning." You yourself once complained: "I can't get no satisfaction." Now you say to your listeners: "You can't always get what you want."

MICK: Now *you* also can't get what *you* want. The same goes for me. I'm saying the same thing as when I said "I can't get no satisfaction," only articulated differently. It's all a question of personal orientation. As one gets older and has read more, as one knows more, one is hit with a variety of influences, one naturally writes different texts. I think back for example on a demonstration in London where people were chanting "Ho Chi Minh" through the streets. At that time I was a participant. Today I find the whole think simply ridiculous. Young people are just so naive.

Q: You sing "I can't get no satisfaction." Can't you, against this lack of satisfaction, since you can demand from society—do more than make music? After all, you aren't the poor kid anymore, who can only sing in a rock 'n roll band. Do you, for example, help subsidize any of the opponents of the war in Vietnam or

any other protest groups?

MICK: I have given money for large concerts that were for the benefit of conscientious objectors and the anti-Vietnam war movement. Nonetheless, I am no Marxist-Leninist, and I also don't wish to live under a Communist government. In America, many young people think Marxism is the only alternative to the present society. But Americans don't have any of their own personal experience about the practice of a Marxist system. That makes it easy for them to be members of such left-wing movements.

Q: For the majority of successful rock musicians, the following seems to hold true: the more famous they become, the more they forget their political and social mission. The Beatles began as young working-class . . .

MICK: They are no proletarians, they're bourgeois. Practically all rock 'n roll musicians come from middle-class circles.

Q: You don't have anything better to offer?

MICK: I can naturally offer no simple naive alternative. But you're right. In a peculiar way, we've all changed. Bob Dylan today seeks to express what currently interests American youth: to move to the country, to provide your own food and nutrition and so on. They want to follow his example, marry, start a family and set up a house in the country. In this way Dylan tries to show people how to live . . .

Mick has also said: "If I'd been a French rock 'n roll singer, I'm sure we'd all have been very involved in the revolution in France. Put in that position, we'd probably have thrown all to the winds and been there at the barricades, so to speak. But in England it's always terribly difficult to see, to find out where the barricades are. The barricades are just clowns."

But in the end, the stagnant climate of England's political weather allowed the princes of rock 'n roll to dream ultimate adolescent fantasies, the apocalyptic fire sweeping all the rubbish of civilization under its red coal carpet.

Souls in Stone

"The Rolling Stones are more than a group, they are a way of life," as Andrew Oldham wrote in the liner notes to their first English album, and the Stones' life-style was adopted by more adolescents than any other posture of our generation.

But myths involve complicity. As Mick Jagger, the Pied Piper of this revolution, said, "All this stuff about

my leading and perverting them . . . we just sort of went along together, didn't we?"

The fanaticism with which their followers identified with the Stones transcended even that of the Beatles (because the Stones were a more exclusive cult) and it superseded the hypnotic attraction Dylan held over his audience because the Stones' style was more visceral. It was street cool and psycho-synchronistic! Like a second skin you could put them on as easily as you put on a record and they were never out of time.

"The Rolling Stones, during their fat years, constantly gave and then reinforced the impression that they were going through the exact same life experiences as me and coming to the same conclusions—and that at the same time that they were precisely me they were also infinitely-more-than-me, all-wise, all-experiencing, all-encompassing," wrote Paul Williams in *Crawdaddy*.

"At any rate we/I identified fiercely with the Stones (as they came through on the records; nothing else mattered—maybe because there was less rock media in those days) from 1965 in my case through the end of 1969, when I felt I knew *exactly* what they meant by 'I hope we're not too messianic, or a trifle too Satanic, too . . . I am just a monkey man, I'm glad you are a monkey woman too babe.'"

The Stones "image," the personalities of Mick and Keith especially, was always crucial to their music. We had cloned ourselves from that implant and so it seemed particularly cynical of them to lead us out into the California scrubland and abandon us.

A little over a year after Altamont the Stones played a farewell tour of Britain (March 4–14, 1971) and on the advice of their business adviser, Prince Rupert Lowenstein, announced that they would be leaving England to live in the south of France; they were receding from us. The Stones had been telling other people to get lost on record since "It's All Over Now." Why not us? However coolly the Stones reacted to the death at Altamont, it *had* affected them. The symbiotic relationship between the Stones and their fans had become personally dangerous. We listened to their albums, like those of Dylan and the Beatles, as if they were seismic readings from an impending apocalypse.

There was the eerie impression that the Stones were no longer quite themselves; they were beside themselves perhaps. Like theories claiming that James Dean or Amelia Earhart

or Hitler are not really dead but live or in semi-comatose conditions on the "XX" floor of some high-rise building, a crank hypothesis began to develop that the original Stones, by now incurably insane, had been hidden away in a Swiss sanatorium along with Brian Jones who, of course, had not actually died.

To the lunatic fringe this seemed the only possible explanation for the drastic change that had taken place in their former idols.

Metamorphosis

Like Darwin's finches on the remote Galapagos Islands, the Stones in exile on their compound in the south of France adapted themselves to new conditions and evolved into a new species of band with exotic plumage. The history of the Rolling Stones after the bluesy synthamesc-spiked *Let It Bleed* is the history of another band or a series of other bands, inflecting, augmenting, adapting and adopting the styles of their contemporaries. As they absorbed trends from reggae, disco and New Wave, the Stones become almost chameleonlike in their digestion of new forms. With new configurations of the band—the horns of Bobby Keyes and Jim Price, Billy Preston's keyboards, Sugar Blues' harp playing, Ollie Brown's percussion, plus grafting onto the band first new breed, blues virtuoso Mick Taylor's lead and five years later Ron Wood's parallel line rhythm guitar—the Stones shifted away from their once monolithic sound.

With these new movable components and the use of more layered and sophisticated recording techniques, the Stones became a corporate concept rather than the "amateur professionals" as they had once described themselves. With Mick, following Brian's death, pushed into a solo stance onstage, some of the collective force of the band was diminished. But they were now consummate professionals and their performances were as rich, polished and remote as their records.

MICK: We're not *that* band anymore, anyway. We're a bunch of different bands. English reviewers seem to have this weird idea of the Rolling Stones as being this band and we've never been *that* band, but they imagine we are. We can do *that* band if we wanna . . . I don't see why we can't make a record that *doesn't* sound like the Rolling Stones. We're not a *brand*, like H.P. Sauce or something.

The Stones rolled through the seventies like tumbling dice, a gypsy band constantly on the move, with new players tagging along for a couple of tours and the odd record and then falling by the wayside as casually as they had come. Their wayward progress continued through the rock 'n roll locomotion of *Sticky Fingers* in 1971. When *Exile on Main Street*, which had been recorded at leisure during a year at Keith's villa in the south of France, appeared a year later, it was an enigma. Its polished sound and its composed, controlled and unified structure framed the Stones in an unexpected mood of reflection as they took stock of their first ten years. *Exile* contains some of the most intimate glimpses the Stones have ever shown us through Jagger's opaque lyrics, yet on the whole it is the band at their most impenetrable. It remains *the* Stones' album of the seventies, tending to overshadow what followed by its awesome authority.

As the seventies progressed they continued to accost the most pervasive new musical idioms—disco, punk, reggae—with shameless zeal. These love affairs were not always reciprocal. Punks took to calling the Stones "boring old farts" and discoids condemned their flirtations as "disco for people who don't go to discos." Their perennial ability to redefine and personalize everything they touched often proved a liability when applied to such tightly structured musical forms.

Punk inspired them to strip down their sound to hard-core rock on *Some Girls* and no doubt had something to do with Jagger's F train outfit on the '78 tour. Reggae, because it is universal in the same sense that rhythm and blues is, proved more susceptible ("Sweet Black Angel," "Crackin' Up" and their cover, "Cherry Oh Baby").

The most unexpected development —perhaps because songs like "As Tears Go By" and "Lady Jane" always seemed to have an element of camp—was the Stones' mastery of the ballad form in a string of lyrically beautiful and moving songs: "Wild Horses," "If You Really Want to Be My Friend," "Memory Motel," "Fool To Cry" and the graceful "Moonlight Mile," "Winter," "Beast Of Burden" and "I'm Gonna Walk Before They Make Me Run." These songs exemplified not only a new direction melodically for the Stones, but—and this would have alarmed the group who made *Out Of Our Heads*—reflected a new maturity.

A major shift in gears for the band, early in 1975, was the "defection" of Mick Taylor after 5½ years' service. As a second-generation blues/rock virtuoso Taylor often seemed to fill an ornamental function in the Stones, embellishing the live versions of "Love In Vain" and "You Can't Always Get What You Want" with soaring solos and adding a final gloss in the studio to tracks like "Winter" and "Sway." The Stones have never been a jamming band—neither Brian nor Keith were essentially lead guitarists and the beauty of the Stones was that they never needed one—and Mick Taylor's technical contributions seemed to subtract from the Stones' basic roll and raunch. When rumors in the British trade press began to imply that Taylor's departure was due to his own dissatisfaction, Jagger gracefully deflected the obvious implication—who would *willingly* leave the Rolling Stones?— with "I mean it's not the bloody *army*, it's just a sort of rock 'n roll band."

While no one could replace the anarchistic and prolix Brian, Ron Wood came closest to being a Stone by virtue of his raucous history with those mod rockers, the Faces; his onstage antics fit in with the prankish theatrics of the Stones, as did his riff-oriented playing style. While he often seemed too much in awe of Keith's spare style, to the point where they almost became indistinguishable, his presence revived Keith. Not since 1969 had the Stones been such a metallic guitar band as on the 1975 tour when Keith returned to prominence in the band with his searing, supple guitar licks.

Every Distance Is Not Near

Sophisticated, worldly-wise and consummate performers, the Stones have always been too aware of their role as entertainers to fall into the lethal fallacy of living out their vinyl fantasies on the street. As Mick says: "I'm a dedicated show business person and I chose rock 'n roll as my career."

Put-on, detachment, irony, mimicry, have always been principles of the Stones "dry as ice" cool. It gave them a biting ambivalent edge. "We are always at one remove in everything we do," said Mick of the Stones. "With their eerie dual commitment to ecstasy and irony," the Stones have always equivocated about the distance between themselves, their songs and their audience.

Like remote planets revolving in space, the Stones throughout the seventies continued to exert a magnetic pull known in physics as *action-at-a-distance*. Their own removal from action infused their albums with a diffuse, electric, reflective, anomalous, and prolix sound and the lyrics, especially on *Exile* were now no longer buried but hermetically sealed beneath its murky grooves. They developed a disembodied intimacy that was not only the opposite of the punch, drive and clarity of their great albums of the sixties but precluded any contact.

In a review of *Exile*, John Kreidl wrote: "There's a distance which has grown up between the Stones and what's real—like a liberator fallen to the feudal temptation, or a benevolent king to decadence.

Kick me like you did before
I can't even feel the pain no more
"Rocks Off"

It was their distance from black American music and culture that had permitted the Stones to develop a radically new form of rock in the first place. Distance induces fantasies. The USA was to the early Stones a blank screen on which dreams could be projected.

Mick and Keith have been conspiring to re-invent the USA, a giant topographical fantasy, hardly less enveloping than Bertolt Brecht's and Kurt Weil's imaginary vision of America in the opera *Mahagonny*. It's become such a part of our mental furniture that we recognise it immediately as, at least, a parallel universe. Naive in the extreme, often exotic as a Japanese western, it's still funkier than the one we've got.

Where once the USA seemed an unobtainable and fantastic kingdom, it was now the Stones who appeared unobtainable to the constituents of the rock fantasy kingdom that they had invented. Although they had restored a lost American music to America, the Stones and their fans were not running along parallel lines. They came from different societies which did not share the same expectations.

But their new change into something so *literally* rich and strange was too much for some who had previously seen them as "figureheads" for a rock and revolutionary lifestyle. Richard Neville, editor of the radical psychedelic magazine *Oz*, and a prime mover in the English underground movement of the late sixties, reacted to their betrayal with a hysterical fury almost as petulant as the style of protest he was ascribing to Jagger: "On The Day The Stones Stopped Rolling," he wrote, "The wedding was stark public confirmation of the growing suspicion that Mick Jagger has firmly repudiated the possibilities of a counterculture of which his music is a part. At the church of St. Anne, Jagger put his signature on a declaration of allegiance to the system, spreading his velvet arse for the ruling class, wedding himself to the lethal values of property personal and perpetuation of an oppressive mythology. It was not the act of marriage (civil contracts being a justifiable compromise in an age of confusion) but—as with his music—

the *style* of its performance. Street Fighting Man found. Satisfaction in every pitiable cliche of la dolce capitalism, from snacks in the Cafe Des Arts ('favorite haunt of Brigitte Bardot, Sacha Distel, Noel Coward . . .') to the 75 ft. yacht hired for £3000; the kilos of caviar washed down with champagne, two gold wedding rings from the exclusive Parisian jeweler, a charter flight laden with celebrities and sycophants, all immortalized on film by good friend and Queen's cousin, Patrick Litchfield . . . The Rolling Stones have almost studiously associated their behavior and their music with the forces against law and order. Throughout the sixties both their behavior and music jostled for our attention, each in mutual reinforcement of the Stones' image. The animosity of the authorities seemed in direct proportion to the fans' affection . . . And so it happened—the Jagger myth—epitomizing multi-level protest for nearly a decade, the myth which two weeks ago exploded with the champagne corks."

Neville concluded his indictment by quoting as ironic commentary the chorus to "Dead Flowers":

'an you can send me dead flowers
ev'ry mornin'
send me dead flowers by the mail
send me dead flowers to my
wedding
and I won't forget to put roses on
on your grave

In his dogmatic diatribe, Neville seemed to miss the Stones' irony, losing his own sense of humor. "Dead Flowers" was the Stones' mockingly affectionate farewell bouquet to a wilted counterculture. With the line "I know you think you're the queen of the underground" they had buried their past connections in a graveyard pun as ghoulish as anything in Screamin' Jay Hawkins' boneyard.

All Sold Out

The Stones, through their transformation of morals and manners had become *the* aristocrats of the "adolescent mode" as sociologists referred to the age of perpetual puberty that sixties rock had brought into being. Rock stars had now replaced the old Hollywood hierarchy as a new elite in society and the Stones were *the* Princes of Pop. For the creators of a new society of perpetual adolescent *stardom*

amounted to an acceptable form of coming of age, and with their own maturity as a band. And for Mick, this was a viable compromise, because, as George W. S. Trow points out: "*Stardom* is the one adult state that inhabitants of the adolescent mode can imagine living in—because, of course, it is not really an adult state but is, rather, the ultimate adolescent fantasy of adulthood, and partly because there remains a wistful regard for the vanishing world of adulthood."

They were now, need they remind us, men of wealth and taste. Their fame and fortune had released them from the oppressive English caste system; the Stones had transcended their working class and bourgeois backgrounds that they may have considered more repressive than where they were headed. Their wealth had set them free. They were always realists, "the dividing line between art and commerce," Andrew Oldham had called them and they had never harbored any of the pieties of their more privileged counterparts, American folkies or the counterculture, about money. Their attitude towards money had always been closer to Barrett Strong's than Abbie Hoffman's. Anyway, getting that Solid Gold Cadillac (or Rose

Pink) was always part of rock dreams.

On April 6, 1971, Ahmet Ertegun, head of Atlantic Records, threw a party to celebrate the signing of a distribution deal with the Kinney Group for Rolling Stones Records. Mick's coming of age in Cannes was appropriately described in *The New Yorker* by George W. S. Trow with a sociological delicacy of perception worthy of Claude Levi-Strauss's structural analysis of Amazonian tribal caste system.

"Although the party took no coherent direction, it was interesting in that it marked the first time that Ahmet and Jagger had paced out together the territory they held in common. The exact boundaries of this territory were yet to be determined but it was clear that there would be room enough for Prince Lowenstein, Mica Ertegun and a number of other more or less well-known figures from the international cafe society including a striking American girl named Bianca Perez Morena de Macias, who was engaged to Jagger. It was clear, in fact, that in the territory in which Jagger was now to be based, he would have a certain amount to learn from Ahmet— more, perhaps, than Ahmet had to learn from him. Jagger had for years gone to parties given by rich people, and for years he had been courted by them, but he had usually made it a point to keep his edge—and his bad manners. The attitude he sought to establish was best seen, perhaps, in his song 'Play With Fire,' in which he, of course, was the fire.

"Control was what Ahmet and Prince Lowenstein had to offer the Stones. Both offered access to productive adult modes—financial and social —that could prolong a career built on non-adult principles. To make use of those modes, Jagger had only to accept the fact that he was now a known quantity: not static, exactly; capable of surprises, perhaps; but formed, established, *known*. As a known quantity, however bizarre, Jagger had something to contribute to the hegemony of the eclectic, perverse segment of the international upper class, and would be assured some permanent standing, if only as a picturesque bit. Andy Warhol, who has understood almost perfectly the social temper of his time, had successfully made this subtle move to a formidable adulthood by effecting the most minimal compromise, and Jagger was offered the same chance.

"Mick's mate, the Jaded Weasel, wasn't so eager to have his tail cut off, and socialized with the only other guest who still had one to wag. Keith Richards, the other essential Rolling Stone, left the party early. His rapprochement with society was less well established. He was looking for his

dog. 'I have to find that dog,' he said. 'That was my only friend at the party, man.' "

To the Stones' audience this new development often seemed like a betrayal. To many the Stones had become the very people they had once warned us against. Their image as jaded socialites parading an entourage of jet-set hangers-on seemed to trivialize them.

The irony of this has not been lost on the Stones themselves. "Respectable," which most listeners interpreted as a scathing portrait of Bianca, Margaret Trudeau or Jackie Kennedy, was according to Jagger originally written about the band themselves, "about how respectable we are supposed to have become as a band."

But what does an outlaw band do when it becomes *the* rock establishment? A group who in the past thrived on juxtaposing themselves to their peers with the disbanding of the Beatles and Dylan's retreat now found themselves alone in the ring. Disconnected from a counterculture they had helped to create, they often had to resort to phantom sparring partners. As their symbiotic relationship to their audience, through affluence and arrogance, began to break down, the reflections in their collective Stoney eye have (inevitably) been themselves. As Mick, especially, took narcissism one degree further than previously imaginable, he entered the most solipsistic stage of his career soon after marrying a mirror image of himself. Once prescient mediums, in their seances of blues, R & B and soul music they were now forced to distill their sound from the air-. waves.

In their second decade and with the weight of their monumental history behind them, they have had to maneuver skillfully to avoid the most insidious and insistent demand on them "to turn back the clock." Nevertheless the Stones have indulged us in this ruthless anachronistic obsession in a number of ways, tauntingly on the title song of *It's Only Rock and Roll* and literally on *Some Girls* on which they went back a dozen years for their sound.

With the release of *Some Girls* and the '78 tour, the archetypal Stones reemerged as a lean hard rock band with an album recorded close to live. Although their sound recalled the Stones of the mid-sixties, their intuitive grasp of rock dynamics enabled them to reconnect to their roots without resorting to nostalgia. If they lacked the urgency and delinquency of old, they now displayed the technique and confidence of a band that has come to terms gracefully with its own history even if we have not.

The mystery of the Stones' mechanics of ecstasy was slowly stripped down in the seventies to a series of isolated poses which called into question their original premise. But the Stones albums, through *Exile*, are for the most part a seamless, monolithic monument to white rock at its purest and most intense.

Mick's putting on of different appearances, once a genuine curiosity about trying on of interacting masks, was often reduced to foolish vanities. His fascination with surfaces, reflecting refracted images of himself and the boys in the band, once an involving narcissism, often seemed pure camp and proved embarrassing.

The enigmatic cool of those Stoney-heads of Brian, Mick and Keith, which exerted such a luminous magnetism in the sixties, dissolved, on stage at least, into Mick Jagger *and* the Rolling Stones.

This very ambivalence when combined with mimicry, archness and distance amounted, in the second decade of the Stones' history, to disconnection. If Keith with his travelling Moroccan tent, his riffs, reggae and smack had become a hermetic shadowy presence, Mick seemed the most remote.

"Well Pick Your Own Mind and Don't Touch Mine No More..."

We passionately believe that all that really matters in human life is precisely what we should be silent about. The unsayable alone has genuine value.
—Ludwig Wittgenstein, *Tractatus Logico-Philosophicus*

We have accumulated around the Stones more images than can be reconciled among themselves. We have an obscure feeling about them overlapping and want somehow to have things cleared up. But the answers we want to these questions (Who are the Stones? What did/do they mean?) are not really the answers to the questions that underly them. It is not by finding more and fresh revelations about the Stones and the connections between these enigmas that answers can be grasped, but by removing the contradictions existing between those already known and reducing their number. But will our minds, no longer vexed with Stones Static accept the obvious, and cease to ask illegitimate questions?

Illegitimate questions about the meaning, relevance and impact of the Stones songs, which began to be asked as early as the Fall of 1964 (the Stones' second U.S. tour) already alarmed Mick (slightly). With the arrival two years later of the fanzines (mimeographed magazines distributed among rock fans) *Crawdaddy* and *Mojo Navigator*, professional critics like Jon Landau emerged with the first intellectual examination of the Stones' music.

The rise of rock criticism, often accused of being a reflection of a pervasive self-consciousness in rock 'n roll, was really only a symptom of the acceptance of rock. Like the Stones, rock, through its own massive success, had ironically undermined the original antisocial stance which had given sixties rock its charge.

Illegitimate, too, are comparisons of the Stones of the sixties with today's Stones as inheritors of their former mystique. All comparison of the music of the two decades is artificial and arbitrary. The juxtapositions further contaminate the question. "All these theories about the music of the sixties and the seventies . . ." says Mick sagely, "the whole idea of decades having anything to do with it is just a journalistic convention in the first place."

Meaninglessness was a method of answering the question of meaning as each new Stones album was released. Lester Bangs on *Black and Blue*:

STATE OF THE ART: BLAND ON BLAND

There are two things to be said about the new Stones album before closing time: one is that they are still perfectly in tune with the times (ahead sometimes, trendies) and the other is the heat's off, because it's all over, they really don't matter anymore or stand for anything, which is certainly lucky for both them and us. I mean, it was a heavy weight to carry for all concerned. This is the first meaningless Stones album, and thank god. (Creem)

For a generation that had used the Stones as their autonomic nervous system for over a decade, the apparent disposability of albums like *Black and Blue* seemed a kind of relief for some from the awful tension of being locked in each other's holding patterns. But by the end of the seventies the Stones, with *Some Girls* and *Emotional Rescue*, showed they had at least one more incarnation left in them.

At the close of the Sixties the Stones had achieved an awesome status that would prove impossible, after *Exile*, to live up to. Almost nonchalantly they declined the responsibility. However, as the *Only Thing Left*, the Stones could not abdicate so easily. Over the last ten years the Stones' health or decline has taken on a symbolic significance to the rock culture as a whole. With them the fate of rock itself seemed to hang in the balance.

The Last "Last Time"

In 1977 the Stones indulged a nostalgic, revitalizing ambition to play more intimate clubs, but this was to have an unfortunate side effect and lead to the most ominous situation for the band since the London busts of Keith, Mick and Brian in 1967. Keith Richards was arrested by the Mounties on a charge of heroin possession with intent to sell, which carries a maximum penalty of life imprisonment.

The incident demonstrated that the Stones as the prime carriers of rock 'n roll anarchy were still considered a political threat by the powers that be. On their brief visit north of the border they had managed to disrupt the country, monopolize the media, "abduct" Premier Pierre Trudeau's wife and create an international incident which looked for a while as if it might topple the government. Not bad for a week's work.

Rumors of the possible survival of the Stones minus Keith, in itself an apparent contradiction in terms, led to the first serious contemplation of Life After the Stones. However, Keith said: "It was one of those weird things in Toronto. Everybody's going around talking doom and disaster, and we're up onstage at the El Mocambo and we never felt better. I mean, we sounded *great*. People were down, asking, Is this the end of the Rolling Stones? In actual fact, it was a real period of activity for us, and everybody in the band was confident. In a way, these things always bring you closer together because you've got to deal with them. What happens to me affects the whole band. But things are coming together real good now."

The specter of the last time kept recurring throughout the seventies. With it came questions about the teleology of rock itself:

KEITH: "The last time? I don't know where that comes from. Nobody in the band gives off that impression or even *thinks* that. They said it in '69, they said it in '72; why the fuck should *this* be the last time?" he asks with controlled rage. "What else are we gonna do? Get a job in an ad agency?"

CHARLIE: "Not amazed that the band is still going, just amazed they get anything together. That's our claim to fame. We're a terrible band, but the oldest. I feel like George Lewis. Yes, I know he's dead. Thanks. You know —I never got into George Lewis much. Ed Hall, now he was my favorite on the liquorice. (*New Musical Express*)

Q: Can't keep up forever?

MICK: You can't keep up with sixteen-year-old girls forever. They're demanding!

Q: People are saying rock 'n roll is dead.

MICK: My line is that rock 'n roll is a dead end for dead end people.

Ne Plus Ultra

I think of the Grateful Dead as a force field, a solid wall of energy moving forward and sweeping everybody in its path, but the Stones are very different. They work with spear thrusts, breaking through to people's minds with penetrating flashes of consciousness.—
Chip Monck

Like the speed of light in physics, Proust's grandmother in *Remembrance of Things Past*, like Muhammad Ali, Picasso and Einstein, the Rolling Stones are the constant against which all others are measuréd. They have defined what a rock band is. Keith, as the epicenter of the band, "*is* rock 'n roll"; Mick is the ultimate performer. Even the usually arch and detached *New Yorker* had to admit it:

"The Stones present a theatrical-musical performance that has no equal in our culture. Thousands and thousands of people go into a room and focus energy on one point, and something happens. The group's musicianship is of a high order, but listening to Mick Jagger is not like listening to Jascha Heifetz. Mick Jagger is coming in on more circuits than Jascha Heifetz. He is dealing in total, undefined sensual experience of the most ecstatic sort. Wagner was interested in

the idea of total art—total effect, total experience. The Stones are doing something similar. They have created something that is much closer to a complete experience than any other public entertainment available. It is compelling and it is very satisfying." (February 24, 1973)

If it is unsettling to think how inextricably meshed we are with these masters of illusion, ecstasy and irony, it is their genius and our greatest compliment to the Stones that sustains the idea that we are symbiotically, if not parasitically, connected to them. And it is hard to believe that with their dis-

banding the astral light of rock would not flicker for the last time, and with it our whole mutant life-style.

DAVID DALTON

DARK HORSES ON PARADE

RIDING
THE LAPPING TONGUE

Whether it's New York or Tuscaloosa, Norfolk or L.A., one factor is constant: The dressing room of the Rolling Stones is always Groove City—the juice flows, smoke rises, crystals crumble, poppers pop, teenies hang in and Mick knifes through like a ballet-dancing matador . . . all to the funky wail of Keith's guitar tuning up, and sometimes the honking sax of a solid, down-home pickup sideman, like Texas Bobby Keyes. And in Buddha repose, Charlie sits twirling his sticks Sid Catlett-style. Scene of good karma.

SLOW ZOOM IN ON MIRRORED FACE OF FALLEN ANGEL as Mick sits down at the lighted glass, and the make-up man leans in intensely to begin his magic ritual—transfiguration toward sympathy for the devil.

Outside in the Washington, D.C., stadium, fifty thousand fans are stomping it up to the screams of Stevie Wonder . . . while they wait it out. Like the teenies, they've been hanging in—since two o'clock this afternoon, many since the night before. Now it's 10:30; they'll soon be impatient.

Just beyond the dressing-room entrance I squeeze through the gauntlet of cops, and one of them asks for my pass. I flash it: a small, white silk banner, lettered in red, glued to my sleeve:

ROLLING STONES ACCESS GUEST
Washington, D.C. July 4, 1972

It occurs to me he should be checking sleeves in the other direction. Without the pass, would I be forced to stay in the dressing room indefinitely?

But now I'm a part of the milling crowd, and almost at once a curious man lays a hand on my sleeve, his face like that of a red fox.

"I'd read this if I were you," he says in a voice with neither warmth nor accent, and he hands me the following mimeographed sheet:

THE STONES AND COCK ROCK

If you are male, this concert is yours. The music you will hear tonight is written for your head. It will talk to you about *your* woman, how good it is to have her under your thumb, so that she talks when she's spoken to. Men will play hard, driving music for you that will turn you on, hype you up, get you ready for action . . . like the action at Altamont, San Diego, Vancouver. This is your night, if you are male. . . .

The Stones are tough men—hard and powerful. They're the kind of men we're supposed to imitate, never crying, always strong, keeping women in their place (under our thumbs). In Vietnam, to save honor (which means preserving our manhood), our brothers have killed and raped millions of people in the name of this ideal: the masculine man. Is this the kind of person you want to be? . . .

We resent the image the Stones present to males as examples we should imitate . . .

If you are female, you don't need this leaflet to tell you where to fit in. You will get enough of that tonight. If you choose to be angry, to fight, to unite with other women to smash the sexist society that has been constructed to oppress you, tonight, here —and every day, throughout America —we, the men who wrote this leaflet, will attempt, to the extent we can successfully attack our own sexism, to support your struggle.

—Men Struggling to Smash Sexism

Later, on the plane, I show this bit of weirdness to Keith. " 'Cock-rock,' " he muses with a wan smile. "So that's it. Right then, we'll use it," and he begins to beat out an eccentric tattoo on the glass holding his Tequila Sunrise, chanting Leadbelly style:

Ah'm a cock-rockin' daddy,
an you oughtta se me bla-bla-bla. . .

But the smile reflects the weariness of one too long and too profoundly misunderstood, and it doesn't sustain. "It's a drag, man, the way people dig evil— not evil itself, but the *idea* of it . . . grooving on the vicarious notion of it . . . it's *their* fascination with evil that locks us into this projection of it."

The Tequila Sunrise is a drink of exceptional excellence in every regard:

two parts tequila, three parts orange juice, one part gin, dash of grenadine.

Thus, your basic Tequila Sunrise is not merely one of those chic, absurdly yin, innocuously thirst-quenching drinks (so prized by dehydrated athletes, entertainers, and heavily dexed writers working against viciously unfair deadlines), it is also Bombsville-oh-roonie. Moreover (and here's another definite plus), the scarlet dash of grenadine into the orange, unstirred and allowed to seek its own cloudlike definition, lends the whole (in certain half-lights) an effect of advanced psychedelia.

In fact, some of our finest moments were aboard this plane, Sunrise in hand, hopping from one gig to the next—Fort Worth to Houston, Houston to Nashville, Nashville to New Orleans —short flights, and, like the dressing rooms, a boss groove and comfort to us all. The craft itself was a regular four-engine passenger plane, refurbished somewhat toward the concept of comfort and groove. A few seats had been replaced with a large buffet, always laden with endsville goodies, mostly to eat. The fuselage was emblazoned with the Stones' symbol, fashioned by Warhol, a giant, red extended tongue, not outthrust so much as lolling or lapping. Hence the craft's name, unofficially, *The Lapping Tongue* . . . or, more familiarly, *Tongue*.

The stewardesses—two fabulous teenies nicknamed Ruby T. and Brown Sugar—would begin mixing the Tequila Sunrises as soon as we started up the ramp. On most planes, of course, you can't get a drink until you're in the air—aboard *The Lapping Tongue* you usually had a drink in hand before reaching your seat.

The fantastic T. Capote joined the tour in New Orleans, and together we were soon contriving a few chuckles by way of fantasizing a nifty skyjack action and subsequent media coverage: CAPOTE SKYJACKS ROLLING STONES

WRITER'S DEMANDS FOR RETURN OF GROUP DESCRIBED AS "EXTREMELY BIZARRE"

NEW ORLEANS (AP) June 30—Well-known author Truman Capote, in what authorities termed "a curiously worded document," made known today the "conditions" under which he will release the English rock group, "The Rolling Stones," after having commandeered their private DC-7 by claiming to have "a laser beam concealed on my person." His first demand was that the plane and its passengers ("kit and caboodle") be flown at once to Peking "for immediate acupuncture treatment of the eardrums." Subsequent demands were of more complex nature, though often quite general. "Grotesquerie in high places," stated one such condition, "to cease tout de suite." Another demand concerned "authors Vidal and Mailer" and referred to "an unnatural act," though it was not specific, saying merely "as shall become them." . . .

et cetera, et cetera, building, gathering momentum, reaching out, even into areas of possibly questionable taste—certainly beyond the purview of a quality-lit mag of *SR* stamp and kidney. Suffice to say we grooved in this odd manner until the real thing came along—namely, the fabulous Brennen's restaurant where the great Tru used to dwell and it was red-carpet time for the prodigal's return. *Gumboville!* Louisiana gumbo. Surely the supreme funkiness of *haute cuisine* the world over. HOLD ON GUMBO, SHIMMERING DISC OF AROMATIC DELIGHT, MOVE IN ON SLOW WAVERING DISSOLVE, back through time and space to the Coliseum in Vancouver, on Saturday, June

3, where the tour began, as the announcer says to a hushed and darkened house: "Ladies and gentlemen, the greatest rock-and-roll band in the world—the Rolling Stones," while from the top balcony someone drops a long string of exploding firecrackers, and Mick leaps into the purple pool of light. *"Dig it!"* he screams and Jumping Jack Flash is on.

With the American tour completed, it has become apparent to certain persons who did not previously recognize it—critics and the like—that Mick Jagger has perhaps the single greatest talent for "putting a song across" of anyone in the history of the performing arts. In his movements he has somehow combined the most dramatic qualities of James Brown, Rudolf Nureyev, and Marcel Marceau. He makes all previous "movers"—Elvis, Sammy Davis, Janis Joplin, and even (saints protect me from sacrilege) the great James B. himself—appear to be waist deep in the grimpenmire. This tradition (of movin' and groovin') had its modest beginning with Cab Calloway at the Cotton Club in Harlem, where he would occasionally strut or slink about in front of the bandstand by way of "illustrating" a number. After each, he would take his bow, mopping his forehead, beaming up his gratitude for the applause as he reverted to his "normal" self for the next downbeat (and invariably a change of pace). The phenomenal thing Jagger has accomplished is to have projected an image so overwhelmingly intense and so incredibly comprehensive that it embraces the totality of his work—so that there is virtually no distinction between the person and the song. This is all the more remarkable when it is realized that there is also virtually *no connection* between the public, midnight rambler image of Jagger and the man himself. On the contrary, he is its antithesis—quiet, generous, and sensitive. What this suggests, then, is an extraordinary

potential for *acting*; and this is, in fact, his future—a future that began with his superb characterization in *Performance*, and that would have included the role of Alex in *A Clockwork Orange*, for which he was ideal, had it not been for Kubrick's aversion to big guns.

While his movements are the synthesis and distillation of all that has gone before or all that appears to be possible in and around a song on a stage, his *sound* is uniquely his own. Its roots, of course, are in the music of the black South—and, with the exception of Elvis Presley, he has done more than anyone else to liberate it from the "race record" category of limited pressings on obscure labels distributed solely in the black ghettos of America.

SLOW PULL BACK REVEALING MICK NOT ALONE ON STAGE BUT WITH SEVERAL OTHERS. PAN LEFT, IN ON KEITH. Keith creates the music to which Mick moves, and while the heaviest impact of the group is undeniably audiovisual, the sound alone has made the Stones the only white band played on a number of otherwise exclusively "black music" disc-jockey programs around the country. "I usually do it," says Keith, "with the idea of its being moved to." Yet when you hear the sheer, drifting lyricism of things like "Ruby Tuesday," "Dandelion," "She's a Rainbow," or the intricately haunting beauty of "2,000 Light Years" and "Paint It Black," one is amazed that Keith's body of work hasn't received more considered critical attention. It is certainly as deserving of such as Paul McCartney's or that of any other contemporary composer.

QUICK SLAM CUT TO BACKSTAGE IN the heart of Dixie. A short, fat man in a business suit, face perspiring, big white handkerchief in hand, trying to get into the dressing-room area and being circumvented, in a coolly muscular way, by our two black security chiefs, Stan (The Man) Moore and Big Leroy Leonard. Ever ready, I switch on my Sony cassette and move right in.

Stan (to Leroy): "Well now, he *say* he the *mayor*."

Leroy: "Shee-it."

Stan: "He *say* he want to present them the *keys to the city*."

Leroy: "Shee-it."

Turns out it *is* the mayor. So the lads dutifully assemble, and somehow (*noblesse oblige*) manage to keep a straight face while he addresses them (verbatim transcript):

Wal, ah tell you *one* thing—them boys you got there [referring to Stan and Leroy] sho do look after you, and that's a fact . . . [winks] . . . wouldn't

mind havin' a few like that mahself, hee-hee . . . wal, now then, ah got to tell you all when it comes to *music*, Law'ance Welk is moah to *mah* taste, not to say *undahstandin'*, hee hee . . . but mah daughtah, Thelma Jean, says you awright, an' ah reckon anything good enuf foah Thelma Jean, wal now, er, uh, is good enuf foah me . . . so ah want to present you boys with the *keys to this heah city*!! Now y'all enjoy yourselves, ya heah?

CLOSE UP MAYOR'S GRINNING FACE, CURIOUSLY MALEVOLENT. DISSOLVE THROUGH TO MATCH WITH SIMILAR PERSPIRING ROUND WHITE FACE, GRIM. This time it's a policeman. He's got an armlock on a young man, hustling him up the exit ramp with what appears to be undue urgency. It put me in mind of a Perelman satire on Kipling, and I wondered what the cop would think if I began jumping with glee and yelling: "Frog's march him! For God's sake, frog's march him!"

Stan looked on sadly. "Man," he sighed, "that's the hardest part of my job—trying to cool out the cops."

"Overreacting?"

"I used to call it that, but that doesn't tell the story. You see, if a man is *aware* that he's overreacting but he does it anyway, then you're into something else. The other day a police chief told me he wanted to have fifteen officers, in riot helmets, standing shoulder to shoulder in front of the stage, facing the audience. Can you dig it? *They* become part of the spectacle, like if you're playing inside a prison, or at a Hitler rally. I ask him: 'Will they have their guns drawn?' I don't think he knew I was kidding. 'They can get 'em out quick enough,' he said. You see, he was probably hoping they'd *charge the bandstand*. I mean, why should the Hell's Angels get all the publicity? That's where he was at."

MONTAGE, SERIES OF QUICK CUTS: TOP SHOT, 2,500 screamers storming the backstage area (Vancouver) after being told the concert is sold out, sending thirty-one police to the hospital. Crowd and fighting dissolve when opening chords of "Brown Sugar" are heard. CLOSE UP, Botticelli face upturned at the edge of the stage (Seattle), radiantly ecstatic as she screams at Bill Wyman: "Bill, Bill! Oh my God, you are so *stone beautiful* I can't believe it!" MEDIUM SHOT, sea of astonishment as audience stares up in narcissistic enchantment (San Francisco) at Chip Monck's fantastic forty-foot mirror slowly turning above the stage, affirming existence and placing them, for a fleeting moment at least, in the same glittering picture as the Stones. LONG SHOT from top balcony (Los Angeles) Mick Jagger quells fifth-row disturbance by taking a drink from his water jug, then dispensing contents, benediction-style, over the fray, calming them wondrously. CLOSE UP, face in twisted anguish (San Diego), screaming like a character out of Burroughs: "*I got the fear!*" while being forcibly subdued by three big cops. A red-haired girl tries to help him, is dragged away by the hair. Others join in; fighting begins. LONG SHOT, Keith swooping in and out of purple-haze spot (Tucson) with extraordinary birdlike movements. MEDIUM SHOT, young man clutching harmonica hurls himself on stage (Albuquerque) and practically into the arms of Stan the Man. The young

man's eyes are wildly alight. "I gotta blow with Mick," he's yelling. "You gotta let me do the gig with Mick!" Stan firmly escorts him away, murmuring. "Hey, baby, this isn't cool— let the cat do his thing, you do yours." A giant harness bull rushes over, truncheon at the ready and eager to use it. "No, it's cool, it's cool," says Stan and leads the boy off the stage. EXTREME

CLOSE UP, the groove and gas crag-like features of the great Chip Monck— now in gnarled concern, as he points to a jagged opening in the concrete foundation of the bandstand, where a bomb had been placed earlier in the day and had gone off prematurely. Don't tell Mick. SLAM CUT to Mick leaping into "Jumping Jack Flash"—a satyr possessed, mad dervish, speed beyond the point of no return. . . .

CLOSE UP, slender fingers racing back and forth, Paderewski-style, on edge of stage (Denver), belonging to young mystery man who follows Stones everywhere, manages to get practically *under* Nicky Hopkins's piano at each concert. Has never tried to meet him.

"One thing about Mick," someone muttered, "he goes all out—every time."

Later, over a big Teq Sun on the

Tongue, in the extreme rear of the plane (banqueted for boss comf and conviv), I gave it certain thought. True enough, I decided, there's not been one like him, nor is there apt to be. I was quaffing off the last of the T.S. in a silent toast, one hand raised toward our fabulous nifties for the old refill, when who should fall by but the great Keith himself—snarling he was, and out of sorts by bloody weirdo half.

"Have a look at this then, mate," he said, affecting a curious accent, and tossed a copy of a pop-Sun-mag-sup (*NYTimes Mag*, July 16). It was one of those stories written by someone so far removed from the scene as to be remarkable for *any* truth at all. The author was described in the square below as "the rock-music critic for the *Times*."

Then I read with some amazement that the Stones (especially as represented by Mick) have copped out, have joined the genteel elite, indeed "*have used their radicalism to gain admittance to the easy good life of wealthy members of the entertainment world's establishment.*"

I laid the rag aside and went for another Teq Sun. While standing there at the bar, I became aware of a foot-tapping melody nearby.

"What's that then?" I asked.

"Oh well, that's the Mick's new thing," was the answer. "You know, like the successful young poet asked the old poet, 'What shall I do now?' and the old poet said, '*Etonnes-moi!*' "

I listened more carefully. It was a full-on studio-type recording, quite impressive—as indeed were the lyrics. It was the title song of an album in progress, to be called *The ——— Blues*. For those readers who are into literary anagrams and the like, the omitted is a ten-letter word beginning with a "c" and ending with an "r." And it isn't "*contractor*."

TERRY SOUTHERN

OUTCASTS
ALL THEIR LIVES

Keith Richard swaggers back and forth, his eyes closed, his mouth open—displaying a distressing paucity of teeth.

He is oblivious to everything, straining in front of the microphone, grinning when he hits the right notes.

The Rolling Stones revue has finally set off on its travels around the provinces of dear old England. The first night at Manchester found the Stones adhering to the peaks set on the three-day stint held at Wembley.

The format is much the same; the band attempt an acoustic version of "Sweet Virginia" which quickly falls apart owing to faulty pick-ups, and "Silver Train" has been dropped altogether—"It sounds just a little too much like 'All Down The Line' when played live," stated Mick Taylor.

The audience for the first night leaves satisfied, a smell of sweaty denim and plimsolls hanging over the hall after their departure.

The Stones themselves travel back by coach to the Post House, an out-of-town Holiday Inn look-alike which Taylor claims was the only place that would allow the Stones to stay under its roof for two nights.

"It still goes on," he states. "None of the hotels in the center of Manchester want anything to do with us. Same with the taxi-ranks. I had to pretend I was one of Billy Preston's band to get here in the first place."

Compared to his cronies, Mick Taylor has the air of a successful worldly young executive. Dressed casually, he is both eloquent and genuinely charming, a fact that will surprise those who heard the first extremely self-conscious and awkward radio interview that Taylor was forced to take part in once he had joined the Stones. And consequently compounded their vision of the young guitarist as a timid, unworthy pretender to Brian Jones' crown.

He sips brandy and discusses the Stones' current affairs with the same measured ease and concern for precision that stand out as dominant characteristics of his peerless guitar work on stage these days.

Meanwhile, Charlie Watts aimlessly wanders around the lobby with his family in tow while Bill Wyman sits in the restaurant, his dour face contemplating the menu.

God knows, enough tall tales and horrendously murky image-weaving have been constructed around Richard since his transformation from the awkward punk Chuck Berry-Slim Harpo-styled rocker who always seemed to lose out to beautiful Brian Jones and sensual Mick Jagger when it came to getting the action, to the bone-faced hoodlum raunch connoisseur toting a powerful drug-oriented mysterioso, topped off with a hornet's nest of black hair and a bone earring.

Remember when Kenneth Anger called him "the devil's right-hand man"? Or the grandiose tales of decay and debauchery that followed the Stones, and particularly Richard, on the 1972 American tour, which were borne out in part by a constant stream of photographs that appeared throughout the media displaying Keith splayed out on a sofa unconscious, eye-makeup running and a look of total collapse on his wasted features.

No one quite knew which member of the Stones would take over as the most publicly persecuted of the band,

but Richard has certainly taken the lion's share this time around to the extent that many have almost seemed to will their own perverse death-wish fantasies on him.

We all need someone we can bleed on, but Keith Richard is in no way a wasted victim of his own image, nor is he some incoherent zombie biding his time.

Richard sniggers hazily and stares down at the table focusing on nothing in particular. He's swaggered over to Mick Taylor's table and now talks in a stoned drawl which never seems to lapse into the realms of incoherence, though it sometimes teeters on the edge.

No clumsy pauses occur during the conversation either: in his own excessively laid-back zone of activity, Richard is an animated conversationalist.

"Y'see, I don't really give a damn what they—what the Media or whatever you call 'em—write about me.

"Y'know, I'd just like to see all those cocksuckers spending an hour on stage doing what I do, and see how they stand up to it. I just presume they

are just the lowest as far as I'm concerned. I mean, the guy on Sunday, who was causing that disturbance, was just looking for a chance to get into some violence. He must have been frustrated or something.

"Anyway after the show, he had all his commissionaire chums standing on some scaffolding going like this (he pulls a particularly ludicrous grimace). So Mick and I threw some coke bottles at 'em."

Richard drags a hand through his black, matted locks and lights up another cigarette:

"I suppose I should add that the press have also helped me. I mean, the *Sunday Times* helped us obviously over that bust, but another time, a few years ago when I was on tour, the Home Office were getting very stroppy about Anita being in the country and were all ready to throw her out. So we went to the *Daily Mirror* or one of those papers, and afterwards the Home Office dropped it like a hot brick. So they can help too."

A plate of pancakes was ordered, and Keith starting digging into them lethargically with his fork. How did

"I mean, all those jet setters must be bored or something. They seem to be on this massive ego trip anyway, which I just don't want to know about.

"All I can say is—those people will not be around a second time. *There's no way they're going to be in our company ever again.*"

How did Richard's much-vaunted meeting with Bob Dylan at Jagger's 1972 Birthday Party go?

"It was very nice actually. I hadn't seen him since the *Blonde On Blonde* era. Changed a lot. Yeah, he seems to be very domesticated. Hard to say from meeting the cat at a party."

"I think everyone expects too much from Bob Dylan," added Mick Taylor. "You can't keep on creating the things he was doing at that intensity."

Keith: "He'd have to put himself back into a very fragile position to create anything like that again. He just couldn't do that, because if he hadn't stopped in the first place, he would have been dead."

Surely, though, the Stones are legendary for their sustained journey close to the edge these past ten years?

Richard continued: "Yeah, but you

pretty old. 'A Hundred Years Ago' was one that Mick had written two years ago and which we hadn't really got around to using before."

Keith: " 'Comin' Down Again' is my song, yeah—no, 'Starfucker' is all Mick's. 'Dancing With Mr. D' is my riff and Mick's lyrics. I tend to work more on riffs while Mick has finished songs.

"Definite guitar parts? Well the thing is that on most tracks there are a number of guitar tracks so you can really distinguish who's playing what. Mick Jagger plays guitar on 'Silver Train' and 'Winter,' while the other line-ups always seem to be different. Like, 'Heartbreaker' has Billy Preston on keyboards, Mick Taylor on wah-wah, and me on bass."

Why were the Stones not including any material predating "Jumping Jack Flash" in their current live set?

"Actually we were doing a bunch of old numbers when we were touring Australia. 'Route 66' we did, uh . . . 'Bye Bye Johnny' and 'It's All Over Now.'

"One thing about working up the old songs is that Mick Taylor doesn't know 'em and would have to learn 'em

have nothing better to do, or that they're hard up for a story, or whatever.

"It still goes on and I just go along with the 'Bad publicity is better than no publicity' idea. I mean, if they wrote about me as the sweet, gentle, loving family man, it would probably do me more damage! And be equally untrue.

"They don't know anything anyway. They'll just blow anything up out of all proportions like that 'Ron Wood to replace Keith Richard' story which started off as a mildly funny drunken joke we thought up at Tramps one night, and which Fleet Street got hold of and blew up.

"Same with the busts. Everyone thinks I've been busted hundreds of times when in fact this now is only the second time I've ever been brought up before a court. I mean Mick Jagger's been busted more than I have, but because you're a celebrity or whatever, everyone gets to hear about it.

"It's the same with jobsworths, who

he and Taylor feel about the reputation the Stones had picked up, particularly on the last Stateside tour, as being the latest international playboy-jetset elite chic thrill?

"Personally I just don't want to know about 'em. I mean, how they get in there and why they're there in the first place, I don't really know."

Taylor broke in: "They seem to like indulging in the popular extravagances of the time, especially Americans who are very publicity-conscious anyway. Now we leave it to Pete Rudge, and as you must know, the organization is incredibly tight."

Richard came back into the conversation: "It's a difficult thing to handle anyway, because it starts with things like—'Oh, Truman Capote is going to come along and write something on the Stones'—and he comes along and brings along Princess Lee Radziwill and some other socialites from New York and you're surrounded by those people. And it just takes one guy like Capote to trigger it off."

see Bob Dylan was by himself. With us there's always been someone there to grip the reins when it's necessary."

Richard seemed slightly more comfortable discussing the Stones' music.

"I guess I like *Beggars Banquet* the best of everything we've done. *Let It Bleed* was a good album too. I'd like to have a single album compilation of my favorite *Exile On Main Street* tracks, though I still feel that the amount of material we had at that point warranted a double-album, even if they are always too long. I really like the new one actually. I enjoyed recording in Jamaica."

Mick Taylor stated that the album was recorded relatively quickly: "The backing tracks were all done in Jamaica. We started off with 'Winter' which was just Mick (Jagger) strumming on a guitar in the studio, and everything falling together from there.

" 'Angie' and 'Dancing With Mr. D' were recorded in the middle of the sessions and 'Starfucker' was about the last. Some of the songs used were

from the beginning. I mean, there are songs like 'Have Mercy' which I'd love to work up again.

"Another reason for us not doing old songs is that Decca have stopped us from releasing new live versions of material recorded on their label.

"A whole live album with Stevie Wonder on it recorded on the American tour has been scrapped because they've ballsed that up. They've got those songs for six years or something.

"I mean, if we're recording a live show with old numbers on it, we just can't put the motherfucker out in the first place because recordings of those songs belong to them until 1976 whatever.

"Sure, I don't really mind them packaging old stuff if they use a little bit of imagination, but putting out old flipsides as singles is shit.

"Decca are supposed to be making records but they might just as easily be making baked-beans."

So how were relations currently with Atlantic records?

"Uh, comfortable, y'know. They've tried to balls about a bit with this latest album.

"They've given us a lot of trouble over 'Starfucker' for all the wrong reasons—I mean, they even got down to saying that Steve McQueen would pass an injunction against the song because of the line about him. So we just sent a tape of the song to him and of course he okayed it. It was just a hustle though. Obstacles put in our way."

What about the notorious incident when Jagger and Richard were both ordered offstage during a Chuck Berry concert by the man himself?

"Ah yes. I don't know the real reasons because Chuck Berry is real weird.

"But the situation arose, I imagine, because I was given this huge great amplifier and he had this tiny Jewel reverb, so there was no way I could turn down and still not over-power him.

"I was just trying to play as quiet as possible—anyway I came on with Dr. John and Mick was standing at the back of the stage, and it developed into a little ego thing where the people were paying more attention to his backing band than they were to him. It's a shame actually because the two numbers we actually played together were great, y'know."

Richard shrugs and orders a final vodka. Anita has disappeared from the lobby.

"Right now, I'm sticking pretty much to playing rhythm onstage. It depends on the number usually, but

since Brian died I've had to pay more attention to rhythm guitar anyway. "I move more now simply because back when we were playing old halls I had to stand next to Charlie's drums in order to catch the beat, the sound was always so bad.

"I like numbers to be organized— my thing is organization, I suppose— kicking the number off, pacing it and ending it.

"Either I fuck it up completely or it really comes together. Like, last night I dropped my pick twice and stepped on my leads in the last number."

He grins, scratches his head, extends a handshake and leaves to get changed for tonight's show. "Gotta put my make-up on 'aven't I."

On the coach, Charlie Watts and wife are entertaining his parents who have come down for the gig. Mick Jagger wanders in and partakes in an animated talk with a juvenile brat wearing a David Bowie hair-cut and the looks of a barely pubescent Gary Glitter—"Wanna souvenir? Want my shoes? Get away with ya. Y' not 'avin' my watch! Wan' my cock?"

The show that night is somehow now stupendous. The crowd are up the moment the band saunters onstage. The Stones transcend all peaks previously set at their current English gigs and perform a beautiful version of "Angie" with Jagger actually singing it in key.

A wild, wild evening indeed and, y'know, throughout the show Keith never dropped the pick once.

NICK KENT

ON THE ROAD TO BUFFALO

There's a lot of difference between being in the studio, or sitting around your hotel room and and sweating it out onstage every night for two hours," Keith said. "The band plays every night and the musicians trim off all excess flab . . . all the bullshit. And you end up with the basic fundamentals glowing brightly."

"I don't consider myself the best rock star and I never have," said Mick Jagger. "There are a lot of people who are good, and since I'm not really interested in white rock and roll I never go and see 'em." But you do, you've seen Clapton, and Zeppelin, and Bowie. "Well, to be honest, I'm checking out the sound systems," Jagger laughed.

"I'm sure there are people who are better than I am, there must be, because I'm not very good. But I don't really care. The Rolling Stones have never said they were the best rock and roll band or the greatest, ever. If you can find me a quote where we said we were . . ."

May 15, 1975: Peter Rudge's office: Discussing what to do to open the outdoor shows, Jagger said, "Those kids are all on downs, aren't they? They take some quaaludes and then some more downs and smoke pot and then they take heroin and then some cocaine and then some Ripple wine, right? Maybe we should all get together in here and take all of that stuff and see what we would feel like and what would entertain us . . ."

Someone mentions Altamont and Mick looks weary. "Oh, I don't know," he said, "People tell me all the time that they had a good time there. Kids arrivin' the day before . . . campin' out and all that. Sometimes I think the only two people who didn't have a good time there was me and the guy that got killed.

"You know, I tried to explain this to someone the other day," Mick said, "and he couldn't understand. I said that rock and roll exists on all these different levels of music, and music exists on different levels. I've been playin' rock and roll and blues, and I started playin' blues when I was very young. 14 . . . and that was mature music compared to 'Venus in Blue Jeans' which was the hit at the time I started. The band I was in at the time was playin' music written by 40-year-old men. So this guy says to me the other day, 'You're over thirty, how can you write rock and roll songs?' But I started off by singing songs written by 40, 50, 60-year-old men . . . 'You Gotta Move' was written by a 70-year-old man, I mean what does it matter. The thing about rock and roll is—I never wanted to be a rock and roll star. I've never been into singing teenage lyrics, and when I started I did these songs written by old people. Perhaps that's why people were sometimes shocked by my lyrics . . . well, not shocked, but interested, at a point where there was no real interest in lyrics . . ."

Baton Rouge, June 1: The assembled journalists spend a lot of time sitting around discussing whether the Stones are still relevant while they wait to talk to Mick. Jagger is shown an article that claims he doesn't want *Cocksucker Blues* to be shown. "I'd like to reply to that actually," he said, "I *would* like to get it out. But there's no way we can get releases from some of the people in it."

Kansas City: In his room alone, watching Elvis on TV, Jagger makes a face. "Owwwh, he's *awful*," Mick says, "No, he's *not* a parody of himself, that's what he *is*." At three a.m. the band rehearses in a basement ballroom. Jagger leans back in a chair at the very end of the room, watching the others. "This is when this band sounds the best," Ian Stewart says, nodding his head in appreciation.

On the plane to Milwaukee: Keith dashes on, grabs the *New York Times* out of Jagger's hands. "Aha!" Keith says, "the reviews . . ." Mick cracks up then, in his very best Monty Python high shriek says, " 'He wrapped his mystique around him like a Gothic cloak' . . . not bad, actually."

Then, "Uh . . . do you feel that you are a member of this group as much as . . . uh . . . you felt when you woke up or do you feel that your rebellion is less than when you . . . uh . . . formed the group last night?"

Attempting to talk seriously about the press, Mick said, "I don't read any of the analytical stuff, those are the ones that I skip. I only look at the front pages or the pictures, actually. Someone asked me if I minded bad reviews, and I said no. As long as my picture is on the front page, I don't care what they say about me on page 96."

"Well, I don't have that many problems, so if others do, then I don't mind dealing with them. Maybe I just ignore my problems . . . I mean, of course I have problems, but not really day to day ones because I have people to look after me, y'know? I'm very lucky, I don't have to pack my bags, I don't have to worry about my airplane, I don't have to worry about my cars. But then you have a lot of people who have emotional problems, and I don't." No tragic lost love? "No . . . it just doesn't exist . . . you know what I mean. I'm very happy." No loneliness? "Lonely . . . no, not lonely at all. Why should I be? I have my dearest friends with me, Keith, Charlie . . . most of the band are my friends, and a lot of other people who have been my friends for years . . . It's not like I'm on tour and I'm the Lonely Rock Star. I mean forget it, doesn't apply to me."

Boston: Jagger is in his room, preparing to go to the gig around five in the afternoon. Clutching a copy of *Creem* and laughing, he says, "*Look* at what she did to this poor boy from Aerosmith," he gasps to Annie Leibovitz. Well . . . he thinks he's doing you, I venture. "She is dear, she is." In a rare appearance on this tour Marshall Chess is practically *onstage* at the Boston Gardens . . . halfway between an amp and . . . right in the *spotlight*; grinning, bobbing in time to the music. ("Didja see Marshall on drums?" Rudge said later.) Racing out of the Boston Gardens Rudge turns and yells to some music business types, "*Come* on . . . you gotta keep up wif' us . . . this ain't fuckin' Slade, y'know . . ." and then, "Oh! . . . There's someone from Yes. Run him over, they beat us in the *Creem* Poll. . . ."

Mick: "When you're on a big tour, and people expect a lot from you, there's a lot of pressure. You have to learn to relax certain periods of the day. The more you bring yourself to relax, whatever method you use to do that, the better it is. Because when you're trying to make it, all your energy is put into trying to make it. Then you realize you have to spend a lot of time cooling out. You have to be calm and effective and all your judgments are balanced because after awhile the pressure gets so much that a lot of bands just freak out on the road. Which has always been a thing of humor with us . . . if you can keep the humor it's all right. People have a lot of different ways of letting out their inhibitions. Sex . . . like they fuck a lot, or destroy rooms . . . all this frustration. One takes it out on things —another on people. I don't honestly think that those are the best ways of doing it. I think sex is quite important, sex does give you a lot of release from tension. I get a lot of release of tension just physically anyway . . . onstage, so I don't have a physical problem like that. If I was standing still like Bill I think I'd go mad."

"I'm an introverted person," Bill Wyman said when asked about his lack of movement, "I don't really move because I don't feel natural movin'. If I did move it would look wrong . . . very false. But there's no *tension*, really. I sort of just get right into whatever's happenin' in the audience . . . things that happen between people in the audience, reactions to what Mick does . . . I think that's really interestin', it's a lot of fun. Especially if the audience is aware of me watchin' them, then some funny things happen. But none of the rest of the band is aware of that either, y'know. They think I just stand there as well, and don't sweat all over. I present myself to the audience performin', but not in a jump-around way. I get off on a few things, I dig it, I really do. But Mick isn't aware of that . . . or Keith, or Charlie, and probably eighty per cent of the audience isn't. But the people around my area are."

In the Milwaukee hotel Keith and Ronnie are being "interviewed" by some Chicago journalists in Keith's room. Huge red carpet-covered speakers, tape recorder and stereo take up half the room. The atmosphere is smoky; red scarves cover the lamps and dim the lights. The smell of incense as well as a pungent French perfume fills the air. "I'm going to put some of the new Stones tapes on and see if any of 'em pick up on it," Keith mumbles, aside, and of course the reporters, having to practically lean *into* Keith's face to hear what he's saying, don't. Someone asks him why so many other groups give more access to the press and Keith smiles and says, "Less people want to write about 'em . . ."

In 1963 a "bio" penned by Brian Jones and sent to Stones fan club head Doreen Pettifer described his eyes as "Red (and bloodshot)." One inquired as to Keith's health: "I couldn't possibly do what I do onstage if I didn't care," he said. "People worry about you; they should worry about themselves. I haven't heard too much of that on this trip, however." Well . . . perhaps it has something to do with the fact that you and Ronnie smile at each other onstage so much. "Yes, but does a smile mean you're healthy? I mean you could be dying of cancer and still raise a smile occasionally. Fuck . . . yeah, I'm very grateful for people that worry about me and all, but it's really a waste of time. I've got it under control as best I can, as well as anyone else. Probably better, if I can exercise the ego for a minute . . . and anybody that worries about me really shouldn't." Are you ever scared onstage? "Scared? No, what is there to be scared of? It's the best part of the day."

Washington, D.C.: Talking in the dressing room to the Russian cultural attaché, Mick tells of when they first tried to set up a Russian tour and he was asked what he would do to improve cultural standards of Russian youth. "I said that I thought they could improve their own cultural standards without any help from me," Jagger said. "Oh, that's too philosophical for me," the Soviet diplomat replied. "Got out of that one, didn't he?" Jagger said later.

Peter Rudge has an idea to use elephants in Memphis, as security, perhaps. Someone suggests that Mick ride one onstage. "This is beginnin' to sound an awful lot like Chip Monck," one of the stage crew mumbles under his breath. "But what would the elephant be wearin'?" Rudge asks slyly. "Better ring up Giorgio and get a bit o' chiffon . . ." Determined to get the elephants in somehow when the day finally arrives, Rudge asks, "There's no way we can get 'em walking around through the crowd? No? Well, can one elephant stand on top of another one?"

Los Angeles, the L.A. Forum: Photographer Christopher Sykes crashes into Bill Wyman coming out of his dressing room. "Ah!" Wyman shouts, "spoiling my solitude before the show!!" In Brian Jones' 1963 "bio" Wyman is listed as: "Bass, works during the day as storekeeper or some-

thing equally horrible. Only member of band married, only one who'll ever be married." Wyman, described in the Boston *Globe* as "his onstage demeanor akin to that of your friendly undertaker" is actually one of the wittiest men on tour. Surveying himself in the mirror in a skintight lizard and leather outfit he said, "If I wear pants like this for the whole tour I'll never be able to produce another child."

Ryan O'Neal is insulted that he has to pay for his tickets, so he returns them. Lorna Luft seems bedazzled by Bianca Jagger. She follows Madame around for several days like a puppydog until Bianca is compelled to remark to a friend, "I do think it a bit strange that all we ever talk about is me."

In the dressing room one night I hear the strains of "Happy." Ah, Keith's song I say, jumping up. "Are you kidding?" laughs a friend, "they're *all* Keith's songs."

Keith has received a letter from a girl who says she's a great guitar player *and* a great fuck. She has stopped by to see him and will hopefully get to play for him. While he's still asleep in the other room she sits on an amp and plays some Chuck Berry styled guitar. It soon becomes apparent that her desire is to play . . . *onstage*—with the Stones. At the *Forum.* "Are you kidding? They'd *never* do that," says a friend. "A chick?? Onstage? With the Stones?" he goes off chuckling. "I just want to strut," she says. "I know if I played with them they'd dig it . . . I could take them into a whole other thing, the thing of a girl onstage with them. Listen, I've jammed with a lot of people . . . Fanny . . . Isis asked me to be their guitar player. I'm not a groupie, and I'm not impressed. I'm a player, I was asked here, I thought I was going to play. At least jam with them . . ." Later Keith is leaving for the gig and leans out the car door to say to her, "Look, come around, or call me later, but about joining the Stones—I mean forget it, it's done.

"You know with Ronnie we seem to be able to get back to the original idea of the Stones, when Brian was with us in 1962, '63," Keith tells me. "Two guitars has always been my particular love because I think there's more that can be done with that combination than almost any other instrument. But what screws most of that up, and this is the bag I fell into with Mick Taylor—whom I love dearly and I think is one of the most incredible guitar players in that kind of music you'll ever get a chance to hear—is that there's this phony division between lead and rhythm guitar. It does not exist. Either you're a guitar player or you're not. And if you are a guitar player playing with another guitar player, there's no point in designating one thing to one . . . there's no freedom there.

"This way with Ronnie is more like what is was with Brian, because we had basically the same ideas about guitar when Brian was still very interested in guitar. It's two guitar players and one sound.

"I always love how sometimes you say, 'So glad to be here in . . . ummmm . . . errr . . .' and then you clear your throat," Annie Leibovitz laughs with Mick, "when you forget where the hell you are . . ." It always gets such a huge response, I say. "I know," Mick cracks up, "they're all so proud of their grotty old towns . . ."

"Every night I go out there and say to myself, please God please, don't let Jagger pull my wig off," Preston laughed. Following an introduction at Madison Square Garden where Mick introduced Billy as *This is Billy Preston, he's staying at the St. Moritz and he likes white boys!* " Jagger later laughed, "I can't say *anything* at all about boys . . . blacks . . . faggots . . . white boys . . . onstage, *or* off."

THE ACTS MICK JAGGER IS SCARED TO PERFORM

"I am inhibited onstage," Mick Jagger admitted. "To a certain extent, yeah . . . I mean there are certain things you wouldn't do. I wouldn't throw myself into the crowd . . . sometimes I feel like doin' that though. When we played that really hot gig I just felt like takin' all my clothes off." Why didn't you, then? "Well, I'm inhibited. Besides, I'd probably get arrested.

"I can't say that I feel like that every day, it's just one thing I can think of. Physical limitations and yes, I have inhibitions because I have to play within a musical reference. If you wander too far away from it, then the band gets lost and I mean if I just completely went off, which I can do at certain points, and lost control then it would be very exciting, but the band wouldn't know what I was doing. And I mean you can't *warn* the band and say, 'Well, I'm going to lose control *here*,' because you don't know if you will or where.

Jacksonville: Later Mick was talking about women: "People always give me this bit about us bein' a macho band," Mick said, "and I always ask them to give me examples . . ." "Under My Thumb" . . . "Yes, but they always say 'Starfucker', and *that* just happened to be about someone I knew.

"There's really no reason to have women on tour," he continued, "un-

less they've got a job to do. The only other reason is to fuck. Otherwise they get bored . . . they just sit around and moan. It would be different if they did everything for you, like answer the phones, make the breakfast, look after your clothes and your packing, see if the car was ready, and fuck. Sort of a combination of what Alan Dunn does and a beautiful chick."

Hampton Roads, Virginia: I'm drinking white wine in the dressing room and Bill Wyman says menacingly, "Don't drink that." What? "No, seriously," he says, deadpan: "Y'know sometimes we can't control ourselves. Once me and Brian and Keith were in Germany and these cops outside the dressing room were hassling the kids and we got so annoyed with them that we poured out half a bottle of whiskey and pissed into it, and offered them the bottle. 'Here,' we said. 'Have one on us,' and they said 'Thanks man' . . . raised the bottle, and drank it."

Jacksonville, Keith's room: The sound is down on the TV set and people (some members of the band and a few friends) listen to new Stones and reggae tapes. Jim Dandy comes on the screen and everyone watching cracks up at his facial grimaces. "Well . . . so far I *like* his *face*," Mick camps. At the end of the song he mumbles, "It's a living . . ." Linda Ronstadt is on next, and Ronnie yells *"Hurry* up ! ! !"

Buffalo, last stop on the Tour of the Americas: Again, Keith's room, eight or nine in the morning. Billy, Keith, Mick and Ronnie have listened to Rod Stewart's new LP, made copies of tapes for each other to take home, talked for hours about music, ordered breakfast and now watch Frankie Valli being interviewed by Dinah Shore. "No wonder they didn't put your picture on the Four Seasons album cover," someone says, "LOOK AT HIS JEWELRY ! !" Mick screams. "C'mon Frankie, show us your belly chain ! !" Keith yells. Collapsing into giggles all around.

"I've had two showers and one bath since the start of the tour and I still smell sweeter than Jagger," Keith laughed on the way to the final concert.

"There is a perpetual adolescent influence," Jagger said during the tour, "because what I was doing when I was eighteen I'm doing now. I mean the room I had at the Olympic Hotel in Seattle is the same room I would have had in 1964. I mean it wasn't any grander, it was the same room. And I'm doing the same things, slightly different of course. Instead of traveling on commercial planes we've got our own, but it's still the same thing. And the responsibilities I have are much less than someone who used to come to our concerts when they were 17 and now they've gotten married and have five children and two cars and three mortgages. I'm married and have children and all that, but I don't sort of worry about it because I'm doing what I did before . . . when I was an adolescent. I only discovered this really by looking at other people in rock and roll . . . it perpetuates your adolescence, for good or bad.

"I don't know if it's good or bad, because I can't evaluate it. It feels real nice and I don't give a shit . . . I don't feel responsibilities other people feel. Obviously, bein' in a rock band makes you more adolescent than if you worked in an IBM company and really had to worry about your future. I don't worry about the future. I'm living out my adolescent dreams perpetually."

LISA ROBINSON

TOO STONED TO ROLL?

The Continuing Stones' Saga, Live from Frankfurt, Germany

The nice thing about the law of gravity is that it applies to *everybody*. You mess with the law of gravity, man, you get your center of gravity at too acute an angle to your feet and bubeleh, you're gonna fall on your rosy ass, and that's *fact*. Basically, the law of gravity don't give a flying one if you're President of the United States or Princess Anne or—da da ba da daba da da—Keith Richard. The guitarist, songwriter and social arbiter to a whole generation of middle-class drug abusers, skids wildly on the polished, dragon-painted portable stage that the Rolling Stones are using on their '76 Tour of Europe and takes a dive in front of 10,000 earnest young Frankfurters right in the middle of "Jumpin' Jack Flash."

It don't faze ol' Keith none, though.

Ol' Keith just collects his legs until he's sitting in some kind of weird discombobulated lotus posture and continues whacking away at his guitar, not missing a single saw-toothed rusty chrome chord the whole time.

It don't faze Mick Jagger either— Mick Jag-gur *performing* on the ramp that leads down into the audience from stage center like the tongue on the Stones logo. Jagger just flounces over to his fallen comrade, or something and he bends down oh-so-graceful and hands Keith his pick—which the maestro has dropped on his journey from here to there—and helps him locate his legs and jack-knife back on to his feet.

The new Stones show is prefaced by an admirable cassette tape of exclusively black and mostly pretty tough dirt-yard black music. It's got Bo Diddley doing "You Don't Love Me," and some Robert Johnson and Earl Hooker, plus some real dirty-ass JA juice, intermingled with some soupy modern falsetto creamy pimp-suit crooning.

The journalistic herd in the cattle-pen press section right under the left speaker banks plays conjecture poker and comes to the conclusion that the drunk-and-dirty-mo'-dead-than-alive stuff was Keith's choice and the well-groomed shot-silk pimpmobile muzak was Jagger's, which is about 50% correct, since we later ascertain that our phantom deejay is none other than Honest Ron Wood, with a few additions made by Big Mick.

Charlie (ah, Charlie's good tonight, inne? Whaddya mean, scumbag, Charlie's good *every* night) lights the fuse on that snare-bass drum-and-cowbell intro to "Honky Tonk Woman." Keith, leaning backwards from the knees, methodically chops out those measured opening chords like each chord was a white line on a mirror, Jagger prowls the stage like he's sniffing each bit of it for a particular odor—like a dog trying to remember just where he pissed the night before —and yep, it's the Rollin' Stones right enough. Know 'em anywhere.

The Great Charlie Watts is playing so clean and crisp and precise that it's almost a shock to pick up on the fact that there's also a ridiculous amount of muscle in his barebeat. Even allowing for the fact that Ollie Brown, a lean black denim percussionist, is whoppin' ass on various passive objects right behind him, it's clear just who's down in the engine room hefting the coal

into the furnace.

Next up they do "All Down The Line" off *Exile On Main Street*, and halfway through someone wakes up behind the mixing desk and cuts in the afterburners on the guitars. It happens in midchord and suddenly a Keith-chord comes scything out of the speakers and slices the top of my head off. I suddenly feel that my skull's just done bin metamorphosed into a two and a half minute softboiled egg and that some intensive bastard is about to dig in with a spoon and eat my brains up.

Messrs. Wood and Richard flanked Jagger, looking for all the world like a pair of diseased crows.

They're a remarkably well-matched pair both eyewise and earwise. Eyewise, they were like bookends propping up the Jagger Library Of Poses; and Wood's extrovert contrast to Mick Taylor's studious angelic self-effacing whiz-kid-in-the-shadows-next-to-Bill concentration erodes Richard's previously obvious Number Two Son position. He's taken over some of the backing vocals that used to be Richard's, and his cheery scampering about and winning ways with a cigarette butt set off the traditionally limned legendary Jagger and Richard stage mannerisms.

Earwise he works out infinitely better than I'd foreseen (or foreheard).

Here, operating as an extension of Richard, filling out Rock and Roll Himself's riffs and squeezing curlicues out of the lead guitar tube to put the icing on the cake, he got it on with a ferocious energy and a commendably disciplined and canny channeling of same. Nobody gets to be self-indulgent except You Know Who.

Jagger prowls and struts and minces and flounces like a faggot chimpanzee, his whole body one big pout. His moves are athletic/gymnastic rather than balletic, like a calisthenics programme designed by the Royal Canadian Air Force.

He shoulders into Ronnie Wood, limpwrists so extravagantly that the movement spreads right up his arm to his shoulder, and niggers outrageously between numbers, going "All *right!*" and *"Yeah!"* and "Ssssssssu*guh!*" like he was Isaac Hayes or somebody.

The only time he stays still is when he sits down behind the electric piano for "Fool To Cry," one of the four numbers they do off *Black And Blue*.

They do "Get Off My Cloud," "You Can't Always Get What You Want," "Happy" (which Jagger caps with a heavily sarcastic, "Fank you Keef. That wos *great*"), "You Got To Move" (with Keith standing back to spin out the guitar lines and Jagger, Preston, and Wood clustered round the mikes),

"Brown Sugar" (audience really picking up on the "Yeah . . . yeah . . . yeah . . . shooooo!" bits) and an oddly perfunctory "Midnight Rambler," which doesn't really play tug-o'-war with your nerves the way it oughtta despite the ritual whipping of the stage with the hallowed silver belt and not-quite-dramatic-enough lighting changes. Wood doesn't have the crystalline snaky lead/firing from the hip rhythm purity as Richard/Taylor, but it's so raunchy that if it moved in next door your lawn wouldn't even wait around long enough to die, it'd move to a nicer neighborhood.

The trouble is that Jagger's cosmic inflation of spoiled brattishness has been so crudely exaggerated that it's stylized itself up its own ass. It's a good show, sho' nuff, but he comes on so strong that it just degenerates into hamming.

After the show I went back up to my room and had a smoke. Somebody spoke and I went into a dream. I had me a dream that made me sad, about the Stones and the. . .

In my dream, Dave Walters from WEA ushered me and three other rockpress folks into Ronnie Wood's room so that we could like *hang out.*

The end of the room we're in is occupied by a sofa, a table, a gang of chairs and a mammoth sound system blasting out Maceo Merriweather, Fury Lewis, Robert Johnson and good reggae. Over at the big table, Keith Richard, who looks—let's just say "tired"—is giving an interview to a Swedish radio guy.

A seat at The Captain's Table had fallen vacant, so I annexed it just as Keith started into answering someone's question about why all the stuff on *Black And Blue* was a year or more old.

I asked him what happened to the stuff they'd cut with Jeff Beck.

"We didn't do any songs; we just played and sometimes the tapes were rolling and sometimes they weren't."

So how was it?

Irritable flicker of the eyes. "You know Jeff. Sometimes 'e was brilliant and sometimes it was rubbish. Ronnie can tell you far more about Jeff Beck than I can anyway."

Richard assembles refreshments delicately on the table in front of him, emits a resounding *snfff* and leans headlong into the next question.

"I only really listen to black music these days." says Richard, *snfff.* "I ain't too interested in white bands who rip off white bands who ripped off black bands."

Ronnie Wood wanders over and hands Richard a fragment of cigarette packet with something written on it. Richard scans it, *snfffs* it, and looks at me very hard. He also makes no attempt to pass his refreshments around.

That fragment of my conscious mind which is monitoring the dream wonders, "Is this some masterly demonstration of Zen and the art of Cool Maintenance, or is the guy the most outrageous bogarter in Christendom?"

Keith looks at the note and then back at me.

Though I'm sitting opposite him, in some weird floating dream way I can read the note. It says, "Keith—do you realize that you're talking to Charles Shaar Murray?" [*Murray gave* Black And Blue *a bad review in the English weekly* New Musical Express—*Ed.*] I *must* be dreaming—big rock stars passing notes in class.

"I read your review, Charles, and I thought it was rubbish," Keith says suddenly and, staring defiantly around the table to dare anyone to call him out, snarfs loudly. Weirdass dream. Nick Kent told me that when Keith gets annoyed he throws ashtrays.

"Yeah, well," I say, "I thought the album was pretty disappointing."

"Most people like it," he comes back. "Did you write that just to be different, then?"

"Naw, most people I know thought it was dreadful too."

"Maybe you ought to broaden your circle of acquaintances," he said.

"Oh, I dunno . . . it's getting broader all the time."

"There was something in your review," sez Honest Ron, "that Keith got really upset about. I can't quite remember what it was, but . . . I'm surprised that he didn't take it up with you."

From beyond Wood comes a sound exactly like Mick Jagger saying in his proletarian voice, "Ol fort your review was bahluddy stoopid."

Mentally shutting out these disturbing hallucinations within the dream, I carry on talking to Wood.

"OL FORT YOUR REVIEW WOS BLAHHDY STOOPID!"

Louder this time. Omigawdomigawdomigawd. This is a dream. This is a dream. Even if it wasn't, that bit wouldn't be happening. Do not panic. Think only of yourself. Do . . . not . . . panic.

Jagger gets up and flounces away to talk to Paul Wasserman, a heavy-set bearded very straight looking American who's doing the tour P.R.

Shortly after Dave Walters from WEA comes over to me. He's turned green.

"Paul Wasserman's just told me that Mick said that if you're not out in 30 seconds he'll get the heavies to throw you out."

Just past the threshold, Keith appears looking placatory.

"Look," he says in conciliatory tones, "*Jagger . . .*" he enunciates the name in less than admiring tones, a sort of aw-come-on-you-know-what-he's-like intonation. "*Jagger* wants to go over some songs and rearrange the set. We're probably havin' a party in Billy Preston's room when 'e gets back from eatin' . . . give us yer room number and I'll give you a buzz later on."

We roll a smoke, light it up.

As soon as it gets to Keith, he says, "What's your number? 572? Okay, talk to you later," and vanishes into the

room with it. We are left staring at the door.

Then, just after I'd checked out, the porter rushed over to the cab and handed me this envelope marked "Charles Murray Room 572." Inside was a note scrawled in red felt-tip on a torn-out page of the tour program.

And this is what it said?

"Dear Charles (The disappointed man):

"Just to say that we hoped you get yourself and your critical faculties safely back to Tinpan Alley. How come you don't get high? You sure work at it hard enough. That's what London does for you. Enthusiasm-unship (an equation from the smoke). Did you ever write a review of 'Exile'? If you did, and still have a copy, I'd like to see it!

"Anyway, thanks for the number at the door! Come see us in London and we'll get you mighty high (you deserve it; hanging out with neurotic

queens from the provinces is gloom by the bucket). I'd love to see a review of your visit to Ronnie's room, now we understand it all. Death to Eddie and the Hotrods!"

It was just signed "Stones," but that "number at the door" bit just had to refer to the final encounter with Keith in my dream. But that was impossible unless Keith had had the same dream I had.

Hey Keith . . . we can't go on meeting like this.

CHARLES SHAAR MURRAY

Fame is like a river that beareth up things light and swollen, and drowns things weighty and solid.

——Francis Bacon, *Essays*

LOVE AND HOPE AND SEX AND DIRTY DREAMS

CELEBRITY DEBRIS

"All I need is more rumors," sighed Jagger when he heard gossip columnists had discovered he was living in Linda Ronstadt's house.

Columnists tintyped the two of them as a tasty tidbit just the year before. So had Jagger and the prime minister's wife, so had Mrs. Jagger and the president's son, so had . . . it rolls on and on.

After a decade and a half, Mick may groan at the thought of yet another installment in his "ongoing soap opera," but in the beginning the Stones were willing accomplices in their own notoriety. Having fashioned their "bad boy" into the perfect press artifact for the headline-hungry hacks of Fleet Street, the Stones' story, an irresistible melange of "Sex, Drugs and Defiance," rolled on under its own steam. Abetted by Andrew Oldham's prepackaged "plants," all this publicity played no small part in their infamous career. But, as Mick somewhat disingenuously complains, "It's almost impossible to get out of the gossip columns once you've gotten in."

In the pages of the muckraking British press, where all parties are "wild" (or "injured") and their guests "frolic at all-night bashes," "punches fly," "insults are hurled," "offenses alleged," "rumors denied," "police alerted," "neighbors shocked," and chaos always about to "erupt," the Stones with Mick as ringleader were a tabloid ready-made.

Mick had always been a gossip columnist's dream scandal. Simultaneously attractive and repellent in his arrogance and androgynous appearance, his presence generated attention: "With his outlandish personal appearance, his long hair, his huge mouth, his minute hips, his girlish face already a caricature, he came to mean all sorts of different things to different people. He was uncommunicative, unforthcoming, unco-operative; nobody knew anything about him; all he had to do was stand there for the theories to form," commented Maureen Cleave in the *Evening Standard*.

Mick's personal life ("spat in posh club," "in tiff with model") began to appear in the society columns. His affairs with Chrissie Shrimpton, Marianne Faithful and Marsha Hunt interested the British reading public as much as the dalliances of Princess Margaret.

With his wedding to Bianca in 1971—an event which managed to fulfill the media's wildest fantasies—Mick became the permanent property of the international wire services. While Mick protested that "this is not a goldfish bowl and I am not the king of France," the press had a field day with the old ultraviolence: "MICK WEDS IN HIPPIE CHAOS," "FANS CLASH WITH POLICE IN PITCHED BATTLES," "BEST MAN SHOWS UP IN NAZI UNIFORM," and pandemonium, his old companion from the Stones' tours, obligingly threatened "to break loose" at the slightest provocation. The predictable puns popped up ("ROLLING STONE GATHERS A BOSS") as well as a touch of soft-core porn: "His bride, radiant in a bra-less Yves St. Laurent white costume, cried 'Oh no!' Her brown eyes were moist with frustration."

Together Mick and Bianca were double trouble, a split-screen scandal. Socialites, movie stars, gilded sweethearts of the chic and glossy, jaded darlings of the Concorde crowd, top of the Best-Dressed lists, paparazzied dining at Maxim's, leaving Studio 54 with Andy Warhol—as mirror images of each other the Jaggers were CELEBRITY CLONES! Reflecting each new trend, frisson, or fashion as it came along, their celebrity stocks rose and fell like shares on multinational commodity exchanges; the latest whisper of scandal about them was read by breathless brokers from Bangor to Bangkok. Mick: "They'll print anything you say, anything. And by the time it gets to Hong Kong, it's ridiculous. Before you know it, you've gone

out with Mrs. Trudeau, which is rubbish. The only reason I'm known in Turkey is because I'm supposed to have gone out with Mrs. Trudeau."

In the fan food chain, gossip is the plasma craved by celebrity-crazed fame junkies with their insatiable appetite for phantom phax, and Mick and Bianca joined the company of the Olympians on the pages of the *National Enquirer* and the *Star*—along with the those old warhorses Liz, Jackie O., Farrah, the Fonz, Elvis, cancer cures, and psychic dogs in the Soviet Union. "SEX IN SKY ON JAGGER JET," tattled Truman, "in every conceivable position." Or "STRIP ROW AT JAGGER PARTY" and "NAMES JAGGER OVER LOVE CHILD."

"It's what I call my fictional life," Mick says wryly. "Someone called it the 'longest-running rock 'n' roll soap opera,' and they're probably right. I get into trouble with journalists when I tell them the media are just a joke, especially in England. But they'd know what I meant if they had to live through what I have to go through. I'll be sitting in New York and read about what I was supposed to be doing the night before in London or someplace. You just try to ignore it."

Part of the fascination of gossip columns is that they are obituaries of the living. Those talked about have little to do with what is said and the gossip column's celebrity caricatures take on a fantasy life of their own. Divorced from reality, these "legends in their own time" carry on as usual, even (or especially) in death: "ELVIS PHONES FAN FROM BEYOND THE GRAVE!"

Brian made a brief visit from the Beyond to impregnate the "Black Magic Girl from Melbourne": "MODEL WHO PRACTICES DEVIL WORSHIP CLAIMS DEAD ROCK STAR BRIAN JONES IS FATHER OF HER ILLEGITIMATE SON." What did it matter that the child was five and Brian dead eight years?

Bianca seemed to actively encourage the constant fascination with her behavior or at least accept it as the "price of fame": Bianca "has tantrums," "raised eyebrows," "innermost thoughts," "TELLS ALL," "I WANT IT ALL," "I'VE HAD IT WITH," and "GETS BLOOD FROM A STONE."

Her every movement, social or intestinal, was examined with pathological intensity.

VIVA: They had dances in the morning and the night . . .

BIANCA: To do it? Yeah.

VIVA: They said constipation was the source of all mental illness, all social ills and . . . lousy sex.

BIANCA: It's one of the main things with women who don't have beautiful skin.

VIVA: How many times a day do you shit, Bianca?

BIANCA: I only eat once. I think it's important how many times you eat . . . (Interview)

Like Oscar Wilde (who replied to a reporter prying into his private life: "I wish I had one"), Mick seemed to incite prurient interest in himself as effortlessly as he dismissed it: "I don't put out wild pictures of me and whomever I'm going out with. I try to avoid going to openings as much as I possibly can. Even before I was married, with girls I was seeing or living with—most of the stories were completely untrue, and it's hopeless trying to tell people that it's not true. I don't tell them anything I'm doing, what I'm reading, where I'm going. They don't know anything about my private life. I have no respect for people who earn their money peeking through keyholes. This takes in most journalists."

However, this prankster prince of pop rarely resisted the temptation to turn the tables on the press. Handed a copy of the Star containing a blistering broadside on him—"Where have we failed that this pimply-faced disciple of dirt is a rootin' tootin' hero to our teenage kids? We can't tolerate seeing him come to these shores and bombard our kids with filth!"—Mick momentarily considered suing, then grinning wickedly said, "Add it to the press kit."

Keith: "You only ever hear about me when the warrants are out" . . . or when "UFO'S LAND IN HIS GARDEN!" As one who has been brushing headlines off like flies for a dozen years, Keith finds the Transylvanian stereotype of him in the press only mildly bothersome: "It still goes on and I just go along with the 'bad publicity is better than no publicity' idea. I mean, if they wrote about me as the sweet, gentle, loving family man, it would probably do me more damage. And be equally untrue."

The Stones continue to be amused at the literally unbelievable literary fantasy life they have inspired in others: "To think that people are actually going to buy these books, read them and believe every word is even funnier—but it's nothing for me to worry about," Mick says about excerpts from Everybody's Lucifer in the News of the World. "There's this whole scene which, when you read it, is like the script for some terrible B movie about Brian and me having this knife fight. Now if it had happened, I'd say 'Yeah' and admit it, but the truth is that it just didn't happen. But I gotta admit that it all sounds quite amazing and I suppose makes good copy . . . gossip is always bigger than music."

DAVID DALTON

MIDNITE 40¢ RAMBLER

MICK WEDS IN SECRET!

Full details inside

Brian Jones' sex after death saga... Australian witch says she has child to prove it!

UFO's ARE LANDING IN MY GARDEN SAYS KEITH RICHARD

BIANCA JAGGER: why she wants blood from a stone

EXCLUSIVE STAR STRUCK ISSUE

Psychic dogs of the Soviet Union discover miracle cancer cure

Why Ron Wood says he is the only straight Stone

Learn about Secret Society to which Bill Wyman belongs

Is Charlie Watts the re-incarnation of Ulysses S. Grant?

The Stone that never rolled says "I hate rock and roll"

Mick Jagger's Rebel Image Is A Gimmick

IF HE had put his mind to it, Mick Jagger could have become a star cricket player in England.

So says his father, Prof. B. J. Jagger, who teaches the philosophy and comparative history of physical education at the University of London.

"But other things got in the way," says the senior Jagger. "Mick was in business administration at the University of London when he decided to take two years' leave to start the group. He did it because he thought it was something pleasant to do, but he also realized it was a way of making money.

"Since he was in business administration, he decided to put what he had learned into practice. That was 11 years ago. His leave from university has long since run out and he has made himself a fortune."

The professor says the Jaggers are a very closely knit family.

Despite the fact that he projects the image of rebellious youth to his millions of fans, Mick was never overly difficult to handle, says Papa Jagger.

"The rebellious thing was put on him by promoters as a good gimmick," he says. "He's a little against the establishment, of course, if the establishment is wrong, and so am I, naturally. In many ways I agree with Mick."

Prof. Jagger also speaks well of his other son, Chris, who has been touring the U.S. with his own group.

"Mick and Chris must have inherited their musical talents from their mother," he says.

"My parents were also musical. My father was the choirmaster and organist in the little village where we lived."

Currently visiting the U.S. to lecture to students at George Washington and Purdue universities, Prof. Jagger lives with his wife in a small English village in Kent.

"We live in an ordinary straight style," he says, "in a house we've been in for 25 years. It's a cottage in which Mick and Chris grew up. The youngsters in the locality are their friends.

"Both Mick and Chris come to visit us there, but of course, it's easier for us to go and see them in their house in London. I'd say we go twice for every time they come to us. It's about the same as any family, I would say.

"Mick talks very pleasantly. I feel a little small at times, with the experience he's had and made use of. The different cultures he's appreciated—he can absolutely floor me."

Mick's mum and dad, Joe and Eva Jagger.

Boy, You Stink, Man, Says Jagger's Mother

MICK JAGGER'S mother was unhappy the first time she saw her son perform with his raunchy rock group, the Rolling Stones.

Although her son is now a superstar, Mrs. Eva Jagger still doesn't like Mick's image. In fact, she doesn't even think he sings very well.

Says Mrs. Jagger: "I was disgusted with the way Mike was wriggling his body about and gyrating." Mrs. Jagger isn't what you'd expect a wild rock singer's mom to be—she's charming, sophisticated and vivacious. And her maternal reminiscences about her son "Mike" (as she still calls Mick, whose real name is Michael) belie the claim once made by a Rolling Stones publicity agent that the Stones weren't born, "They just happened. They don't have mothers!"

So, it's no wonder that Mrs. Jagger isn't enthusiastic about her son's reputation as a user of soft women and hard drugs. Still, Mick is an immensely popular performer. And not even a disapproving mother can complain about that. "You can't argue against success, can you?"

UFOs are landing in my garden

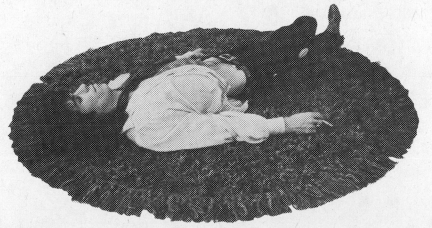

KEITH RICHARD, Rolling Stones guitarist and co-writer of songs with Mick Jagger, believes that he lives on a UFO landing site.

There's a growing interest among pop people in the existence of unidentified flying objects (UFOs) and Keith claims to have seen several down near his country home in Sussex. "I've seen a few, but nothing that any of the ministries would believe," he told me this week "I believe they exist—plenty of people have seen them. They are tied up with a lot of things, like the dawn of man, for example. It's not just a matter of people spotting a flying saucer.

"I'm not an expert. I'm still trying to understand what's going on."

But he believes that something is happening. And he says, he has it on good authority that his house is a landing site for UFOs.

Meanwhile, back on earth.

'EFFEMINATE' POP SINGERS SCORNED

LONDON, Saturday. — Pop singers Mick Jagger and John Lennon are disliked by working-class teenagers, who regard their long hair and unisex clothes as effeminate.

Singers such as Jagger, Lennon and Jimi Hendrix are more the idols of middle-class teenagers, who see hippie-style underground music as an expression of protest against their parents' values.

These are the findings of a survey of nearly 200 British schoolchildren aged between 12 and 15 by the University of Leicester Center for Mass Communication Research.

Two researchers, Mr. Graham Murdock and Mr. Guy Phelps, claim their survey shows that pop music—not television—is the dominant influence on the life of the average adolescent.

They found that teenagers from different social backgrounds had different tastes in pop.

Teenagers, they say, see pop divided between "mainstream" and "underground."

"Mainstream" pop comprises romantic ballads and is identified with the life-style of singers such as Cliff Richard. "Underground" music includes songs that grew out of the protest movement and is identified with singers such as Jagger, Lennon and Hendrix.

Working-class teenagers were more likely to be fans of "mainstream" pop singers such as Cliff Richard, Stevie Wonder and David Cassidy, the survey found.

Only 8 percent of teenagers from working-class homes liked "underground" pop, compared with 43 percent of middleclass teenagers.

One of the main reasons for working-class boys' rejection of the music and life-styles of Jagger and Lennon was "that they perceived the hippie emblems of long hair and sexually ambiguous dress-styles as essentially effeminate and homosexual," Mr. Murdock said.

"This was also true of the working-class girls, who shared with the boys a very rigid view of the appropriate forms of sexual self-presentation."

Another study by the center has concluded that violence on television does not make children more aggressive.

Dr. Richard Dembo, who conducted a survey among working-class boys at a comprehensive school in Britain's northeast, said: "Figures give no support to the quest for the banning of specifically violent programs in the effort to clean up television."

Dr. Dembo found that boys with a reputation for being tough at school watched almost exactly the same films and television programs as calmer boys.

One of the most popular programs among both groups was "Blue Peter," a highly rated children's television show on the BBC.

Most aggressive boys preferred to watch football matches on television, and only 12 percent of their viewing time was taken by programs of violence.

Dr. Dembo said it was wrong to imply that young people could not use their judgment on the mass media.

Model Who Practices Devil Worship Claims Dead Rock Star Brian Jones Is The Father Of Her Son

IN 1969, Rolling Stones lead guitarist Brian Jones was found dead in his swimming pool, possibly from a drug overdose.

Now 25-year-old model Loriann Faithless is claiming Jones made love to her one night after a party in an Australian hotel.

The result of that solitary union, she says, is her son Timmy.

"My girlfriend and I went to one of the Stones' concerts in Melbourne, and were given passes to go backstage.

"The Stones invited us to a hotel for a party. We were ushered into taxis and went up to the third floor of this hotel.

"I was very drunk, but I remember this little blond fellow coming up to me. He turned out to be Brian Jones. He'd been very quiet at first, but, once he got drunk, he became very friendly."

Loriann asked Jones what it was like to be famous, but Jones wasn't in the mood for talking about fame.

He had something else on his mind. He suggested they have "some fun."

"When Timmy was born, there was no mistaking who the father was," Loriann insisted. "With his blond hair and blue eyes, he was the image of Brian."

Loriann is a part-time model—but her true interests lie in the occult. She practices black magic and devil worship, and swears she is a black witch.

She and Timmy live in an apartment in Melbourne that doubles as a temple for worshipping the devil. The living room is stacked with altars to Satan and miscellaneous witchcraft equipment.

STRANGE SINGING

Anita Pallenberg flashes a bewitching smile while dining out.

IT WAS two a.m. on the night of a full moon recently when Ridgefield, Connecticut, police officer Michael Passaro stopped his patrol car about a quarter of a mile down the road from Keith Richards' house to investigate "some strange singing" coming from the nearby woods.

Keith's common-law wife, Anita Pallenberg, has been linked to a witches' coven in Westchester and was the central figure in a circle of witches in the county.

"I didn't even know at the time that Richards' house was nearby," Passaro said. "No connection between them has been brought to my attention." According to residents, there have been several bizarre satanic rituals in the area over the past five years. A local reporter attributed the outbreak of occultism to "rich people taking acid."

TAMMY TELLS...

Tammy Tells...Now hear this. When the Swinging Jaggers, **Mick** and **Bianca**, are lying there in bed (on the rare occasions when the married couple get their peripatetic life-style together) they talk about—are you ready—cricket, the favorite sport of the English. Mick revealed this in a recent interview with Cricket magazine, saying Bianca often turns to him sleepily to ask the latest about their mutual passion...Who says a Rolling Stone gathers no moss: Mick Jagger was hit with another paternity suit: by an airline cutie he flew...-

Paint It Red, folks. Mick and his Stones will gather no moss in the Soviet Union. In reply to a reply to a Russian newpaper reader's question, **V.M. Kokonin**, artistic director of the Soviet concert agency, said the English rock group lacks glamor, attractiveness, naturalness and novelty, and he did not think the group would be able to "help people achieve self-perfection"...Mick and Bianca reportedly had another whopper of a fracas. And this time sources tell me Bianca tore to shreds a dozen of Mick's $70 silk shirts

—with her teeth. Last time she was a bit more conventional. She cut those with scissors...He was wearing a striped blazer decorated with a yellow rose, she a big-shouldered coat, sequined **Chiquita Banana** shoes and a green straw hat. After presenting the $350,000 they had raised for earthquake relief for Nicaragua to the Pan American Development Foundation in Washington, Mick and his look-alike wife decided to try the exclusive Sans Souci restaurant. **Paul Delisle**, the maitre d'hotel, was not impressed. "No reservation: no tie," he said, turning them away...Poor Mick threw a huff and disappeared from his own party at Ashley's, the

New York restaurant and disco, when the doorman failed to recognize him last week. **Keith Richard** and **Ron Wood** were freely admitted, but when Jagger arrived he was stopped at the door. "Who are you?" demanded the doorman. "I'm **Gary Crosby**," said Jagger, smiling weakly. "Pleased to meet you." And with that he got back into his limo and drove away. But the group threw a party exclusively for their road crew at Le Jardin, the leading gay disco. The roadies were served omelettes and slices from a giant cake three feet high, crowned by the Stones' eagle logo, moulded, unfortunately not in birthday icing, but plastic.

MICK JAGGER TO GIVE UP ROLLING STONES SO HE CAN STAY HOME AND MIND THE KIDS

NEXT to the Beatles, the Rolling Stones are easily the most popular rock group of all time. Mick Jagger seems to say everything any kid ever wanted to scream against his parents.

The group has enjoyed incredible success thanks to the young fans who identify with Jagger's scowls of protest. While the Beatles have long since disbanded, the Stones just keep rollin' along gathering lots of greenbacks. Sometimes it seems as if they'll last forever.

Well, sit still because the word is out in London that the Stones might break up! That's right, and it's Mick Jagger who's leading the way.

Why would anybody want to tamper with such a successful combination? The reason is pretty plain and simple—you might even call it old-fashioned.

Mick Jagger wants to become a family man.

Surprising? Well, ever since the birth of his daughter Jade in 1971, Mick has been sounding strangely like a homebody. And now he's discovering that he'd like to spend more time raising his daughter in a proper domestic atmosphere. To do this, the band would have to split up. Mick puts it this way:

"As for me, the end of the road's coming on the pop scene. I've given myself four more years, then I quit. For a family it's not the scene."

Surprising words to come from the lips of a man who's been idolized by an entire generation of rebellious teenagers.

Jagger doesn't talk much about anything these days without somehow bringing his wife and daughter into the conversation. He'll smile tenderly and say:

"I've settled down—well, almost to domestic bliss." His praise of his daughter knows no limits and she fascinates him with her smiling and gurgling. He says that he really likes children and wants more, lots more.

Little Jade has been a pretty lucky girl so far. Mick and Bianca have taken her on the road with them. She's already seen more of the world in her short life than most of us ever will.

Parents around the world have wanted to see the Stones break up for a long time and it now seems as if they may soon get their wish. After all, Mick is getting a little old to be a rock idol and the thought of staying on only to become a second Elvis Presley in Vegas doesn't appeal to him at all.

Besides, he'd rather spend his Sunday mornings strolling with his daughter through a quiet park.

ROLLING STONES AT A NUDE SWIM PARTY

By DAVID DAWSON

SOME members of the Rolling Stones pop group attended a nude swimming party at a North Balwyn mansion on Friday night.

Guitarist Keith Richard was guest of honor at the party given by a beautiful young female journalist for an underground newspaper.

Most of the guests went to the party after a banquet by WEA records for the Stones at the Montsalvat Artists' Colony, Eltham.

Guests included pop musicians, actors, poets, artists and journalists.

Many guests, fortified by an abundant supply of liquor, stripped each other naked and plunged into the pool.

Other guests took poolside seats and called encouragement to the nude swimmiers as they kissed and caressed in the glow of soft lights from the house.

Some clothed journalists were thrown into the pool by members of opposition publications.

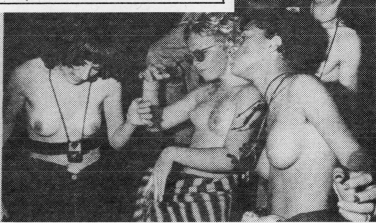

THE NIGHT MICK JAGGER GOT INTO MY PANTS

By LISA ROBINSON

IT WAS quite hot the second night the Stones performed in Toronto, and the scene backstage was the usual. Crew members setting up, the band and their guests enjoying food and drink in the hospitality suite, Peter Rudge overseeing everything, Keith and Ronnie tuning up, Jagger getting dressed. Then — and imagine my surprise — logistics expert Alan Dunn approached me with the most unusual request. "Got any spare knickers, Lisa?" What? It seemed as though Mick had lost his athletic supporter, the one he likes to wear under the gray and white striped cheesecloth outfit, and the only available extra one belonged to the man from Atlantic and was found to be...unsuitable. So...

After much consultation and attempts at other alternatives, it appears that either I offered mine in the line of duty or Mick's usual underwear would show through his costume. As that would never do, I removed the item, (privately) took it to a wash basin where Dunn had set up soap and hot water, and washed the panties under the watchful eyes of Anna Lou Liebovitz and Christopher Sykes' cameras. Then, Alan Dunn, with Jagger's assistance, took the bikinis and dried them with a large electrical fan. Mick put them on—backwards. (They didn't fit badly, actually, size small.) "With girls' ones you have to wear them back to front," Jagger said knowingly, "'cause they're bigger in the back..." Everyone breathed a sigh of relief as a Crisis on the Stones Tour of the Americas was avoided. And I must add, Annie Leibovitz and I looked very closely during the entire performance and my panties held up rather well.

SEX IN THE SKY

Young Fan Seduced on Rolling Stones' Jet

Truman Capote, Mick Jagger
Watch, Shrug
As Movie Camera Rolls

AN ANONYMOUS "Lolita" stripped naked and made love to a young doctor "in every conceivable position" while passengers aboard The Rolling Stones' personal plane gathered to watch and the pair were filmed under movie lights in mid-air.

The shocking sexual encounter between the physician and a delighted but underage groupie took place on the Stones' DC7 jet during a Pittsburgh-Washington, D.C. flight, according to world-renowned author Truman Capote.

Spokesmen for the Stones rather lazily evaded denying that it happened. One said Capote wasn't on the flight and another said it didn't happen "as far as I have been able to find out."

Capote himself found the whole thing mildly amusing, according to an account he gave the rock magazine "Rolling Stone." He is the author of "In Cold Blood."

"They had this doctor on the plane, about 28 years old, rather good looking," the writer was quoted.

"He would pass through the plane with a great big plate of pills, everything from Vitamin C to vitamin coke," said Capote, who was traveling with the group on their last American tour.

"At whatever city we would arrive at, there would always be these hordes of kids outside, and he would walk around...and say 'You know, I'm Mick Jagger's personal physician. How would you like to see the show from backstage?'

"He would get quite a collection of them. Backstage, he would have them spread out, and every now and then he would bring one back to the plane.

"The one I remember most was a girl who said she'd come to get a story for her high school newspaper...she sure got a story, all right," Capote said, laughing.

"They fitted up the back of the plane for this. Robert Frank (a movie photographer) got out his lights, the plane was flying along, and there was Dr. Feelgood —ing this girl in every conceivable position."

"The Stones improvised some bongo music to go with it," Frank told another newspaper. "But they got bored after a few minutes and went back to their seats."

The passengers flocked about to watch the "fun."

"The plane was flying at some really strange angle," Capote said, "and the stewardess kept saying, 'Would you please mind moving forward?' "

When the plane started coming in to land, the couple was still at it," Frank said. "The doctor took the girl, still naked, on his lap and fastened the seat belt around them both."

Dr. Feelgood had a terribly hard time getting his trousers on" when the plane landed, Capote said, "and in the end he had to come off the plane holding his trousers in his hand."

"The girl," Capote said with just a trace of envy, "was apparently enjoying the whole experience."

IS JAGGER FINISHED AS ROCK IDOL

By DOROTHEA TAYLOR

HAS super-swinger Mick Jagger finally turned in his Scandal-ous-Conduct medal?

Is the teeny-bopper's fire-breather really "going straight" — or is the Pied-Piper of a generation of rock music fans just bidding his time, quietly stashing away his musical dynamite, preparing for one last world-shaking blowup?

"It's just the lull before the storm," say the quivering disciples of the unholiest roller of them all.

Mick is still the same old **Menace to Society** that their fathers always said he was, they claim.

Outlaw saint

The faithful can't believe that the Mick, the outlaw saint, would stop poking pins in his personal society doll just because he got married.

They can't believe that the **Boss Man of the Rolling Stones**, the man who had convinced millions that the good life meant getting stoned and running naked in the streets, would abandon all that depravity and anarchy for one chick and a kid.

Now that the look-alike couple are expecting a little Jagger, parents of the stoned generation expect Mick and the missus to produce a real-life Rosemary's Baby.

If the kid isn't born with horns, there'll be enough bets lost among the over-30 crowd to start a new market plunge.

The gossip about the new Mrs. Jagger started even before the weird Riviera wedding.

"They called her Super-Groupie," said many of the 200 hip Londoners Mick had flown in just for the occasion.

"She got tired of sleeping with **Michael Caine** through two of his movies," said another, "and started camp-following with the Stones."

Such talk!

"Such talk!" said Beatle **Ringo Starr**, who showed up with his wife and baby for the wedding in the tiny St. Tropez town hall.

Another member of the disband-ed Beatles, **Paul McCartney**, joined with his wife and two children in trying to make the occasion respec-table.

Almost as if to prove all the vicious rumors, Bianca showed up in a classy white bridal outfit, with two bare pink breasts hanging out for all to see and admire.

But despite the fistfight, obscene guests and topless bride, the Jagger wedding was nothing compared to "the old days."

Even the brassy bride seemed like a nunnery graduate when compared to some of Mick's old flames.

WHY JAGGER HIT A WOMAN

BRITISH rock star Mick Jagger admitted in an American court that he slapped a woman in the face as she tried to serve a summons on him.

The woman Mrs. Vivian Manuel, carried papers claiming $328,500 damages for farmland trampled by fans at a Rolling Stones concert in 1969.

She told the court at Alameda, California, that 32-year-old Jagger struck her several times as he was about to board an air-liner.

Sorry

Jagger said that he slapped Mrs. Manuel in the face because "she threw the papers at me...I reacted quickly. I was sorry later."

The clash occurred three years ago, and the following year a court gave judgment against Jagger in his absence.

He now seeks to have the judg-ment set aside because he claims he was not served with the summons.

A decision will be given on Fri-day.

ROLLING STONE GATHERING LITTLE NOTICE

ST. TROPEZ, France—For four weeks Mick Jagger of the rock group Rolling Stones has been taking religious instruction in the Catholic faith to prepare for his marriage this week to Nicaraguan beauty Bianca Terez Morena de Maccias.

The instruction—one hour, two evenings a week—takes place in the shabby, cream-washed office of St. Tropez's Abbe Lucien Baud who is to marry the couple in a simple 40-minute church ceremony.

Abbe Baud said he had no real idea of the identity of the solemn young man in the psychedelic patchwork trousers who sits opposite his old oak desk and discusses religion with him in very passable French.

"I only realized he was a celebrity of some sort when the commissioner at the town hall called on me and said that I should not say anything about him because he was

Mick, the mayor and the missus.

arranging for a quiet wedding," the abbe said.

"I am afraid I have never heard of these Rolling Stones. Do they play rock? Super pop? I never have much time for these things here, you know. This is a busy parish with 6,000 souls and my day is very full."

MICK WEDS IN HIPPIE CHAOS

Introducing Marlon...son of Rolling Stone Keith

LIKE ANY other father, Rolling Stone Keith Richard was mighty proud to show his son Marlon to the world yesterday.

He cooed. He cradled Marlon in his arms. "I am positively delighted," he said with a smile.

Mother, 25-year-old German actress, Anita Pallenberg, was even more ecstatic.

"He's gorgeous," she said, gazing down at Marlon, who weighed 7lb., 4oz., at birth.

Expansively, she added: "I'm going to have thousands more."

PARIS, Wed.—Gaudy St. Tropez has seen some bizarre sights but none as way out as the wedding of Rolling Stone Mick Jagger to former Nicaraguan model Bianca De Macias today.

The guests from London were so eccentrically dressed that the far out St. Tropez hippies said: "We look like cabinet ministers."

Well, the police chief told us to get Mick and Bianca to the church on time.

And we certainly tried.

Confronted by jostling crowds, police chief Jean-Pierre Haramboure found his entire force totalled only four gendarmes.

Somehow, we managed to channel a fifty-yard pathway through the square for the couple to get into the town hall chamber.

But waiting inside was a battery of cameramen and a strong corps of radio commentators.

Mick's face flushed with anger.

His bride, radiant in a breathless, bra-less, Yves St.-Laurent white

costume, cried: "Oh, no!" Her brown eyes were moist with frustration.

The 28-year-old Rolling Stone refused to go ahead until the room was cleared.

But after advice, he changed his mind.

Love Story

As the couple exchanged rings, part of Bach's wedding march was played and then, at the request of the bride, a medley of themes from the film *Love Story.*

A different kind of music was heard when the reception turned into a "jam" with the celebrities joining in, includung our Mick! Bianca finally returned to her hotel alone, leaving Mick on stage. Mick's parents, Joe and Eva Jagger were last seen still clutching their son's carefully wrapped wedding gift. Commented Mrs. Jagger: "I hope my other son doesn't become a superstar!"

The mayor, commenting on Jagger's wedding day rough-house, said "He is a victim of his talent and fame."

It May Be Sour Grapes, But...

Michael Caine Says Rolling Stone's Wedding Won't Last

By LOU KEMP

AFTER THE BALLYHOO and gaud of Rolling Stone Mick Jagger's wedding, Michael Caine has come forth to declare Bianca Perez Morena de Macia and Mick shouldn't have married.

Caine ought to know. He dated the beautiful and mysterious 26-year-old Nicaraguan girl like he wanted it to last.

Unlike the guests at the pop marriage, Caine has an inside track on Bianca—who might have gone unnoticed at her own all-night wedding bash had she not donned a see-through blouse.

"I was with Bianca for quite a long time," Caine confessed with gusto. "We enjoyed the relationship very much, and I was a bit upset when I read about her marrying Mick Jagger."

CAINE WASN'T invited to the St. Tropez wedding, and sour grapes may play a large part in how he views the wild vow-taking of Mick and Bianca.

He admits that Bianca left him, for instance.

Yet he insists there's trouble ahead for the newlyweds. "This is all wrong," he said simply.

"She'll argue about everything until you feel you're going mad. I'll bet they're fighting like cats and dogs already," he added, looking up from a magazine account of the wedding.

CAINE MET the new Mrs. Jagger in Paris, where she was studying.

At 18, Bianca had had enough of Central America and flew to Europe.

Two years later she returned to

Bianca; she was Caine's steady . . . until Mick moved in.

Nicaragua and took a job in the foreign office. But she disliked the job and couldn't stand her drab homeland.

Returning to Paris, she went from one job to another until she finally landed in the Nicaraguan ambassador's office. She was a hit in the diplomatic circles. There, she met Caine.

Soon after, the two were off on a

whirlwind romance.

WHEN HE was making "The Italian Job," she was his live-in chickie on location in Turin.

While Caine was filming "The Battle of Britain," a Rolls always stood outside Bianca's door, motor running. When Caine called Bianca to come to the set to share his rest periods in his dressing room, she went running.

Raised a strict Roman Catholic, Bianca lost most of her inhibitions in Caine's presence. Her nude and see-through fashions were the talk of the Riviera.

"The subject of religion never came up between us," Caine recalled. "It never worries me what religion a girl has, because women only bring up religion when they're thinking of marriage."

JAGGER AND Bianca had two ceremonies: one civil and the other Catholic.

"Women know I'm not looking for marriage because that means a permanent, lasting relationship. I never met Bianca's family, either," Caine allowed.

But Mick Jagger did. Shortly before their excursion into wedlock, Bianca took Mick in tow to Nicaragua. Her mother was upset by her lustrous daughter's wardrobe, but she said: "I think Mick is a nice man."

Caine has a rule about old love affairs. He never gets in touch with the girl again, so he didn't even send Bianca best wishes.

"I PREFER not to see a girl again," he said sharply. "I don't see the point. The memory is much more pleasant than the reality, which often isn't so glamorous."

HAIR STAR NAMES JAGGER IN LOVE-CHILD CASE

By TAMARA BLACK

POP SINGER Marsha Hunt, who for two-and-a-half years has kept the identity of her baby's father secret, named him yesterday as Rolling Stone Mick Jagger.

Now 29-year-old Jagger is to be blood-tested to help determine whether Miss Hunt's daughter Karis is his child or not.

Twenty-six-year-old Miss Hunt, colored American former star of the rock musical "Hair," made the claim in affiliation order proceedings at Marylebone Court, London.

Later a spokesman for the Rolling Stones stated that none of Miss Hunt's allegations were admitted.

During the three-minute hearing, which was adjourned to July 31, Miss Hunt sat behind her solicitor Mr. Michael Seifert.

Jagger, the magistrate was told, was on his way to Italy. He was represented by counsel Mr. Bruce Blair.

And Mr. Blair successfully applied, without any objection from Miss Hunt's lawyer, for a court order for blood tests.

She now sings with a new pop group and lives with baby Karis in Marlborough Place, St. John's Wood.

Recently, she said in an interview: "I don't even discuss the father. He was just a friend. We just had a baby. We weren't living together."

Mick Jagger married 25-year-old Nicaragua-born Bianca de Macias in May 1971. They have a daughter, Jade.

PRESIDENT'S SON JACK DATING WIFE OF MICK JAGGER

PRESIDENT FORD'S son Jack is following in the footsteps of his sister and having an affair with someone connected with the rock music world, singing star Mick Jagger's wife Bianca.

Only a few weeks ago, reporters on both sides of the Atlantic were gathering information about Susan Ford's involvement with Rod Stewart, lead singer of the Faces, a popular British group.

Now, INSIDER operatives have spotted Jack, 23, walking down the streets of New York with Bianca.

Ford and Mrs. Jagger spent most of the night at the posh El Morocco Club, where they danced and quaffed beers until the early hours of the morning.

With two armed Secret Service men following close behind, they left El Morocco for nightcaps at Le Jardin Club. Ford then returned her to her downtown hotel and made a quick departure.

A recent graduate of the University of Utah forestry school and the wife of one of the best-known entertainers in the world, they made an odd couple, the source said.

KEEPING UP WITH YOUTH:
JAGGER'S LOVE LETTERS

By PAMELA SWIFT

WHAT DID Mick Jagger write in his love letters to Christine Shrimpton, younger sister of British model Jean Shrimpton?

It must have been torrid stuff, or why would Mick, leader of the Rolling Stones, have gone to court in London to stop his former girlfriend from making them public?

Some months ago, Jagger obtained a temporary injunction forbidding Christine from selling or publicizing his letters. Now he wants a permanent injunction to make sure they don't appear in print. He's also asking for damages, alleging breach of confidence and infringement of copyright. Moreover, Mick wants his letters back, which raises a ticklish and technical question: To whom do love letters belong, the writer or recipient?

In any event, Jagger, now married to the former Bianca de Macias, does not want his love letters exposed.

Chrissie Shrimpton: Off the hook?

BIANCA BLITHELY BITCHES!!!

BIANCA'S been telling tales out of school these days and aren't we glad! One of the most talked about women of the decade has been doing most of the talking herself and the details are delicious: "When Mick first saw me, it was in Paris. He admitted that he had a shock. He had the impression that he was looking at himself. I know that people theorize that Mick thought it would be amusing to marry his twin. But actually he wanted to achieve the ultimate in sexual experience by making love to himself."

And get this, our Bianca doesn't dig marriage at all: "As far as marriage is concerned, I was frightened of the whole idea. Actually it is Mick who is the bourgeois sort about this. He insisted on having a proper ceremony and becoming man and wife in the conventional sense." And guess what, pregnancy's no joyride either! "I hated my pregnancy. It was horrible. I was three months pregnant when we married. Mick was quite difficult about the whole thing. No, I didn't have stretch marks, I am not marked in any way by the birth. And I don't carry around any pictures of Jade."

Well, needless to say, this sort of talk indicates trouble in paradise and Bianca admits as much: "Perhaps Mick isn't attracted to me anymore. When I first met him I knew who he was. But I don't know now. He has changed." Oh, well, not to worry because Bianca's "not a typical woman anyway." She's said to enjoy the adulation of fans herself and her nights are never lonely, no? "What is wrong with that? I like men's company and Mick is not always with me." An added bonus is that she is part man herself! "I know that inside me there is a desire to be a man. I would have preferred being born a boy. But I also enjoy the power of being a woman." Well, more power to you, Bianca.

'Darling, I want it all'

By ROBERT KIRWIN

MUNICH: "I am very vulnerable woman. I am not strong, tough Bianca everyone imagines. I am little girl."

She sits at a table in the bar of the Hotel Residence—Bianca Rosa Perez Macias Jagger—the Bianca Jagger.

She has just finished her first big-budget movie, "The Ringer," which co-stars Jeff Bridges and is about a rich young man and his problems with women. Number one problem: his wife. Number two problem: a tart.

Bianca plays the tart.

"I make her different kind of whore than you usually see on screen. I make her sympathetic—a good, high-class whore. I make her whore with a heart of gold.

"I mean, I fell in love with this character myself, she became my friend because I understand her and she understands me. She's simpatico, you know? She moves you. She is not used to this, being whore. Not used to getting close to her tricks. *But—but*—this man comes to her and asks her to teach him to be better lover, no? And they establish a relation that grows. And you know what? She falls. At the end, she falls.

"I mean, don't make no mistakes. People think that prostitute have no feeling. This is wrong. Prostitute do have feeling. They human. Who can say what kind of background they come from? They were young once. They are human. Vulnerable."

Bianca grows on you. You expect all glitter and flash and coldness. What has she to say about all this jet-set nonsense?

"The image of mine I never have liked. And it is not true," she says, the black eyes flashing. "I could not be in all those places you see me all over the world, in the photos. Could I? All those places, dancing and having a good time? No. Jet-setter? I do not like that."

But Bianca—don't you play along even a little bit? You don't disdain the entire thing, do you?

"No. It's the press." She pouts nicely. "They are nice, but they do not leave me alone. The press chases me, they try to catch me in embarrassing positions. They are always there—when I step off an airplane, step into a hotel, when I'm dancing at a disco or a party. Flashbulbs, flashbulbs! They even post themselves constantly outside of my home. Around the clock. I know they are merely doing a job and I tell them that I realize that. I go out to them on cold nights with coffee, and I say to them: 'Allo, boys, I bring you hot coffee.' And they say to me: 'Gee, thanks, Bianca.' And they say: 'We're sorry, Bianca, to be staying around your home like this all the time, but our editors pay us for doing this.' I say to them: 'I know, boys, I know. It's merely your job to follow Bianca, wherever she goes.'

"Of course I get bad press all the time, too. I don't like it, and I don't like the Bianca type that people see in the papers. I don't know that Bianca—she's a frivolous person, she goes from one place to another and does nothing. That is not me. I live a normal life. I have a child."

Bianca has a reputation for falling in love with a different man every 20 minutes. Is this merely part of the false, jet-setter image?

"Ha ha ha, it is true that I never really fall in love for a long time with anybody. I'm afraid to. I have fear of doing that. But I have my freedom now, the freedom to be able to refuse, to say to any of the men who try to hit on you, that maybe you don't want them hitting on you.

"However, I am not saying that men do not still play a big part in my life. Men play a big part always in every woman's life. I mean, what are you supposed to relate to?"

DIVORCE? IT'S NEWS TO ME

ROLLING STONE Mick Jagger dashed out of London for New York yesterday, claiming he knew nothing of a divorce action by his wife Bianca.

He checked in at Heathrow Airport with girlfriend Jerry Hall, just as a Concorde flight was about to leave. As the couple ran through the departure lounge Jagger denied he had been served papers by Bianca's lawyers.

"It's news to me," he shouted. "Nothing has been handed to me. I saw Bianca a few days ago. We had a party for my daughter."

The End Of A Beautiful Friendship

The Jealous Rivals

Caroline Kennedy . . .

. . . Princess Caroline.

By HARRY ALTSHULER

Carolines Fall Out
Over Pop Star
Mick Jagger

THE battle of the century at the Olympic Games in Montreal in mid July won't be on the program. Instead, it promises to erupt from the spectacular clash of two world-famous girls named Caroline—who used to be the best of friends.

Caroline Kennedy, daughter of Jackie Onassis and the late JFK, will be there as a photographer. Sultry-looking beauty Princess Caroline of Monaco, whose French is as fluent as her English, got herself appointed an official interpreter.

But cameras and languages are just their stock-in-trade; the real determination of each girl, they've both told their friends, is to put the other one in the shade.

They'll both be out to corner celebrities, grab the limelight, and shine at the V.I.P. parties as each strives to better the other.

Their friends have told MIDNIGHT that like any such fracas between teenage girls and former friends, it happened over a man.

Not even a single man, at that. It's Mick Jagger, who has just made a spectacularly successful singing tour of Europe and Britain with his Rolling Stones, and with his wife Bianca along.

Princess Margaret was there; so were both Carolines and all of swinging London. At one point Mick was so mobbed by females clamoring to get near him that he had to take refuge in the men's cloakroom to catch his breath.

The First Lady and the Rock Star

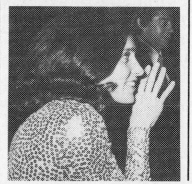

"I'M VERY FOND of him," said Margaret Trudeau. "I'd like to think he's a friend. But after all, I'm a married lady."

The wife of the Canadian prime minister was referring to **Mick Jagger**, lead singer of the Rolling Stones. She was interviewed last night in Manhattan's City Center. It was her first public appearance since she left a Toronto hotel Tuesday where the Rolling Stones were also registered, leading to widespread press comment in Canada and one report that she was traveling with the rock group.

HAVING BIANCA: JUST LIKE HAVING MICK

MICK JAGGER is "androgynous enough for almost anyone," and a visit from his estranged wife, Bianca, is "just like having him over . . . she's the female Mick."

So says **Andy Warhol**, whose new book, *Exposures*—due out October 15 in both $100 and $500 editions—chronicles life among the Beautiful People (**Liza Minnelli, Truman Capote, Salvador Dali,** et al.) in both words and more than 350 previously unpublished pictures.

Warhol contends that Bianca "could be the next **Rita Hayworth**," but he seems most taken with the Jaggers' eight-year-old daughter, Jade, who taught him how to play Monopoly. Says the admiring author: "She always says 'Andywarhol', as if it were one word or a brand name, which I wish it were."

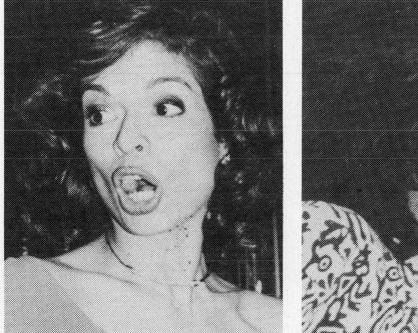

THIS I BELIEVE by Steve Dunleavy

It's time we exorcised this demonic influence over our children!

MICK JAGGER should come to America more often. I say that because it does us good, really good to look at ourselves squarely in the eye and see where we have failed.

Where have we gone wrong that our twelve and thirteen-year-old daughters are making him a millionaire—YET AGAIN?

Where have we failed that this pimply-faced disciple of dirt is a hero, a rootin', tootin' hero to our teenage kids?

We have this pale-faced foreigner, this Englishman, getting $10 a seat from our kids to see him perform.

And what do they see?

They are blitzkrieged by a tightly packaged excess of four-letter words.

Mick Jagger is a multi-millionaire, by the grace of the people and society which he scorns.

Okay, squares like me can live with that outrage.

But what I can't tolerate, and won't, damn it, tolerate, is seeing him come to these shores and bombard our kids with filth.

Perhaps you think I'm exaggerating.

Sick surprise

Well, let's take his first show in Baton Rouge, Louisiana, an event meticulously covered by the limp wristed corps of rock critics who raved about his music but failed to report exactly what he did.

Some newspapers, because of old-fashioned and commendable shyness, refrained from the report. Others just didn't know about it.

But at the height of his first show, a giant 20-foot rubber phallus exploded from the heart of the $4 million mobile stage.

Later in his dressing room he sipped gleefully on a glass of chilled red wine and boasted:

"I designed the thing to surprise the rest of the group.

"And it really worked. They were so stunned they lost the first verse of the song entirely."

Thirty-six-year-old Detective Lieutenant Bobby Carr of Baton Rouge said simply in his southern drawl: "I just don't appreciate that kind of business."

Tony Scaduto, who wrote the best selling book *Mick Jagger: Everybody's Lucifer*, says it all rather crisply:

"I frankly don't like Jagger as a person. Here is a man whose two great loves before Bianca (his wife) both tried to commit suicide."

Scaduto then points out that Jagger's colleague Brian Jones died mysteriously in his pool in 1969. "The three closest people in his life either died or tried to die."

At the height of Jagger's demonic splurge, the world was shocked by his rock concert in Altamont, California, where his Hell's Angels bodyguards stabbed a fan to death.

Three other people died at that concert and scores were shockingly injured.

"Weird, isn't it?" he shrugged. "I mean they did their thing, didn't they?" And then he bought himself another suit or was it a Rolls-Royce?

Author Scaduto continued: "I guess a great artist must be amoral and push aside all friends and lovers...

"Jagger is unfortunately sucked into his own image...sometime during that 1969 tour he began to get into the whole evil-dirty-rapist-drag queen image.

"Above all he just doesn't care about people."

Drug offender

Here is this person, a convicted drug offender, preaching the gospel according to Jagger to our teenagers.

Here is this person who spits on a free-enterprise society but shuns his native country of England to live in France so he can avoid taxes.

And here we are filling his pockets...And here we are with our kids hanging onto every dirty word from his lips.

No, it's not our kids' fault. It's our fault.

Somewhere between telling ourselves that we must "be modern," must "keep up with the changing world," must "move with the times"—we forgot to tell them about a few things—like the timeless values that have made us a great people.

Things that have a lot to do with God, a flag and a country. Corny? Well, maybe.

It's our fault, Mr. Jagger, not yours.

Bianca: Why she wants blood from a Rolling Stone

Bianca gets carried away by Sterling St. Jacques.

BIANCA JAGGER is out for blood in her divorce action against hubby Mick — but she'll settle for $12.5 million, according to her lawyer Marvin Mitchelson.

Bianca, 28, is really after EVERYTHING Mick earned during their eight-year marriage. And in a new claim before a Los Angeles court, she estimates that to be a cool $25 million.

But under California's Equal Property Law, she's entitled to only half.

"Bianca is furious," according to Mitchelson, "because Mick has put the financial squeeze on her—closing her bank accounts and returning her bills unpaid."

In her Los Angeles superior court suit, Bianca also charged that Mick has "bragged that he's never given any woman anything and never would, no matter what the circumstances."

Lawyer Mitchelson, who made headlines by representing Lee Marvin's ex live-in lover, Michelle Marvin, in her landmark breach of contract suit against the burly actor, told MIDNIGHT/GLOBE:

"Mrs. Jagger filed for divorce in London last May, but she never did serve Jagger with legal papers because she hoped for a reconciliation—especially since they have a little daughter.

"Of course, it becomes impossible to get a reconciliation when your husband is living with someone else."

Bianca did not charge Mick, 35, with adultery, but noted in her petition that he's been living with Texas singer Jerry Hall for two years.

The divorce, she said, was because of "irreconcilable differences."

Jagger has tangled with Mitchelson, the reigning prince of high-priced Tinseltown alimony settlements, before—and lost. The lawyer represented singer Marsha Hunt in her paternity suit against Mick.

While waiting for the settlement of her $12.5 million claim, Bianca has asked the California court for $13,400 a month to cover expenses.

She also wants Mick kicked out of the London, England, town house they occupied together.

And she wants him to pay—right now—$9,000 in bills she has run up with designers Yves St.-Laurent and the House of Dior.

In addition she wants immediately custody of their seven-year-old daughter, Jade. And, to add insult to injury, she wants Mick to pay a $50,000 advance on lawyer Mitchelson's fee.

Bianca and legal big wig, Marvin Mitchelson.

THE THOUSANDS BIANCA WANTS

HERE'S HOW Bianca's $13,400 monthly claim for expenses breaks down:

- Rent or mortgage payments...$4,000
- Food, household supplies...$1,200
- Clothes...$2,000
- Utilities...$200
- Telephone...$300
- Transportation...$2,000
- Entertainment...$1,000
- Laundry and cleaning...$200
- Child care, chauffeur, nanny and live-in maid...$1,500
- Auto expenses...$500
- Incidentals...$500

MICK'S SONG 'MAKES HERO OF BOSTON STRANGLER'

Author blames Jagger for provoking sex crimes

MICK JAGGER and his Rolling Stones are glamourising sex killers like the Boston Strangler, a woman author claims today.

The writer, American Susan Brownmiller, accuses the Stones of turning the Strangler into a hero in their song' "Midnight Rambler."

And she says in her new book that the Stones' other numbers like "Satisfaction" and "Let It Bleed," indirectly incite sex crimes.

They put the emphasis on aggressive sex and are as bad as hard porn and blue films, Miss Brownmiller claims.

The Boston Strangler strangled, stabbed and sexually mutilated 11 women between 1962 and 1964.

A man confessed to the crimes, but later retracted. So police files on the case are still open.

Miss Brownmiller says the Strangler is now challenging Jack the Ripper as "the mythic hero of sexual violence." A book and a film have already been produced about him.

Stabbing

The Stones' "Midnight Rambler" contains several explicit descriptions of rape and stabbing, and has the line: "Well, you heard about the Boston...aghhh!"

"Mick has become the mythic Strangler," she claims, and audiences link Jagger's colorful stage scarves with the Strangler's garotte.

Miss Brownmiller's book *Against Our Will* (published by Secker and Warburg at 4.9 English pounds) demands stiffer penalties for rape. Most men still consider women are "fair game," she says.

Ayatollah Khomeini Strips Iran Of Music

AYATOLLAH Rubollah Khomeini banned all music from Iranian radio and television yesterday because, he said, it is "no different from opium."

Music, the revolutionary leader said, "stupefies persons listening to it and makes their brain inactive and frivolous."

Music thus joined alcoholic drinks, most Western movies, and the practice of men and women swimming or sunbathing together as artifacts of the previous "satanic" regime that will not be tolerated under the Islamic Republic.

Saying that musical programming had "corrupted Iranian youth" and robbed them of their "strength and virility," the Ayatollah declared:

"If you want independence for your country, you must suppress music and not fear to be called old-fashioned. Music is a betrayal of the nation and of youth."

Hosney Gaber, the director of the Islamic Center of New York, said that music was approved under Islam "if it is innocent and used for special occasions like marriage" or "during a war or for national songs."

Forbidden, he said, was "music which might excite youth, if it's conducive to something which is not proper between the sexes, like inciting people to dance or creating some kind of feeling."

Ayatollah Khomeini was more firm on the issue, saying that "a youth who listens to music can no longer appreciate realities."

So Keith asked me if I could make him a five-string guitar. I said sure, and it was like a new instrument. It was an actual instrument, a real five-string instead of a standard guitar sort of modified. He really got into it, started to play a lot of rhythm licks on it which most people hadn't thought of and don't like to do with an electric guitar because unless you're careful you can really go over the top with it: so it's not paced right, it's muddled, there are too many things working at once and you lose your clarity.

Now it's almost impossible to give a list of the guitars in Keith's collection that's going to be the same in six month's time. They have a very high rate of attrition. In the *Guitar Player* interview with Keith, I said his current collection consisted of six Les Pauls, a Les Paul Junior, an L 6S, four Telecasters, two Stratocasters, one Zemaitis five-string, three five-strings made by me, one acoustic by me, two Travis Bean guitars, a Travis Bean bass and a Fender Precision bass. I could add another ten guitars that I know he's got, including a few of mine. One six-string is a copy of a Fender Telecaster with Fender Telecaster electronics. I just made it because I had a beautiful piece of mahogany and a beautiful Fender rosewood neck that just seemed to want to be together. The other six-string was an improvement on the design of the padouk and bird's-eye maple five-string that I had just made for the New Barbarians, it was cherry in bird's-eye maple. It's the prototype of my new ("Keith Richard") production model. It's a six-string limited production model, 25 quarterly—100 a year! The one or two that burned up or something I'm not sure of—one five-string electric and one five-string acoustic. Then I made Keith a walnut five-string. I haven't seen that one since so I don't know what happened to it. The next to the last one I made him was padouk (it's a kind of red wood from Burma) with bird's-eye maple top and the stainless steel bridge. It has an ivory nut and EMG electronics. It's just a new, new guitar. It takes me about eighty hours to make one guitar, it's not very economical—if they're done one at a time!

Given that he wants a great overall guitar there are different things that Keith might specially ask for. For instance, he'd maybe want one just for slide, or one for just playing open tuning on, whether it be a five- or six-string. On a slide, say, he would probably ask for a single cutaway solid body, neck through the body, solid all the way through, a single pickup, high action bridge. Or for a lead guitar, he'll want something with

lower action, more pickups, and more control. On the matter of wood, Keith's last comment was a laughing "Oh, I don't care as long as it's wooden." For a country guitar he'd want a twangier sound. That has to do with the pickup and what material the guitar is made of and amps, etc. Keith's demands for his instruments tend to be different from other guitar

players' because half of them are five-strings. Other people want specific things too depending on their style. And of course different people want different kinds of inlays and decorations. Dylan wanted hearts, crosses, diamonds and spades, Tom Petty wanted broken hearts and there's the guitar I made for Woody where I got this friend of mine to cut out different Woody Woodpeckers out of different kinds of wood and inlay them. Woody wants his like Keith's exactly except six-strings. I also make 'em for Jagger and Bill. I made a bass for Bill years ago but I think he only uses it in the studio.

As for strings, Keith's been using Ernie Ball, but I make up my own gauge. It's a different gauge for the

five-string tuning. It's odd strings, instead of a premade set of what people think you ought to be playing. You can get a stronger sound. Keith breaks strings a lot so I just beefed up the gauge. The gauge depends on the diameter, the smaller they are the easier they are to bend. For Keith, I make a medium light—there's no such thing, actually. You take light gauge and

some medium and mix 'em, or heavy lights. Sometimes he doesn't know what he's using on stage but it helps out, he doesn't break so many strings and it strengthens his fingers.

As for amplifiers, on tours they use Ampeg SVT's, pre-amped by a Mesa Boogie. SVT is just a particular kind of Ampeg model. Also, various MXR's, they're like a box that has two knobs an' a foot witch that allows you to vary intensity, phasing, delay and vibrato—whatever you want. They're phase shifters or distortion monsters, they've got about ten of them. The Stones, as for electronic gadgets, tend to play pretty practical, they use whatever's available that suits their purpose, which is to say as basic as possible. But they love to experiment! These

pickups I'm using are active, meaning they have a pre-amp built into them, they're driven by a nine-volt battery. Not wireless, but these can be used wireless. They have built in pre-amps which boost the power and cut down the noise. The pre-amp is built into the back of the electronic pickup. It's just like a little integrated circuit chip, a series of different little things along the lines of transistors and resistors—little cartridge as in mini pocket computers—and you put it on the back of your guitar! Now for wireless you have a radio box transmitter that you strap onto the guitar that runs into the guitar's orginal electronics and there's a receiver on the amplifying system that picks it up and that's how it works, transmitters and receivers. Anybody could copy it, there's nothing to it.

On tour Keith will take at least sixteen or seventeen guitars and we'd use at least six or eight of them a

night because of so many songs being in different tunings. Same thing on any one album. The Stones tend to use my guitars in the studio more than on the road because they get banged up and they're expensive. But if I can get them some durable inexpensive ones, like the last two I made, they'll take them on tour. Now there's this one guitar, my old Martin, that I was making into a five-string for myself that he wanted and it just burned up in a fire—now I'm rebuilding it. Like I said, a high rate of attrition!

With the Stones, guitars have to be changed all the time. Some of them can't be used some nights; they get weather shocked, banged up. Generally, the ones we used the most stayed in good shape.

[*And we hope whoever has these guitars tonight is taking good care of them.* —Ed.]

Boy, don't we!

as told by TED NEWMAN-JONES

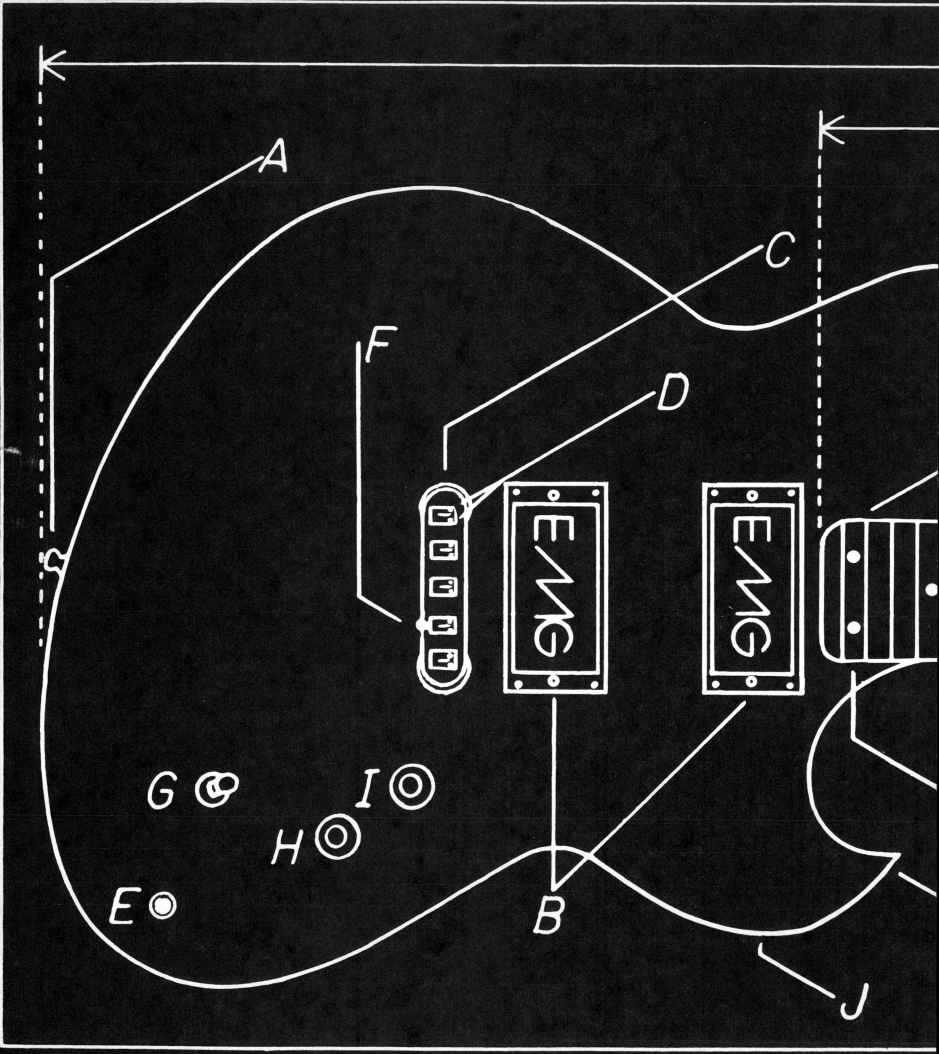

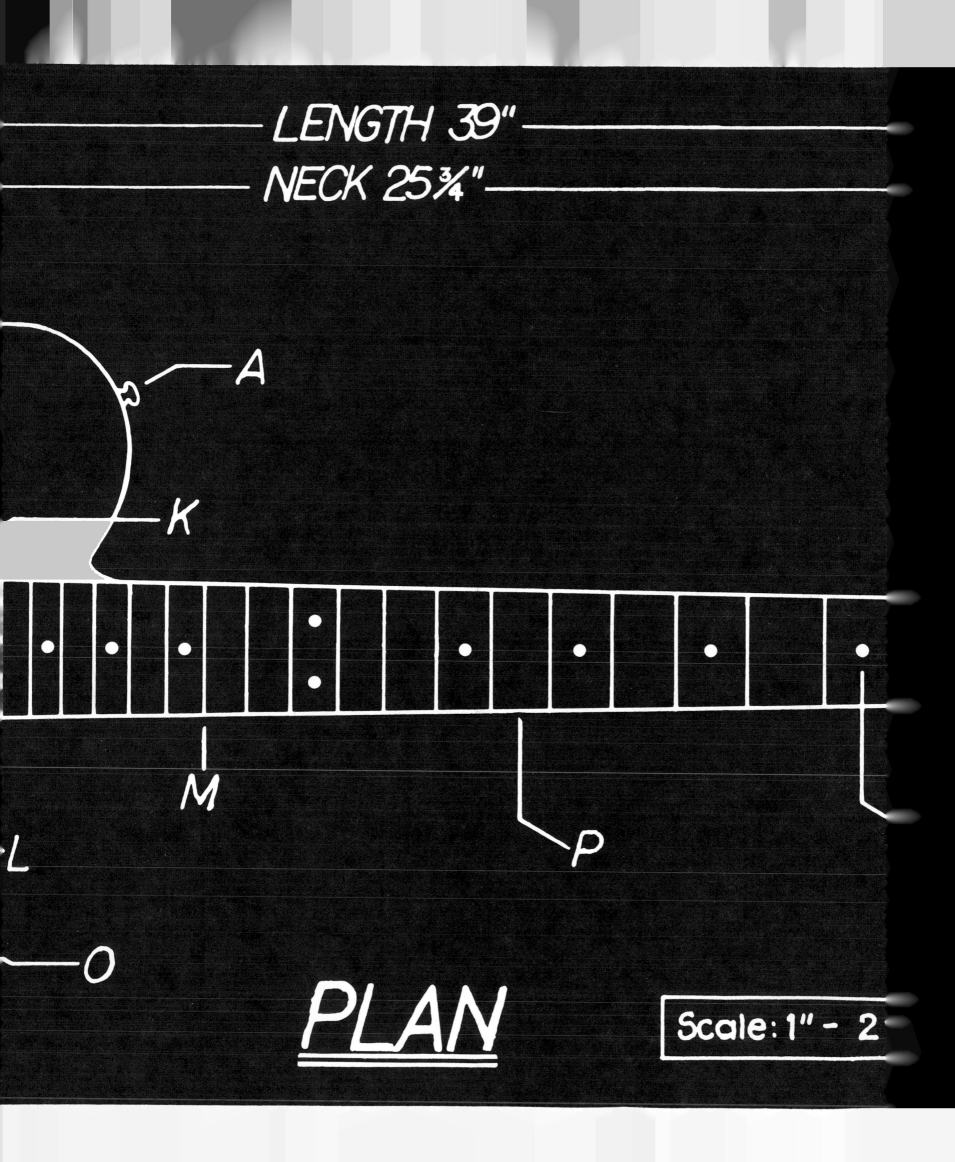

LENGTH 39"

NECK 25¾"

A

K

M

L

P

O

PLAN

Scale: 1" - 2

GUITAR MAKER
BY APPOINTMENT
TO THE ROLLING STONES

Just about the first guitar I ever rebuilt was an old Rickenbacker and I've never seen one like it since. I don't know the number, but I'd know it by the shape anytime. It was a solid body, didn't seem to be a real popular model. Now how this guitar, minus one string, turned out to be the first of many I'd build for Keith happened in a somewhat roundabout way involving a Rickenbacker, the flu, a magazine article and a check someone signed. I'll try to make it as simple as possible so I can tell you about the guitars themselves.

While going to college I'd read an article in *Eye* magazine on the Stones written by someone called Stanley Booth. Later on I ended up in Memphis, selling clothes, and cashed a check for a man who turned out to be Stanley Booth. Told him I thought his article was great, etc. This eventually led to my meeting the Stones in '69 on tour, and spurred me to ultimately go to Europe in '71. Two hundred bucks round trip!

From Paris I called England and was told the Stones were all down around Nice. I ended up on Jo Bergman's doorstep with a bad cold and this flu sort of thing and she took me in and took care of me and I said, "Well, I've got this guitar, a Rickenbacker, that I think Keith would be interested in," and she said, "Well, they're recording and I don't know if you can get in to see them and blah blah blah." So one day she'd gone out to the market and I was sitting around the house and the phone rang and it was Keith and he said, "You the guy with the guitar?" and I said, "Yeah," and he said, "Take a cab on over here," and I said, "Hell, it's forty miles!" Plus that scene how the taxi drivers drove in France, I wasn't too wild about it. Anyway, it would've cost me an arm and a leg to take a taxi forty miles! Keith said, "I'll pay for it," I said, "It's no big deal," and we went on like that for a while . . . Anyway, I finally made it on to the train and then a short cab ride to Keith's house, Nellcôte, right on the coast. It's a big old huge mansion made of stone and columns, pillars and stuff. Probably built late 1700s or early 1800's, by either a British or a French admiral of the Navy and he had a lot of money, I can tell you that. The Stones had the whole basement set up as a recording studio, where they were doing *Exile On Main Street.* Keith met me at the door, and he says, "Well, come on in," and, you know, he was standing there, didn't have any shirt on, it was summertime, he just had his pants barely on, Hummingbird guitar in his hand. We went inside this huge house and he said, "Let me show you my guitars and bring that one," so we went down to the studio, and there's a whole bunch of guitars he showed me . . . old Martin, some old Gibsons, Telecaster he had tuned to five strings. I had this guitar tuned to open tuning but I had it tuned in *E.* Keith immediately took the sixth string off and tuned it to *G,* plugged it in, played it, liked it, said, "I'll take it, how much do you want?" And I said, "Oh, about three hundred bucks." He said "All right." And we looked at all his instruments, had a little bash down there, jammed a little bit and decided to go upstairs and meet everybody. Nicky Hopkins was there and Gram Parsons, Anita, Marlon, and we just sort of hung around for a while, walking around in the sun, and I could tell I was welcome to stay for as long as I wanted, hell, I could have stayed the rest of the summer, there's so many bedrooms, but I didn't want to wear out my welcome. Being raised in the South, there's that Southern thing where rather than just hang around you just be real polite and leave and I did. I guess that made some sort of impression cause later on that house got ripped off, all Keith's instruments got ripped off, and he got in touch with me and he was in tears, told me his guitars were gone and asked if I could replace 'em and fix the ones he'd already replaced. I said, "Yeah," and he told me to come on out to L.A. and I said, "I ain't got no money," and he said, "I'll send you a ticket, just come on out to L.A., you can live with me, fix all my guitars, we can set up shop in one of the bedrooms, kitchen table or whatever," and I did.

While I was in Arkansas, I got a telegram asking me to contact Keith, this must of been February of '72. I got in touch with him and he said, "Hey, man, you wanna come out on the road with us?" I said, "Sure," and he told me they were planning a tour and would keep in touch with me and let me know when rehearsals were. So I sat needles and pins for the whole spring in Arkansas, just ecstatic and elated, and about May he got back to me and said, "Meet me in L.A. for rehearsals, we're going to go on the road and we want you to come with us." I didn't really have a purpose or a job, but I'd always recognized the fact that they were outta tune on stage a lot and spent a lot of time tuning in between songs. So I mentioned that to Keith and Mick and said that it'd look a lot more professional if every time they finished a song and went into another one they were in tune or had a fresh guitar to go on out with. They bought that idea, it cut three minutes off of their show, right off the bat, which allowed them to put in two extra songs, from fifteen to seventeen songs, so the paying public was getting a better deal and they realized, all of a sudden, that's why they'd hired me!

Anyway, at the time I showed Keith that first guitar in France, he was playing open tuning using the top five strings. I don't know the origin of this style of Keith's guitar playing, but it's an old blues tuning. I don't know if it was an accident or what. Maybe he broke a string and he just liked the way it sounded. Aside from playing slide, there's an advantage to using only five strings when you're playing open tuning. With the sixth string you tend to get a drone on it, if it's tuned in *G,* because you may have too many of the same notes in that chord. With five strings on open tuning you don't have that sixth string bottoming you out. For example, Keith plays a lot in open *G* tuning, like on "Street Fighting Man," "Jumpin' Jack Flash," "Tumbling Dice," "Rip This Joint," even "Wild Horses." So with a *G* chord in open tuning you've got too many *D*s. I mean you can only have so many *D*s before the *D* starts dominating and it gets muddy sounding on the bottom end. You tend to get a lot of drone if you play in open tuning on a six-string guitar; tuned to a *D* it would have that sound that Joni Mitchell gets. It's a modal tuning which is not what you want for rock 'n roll. But Keith does it with five strings, generally in *G.* Essentially, your tuning on a five-string guitar is real similar to a banjo, a five-string banjo's tuned the exact same way. I was playing in a real crazy jug band in Arkansas one time and I showed this guy all these Stones' licks on his banjo and he went crazy. It altered his style entirely, you know!

To describe it real simple, on an open tuning you make your chords by sliding your fingers up and down the neck of the frets, as in bottleneck or slide guitar playing. You're playing a chord just by simply barring. This is a good style for Keith because he plays very rhythmically, but it's not particularly good for lead. A lot of old blues guys play open tuning, most of them do, in fact. When a guitar is in open tuning, the first chord you make is correct. Because it's tuned to the chord. And if you know two more positions you can play rock 'n roll guitar or the blues or country tunes without having to make fingered positions on the frets. You've already got a chord to work off of. The other notes you could play in open tuning, aside from the straight slide chords, for instance, would be the complement of the chord, done by adding two notes to the existing barre chord.

When I handed Keith the Rickenbacker he took off the sixth string and showed me how he played five-string tuning. A friend of mine, Jim Dickenson, had told me Keith played in open tuning so I had figured out "Brown Sugar" and a couple of other songs and I thought I had it figured till Keith showed me it wasn't *E* tuning, it was in *G,* five strings!

We started talking and he said that you've got some problems making a six-string guitar into a five-string because you've got a gap where the sixth string used to be, and if you try to move the strings around at all then you're going to miss the pole pieces on the pickup. Those're little dots, they're magnets directly under each string and they're surrounded by copper wire. That's all a pickup is. And if you wanted to space the strings out, a six-string to a five-string spacing, it wouldn't work out 'cause you'd miss the pole pieces—you wouldn't get the right sound, it wouldn't magnetically pick up the signal. Plus the bridge wouldn't be spaced properly. Now they've run a bar completely across. In the pickups I use there's a magnet that runs all the way across, so did Bill's old Japanese bass, by the way. With the bridge with six pole pieces and only five strings on a six-string guitar, they're wrongly spaced for the width of the neck, you're only playing part of the neck. Keith wanted it all to be symmetrical, like it's supposed to be, like God meant it to be!

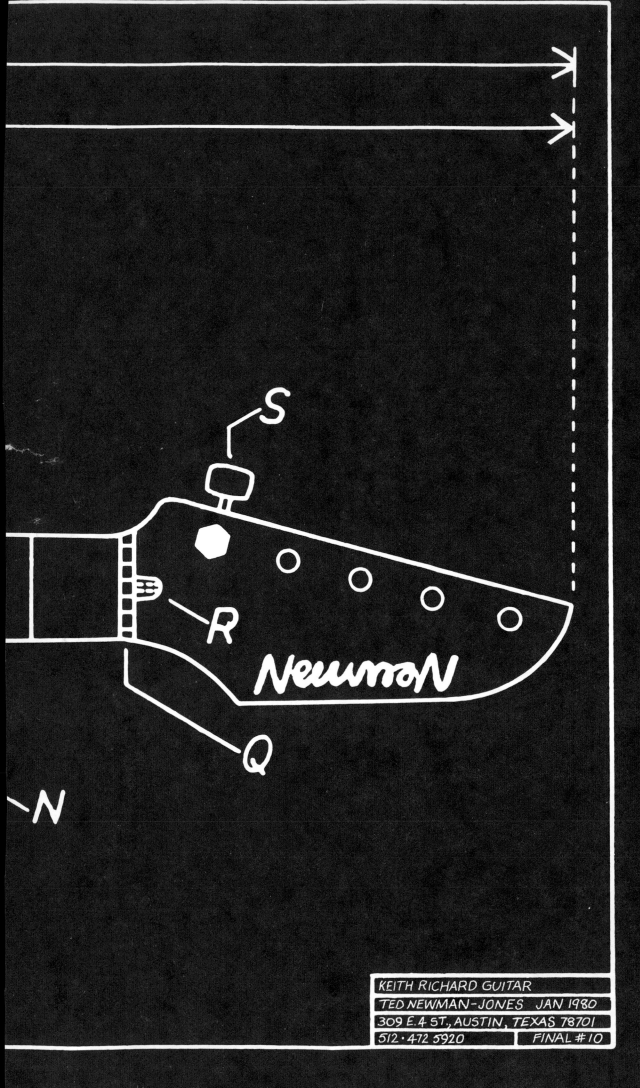

KEY

A. Dimarzio "Strap-lock" buttons for guitar strap.

B. 2 EMG humbucking pick-ups with pre-amp powered by 9 volt battery. Made by Overland.

C. Fully adjustable stainless steel bridge. Individually made by Newman guitars.

D. Dual Allen head screw adjustment for height of bridge.

E. ½" in-put jack. Made by Overland.

F. ⅛" stainless steel longitudinal intonation adjustment screw.

G. 3 way switch. Bottom position activates pickups furthest from neck. (i.e. more bass effect) middle position blends all volume and tone; top position activates pickups closest to neck (i.e., more treble effect).

H. Tone control pot by Bourns.

I. Volume control pot by Bourns.

J. Thickness of body 1 5/8".

K. Neck width at body 2 3/16".

L. 24 fret double octave scale.

M. Frets: nickel and silver alloy.

N. Dots: standard abalone inlays. (Woody has "Woody Woodpecker" inlays on his).

O. Body: cherry wood with birdseye maple veneer.

P. Neck: cherry wood with birdseye maple veneer for fingerboard.

Q. Width at nut 1 5/8".

R. Spine: 3/16" stainless steel truss rod with Allen-wrench end adjustment.

S. Machine heads by Schaller.

S

R

Q

N

Newman

KEITH RICHARD GUITAR
TED NEWMAN-JONES   JAN 1980
309 E.4 ST., AUSTIN, TEXAS 78701
512·472 5920   FINAL #10

SLAVES OF RHYTHM

"AN' I KNOW I PLAY A BAD GUITAR": KEITH RICHARDS ON MUSIC

Q: When were you first attracted to a guitar?

KEITH: Well, apart from looking at my grandfather's for many years everytime I went to visit him, it was when I got sent to art school, in 1959. It so happened in those days, that was where everybody learned to play guitar, for some reason. In art school there are a lot of better guitarists than there are artists. Everybody was doing it. So on top of wanting to learn to play guitar for a long time and not being able to afford it, suddenly I was thrown into this place where there were lots of guys in various stages of learning. And you could always borrow a guitar.

Q: What was the first guitar that you owned?

KEITH: A cheap little Spanish acoustic with gut strings.

Q: How did you learn to play? Did people teach you songs, or did you learn from records?

KEITH: I probably learned more off records. I'd spend hours and hours on the same track—back again and back again. I'd learn the chords and how songs were put together. At the same time, at art school every day, I just picked things up from watching and listening to other guys as well.

Q: Could you read music then?

KEITH: No. Can't now, either.

Q: When did you first get turned on to blues and folk-oriented music?

KEITH: The minute I heard it, you know. The more I got to hear it, the more I wanted to find out about it. Art school, again, was responsible for a lot of that, because there was a whole range of music there. As I say, people are very conscious of music, there at art school. There was a lot of jazz, too, and a lot of Ray Charles at the time, as well as blues and folk music. So I learned two or three different sorts of things all at once. I learned some old Woody Guthrie and Ramblin' Jack Elliott. And at the same time whenever I could get my hands on an electric guitar, I was trying to pick up rock and roll riffs and electric blues—the latest of Muddy Waters. I probably never would have heard of those people if I hadn't gone to art school. Suddenly it was there. It was one of those things where maybe I'd heard two or three of those records over a period of ten years, and they were the links that I had been looking for. Because in England, it just came out of nowhere. We had a sort of different perspective on it than Americans, because before rock and roll, there was nothing similar to it, as far as we were concerned.

Q: When you were learning, did you practice a lot?

KEITH: Every spare minute—just because I wanted to be good at it. I loved doing it. I used to sit at the top of the stairs, because the echo was good.

Q: When did you buy your first electric guitar?

KEITH: I guess it was around the time that Mick [Jagger] and I first got together with Dick Taylor [of the Pretty Things] and some other guys that Mick knew. I managed to scrounge a really cheap old f-hole guitar. A blond thing with no name on it—it was discreetly left off. I bought a Japanese pickup to stick on. Funny thing is, it was based upon the same principle Dan Armstrong has been using, in that the guitars he's been making in the last few years have sliding pickups. And this was 1962! Of course, eventually, the thing kept coming unsoldered.

Q: When you met Brian Jones, was he playing acoustic or electric guitar?

KEIF RIFF-HARD

PETAGNO '74

KEITH: He was playing acoustic guitar with a pickup on it. When I first met Brian, he was doing almost exclusively Elmore James stuff.

Q: How did the two of you relate as guitarists?

KEITH: Really fantastic. But later Brian got fed up with the guitar, and he started to wander around to every other instrument. He found that he had this facility for any instrument that might be lying in the studio. We might be trying to get a tape together, and after two or three takes, he could handle it well enough to be able to use it on the record. He'd play vibraphone, marimba, harp even—he'd never touched them before. He had this incredible concentration, where he could apply it all, and in an hour or so, he'd have it down.

Q: When you two first started playing together, who did what?

KEITH: We were both feeling each other out, because we were all very much into electric Chicago blues. Our styles varied a lot. I was personally more into the, I would say, commercial stuff—from Chuck Berry, Bo Diddley, Muddy Waters, Jimmy Reed. And for some reason, these were the people Brian had never heard of. He was more towards Elmore James. B. B. King, and Howlin' Wolf.

Q: Obviously, a lot of your style comes from Chuck Berry.

KEITH: Oh, without a doubt. When I was learning guitar, I spent so long learning from him and his records, that there's got to be so much in-

fluence in there. And then I've spent so many years playing his songs onstage. We still do some of them, like "Oh Carol" [Rolling Stones] occasionally and "Bye, Bye, Johnny" [More Hot Rocks]. And I still enjoy it. More than anybody else before or since, he has a knack for turning a 12-bar progression into a commercial song.

Q: How about those sessions in the Chess studios [Out Of Our Heads and Rolling Stones, Now]?

KEITH: At first it was almost unbelievable, because at the time the studio was pretty much as it had been throughout the Fifties. Ron Malo—the same engineer who had been doing Muddy's stuff, and Chuck Berry's, and Howlin' Wolf's for the last few years—did our sessions. And there was some incredible music going on in the back

room all the time we were there. Sometimes we would open the door and peep in. Some amazing stuff going on.

Q: How was your playing relationship with Mick Taylor?

KEITH: Always very good. It was a different thing for me. There is no way I can compare it to playing with Brian, because it had been so long since Brian had been interested in the guitar at all, I had almost gotten used to doing it all myself—which I never really liked. I couldn't bear being the only guitarist in a band, because the real kick for me is getting those rhythms going, and playing off of another guitar. But I learned a lot from Mick Taylor, because he is such a beautiful musician. I mean, when he was with us, it was a time when there was probably more distinction, let's say, between rhythm guitar and lead guitar than at any other time in the Stones. More than now and more than when Brian was with us, because Mick Taylor is that kind of player; you know he can do that. He's a great guy; I just hope that he does something for himself soon. The thing with musicians as fluid as Mick Taylor is that it's hard to keep their interest. They get bored, especially in such a necessarily restricted and limited music field as rock and roll. That is the whole fascination with rock and roll and blues—the monotony of it, and the limitations of it, and how far you can take those limitations and still come up with something new. It's the restrictions and the form and the monotony that make it so interesting, let's say. It's the little variations.

Q: How about your relationship with Charlie Watts? Do you play off his accents?

KEITH: Very much. We tend to play very much together. I have to hear Charlie, and I think he has to hear me. I love playing with Charlie; he knocks me out every time. Sometimes I don't see him for six months or so, and we get together, and he's better every time.

He must practice so much.

Q: How do you interact musically with Bill Wyman?

KEITH: I don't really know what to say about Bill, because he is, like, the perfect anchor between Charlie and myself. To me, his strong point is that he's always there, but he's always unobtrusive. And for me, straight ahead rock and roll bass should be there, you should feel it, but it should never stick out so that you actually notice it more than anything else. A bass should be something that you can walk on and not have to worry about whether there are going to be any holes there.

Q: Jean-Luc Godard's film, Sympathy For The Devil/1+1, is one of the few films which actually documents a band working in a studio. Was that just cinèma vérité?

KEITH: That was how it is. I mean, you can hear that. "Sympathy For The Devil" [Beggars Banquet] started as sort of a folk song with acoustics, and ended up as a kind of mad samba, with me playing bass and overdubbing the guitar later. That's why I don't like to go into the studio with all the songs worked out and planned beforehand. Because you can write the songs, but you've got to give the band something to use its imagination on as well.

I don't think you can put music down on paper. You can write down the notes that are being played, but the thing that you can't put down is the "Factor X"—which is so important in rock and roll—which is the feel. There's that atmosphere. Which is one good thing with live recording. At least the technology has made it possible to make good live recordings in the last couple of years.

Q: Today, you use a lot more chords onstage than you have in the past.

KEITH: It's true. Now, especially with Ron Wood, the band's playing a lot more the way it did when Brian and I used to play at the beginning, when Brian was very much into guitar. We used to play a lot more rhythm stuff. We'd do away with the differences between lead and rhythm guitar. It's like, you can't go into a shop, and ask for a "lead guitar." You're a guitar player, and you play a guitar. What's interesting about rock and roll for me, and particularly for guitarists, is that if there are two guitarists, and they're playing well together and really jell, there seem to be an infinite number of possibilities open. It comes to the point where you're not conscious anymore of who's doing what. It's not at all a split thing. It's like two instruments becoming one sound. It's never been the technique with me.

Q: Do you find yourself improvising more onstage, or do you have it all worked out ahead of time?

KEITH: It varies with each song. If you have only started playing a song onstage, you tend to stick very much to what you remembered doing when you recorded it. And as you get more confident with it, after a couple of tours, you start to get really good. The thing you've got to remember with most songs is that when you hear them on record, especially with our band, we could well have only heard that song for the first time a couple of hours before that. So a lot of times our songs get a lot better after a couple of hours of being bashed around the stage, because we knock them into shape, and you begin to realize that's how it should have been.

Q: When did you get into open tunings?

KEITH: I started to use open tunings on *Beggars Banquet*. During that long recording lay-off after *Between The Buttons*, I got rather bored with what I was playing on guitar—maybe because we weren't working, and it was part of that frustration of stopping after all those years, and suddenly having nothing to do. So my playing sort of stopped, along with me. Then I started looking into some Twenties and Thirties blues records. Slowly I began to realize that a lot of them were in very strange tunings. These guys would pick up a guitar, and a lot of times it would be tuned a certain way, and that's how they'd learn to play it. It might be some amazing sort of a mode, some strange thing. And that's why for years you could have been trying to figure out how some guy does this lick, and then you realize that he has this one string that is supposed to be up high, and he has it tuned down an octave lower. Anyway I eventually got into open-*D* tuning [*D, A, D, F♯, A. D*, low to high], which I used on *Beggars Banquet*. "Street Fighting Man" [*Beggars Banquet*] is all that, as is "Jumpin' Jack Flash" [*Through The Past, Darkly*]. "Child Of The Moon" [*More Hot Rocks*] was one of the early open-tuning numbers on the electric guitars, because "Street Fighting Man" was all acoustic guitars. There's no electric guitar parts at all.

Q: Have you had any five-strings custom-built for you?

KEITH: Yes. Around the time I got into them, I bumped into Ted Jones, Newman-Jones III to his family. He said he could make guitars, and we started talking, and he got interested in the fact that I was playing five-strings. So I said, "You've got some problems making a six-string guitar into a five-string, because you've got the gap, where the sixth string used to be, and if you try and move the strings around at all, then you're going to miss the pole pieces on the pickup. The bridge

on mine is a six-string bridge." So he said, "Let me make it a five-string guitar." And then later he turned up with one. It was almost like playing a new instrument—now that it was an actual instrument, a real five-string guitar, instead of an ordinary guitar sort of modified.

Q: Has he been making most of your guitars over the past six or seven years?

KEITH: He has been making a fair amount of them. In fact, he brought two to me recently. One was supposed to be for Mick, but I got to him first and paid for it. Too bad, Mick. Every time he brings these guitars, they keep getting better and better. The neck he's making now, instead of just having a truss rod through the middle, is almost like a Travis Bean guitar, with that aluminum neck, except that it's slightly smaller, and the aluminum is encased in maple; so you've got the strength of a steel neck, but without actually touching cold steel when

you're playing.

Q: Do you still play six-string acoustic?

KEITH: Yeah, I've got a Gibson J-200 that I string with what they call a "Nashville stringing," which is basically a twelve-string set, but you use only the top six of them—except for the *G* string—so you get these strange droning octaves. The thing has notes and voicings of chords coming completely from nowhere. It's strange; there is this one-octave difference. They use this setup a lot in the South. When we did those sessions in Muscle Shoals, Alabama, around '69 [*Sticky Fingers*], there was a guitar strung like that there. In fact, on "Wild Horses" [*Sticky Fingers*], it sounds like a twelve-string that Mick Taylor's playing, but it's a Nashville-strung guitar. It gives it that really nice ring that a twelve-string will give you, without that "boom" underneath.

Q: Do you have any specific recording tricks or techniques?

KEITH: I've not got anything in particular, mainly because the technology is changing so fast. I tend to pick up a new set of things every time I go in to do an album. For instance, it's been two years now since we did *Black And Blue*. By the time we get into the studio again, there'll be at least two or three things that weren't there in 1975, and I tend to get hung up on what's there, and see what there is that's new.

Q: What do you use generally?

KEITH: On a slower side, I like to use a little bit of phase or put it through a Leslie to make the rhythm guitar more interesting. "Coming Down Again" [*Goats Head Soup*] was a mixture of a Leslie and wah-wah. If I'm going to be using two or three effects at once, I try and play them against each other.

Q: What is the difference between your setups in the studio and in concert?

KEITH: Well, I never use an amp in the studio that I use on the stage. I mean, stage amps are far too big. Probably the biggest mistake inexperienced guitar players make is thinking that to have a lot of volume in a studio you need a huge amp. It's probably the opposite. The smaller the amp, the bigger it's going to sound, because it's already going to sound like it's pushed to its limit. Whereas you can never push à Marshall stack to its limit in the studio, because it will always sound clean. I treat each track, each song, completely different. If I'm using a certain sound, a certain amp and guitar, on one track, I'll deliberately break that all down and set something else for the next track. Just so it's not all sounding alike, and because that's the only way you can learn new things—by constantly trying out different things.

Q: Do you use a lot of different effect pedals?

KEITH: Not really, no. Recently, I have turned on to a few things, because I think they're really sophisticated. You can really get some interesting sounds with some of the things that are coming out now. A few years ago, pedals and gadgets were really just a hassle. You'd be lucky if they worked nine times out of ten. Now you've got the MXR phasers that can sound so good if they are handled right. I use them onstage for a couple of numbers. The thing with effects is, I find that it's best if people don't notice them that much. If you overdo it, and everybody realizes that you're using a phaser, then I think you're on the wrong track already. You've got to use those things with a certain degree of subtlety. A graphic equalizer I've found to be real useful, too. The Mesa/

Boogie got me into graphic equalizers, and then MXR came out with a separate one. I've been using that with an Ampeg onstage.

Q: Do you use a lot of feedback?

KEITH: Only unintentionally.

Q: What do you do to control it?

KEITH: It depends on your amp to a certain extent. A lot of the times, it just depends on the position you're holding the guitar in relation to the amp and how much pressure you keep on the string. You can just take a fraction of the pressure off, and you will lose it. And that is the worst thing. If you're going to use a bit of feedback, you've got to be able to make it sustain and hold there.

Q: What kind of bottleneck do you prefer to use—glass or steel?

KEITH: I once went through the trouble of making my bottleneck out of a green bottle. I must say that that was the best one I ever had. I have heard just as good coming out of a length of brass pipe, but for me, there is something about the feel of glass on the string that's just that much more sensitive than a length of car exhaust pipe.

Q: What finger do you use it on?

KEITH: Usually, I wear it on the little finger and damp with the one behind it. It's funny that you should ask that, because I've been using the little finger for quite a while, but I used to use the ring finger. Strange, because I can't remember why or when

I changed. Maybe it had something to do with when I started playing 5-string or open G. It must have been around that period. That's the only thing I can think of. I definitely remember doing it the other way, because Brian used to use his little finger. I must have made some decision a long time ago and forgot about it and just do it automatically now.

Q: What type of fingerpicking style do you use?

KEITH: Travis, claw-hammer—I

used to know the names of them. Generally three fingers and the thumb, except I find if I sit down and get into it, I start to use more fingers, and I find that eventually I can start to use the little finger again. It's like I use it so little when I'm playing and working, you know, that I find it only comes back again slowly and with a lot of practice.

Q: How about fingerpicks?

KEITH: I can never get along with them. I never had long nails, either, so

I really feel that my fingers have sort of grown two inches when I wear fingerpicks, and I'm all thumbs.

Q: What about flatpicks?

KEITH: Yeah, that's what I generally use, the flatpick, and I've done a little bit of picking with that. I like very thin ones sometimes, for recording certain things. My preferences in things you'll have to take with a certain amount of reservation. Because for certain things, I will use totally the opposite. I'll find myself in the studio using heavy strings and a heavy pick, because that sound happens to be working for that particular thing. The key is to not get too locked into something—not if you want to be able to produce a lot of different sounds and have things that turn you on as well. Because that is the kind of thing that keeps you turning other people on.

Q: How about ear damage?

KEITH: Well, I've got really strong eardrums, and so does every other rock and roller. I know that seems like complete rubbish, since you'd think if anybody is going to get their ears damaged by rock and roll, it's going to be rock and roll musicians. But I don't know a single deaf one yet. Mind you, they wouldn't be around if they were deaf. They're worried about the audiences going deaf, but I always thought the first ones to go would be the musicians.

Q: What's your record collection like?

KEITH: A mess. I carry it everywhere I go. My hotel room is usually the center of attraction, because I carry a sound system. I've got a collection of things I'm never without: all the Presley Sun recordings [available on *The Elvis Sun Sessions*, RCA Victor, APMI-1675], a fair selection of Chicago blues, a lot of reggae. I usually keep up with what's going on, like the latest stuff that's coming out of Jamaica, because they're doing a lot of things there which parallel what has gone on here, and they're just doing it now. And they've got that excitement, and they're getting some sounds which they're just not getting over here—mainly because they're not hung up by any sort of recording studio etiquette.

Q: Do you think your style has changed over the years? Do you think that you've improved or are improving?

KEITH: Yeah, I think so, I'm not the sort of person who could carry on in the face of knowing that I wasn't doing better than I was doing a few years ago. That would be time to stop and do something else. And I think for the whole band, both collectively and individually, nobody could or would do it if they felt that they'd passed and couldn't say anymore, and were just going over the same old thing. That's

why I would like to try to break the old tour circuit down a bit. I would like the band to play regularly, you know, like every other fortnight.

Q: Smaller clubs as opposed to the auditoriums?

KEITH: Or at least if you're going to play the huge stadiums, the next day you play a small club as well. There's no reason, not to. I mean, there's no reason why you shouldn't play Madison Square Garden or play the Bottom Line, and do a live stereo FM broadcast from there, to think about the audience in that way. That's a good idea, because there's nothing like it for a band to play in a small room. After all, that's where we put it all together in the first place. In these large auditoriums, half the time you're fighting the environment. In a club, you're hearing what the audience is hearing, and there's no middleman.

Q: Do you have any advice for young musicians?

KEITH: What can I say? If you're going to do it, you got to keep at it. That's all. There's very little advice you can give, because a musician knows, I think, after a certain period of time. If you find that you're forcing yourself to practice, then you're not being a musician for the right reasons.

SCOTT E. KUTINA

BRIAN JONES ON EXOTIC INSTRUMENTS

The top boys are going through a new stage. The immortal blues artistes who they were raving about a short while back have been eclipsed almost completely by the weird and wonderful works of Ravi Shankar, and they've not been content with admiring from afar, but have "got right in there" and set to work on mastering the much talked about sitar. We have only heard of three British artistes who have bought them—George Harrison, Brian Jones and session man Jimmy Page.

Obviously we wouldn't like any of our readers to feel deprived of any knowledge we have on Ravi Shankar and the sitar, so we asked Brian Jones to give us a run down on the Asian instrument.

Being a perfectionist, Brian tried to explain the intricacies of the sitar, but unfortunately our surroundings were rather noisy—like the canteen at the Empire Pool, Wembley.

"I'd like to help you out on this," said Brian, "But what we should really do, is visit a couple of museums so as to get some background history. The knowledge I have is comparatively small to that of an expert—however much you think you know, there is always more to learn. There's this fellow in the States, his name is Hari-Hari, and he taught me the basic history of the sitar. He studied under Ravi Shankar for twelve years, yet he still considers himself a pupil—these people dedicate their lives to the instrument."

The sitar is not the only instrument Brian has recently experimented with, he also plays dulcimer, marimbas and koto (a Chinese instrument, which he purchased in the Virgin Isles).

Why is it you took a fancy to playing these instruments, and not Keith or Bill?

"I've always been more interested in musical instruments than the others, because I'm an instrumentalist. Do you know, I don't know the words of most of our songs, that's why I play the piano, sax and clarinet—because I don't sing!"

I reminded Brian that in one of the musical papers it said that the Stones were copying the Beatles by using sitar on their new LP.

"What utter rubbish. You might as well say that we copy all the other groups by playing guitar. Also everyone asks if it's going to be the new trend. Well, personally, I wouldn't like it to be.

"You don't have to get that weird Indian sound from a sitar. Take 'Norwegian Wood.' Atmospherically it's my favorite Beatle track—George made simple use of the sitar and it was very effective."

I asked Brian if it was necessary to be able to play the guitar before attempting to play sitar.

"Not really, but it's an asset."

Does one tune a sitar like a guitar? I asked.

"No. To a certain extent there is a regular way of tuning a sitar. Out of the eleven resonating strings there are five main ones. The first is tuned to the fourth, the second to the fifth, the third to the tonic, the fourth also to the tonic and the fifth to the tonic of the lower octave. The frets have to be adjusted and tuned like a Western diatonic scale. The melody is played on one string, and the other strings are used for droning. Incidentally, you might be slightly baffled as to why different people state that there are about twenty resonating strings, whereas I have said there are eleven. The answer is that it varies on every sitar—they are not all made exactly alike."

Obviously, my next question was—what is a diatonic scale?

"To get a diatonic scale, you choose between a flattened 3rd (minor) or a natural 3rd (major), or consequently a flattened 7th or a natural 7th—on a sitar you adjust the frets according to what you use.

"Each string can be slurred two inches sideways on any fret over a range of half an octave. On 'Paint It Black' I used a flattened 3rd in fret position.

"The sound you get from a sitar is a basic blues pattern, which resulted in the flattening of the 3rd and 7th as a result of the super-imposition of [the] primitive Eastern pentatonic (5 notes) system on the well-known Western diatonic scale. Indian musical notation is, of course, vastly more complex than either of these systems, but the effect of using the sitar in pop music produces a similar effect."

After that mouthful Brian went on to say that Indian classical music has religious connections.

I asked Brian if he'd tried amplifying it by using a contact mike.

"Not yet, because we haven't used it on stage. It has two sound boxes, one's at the top and the other one is incorporated into the main body. Hari-Hari amplified it on a low level—it gives a good sound."

Brian had just enough time left before going on stage to give me a few notes on the dulcimer.

The dulcimer is a flat piece of wood with banjo strings, and it is played like the sitar by sitting cross-legged on the floor.

"It's an old English instrument which was used at the beginning of the century.

"It gives a kind of blue grass sound, and you pluck it like a harpsichord—I use a sharpened quill. 'Lady Jane' features dulcimer."

"By the way, with a sitar you have to pluck the strings with your fingers—I've been playing it so much that I've lacerated the tops of mine.

"I know everyone's putting the sitar down and making us out to be blasé about the whole thing. A lot of people think we're featuring it to be different. Without giving an offensive answer, all I can say is what's wrong with experimenting?"

Nothing, Mr. Jones. Nothing at all.

SUE MAUTNER

BILL: "BASICALLY IT'S A MATTER OF TIME"

Q: *How did you decide that a seven-fret interval was the right amount to tune down the guitar strings?*

BILL: I'm not exactly sure, but it seemed like they couldn't go any lower without the strings getting too soggy to play. I used to play Chuck Berry riffs under the band or just maybe do a walking thing on two strings. And then I remember going to see a band that was playing at a dance for maybe 800 people in an old cinema that had been gutted to make a dance hall. I remember walking from the stairway and through the door and being floored, just rooted to the spot, by this amazing sound. It took me a moment to realize that it was the sound of the electric bass, and I was just thunderstruck by it. I thought, "Well, I've got to get a bass, because this it where it's at." I could see the difference immediately.

Q: What did you finally choose?

BILL: Well, there wasn't much choosing involved. When I went looking I found out that basses were something like 115 pounds, which you can multiply by two if you want a rough idea in dollars. I didn't have money like that. I was earning about eight pounds a week then and about to get married, so there was no way I could purchase it. So then the drummer said he knew a guy who had a bass guitar to sell. He wanted eight pounds for it, and I thought about how terrible it had to be. But I wanted a bass, so we went and looked at it and, sure enough, it was a mess.

Q: What kind was it?

BILL: I never have found out. It was Japanese and had a thin, flat body with one pickup. The body was big, but it had an incredibly thin neck. The tuners were really bad, and the strings went straight over this solid piece of thing for a bridge and through a hole and hooked on the back. It was also a horrible brown color. But it was a bass, and it was in my price range, so we scraped half of the money together and promised him the other half later. It was a little disappointing, because I'd been looking at photos of Jerry Lee Lewis's and Little Richard's bands, and they had all these wonderful-looking guitars which I had never seen in England. Of course, they were mainly Fenders and Gibsons. Little Richard's band used some really obscure-looking ones.

Q: So what did you do with your prize?

BILL: Well, I got out some of the pictures from guitar catalogs and came up with a drawing of a bass body as I would like it to be. It was kind of a Gibson shape, and I drew it out on a piece of cardboard and cut it out. Then I took the piece of cardboard and put it on the back of the bass and drew around it. There was like two or three extra inches around the edge, and I went down the road to my uncle's house and cut it out with his saw. Then I pulled all the frets out because they buzzed badly. I figured I'd still have the lines in the fingerboard to go by if I took the frets out. Then I rubbed it all down so there weren't too many holes in the fingerboard, and got the body very smooth, with a bit of shape on it. Then I stripped all the finish off and painted it with three coats of shiny black paint and rubbed it down to a fine finish. I bought some Framus strings and plugged it into this tiny little amp I was using. It sounded fantastic.

Q: How long did you use that first bass?

BILL: I still use it even today for recording certain songs, because the sound is so pure and deep and rich. With no frets you can really slide around on it like a stand-up bass, only you can see where the frets are supposed to be. I could never see my way about on a fretless with no markings; on this you can actually see where to put your fingers, but you have to be very careful because you have to be dead on to be in tune. I've used it on nearly every single record with the execption of the *Some Girls* album; I used a Travis Bean for that.

Q: What other instruments have you used?

BILL: After I'd been playing a couple years and started getting the studio gigs, I decided I had to have something that looked a little more respectable. So I bought this big flashy-looking Vox. I think it was called a Phantom. That's what I was playing when I went to audition for the Stones.

Q: So what made them decide you were the man they were looking for?

BILL: By that time I owned a Vox AC-30 amplifier, which was really something in those days. It was like your Fender Twin, if you like, which was quite a valuable asset. So they

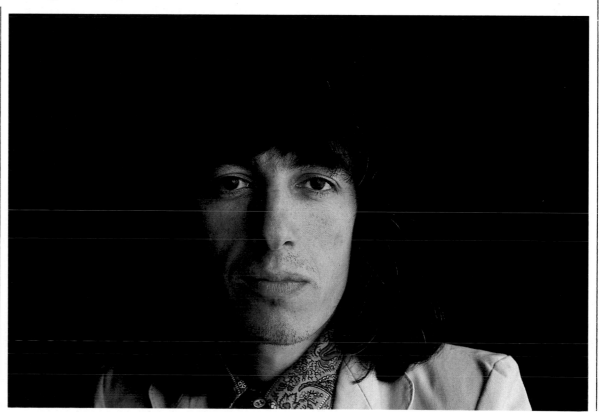

thought, "Oh, really good amp; bass player's nothing special, but we'll keep him so we can use the amp." That was the general opinion, I have since learned. You know, they are real con artists, that lot.

Q: How long did that Vox last?

BILL: I went back to my homemade bass about a month after I had joined the band. It just had a sound that couldn't be beat. After a while I got really scared to take it on the road because I was afraid it would get stolen. That happened a lot in those days, with the kids pouring onstage and all that. I had to find a substitute, which wasn't easy, because my bass had such a narrow neck and my hands are really tiny. I've probably got the smallest hands in show business, at least among bass players. I would say the scale on my bass is at least six inches shorter than a Fender Precision.

Q: So what did you settle on?

BILL: I've never really settled on anything. About the only thing around at that time that was suitable was a Framus Star—you know, with the big cherry body. I played it upright, be-

cause it was still quite a long guitar and my arms are short as well. I just found it physically easier to stretch up and down than sideways. I played one of those way up through about 1968. I tried a few Vox guitars, some Gibsons, and various Fenders, because of the sound. The boys always used to say, "Why don't you try a Fender—

you get a really good sound and it's easy to record," and all that. And I would agree, but I could not play the bloody things. I tried the Mustang, the smaller version, and there were a couple more which I can't remember.

Q: Have you found another guitar suitable for recording?

BILL: Yes. I've now got a Travis

Bean that was built to my size specifications. I played one of their full-size models and was really impressed by the quality of it.

Q: How do you see your development as a musician since those early days?

BILL: I thought I improved very quickly in the first two to three years, as the whole band did. The only exception was Brian, who after a couple of years reached a saturation point and started to deteriorate. Keith, Charlie, and I were improving fast on our instruments and Mick was, of course, also improving as a performer, dancer and singer. We were all trying new things, experimenting on other instruments. Brian was the best at that. Even when he wasn't playing any better on his guitar, he was picking up all sorts of instruments in the studio and playing them well. He'd try just about anything—dulcimers, sitars, flute, full-size harp. We used to experiment quite a bit, but then it kind of leveled out. The scope for experimenting with the band just seemed to close up. Mick

and Keith are always looking for something different, but the songs and the chord structures don't give you much of a chance of doing anything different, except perhaps on the slower ones.

Q: What inspired you to record your own albums?

BILL: I got pretty frustrated about five years ago and felt that I needed to break out. I'd always been aware that I was no Jack Bruce or Stanley Clarke, but I was feeling really cramped by the material we were doing and what was left for me to actually perform on. I wanted to play with some different musicians and instruments. I've always done more outside session work than anyone else in the band because I need that variety. The Rolling Stones have gotten so big that it's just not practical for us to mess about and experiment with new instruments. If you want to mess on piano, Billy Preston or Nicky Hopkins is there. If you want horns, you have to have a horn section. If we want vocalists, we can call up three of the best in the world. So all the fun of playing around on other instruments—like finding a glockenspiel and doing something on that—just faded away.

Q: Did the solo albums satisfy your need to diversify?

BILL: Well, I lost that frustration I'd been living with for two or three years. After I'd done those two albums I felt very differently about playing and recording with the Stones. I became much more confident and unafraid about experimenting in the studio, rather than sticking only to the safely solid. I could experiment more and see what the guys thought.

Q: What do you think gives the Stones their characteristic sound? Why does no other band sound quite like them?

BILL: That's something I've tried to analyze with a lot of people. We have a very tight sound for a band that swings, but in amongst that tight sound, it's very ragged as well. Leon Russell and I finally came up with a theory that goes something like this: Every rock 'n roll band follows the drummer, right? If the drummer slows down, the band slows down with him or speeds up when he does. That's just the way it works—except for our band. Our band does not follow the drummer; our drummer follows the rhythm guitarist, who is Keith Richards.

Q: And that makes the difference?

BILL: Yes. Immediately you've got something like a 1/100th of second delay between the guitar and Charlie's lovely drumming. Now, I'm not putting Charlie down in any way for doing this, but onstage you have to follow Keith. You have no way of *not* follow-

ing him. You know there's no rigorous 12 bars and then we break and do that bit and then we come in with four more bars and then Mick does his part —it doesn't work like that. The tune is basically worked out, but it changes all the time; it's very loose. So with Charlie following Keith, you have that very minute delay. Add to that the fact that I've always been able to pick up chord structures very quickly, so I tend to anticipate a bit because I kind of know what Keith's going to do. We've been playing together for so long that I know without even thinking about it. That's why I might be standing there looking at the ceiling.

Q: What's the result?

BILL: When you actually hear that, it seems to just pulse. You know it's tight because we're all making stops and starts and it is in time—but it *isn't* as well. That's what we think is the reason for our sound, apart from our style. Everyone thinks, "Oh, Rolling Stones" as soon as they hear one of our fast tunes.

Q: How did you get one of your original compositions, "In Another Land," on *Their Satanic Majesties*

Request?

BILL: The only reason that went on the album was because on the night that it was recorded, Charlie and I were the only ones who turned up for the session. Glyn Johns was engineering those sessions, and they seemed to go on forever because the drug busts were on and we didn't know whether Mick and Keith were going to prison for God knows how long or what. Mick was maybe getting three years and Keith was getting a year—we didn't know. They were out on bail and there were appeals, and the tour had been canceled. It was a very, very weird time about then. So on this particular night, I turned up as usual and Glyn told me that the session had been canceled but that I'd already left home before he could reach me. So we listened back to a few things, and then Glyn asked if I had any songs I wanted to do. It so happened I had been fooling about on the piano, and so we had a go at it. We thought we'd use sound effects because we didn't have much instrumentation.

Q: Did you do all the vocals by overdubbing?

BILL: The Faces were recording next door, and [guitarist] Steve Marriott came in and volunteered to help out. I had never sung before, so I used a tremolo on my voice. Nicky Hopkins showed up to play some piano, and we just messed about until we finally got it down. And the next night when the boys come in, Glyn played it back and they really liked it but decided they had to put some backing vocals on. So it came out because it seemed to work with the rest of the songs on the album. But you have to look on it as a complete coincidence. I mean, if everybody had turned up that night, that song would never have appeared on record. That's the way it is.

Q: So what do you want to do to keep from getting bored again?

BILL: Actually, I've been working on an idea for a film score lately. I'd like to do some electronic music. Nothing heavy or complicated, but something very simple. I've got a Polymoog and an ARP synthesizer that I've been using to put some things down on a four-track. What I'm looking for is a chance to write descriptive music for a visual thing. I got turned on by all those spaghetti westerns by Sergio Leone, and they got me trying to write descriptive music. I've gotten quite hung up on that in the last year or so, and I'd like to experiment with it some more with some new instruments just to see what happens. That's really my next goal. Now all I need to do is find a film maker who will trust in me.

JON SIEVERT

jam

IN TUNE WITH CITY LIFE

ジャム

シティ・ライフとロックが出会う音楽雑誌

ジャム4月号・昭和54年4月
1日発行（毎月1回発行）
第1巻・第4号・通巻4
号・昭和53年11月24日
国鉄首都特別扱承認
雑誌第4156号

450 yen

■巻頭インタビュー
ストラングラーズ

■秘蔵写真一挙公開
キース・リチャード

■太陽の使者
アース・ウインド＆ファイアー

■ジャマイカの征服
ボブ・マーリィ

■嵐の予感
ニール・ヤング

■甦るヒーロー
ジム・モリソン

■リン・ゴールドスミスの鮮烈！ショット！
ヴァン・ヘイレン

■ニューヨークの頭脳
トッド・ラングレン VS パティ・スミス

Keith Richard

1979 4 April

人気爆発！新感覚のロック・マガジン

11

GLIMPSES OF GLIMMER

Our motto has always been "Give Us A Glimmer."—Mick
A touch of glimmer can be more addicting than smack.—Keith

The Stones, masters of oblique delivery (the "elegant defensive") and men of many moods, do not give statements. Statements are made by politicians, bankers and "little men in raincoats." Interviewing the Stones can be problematical. They've been asked every conceivable question their wily interlocutors could frame and only the most skillful practitioners have been able to distill the essence of these encounters in print. Lisa Robinson on the subject of "The Last Time:"

"So, Mick . . . how much longer do you think . . ."

MICK: [*Groan.*] Now you're asking the same question as . . . we must be coming to the end of the interview.

LISA: Oh no we're not. Well, in all fairness, there isn't any question that one could ask that hasn't been asked of you before.

MICK: Oh, okay, well by next year I probably won't do anymore. So you better come and see us this year, it might be your last chance . . .

LISA: Humm, it's a rather funny way to sell tickets, I offer. [Laughter.]

Relative and subject only to the well-known Ruby Tuesday effect, they can change their minds at least as often as their tune. Mick and Lisa again:

LISA: You said that when you started you wanted to sound like those old black bluesmen . . .

MICK: Rubbish, I never said any such thing . . .

LISA: I have the tape, I promise you you said it. You said in terms of age, and people talking about age and how when you started you wanted to sound like sixty-year-old men whose records you listened to . . .

MICK: It was Keith who said that . . . I read that he said it the other day . . .

LISA: *You* said it to me.

MICK: Well then, he nicked it off me.

The group hasn't really had "equal time" in the press since the very early days of the *Rolling Stones Monthly*. And Charlie, for one, is just as glad.

Coaxing Charlie from behind his kit on stage is as likely as getting him out of his front door when he's off the road, and he's thankful for the front man who holds the eyes of the crowd. "I'd hate to be Mick," he admits cheerfully. "I'm glad to say he's promoted himself in that direction— always in the magazines—because it helps us. It's great for me because I'd never do that. I hate that sort of thing. I'd hate to go on stage and walk about in front of everyone." A relationship Jack Spratt and his wife would envy.

"Charlie Watts just goes rolling along," wrote Chris Welch, fostering a fluvial pun. "Cheerful, honest, sometimes blunt, never pretentious, Charlie stays much the same whatever cataclysmic events are crashing around his head.

"While policemen, Australians, and journalists work themselves up to fever pitch on the subject of the Stones (Rolling), Mr. Watts remains cool, amused, and only very occasionally annoyed."

Yet zip-lip Charlie, droll, deferential and dapper, never misses a beat (in conversation anyway). Journalist (asking about Charlie's book, *Ode to a High-Flying Bird*): "Who is Charlie Parker, anyway?" Charlie (stone-faced): "I think he's a member of the Yardbirds."

Charlie no longer gives interviews but his Buster Keaton deadpans and absent minded whimsy have always spoken well of him.

Bill is the group's chronicler, "our official historian," Keith calls him. What's not written down he has cataloged in his head. Keith claims that "when you ask him about the date of a session or a gig you can *hear* the tape rolling. He's got it *all* stored up there." A wry wistful wit, Wyman says he's only called "the silent Stone" because he's so rarely asked anything.

BILL'S SCRAPBOOK

Bill Wyman has been collecting cutting on the Stones since the very beginning of their rise to fame, and has twelve scrapbooks completely filled up with items clipped from magazines, newspapers and so on.

He also has enough cuttings, besides these, to fill another twelve scrapbooks but never seems to get the time to do any pasting these days. (Stones Monthly)

Years of stereotyping as the Taciturn Tone has pushed Bill back into the woodwork. He appears in close-up for all of ten seconds in *Ladies And Gentlemen, The Rolling Stones*. On the BBC's history of the group he was not even mentioned during the first three

hour segments and not once personally interviewed during the entire series. "So you can see for yourself," he wistfully told Roy Carr, "that without fully realizing it, you subconsciously push yourself further into the background." *Basically*, one of his favorite words. Bill's answers are as solid as his base line. "You could walk on it," says Keith.

"Great actually—*very* basic" adds Keith underlining the Framus pun, "—that's a compliment. There aren't that many *basic* people around." Bill's description of how the Stones' five-cylinder sound synchronizes (in *Slaves of Rhythm*) is worth every piece of prose (or cons) about how the band works together.

Brian was opinionated, prolix and given to pompous pronouncements, Mick Taylor is a subtle, retiring, gentle spirit with a tart side ("I have the rare distinction of being the only person to have left the Stones and *lived*") and Ron Wood is a horse of another color entirely, to whom a wink is as good as a nod, there are as many pints in the pub as there are bars in the blooze, one of the lads and a Face in the Stones.

Keith, steeped in the "Stones' immaculate past," rambles eloquently, casting a cool eye equally on the darkness and the light, recounting with unerring insight the turbulences, incrustations and whirlwinds that have polished and eroded the Stones in their time. He speaks with the devastating honesty of someone who simply can't be bothered to prevaricate. Anecdotal, ironic, intense and filled with the revelations of an explorer of charged spaces, Keith delivers his cryptic perceptions with a sense of urgency and an instinctive ability to connect effortlessly with the core of things.

It is around this very core that Jagger just as effortlessly whirls his personas before his inquisitors. Mick is the very incarnation of the dandy; and for dandies to seem is to be. He enjoys the game and with all these Micks in the air at once, only an alert player can keep up with his unnerving serves ("Which story do you want?"), his lethal lobs ("Maybe it's *your* eyes that are jaded") and his tautological backhand. "You've got to have all the balls in your court," says Keith. "Jagger has that instinct."

Keith's stature in rock is now so momumental that he resides perpetually in a DMZ whose terrain is largely contoured by hyperbole: The Realm of Unqualified Superlatives! As if hypnotised by his very presence even jejune journalists are reduced to sententious sycophants, a state of near aphasia wittily remarked on by Charles Shaar Murray:

You know the riffs:

There's the one that goes "When Keith Richard comes into a room rock and roll walks in the door," right, and the "Keith Richard the world's most elegantly wasted human being" which comes equipped with hyperbolic virtuoso prose which attempts to outdo the last writer's description of how utterly, utterly *out of* it and cadaverous Mr. Richard looked at the time, and the scholarly bit about Keith's pitiless open-tuned riffing and Newman Jones III and the four hundred and ninety-seven guitars: all of which boil down to a single one-liner terse enough to stick on a telegram and not be hurting when you get your phone bill, and that one goes "Keith Richard *is* rock and roll."

The Glimmer Twins, like binary stars, in the wake and pull of each other's gravity are as enigmatic as the frequencies they emit.

CELEBRITY

In fact they are so different, even from each other, Mick and Keith.

The one is nearly as much a socialite and movie star celebrity as he is a rock singer. Photographed entering Max's Kansas City and leaving it. In Andy Warhol's Interview magazine. On the fashion pages. Top of the ten best-dressed men league. The group's press agent, most willing to talk to reporters. The original rock androgynous.

And the other, pure hundred per cent musician. Apostle of raunch. Equally as fascinating, perhaps more so, in his gaunt and wasted pose. He still best represents the politics of delinquency and the spurious glamour of the drug culture.

The establishment's whipping boy, yet he continues to ride it out, with just a contemptuous glance over his shoulder.

Mick is fidgety, a coil of strung-out energy, his body always posturing, his hands beating at something . . . the flat of his thighs, a tabletop, picking things up compulsively.

Keith is slow motion, almost abstract. Even gentle. A cloak of world-weariness on his shoulders. The answers seem to come from far away, as if the questions have long been considered and debated within.

Close-to he's less raunch. When he shakes hands, his is soft and boneless.

"Contrary to popular legend, Richard is one sharp interviewee," wrote Pete Erskine. "Anyone who's viewed the oft-quoted Robt. Greenfield *Rolling Stone* interview will, if they have any kind of taste, have marvelled at (a) his turn of phrase (b) his humor—prancing about beneath the dry, absorbent facade."

But Richard, when he can be bothered, has always been a true showman when it comes to interviews, and even though the coals were pretty thoroughly raked for Robert Greenfield's supreme *Rolling Stone* interview, Keith still provided a few un-

erring insights during this session. He remains the Stones' premier personal historian, not to mention one of the precious few musicians (Pete Townshend's another) who can verbalize upon the subject of rock 'n roll with any real organised panache.

"Insincerity is merely a method by which we can multiply our personalities," said the ostentatious Oscar

Wilde. Mick has taken him entirely to heart: "I honestly feel I've got to be chameleonlike just to preserve my own identity. I enjoy changing personalities."

"You risk becoming obsolete," Mick told James Fox, who played opposite him in *Performance*, "if you concern yourself with what people think of you in public. It is very dangerous if you begin to believe in what you represent, you are bringing down the curse of the politicians on your head. Instead you project a fantasy between your reflection and yourself."

Roy Carr, in the N.M.E. ruminated on the alarming arithmetic of Mick's doppelgangers:

"Mick . . . (pause) . . . Mick, there's nobody sitting next to you."

"What?" grunts Mick Jagger.

"Mick," begins Anna Menzies of the Rolling Stones' office again, slowly repeating herself in an effort to gain his undivided attention. "I said. 'There's nobody sitting next to you on the sofa.'"

"Oh yeah?" He breaks off his ramblings and, with a sharp motion, jerks his entire body round to face the

lady. "Must be that play I saw on TV last night, it was all about this bloke who keeps on hearing strange voices and who was always talking to himself."

Jagger, suddenly realising the full implications of that last statement, offers a broad smile in defense, but not before an ominous silence fills the room.

Questions simply glance off the mirrored surface of such an elusive entity. "I simply say back to them what they say," Mick says solipsistically, "and they think the Stones said it." This is the displacement theory of interviewing taken to its most refined point: you can never ask a question without including the answer.

He dismisses the cat burglary of gossip, the colloquies of rock critics and the inaccuracies of reporters. If he believes in anything vis-a-vis the press, it is the fallacy of intimacy. "'Are you who I think you are?' Oh my God, that's my unfavorite line of all!" But *Mick*, that's exactly what we want to know . . .

DAVID DALTON

YOU'RE NEVER ALONE WITH A SMITH & WESSON:

A Very Strange Interview with Keith Richard

t's a balmy monoxide breeze that blows off the Thames across from Cheyne Walk. There's a yellow GPO truck slewed up on the pavement across from Keef's front door with two guys in overalls making marathon work of stripping bits of wire with pliers.

Somewhere between there and here —Atlantic's omni-carpeted West End smoked-glass labyrinths—the man is, you might say, in transit.

This, if one is to lend credence to the popularised Richard persona, being no mean feat. Your confidant, having arrived early, is dropping cubes in anticipation. The Big K's newest exploit, as relayed to him in the cab coming over, having been the drawing of a knife during a recent altercation.

"Oh ho—*do I baby*—I see these phoney workmen outside my front door every day; I'm movin' very shortly.

"Mick an' I feel it—but it doesn't bother us particularly. I mean, after every raid one just improves one's security systems, ya know?" A lackadaisical smirk and a quick glance right at Spanish Tony, a tall chisel-faced Aramis king with immaculate grey sprayed hair, expensively-cut denims, shades and a Hawaii Five-O whiff of neat and silent ruthlessness.

Yeah, but how about the latest one, the gun bust?

"Aw *that* saga ended in Marlborough Street Magistrates Court with a very sensible magistrate who *saw* the way the wind was blowin' from our friends at Scotland Yard and—uh—was reasonable enough to understan' that—er—because I had to plead guilty because from everything found in my 'ouse, technically I was guilty . . ."

It happened last year. The cops blew in on Keith and Pallenberg and a friend and this gun and this whole pantechnicon of medicine cabinet marvels.

"There were like—uh—fifteen charges and with every one I had to say 'guilty'—*but then I came out with my mitigation* which was fantastic because it really showed the cops up for what they were. They even tried to string in this old Belgian shotgun that was built in—ah—1899 or somethin'. —obviously one of those fowlin' pieces a father'd give 'is son when he was 12 or 11 or somethin'. And the police tried their damndest to tell this 'ere magistrate that this weapon was a

sawn-off shotgun. From that moment the magistrate saw what was 'appenin'. That I'd walked into my 'ouse which I'd rented to a lot of people who'd been very clumsy and not cleaned up after themselves.

"Actually," says Richard, in his personable nasal tones, "it was a very nice gun, the new model revolver with a hammer guard. It'd been sent to me by a bodyguard on our '72 tour of America, who felt that I should never be without one—'you're never alone with a Smith and Wesson.'"

Contrary to popular legend, Richard is one sharp interviewee. Anyone who's viewed the oft-quoted Robt. Greenfield *Rolling Stone* interview will, if they have any kind of taste, have marvelled at (a) his turn of phrase (b) his humor—prancing about beneath the dry, absorbent facade. Greenfield covered it all —as Anthony Scaduto, who lifted mighty chunks for the bones of his book "Mick Jagger" is well aware of.

The *real* questions you'd like to pose are (a) How many times a year does he have his blood changed? (b) What is the composition of the cocktail menu of congestants that supposedly necessitate this. (c) What in hell happened to his teeth? (viz. The Charcoal Smile). (d) The validity of some of the more outrageous scenes he's supposed to have been involved in. And (e) Why each part of his body appears to function from some several unconnected information centres—thus, for example, giving him the lope of a clumsily handled marionette as yet perfected only by Nick Kent . . . and that after years of study.

"It appears to me," Keef says languidly, "that Anthony (Anthony???) got Marianne very, very Out Of It for a few days and wrote down everything she cared to memorise and—uh—embellish. 'Embellished Memories' I'd call it."

Like the very first time when Keith and Jagger got up together with the band and tore through a ravaged version of Berry's "Round And Round":

"When their single number was completed they received a polite bit of applause from some and a stony silence from many. Cyril (Davies, co-leader and singer harpist with the band) joined them. 'Good voice you got,' he said to Jagger. He pointedly ignored Keith. Dick Taylor, sitting it out as a member of the audience, felt strongly that everyone in the place had hated Keith's disruptive Chuck Berry routine and were anxious to dismiss him as a mere rocker . . . Jagger swilled some beer down his throat and said nothing. He was so overwhelmed by the excitement of his first public appearance that he could not say a word or even con-

sider the dreadful audience response to Keith's playing.

"Jagger had made it. He'd played in front of a hundred people and he was certain he'd pulled it off . . ."

And subsequently Scaduto claims:

"Among some members of Blues Incorporated and their wives, crew and associates, there was a strong feeling that Jagger had abandoned Little Boy Blue and the Blue Boys, that he had broken up the group by becoming a singer in Alex's band. Keith most of all appeared stranded by Jagger, Keith was always tagging along at Jagger's side, the friend with the guitar who watched from a table out front but was never permitted to play because he was a rocker . . ."[*]

"It's an interestin' twist," says Richard, smiling contemplatively. "I never wanted to play with Blues Incorporated and they never wanted me to play with them. The true story about that is that Mick, myself, Dick Taylor from the old Pretty Things and another guitarist who's now an official with the Labour Party, Bob Beckwith, met Brian in this club that Alexis was playing. We'd sit in for a couple of numbers and a few weekend dates, deb dates that Alexis copped occasionally through—uh—kissing the hem of some lady-in-waiting.

"Mick would be invited along on some of these dates to sing just because he was a bit of a freak then and they loved the response. . . getting all these chinless wonders comin' up: 'ay seay cheppie, can yew play 'Mooon Rivah'?'—to Alexis and Cyril Davies, can you 'magine? But I never had any desire to join that band; that band drove me crazy, quite honestly. I thought it was just a very, amateurish attempt by a lot of middle-aged old men, ya know?

"The only period he (Scaduto) touches on with any kind of sensitivity is when there was this period of two months in '62 where Mick was doing quite a few gigs with Blues Incorporated to the exclusion of rehearsals with the embryonic Rolling Stones. Brian particularly was feeling that Mick was just after as much bread as he could—uh, two pound ten a week—and because he (Brian) was a sticker for rehearsals he felt that to a certain extent Mick was deserting us—which was, to any rational person, rather silly because the Stones weren't working at all."

There was no kind of class barrier between the three of you? I mean, Brian and Mick both came from middle-class homes and you were work-

* *Extracts from* Mick Jagger *by Anthony Scaduto reprinted by kind permission of W. H. Allen and Co. Ltd.*

ing class. Scaduto, to an extent seems to play on this. . .

"No. That's. . . that's beautiful. Anthony's surpassed 'imself there—I didn't think 'e'd get down to that one. Mick and I had known each other since we were five years old. We lived in the same street. It wasn't until five or six years later that people realised that those things didn't matter. In those days it was more of an inverted snobbery; it could be held against you. One was proud to come from the lowest part of town—and play the guitar too; grammar-school people were considered to be pansies, twerps. . ."

And the suggestion that Brian was a purist and that his disenchantment stemmed from the band moving away from the original stuff?

"Brian was never a purist. He used to like to pretend he was, when it was convenient. Which was great, it was a great trick he had. In actual fact Brian used to play alto-sax with a Cheltenham rock 'n roll band called The Ramrods who used to do all Duane Eddy stuff—that was *his* claim to fame."

Next?

"Brian played a special role in the band, a musician's musician who seemed to be everywhere at once," Scaduto writes, foaming a little at the nib, "whose function within the band was to use all the instruments he had mastered to create the ringing harmonics that gave to the Stones' music a texture and embroidery and made them the so-called Greatest Rock 'n Roll Band In the World. Brian's music was of such a beauty that it brought the Stones together in the beginning and held the group together like glue through the trip to super-stardom."

"To be fair to Brian . . ." Richard accepts a cigarette and pours himself another drink, "because he's dead I can say 'Oh Brian was a fantastic musician' but it wasn't true. Brian *wasn't* a great musician. He did have a certain feel for certain things, but then everybody in the band has that for certain things too. And there was a nice bit of chemistry there for a while which unfortunately didn't stay. Brian was the least capable of coping with teenybopper stardom and it made him so depressed that eventually he became a liability—and especially because of the pressure we—as a band—were under."

Scaduto, at this point, shifts into fifth and puts his foot down; he suggests that Andrew, Keith and Mick formed a kind of exclusive triumvirate for working up new Stones' material. At one point he even has Bill complaining about it. "Brian," he says, "felt that Jagger and Keith had been engineering his isolation from the group in an attempt to drive him out."

"Not true," says Richard. "Brian as far as I know never wrote a single finished song in 'is life; he wrote bits and pieces but he never presented them to us. No doubt he spent hours, weeks, working on things—but his paranoia was so great that he could never bring himself to present them to us.

"Bill wrote and we did give 'im a chance—on *Satanic Majesties*—which we even put out as a single, goddamn. Bill Wyman is the only cat in the Stones to have singles out under his own name ya know?"

Could you not have approached Brian, though—encouraged him?

"I did. Around '66 I had a change of heart because the pressure dropped off as we stopped touring; for the next year Brian and I became firm friends again—I was living with him and Anita for two years. The thing that blew it was when we went down to Morocco and he was pulling this hard-man number knocking off Moroccan whores—uh —and being absolutely disgustin' and everything, so I said 'C'mon baby, I'm takin' you home' so we left and that was the end of Brian and me as friends.

"All I tried to do with Brian was bring 'im more into the groove because he wasn't really doing anything any more—he wasn't contributing anything to the group. All I wanted to do was bring him back into the mainstream again, but Brian used that fact to create a vendetta against Mick, because Brian always wanted to be . . . like this whole thing of 'Who do the chicks like most' that started with him back in '63.

"I'm sure that goes oh with Slade and The Sweet now."

Well, that's Mr. S. trussed up and deep-fried. One of the things I picked up from scanning old Jagger interviews—particularly those of Messrs Kent and Carr—was that Jagger appears to exhibit this tiny twinkle of condescension towards Richard's per-

haps more tightly defined R 'n' B origins—and in particular his oft-touted love for early Chuck Berry. Like the question-and-answer thing Carr performed with Jagger this year in which he (Carr) leads through with the statement: "He (Richard) still plays Chuck Berry," to which Jagger is supposed to have chuckled and replied, "Yeah—but I try and forget about that."

Richard, not unnaturally, slurs off in a well-disguised sidestep:

"Mick," he says, "plays games with every interview because Mick always has his guard up. Mick is also very conscious, to my mind, of not wanting to be associated with anything that might be considered 'old hat.' He doesn't listen to Chuck Berry any more, but then I don't play like Chuck Berry any more unless Mick comes up with a song that calls for that kind of treatment, and then I'll love it and blow it out like that ya know?"

At which point he launched into a turgid discourse on guitar players from

Mac Gaydon to E. Clapton, whom he refers to as "A chubby bearded lad who will no doubt change into some other form within the next year or so." (He confesses to worrying about the Big C's "current condescending attitude to rock an' roll").

Is it true, then, that you hurled an ashtray at the altar when Mick and Bianca got married?

"Uh—well at one point I did 'eave a rather 'efty piece of metal at a policeman; they didn't know me from Adam. I 'ad to get in somehow . . ."

And your involvement in the '65 Urination Bust (the Stones hit the headlines having been caught one night taking a leak against a gas station wall. They thought it was closed. It wasn't).

"No, that was Brian and Bill. I finished mine first . . . the thing with Bill is—and this is one of the best-kept secrets in The Rolling Stones— that he has probably got one of the biggest bladders in human existence— when that guy gets out of a car to take a pee you know you aren't going to move for 15 minutes. I mean it's not the first time it 'appened to 'im . . .

"In America one night we pull up in the limo—this Cadillac limo. Bill wants a pee. Everyone's gonna have a cup of coffee. Bill's used to it, he's way behind this tree or somethin'. He has a cigarette, reads a paper or somethin'—and he sees this policeman coming. He's powerless, right? And this policeman comes up with his torch blazing on this member which is still gushing away like a fireman's hose . . . and, well, what could 'e do? All 'e can say is 'Well, put it way and wipe it when you've finished,' I think even he was horrified . . .

"To my knowledge, Bill has never done one in under five minutes."

A quickie—then dart for the shrubbery.

"Umm . . . Keith, how about this claim that you are about to become The Next Pigpen?"

"Well . . . I mean, I gave up drugs when the doctor told me I had six months to live . . .

"I mean—if you're gonna get wasted, get wasted elegantly.

"Now the thing is," he says, fiddling with the shattered remains of a premolar so that a small piece comes away between his fingers (he looks at it querulously), "I'm terrified of dentists. You've only got to 'ave one broken tooth for everyone to think you're a villain—but I'll surprise you all next year. I promise you. I'm just waiting for this new technique to come out—there was a point where I could groove on it but—ah—last month another chunk fell off and since then it's fallen outta favor wiv me."

PETE ERSKINE

MICK HITS OUT AT EVERYTHING IN SIGHT

If only it hadn't all been so damnedly, unrelentingly . . . uh . . . *amicable.*

I thought I had it sussed, right. I was after yer grand confrontation—a bit of friction here, a bit of tension there, the subtle application of pressure by means of provocative loaded questions slowly but surely wearing down the facade, until—*eureka*—the interrogator achieves a reasonable, sustained glimpse of The Man Behind The Masks.

And how does it have to end up?

Me and old Rubber Lips closeted in this Japanese restaurant sharing the corner table with photographer Pennie Smith and WEA PR lady Moira Bellas, who very graciously *don't butt in* even though their very presence has put a strain on the Positive Intimacy Quotient I'm striving for, relegating the occasion instead into a cosy minor-league social encounter where servile Orientals ceaselessly hover around.

If you're going to really get into these things, then take it from one who knows: interviewing Mick Jagger, with an eye for pinning down the human element effectively, remains arguably the most tantalizing coup known to the discerning, passably self-assured rock interviewer.

Ultimately you have to respect the sheer style and tenacity of the man, however infuriating it may be. Even if you come to the inevitable conclusion—which is why the hell does Mick Jagger feel the desire to involve himself in these absolutely redundant exercises in media bedazzlement? A man of his stature shouldn't feel the need to face the press *ever*—so why even bother to tangle with these ridiculous charades?

"She makes me," he pouts, pointing to Miss Bellas, before going for a more "reasonable" tack—"Well anyway I don't do 'em very often. It's just that . . . honestly and truly, I do like to keep in touch with some of the press. I actually enjoy their company, like to see how they're doing and that."

The first question asked is the obvious one, of course, which is: what exactly has Jagger got planned for his and the Stones' future in the event of a verdict reached pertaining to Keith's future activities or lack of same? The well-oiled PR machine starts operating with, if not any particular frankness, at least a personable twist to the rhetoric.

"The answer to the question is the same one I've given to everybody else. That however is because it's the truth, and thus the only honest reply I can possibly produce. Which is—I simply cannot hypothesize about the eventuality because so many variables could happen to Keith. If you give me a 'What would happen to Keith if . . .' line then . . . but otherwise, I mean, it could be anything from him being landed with a life sentence, to him having to report to the Canadian authorities every week. I dunno, y'know.

They could do just anything. They could put him in a hospital for months, they could . . . oh, anything. And I seriously haven't made any plans for any of these eventualities (*pause*). I'm going to have to cross that bridge when I come to it."

O.K. then but let's go back to the incident itself. Surely Jagger, who is certainly no fool and the last to function under slipshod precautions, would have made sure that his second-in-command was afforded full impregnable protection at all times, if only for the selfish purpose of protecting his own interests. "You mean, did I know it was going to happen . . . uh, sooner or later? Well yeah, of course. Christ, Keith fuckin' gets busted every year."

Yeah, but it's getting more and more serious now, obviously, until . . .

"It reaches a head. That's what you're saying. Yeah, sure. And then you've got to do something about it. But I'm not judge and jury. I can't morally . . . I can't go into those sort of details. Christ, I can tell you what I *think* of the case but I can't . . . I mean, it's not even my case. I don't know how many needles they found layin' around. I didn't have anything to do with it all. I never even went to see the cops."

The one arguably propitious facet to "Keith's bust", though, is that Jagger can use it as a perfect safety clause to stall off the latest accusations of creative laziness being aimed at the Stones from certain quarters.

"As a result of the bust, 'live' work has been right out of the question. When someone's on bail—as far as I remember when I was on bail—it's just a fuckin' nightmare going out on a tour. The police in every country are just so ready to pounce, y'know—they've obviously been alerted, received special instructions to pay particular attention, to keep an eye out constantly for you, particularly when you're on the charge Keith's on.

"I mean, Christ, I'd never go out on the road with a geezer on a heroin pushin' charge No way. Very problematic, that is."

Jagger refuses to give out even the most trivial details about this latest project, joking around about possible influences or whether the current "New Wave" styles might insinuate themselves into the patented Stones' sound.

He does, however, concede that *Black & Blue* "wasn't very good—certainly nowhere as good as 'Let It Bleed'," which was after all created under similar second guitar-less conditions.

About EMI, the Stones' current European label, he has this to say.

"They're actually not as 'square' as I thought they'd be. I reckoned it'd be just like Decca, y'know."

Then why on earth did you even approach them?

"The money, dear, the money. If you don't go for as much money as you can possibly get, then I reckon you're just fuckin' stoopid!"

Of course there is such a thing as artistic control?

"Aw-w come on. We've got that side well sown up, mate. I mean *(he affects a particularly moronic accent for*

this bit) I told 'em all right there and then, if I go on the telly, like, and do worse things and say worse swear words than what The Sex Pistols *ever* did—will you sack us? 'Cos there's just *no* way you're going to get back any of the money, right. They just said 'No way, Mr Jagger.' "

Ah yes, The Sex Pistols! Very mention of the name heralds the time be right for Mick Jagger Talks About The New Wave Chapter 34.

First off, though, one might as well broach the claim made by one J. Rotten that he actually once slammed the door on Jagger's face, leaving him shaking with fear, outside Malcolm McLaren's "Sex" shop, since re-named "Seditionaries."

"Now this is all total fantasy. Just complete and utter fantasy. I never read it—but oh dear—no, it's not true at all. I don't even know where the 'Sex' shop is . . . hold on, I vaguely recall where 'Let It Rock' used to be.

But there's a lot of clothes shops in the Kings Road, dear, and I've seen 'em all come and go. Nobody ever slams the door on me in the Kings Road.

"They all know I'm the only one who's got any money to spend on their crappy clothes *(pause and then in a venemous whisper)*. Though even I would draw the line on spending money on torn t-shirts!"

Further thoughts on the "new wave" then, Mr J? Have you even seen many of the bands?

"Yeah, 'course I have *(pause)*. Quite a lot of 'em anyway. I've forgotten their names. There's a lot I haven't seen either. I mean, you can't expect me to see them all now, can you."

Ah, but you sound so blasé?

"Well to tell the truth . . . I mean, I've never really liked what goes for white rock 'n' roll, y'know. Never ever, come to that. Speaking as one white person to another *(smirk)* . . . no, I just can't dance to it. I find it very, very difficult to dance to white people playing 'cos they get all the, uh, accents wrong. It's not even that it's too fast, it's just that all the 'accents' are in the wrong places, y'know. I mean, I've really *always* felt like that about white rock—from Elvis to The Sex Pistols—and I'm not going to stop thinking that way because of any new band, y'know *(pause)*. I do like that album very much by The Motors, though. So does Keith, even though he's stopped Anita (Pallenberg) going out to see punk bands *(laughs)*! I've got to talk to him about that. I mean, it's disgusing ordering your old lady around like that in this day and age.

"Nah, but this whole new wave thing, I remember when you used to be telling me about 'em, those *new* bands . . ."

Really? I seem to recall once referring to the merits of Iggy Pop and the New York Dolls y'know, the originals.

"Ugh, the New York Dolls! What a load of rubbish! Iggy's alright. I saw 'im with David Bowie on that last tour—the band was pretty ropey, I thought. 'Ere, but listen, I know who started all that! Lou Reed. Lou Reed started everything about that style of music, the whole sound and the way you play it. I mean, even *we've* been influenced by the Velvet Underground."

Aw, come on, Mick! This is starting to push the bounds of reasonable credibility now.

"No, really. I'll tell you *exactly* what we pinched from him too. Y'know 'Stray Cat Blues'? The whole sound and the way it's paced, we pinched from the very first Velvet Underground album. Y'know, the sound on 'Heroin.' Honest to God, we did!"

Alright, alright, I believe you (thousands wouldn't, mark you).

" 'Course"—he continues, unabated—"the whole thing doesn't really mean a light in the States, mind you. All these new bands think it's all going to drop into their laps and it isn't, certainly not as simple as they reckon anyway. None of 'em have even done any groundwork there yet, haven't even checked out even tentative strategic ways of gaining an audience there yet. By that, I'm not saying that they're not capable of playing big halls and stadiums. Fuck that! Virtually none of 'em have even got round to starting at The Bottom Line! They can't even get around to that. Maybe The Sex Pistols think they can ignore that route or something, I don't know. They gotta do that, though. No one's going to bother with you otherwise."

By stating the aforementioned, Jagger somehow appears not to have fully sussed out how the punk thing happened to catch on in our native Isle—though he may still have a point. After all, I mutter, the States is still besotted with identikit bands like Aerosmith, who are just a poor copy of you.

"Oh Gawd, Aerosmith! They're just rubbish—absolute bullshit. The singer (Steve Tyler) is quite a nice guy, mind you. He's almost too bloody sweet. He's very kind to me, anyway *(smirk)*. Yeah, you know what I mean. He's such a little sweetheart, really—what can you do with him? Punch 'im in the mouth? *'Ere, what are you playin' at, fuckin' impersonatin' me?'*—Slam!" *(laughs)*.

Somehow, this comparatively ludicrous topic draws me to try for a shot at the human being behind the grand facade. I ask why on earth someone like Jagger feels inclined to actually socialize with someone who is nothing more than a pretty arch imitator? Surely it displays a pretty hefty narcissism quotient at work?

"Nah, not really. I just enjoy changing personalities."

Really?

"Yeah, honestly! I feel I've got to be very . . . uh . . . chameleon-like just to preserve my own identity. You have to do it sometimes . . ."

But doesn't it reach a point where you lose contact with yourself?

"Hmm, maybe that's true, but I don't feel threatened by that possible eventuality. I don't want to have just one front. I feel like I need at least two just to carry on doing what I'm doing comfortably. It's acting, sure it is . . . that's what it obviously comes down to. It just gives me the facility to do practically anything I want, see, and even then the most drastic changes of personality don't really af-

fect me 'cos I never felt the need to do 'em that often. It's all part of being a rock 'n' roll star, after all."

Then who do you actually feel the most comfortable with?

"Uh . . . rock guitarists! (Laughs) No, it's true, though. Keith, Woody . . . Jimmy Page."

So it's still a camaraderie thing for you, having Keith in the band.

"God, for more than that as well. I couldn't make a total Rolling Stones album without him. I *could* make another kind of album, of course . . ."

So how necessary is Keith to you?

"Now *that* sounds like an awfully *vicious* question in the full context of this current predicament."

It's not meant to be. It's very interesting, after all.

A pause ensues.

"I've learned a lot from Keith y'know," remarks Jagger, displaying something approximating real concern.

"I mean, actually I could go into the studio and make a Rolling Stones-type album . . . not archetypal Stones music perhaps, but then who needs that all the time? But then again I've always said that Keith could go in by himself and make a great studio album. I believe he could too. But that's not the point . . ."

Then what *is* the point?

"The point is that it's easier having someone else alongside you in the driver's seat taking care of his side of the scheme while you take care of your part. And of course there's that chemistry thing there too . . ."

Okay, so where exactly does Ronnie Wood fit into that scheme right now? I mean, he's in a pretty strange —though potentially very strong— position.

"Yeah, right . . . he's in an aeroplane right now."

That signals the end of *that* little

dialogue. Perhaps it was getting distasteful or too close to some dangerous truth. Or it might just have lost all interest for Jagger. Instead—unaided and unprompted—he starts verbally accosting The Stranglers for some unknown reason.

"Don't you think The Stranglers are the worst thing you've ever fuckin' heard? I do. They're hideous, rubbishy . . . so bloody stupid. Fuckin' nauseatin', they are."

The next moment, he innocently asks:

"Is Roy Orbison dead? Hard to tell these days, isn't it? Pop stars— they're dropping like flies. Droppin' all over the place, mate! I was in Turkey when Elvis choked it, by the way. They started playing all his records one after the other and eventually I sussed the logical thing—he's snuffed it."

NICK KENT

THE HUMAN RIFF PLUGS IN

Incense wafts through his hotel room door and down the corridor as West Indian rhythms turn into the gentle harmonics of "Sweet Virginia." "He's definitely awake now," Ian Stewart explains, a man who knows the Stones' private idosyncrasies better than anyone. As days turn toward night, Keith is becoming whole. The human riff is beginning to resound.

Charlie Watts emerges from his chambers, short-haired and restless, and disappears into the night air for a meal with Jagger before the session begins about nine. Driving towards the shopping center complex that houses Musicland, Stewart describes the band's legendary studio behavior: "It's pretty boring." Stewart ought to know, having played piano on many of the Stones sessions. With his truck-driver smile and bulky frame, Ian Stewart is more the fifth Stone than anyone.

Bill Wyman is already there, also short-haired, healthy and serious, listening to some playbacks, sometimes nodding his head, other times staring blankly into space as hard-hitting raunch, instantly reminiscent of early-day Stones guts and R & B funk, blares out of the studio monitors.

The man who oscillates between wasted elegance and the blunt edge of coming down, continually defying Darwinian principles of survival, is the

last to arrive. Now almost awake, Keith Richard struts in, caught midway between a sway, hair standing on edge in just-out-of-bed disarray. He

affects one of his classic rock postures, running his hands through the prickly hairs with abrupt strokes, then plugs in, leans to the left, lights one of many cigarettes, checks the drink perched atop the amplifier, and kicks up a lethargic reggae riff. The session has officially begun.

Richard is accompanied by a sidekick-*cum*-confidant named George, who speaks in clipped tones and sounds not

unlike Peter Lorre. George rolls joints and lights cigarettes.

The first couple hours are kind of boring in a totally hypnotic way. There is nothing much happening, but it is impossible for a stranger to turn away for even a minute for fear of missing some astounding studio confrontation. (So few people, over the years, have been allowed to observe first-hand the Stones at work in the studio.) On

the other side of the glass partition, Ian Stewart sits in the lounge and reads a book.

"Keith has his own way of working," Glyn Johns once told me. Johns has engineered infinite Stones sessions, from the first primal screams of 'C'mon' to recent sessions in Rotterdam. "He works on his own emotional rhythm pattern. If Keith thinks it's necessary to spend three hours working on a riff, he'll do it while everyone else picks their nose. I've never seen him stop and explain something.

"Keith's whole idea is that it doesn't matter who's in the control room because if the Rolling Stones are in the studio it will be great," Johns had said. "The Stones always produce themselves; they know what they want."

Tonight they want a reggae feel with a style owing less to the Wailers and more to their original heroes like Muddy Waters and Junior Wells, but Charlie is having trouble mastering his drum part.

"C'mon Chawlie, you can do better," Jagger encourages.

"No," Watts says softly with utmost certainty, "I *can't*."

"Yes you can," Jagger says, his definitive tone arising again.

Keith kicks off the riff once more, Jagger drives Charlie along, adding some spontaneous latino funk on a few percussive instruments. Charlie grins sheepishly as he begins to get it. Then they come in to listen to the track. Keith and Charlie light up cigarettes and Jagger bounces about as the tune rebounds around the control room. Bill listens intently.

Four hours pass but the human metronome shows no signs of breaking down, once again starting up the four-bar intro that sounds not unlike the beginning bit of "Tumbling Dice" before it settles into a groove. Breaks are taken, meals eaten, vices indulged in. The Jack Daniel's bottle begins to read empty. But it all comes back to chasing the same riff towards perfection, mastering the feel until all five men are pumping away on the same tempo, symbiotic in the early morning alcoholic haze, beating like one loud heart.

"That's how most of my songs come together," Keith laughs, replenished by a new bottle of Jack Daniel's. "I can't walk into a studio with a song typed out on a piece of paper and say '*this* is it, *this* is how it goes, *play* it.' If that's what I wanted, I might as well hire session men.

"I just go in there with a *germ* of an idea, the smaller the germ the better, and *give* it to them, *feed* it to them, and see what happens." Keith's accents form their own rhythms. "Then it comes out as a Rolling Stones record instead of me telling everybody what I want them to play.

"The band can work it any way they want. If it works, great. If it doesn't, I know I can go in there the next night with another germ. I know I'll grab them some way, infect them somehow. If it's good, then Mick and I can finish it off."

After six hours, they finally agree on one take. The vocals will be done later. The album has a working title of *Cockroaches* and sounds more like mid-period Stones than the band's recent explorations with synthesizer/guitar/piano relationships that resulted in songs like "Can You Hear The Music" or "Time Waits for No One." This development seems clearly linked to Mick Taylor's departure.

"It's funny that you should mention those two songs, 'cause they were my particular riff but got taken up by others in the band," Keith explains, continuing to pour out generous shots of Jack Daniel's. "Those songs got turned into something I didn't even imagine. Whereas something like 'Angie' turned out pretty much as I expected.

"That's another reason why on . . . ," he stops for a moment to think of the album, "on *Let It Bleed*, we put that other version of 'Honky Tonk Women' on, 'cause that's how the song was originally written, as a real Hank Williams/Jimmy Rodgers/Thirties country song. And it got turned around to this other thing by Mick Taylor, who got into a completely different feel, throwing it off the wall another way."

The record player blasts out a tinny rendition of "Tumbling Dice." Of the twenty-odd records in the room, several Stones albums are the only token white music in an Al Green, Stevie Wonder and Jimmy Cliff collection.

A dozen antique scarves are draped lovingly over a room lamp. The back-side cover of *Goat's Head Soup* stands atop one speaker, the haunting photo of Keith peering out at all who cross its path. Keith picks up one of those miniature cameras, playing with it until he exhausts the picture possibilities or grows bored with the toy.

"Basically, the Rolling Stones are a two-guitar band, that's how they started off. And the whole secret, if there is any secret behind the sound of the Rolling Stones, is the way we work two guitars together. As far as records go, it's no big hassle for me not to have another guitar player 'cause I'm used to doing all the parts. It's just I *like* working with another player, that's the *turn-on* for me, hearing someone else fill in the spaces. We crossed the problem of Brian's death so successfully that it's actually harder to cross this one," Keith said, " 'cause Mick Taylor dropped in so naturally. A band doesn't stay together unless

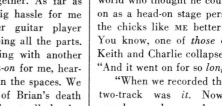

there's a *reason*." He stops for a minute, sliding back like the tide.

"As a guitar player I know what I can do. It doesn't matter about the BB Kings, Eric Claptons and Mick Taylors, 'cause they do what they do—but I know they can't do what I do. They can play as many notes under the sun but they just can't hold that rhythm down, *baby*. I know what I can do and what I can't. Everything I do is strongly based on rhythm 'cause that's what I'm best at. I've tried being a great guitar player and, like Chuck Berry," he says of his legendary idol, "I have failed.

"It's knowing how to live with each other for endless periods of time, and how to live without each other for endless periods of time. That's the *elasticity*. Maybe that's the difference between the Rolling Stones and Deep Purple. Maybe elasticity has something to do with knowing what you want.

"Hey Charlie," Keith begins, re-energized. "When was the last time Brian *really* played on a session with

any real consistency? It really was a *long* time ago," he says as if it seemed so much shorter then. "Once we exhausted all the club numbers, he really didn't function as a guitar player did he?"

"He went through passions," Charlie recalls. "Remember when Coltrane was his idol?"

"Yeah," Keith sighs, hitting a lovely sway, "a contradiction in blonde. He was the only guy in the world who thought he could take Mick on as a head-on stage personality. 'All the chicks like ME better than Mick.' You know, one of *those* confidences." Keith and Charlie collapse in laughter. "And it went on for so *long*.

"When we recorded the first album, two-track was *it*. Now everything sounds so clean and sanitized, like a supermarket, all hygienically wrapped." Richard makes a face as if the bad taste is still in his mouth. "Dolbys," he spits out in digust. "All dolbys do is take all the guts out, then it's not rock 'n roll. Then it's intellectual music. I mean, cleanness of sound is one of rock's biggest enemies.

"There isn't one producer who can handle the whole thing," Keith admits. "You run through them like you run through gas in your car. You burn them out. It's a ruthless circle. Jimmy Miller [who produced *Beggars Banquet*, *Let It Bleed* and *Exile On Main Street*] went in a lion and came out a lamb. We wore him out completely. Same with Andrew Loog Oldham. Burned out like a lightbulb. Andrew wanted to be Phil Spector, meanwhile nobody gives a shit and it's just . . . just ridiculous.

"Suddenly, instead of trying to make records, they're trying to outdo each other.

"Jimmy was great, but the more successful he became the more he got like Brian. You get someone like Jimmy who can turn the whole band on, make a nondescript number into *something*, which is what happened with *Beggars Banquet* . . . . We were just coming out of *Satanic Majesties*, acid, Brian's death, Mick was making movies, everything was on the point of dispersal, I had nicked Brian's old lady. It was," he pauses, "a mess. And Jimmy pulled *Beggars Banquet* out of all that.

"But suddenly he thinks he can do that with any band. Jimmy Miller ended up carving swastikas into the wooden console at Island Studios. It took him three months to carve a swastika. Meanwhile, Mick and I finished up *Goat's Head Soup*." (Or, as Glyn Johns observed, "If you've got any ego at all you'll never be catered to by the Stones.")

"It must be something about us to make them think this is *it*, this is the epitome, I can't go beyond this. If I can do this with the Stones I can do this with anybody. Which is bullshit. Mick and I know that. It's just a matter of realizing your limitations. *That's* why we've outlasted everyone.

"I can't live without being on the road. Every minute spent off the road I either turn into an alcoholic or a junkie 'cause I've got nothing else to do. It's just a waste of time. I can turn into anything: a Dr. Jekyll and Mr. Hyde, a psychedelic treat, a Jehovah's Witness, a junkie—anything can happen 'cause I'm not doing *that*.

"*That's* what I do. I mean, most people that do things at least have the opportunity of doing it pretty regularly. We're in this unique, so they say, position of not being able to expose ourselves too much. So you've got these horrible extravagances of people saying, 'I don't want to work *this* year.'

That's why I did the album with Woody. I couldn't stand it anymore. To write off a whole fucking year in one sentence." He shudders.

"Rock goes 'round the same circuit every year, let's try and widen it. . . . Africa, India, places it's never been before. *That* appealed to their economic sense of balance.

"Onstage, I do what I'm doing. Making records is something I enjoy. But onstage you've only got that one go at it. *That's* what's great about being onstage."

Aside from a new guitarist, the tour (which began June 3 in New Orleans) is a departure from previous outings, as the horn section has been replaced by an occasional sax solo.

"I hope for old times' sake it will be Bobby Keyes," says Keith, who can be nostalgic when he wants. "But he walked out on the last tour. Not walked out, just collapsed. The thing is, the Rolling Stones destroy people

at an alarming rate."

Ask Keith if he thinks he's got a greater capacity for survival and he'll grab some more Jack Daniel's and say, "No, Hitler thought that and eventually had to kill himself."

The food and activity has made him talkative once more. The guitarist professes total fascination with Hitler, excited to be in Germany where all the action from all the books he's read took place. Not that he approves of Hitler's politics, but the man's ability to realize ambitions amidst an atmosphere of total chaos does impress him. And he is likewise fascinated by Hitler's reputedly magnetic stage presence, strong enough to infect mammoth crowds, to rhythmically induce the mystique.

"Rhythm," he sighs. "I saw this incredible thing on television where this guy in Japan recorded the sound that babies hear in their mother's womb. And it turned out to be this

goddamned awful *Gary Glitter sort of drum sound!*" He bangs the glass table hard, three times, making the Jack Daniel's bottle dance. "But within two minutes the babies were asleep. Apparently this is the answer.

"They're making a record so mothers can get some sleep at night. I know I've got two of my own and I know what that fucking problem is. But this thing that puts them to sleep is this," he bangs the table again. "It's fucking rhythm, and rhythm is something you can't put an estimate on. You don't know what value it has for people, what it means. There's something within people pumping away all the time, even if they're not conscious of it. But you know you're hitting it every night when 20,000 people react."

BARBARA CHARONE

MICK JAGGER'S SECRET DESIRES

Chats with Lisa Robinson

It seems that whenever Mick Jagger and I sit down to talk, we end up gossiping, giggling, yawning, drinking; everything but a SERIOUS DISCUSSION about THE MUSIC. Perhaps in the past six years I have provided him with some comic relief from questions like: "Do you think you're Lucifer?" "Is there life after death?" and "How much longer can you keep getting up onstage and doing this rather foolish thing?"

What follows are some of the chats we've had circa 1976-1978 that show our slightly wacky rapport, and give a glimpse of what Mick Jagger is really like. For whenever people ask me that question, I answer: he's smart, clever. . . . We all know this. You don't stay at the top of your chosen field for sixteen years without knowing something that others don't. But more to the point, as an interview subject, Mick Jagger has never let me down, is never boring, and is, in fact, a laugh a minute.

Q: About the songwriting credits, why don't you clarify ever who writes which songs?

MICK: Well, because you can't really. It's not really true that I wrote all of one, and he wrote all of one when you get down to it. Keith or I might have had the initial idea, but after awhile you can't separate who wrote it. We just sit down and do them, sometimes in the studio, sometimes at home.

Like here, this song, "Memory Motel," I wrote the first part, the piano part, which I played. 'Course I had to take time off from the Stones . . . that take a lot of my time, let me *tell* you. I have to make sacrifices, let me tell you . . . but I don't mind, it's my own time—to do my own solo stuff on the LP, but more of that later. So anyway . . . I play the bloody piano, right? Okay, so I'm going "mmmmmm-mmmm, a-mmmmmmm," and Keith goes "hmmmmmggghhh . . . uhhh . . . that sounds awright. . .," and I say, "well, I only just started it, I ain't finished yet," 'cause I like to get everything finished, done, written on paper, typed up, all written out. But he doesn't like that so he says, "I've got a middle bit here," and he sits down at the other piano, the electric piano, and he plays the middle bit. Then I learn that and he learns my part, and *then* we make the track, and I sing what I've got. And then I go and finish the words. They're all done in one day.

And in fact, when Keith wrote the middle bit, he did those words . . . he goes . . . "mmmmmm . . . she's got a mind . . . of her own . . ."

Anyway, that's how, for instance we wrote that song. Boring, isn't it? I told you it would be *dull*.

Q: A lot of people didn't realize at first that that was Keith singing.

MICK: Well, we've got similar voices, we're from the same town.

Q: Do you anticipate any problems with this one, this "Hey Negrita"? The title?

MICK: What? "Hey Negrita"? It's a compliment. I mean, it's not a putdown. I mean, what's the problem, the "hey" part? Hey? No, I think "hey" will get past. What, you think colored people won't like it? Well . . . only the most sensitive ones. It's about South Americans, that's just what you say, you know? You say, "hey negrita" . . . one negri . . . negrota . . . you say to a lady one, a lady negress . . . "hey, negrita!" In fact, it's been done, been said to my old lady, you see?

Q: How did she react?

MICK: She said, "That would be a good song title." So there it is.

Q: Do you think people don't expect the Stones to write a song about "my daughter on my knee"?

MICK: Oh, I know, it's *surprising*, isn't it? It's the *family* side, Well, it *is* true, the Stones *are* getting on, and and have done it with a lot of girls and what could be surprising if you've got children, eh? At the end! Keith's had *so* many, I dunno . . . and other girls have claimed that they've got my baby and it's not true . . .

Q: But you know, don't you, that people really think of you in a totally different way than you REALLY ARE?

MICK: Yeah . . . mmmmmm . . . yeah, yeah, yeah . . . But what can you do? You can't go around worryin' about what people think and what their impressions are. Shoutin' I'm not *really* like that, if you *only knew* me! You'd think I'm such a *nice person* . . . I write about my *daughter* . . . and, I'm really very funny, actually, according to Lisa Robinson. I'm not really the person you think I am.

We sat down in the Atlantic Studios where Mick had been listening to the tracks of Love You Live. *It was sometime early this summer, and we attempted, once again, to try a serious interview. Fortunately, that's not possible.*

Q: Okay. Tell me about what you think of punk rock. Is it what you were when you began?

MICK: Yeah, a bit. Not completely. A lot of it . . . not the politics . . . We got into that later, I wrote songs against the Queen later on.

Q: Well, I guess "Street Fighting Man" was pretty political, but why wasn't the reaction against it as intense as the Sex Pistols' "God Save the Queen" . . . ?

MICK: Too subtle.

Q: WHY do you go to see these bands?

MICK: Well, because that's what I DO. I go out. I just go out. I just go out and have a drink and see a BAND, it's a sort of *evening*. What do you think I do? Eat at Grenouille, or something?

Q: Yes, actually . . . you do have that image . . .

MICK: Well I don't. I lunch at Grenouille.

Q: Well, I've seen you sit up

until dawn talking with Billy Preston about Arp synthesizers and playing four chord blues or whatever that is . . . and people just don't see that side, I guess.

MICK: Well it's what we've been doing for the last two months, it seems . . .

Q: When people say "oh, they're older now, they're not as good as they were then". . . you told me that you thought you were a bit "ingenue" then . . .

MICK: Well it's different. Ingenue is ingenue. You can only be ingenue once, it's a thing of its own. When you're ingenue that's great, because you're so sort of dumb . . . and enthusiastic, and then you get better. But with those old numbers, they were a bit ingenue, because we hadn't really done them . . . like "Mannish Boy" we only rehearsed once, and then only half. And I don't think we ever played it onstage.

Oh yes, Lisa. I reaaallly think that there's a LONG way to go and I've got A LOT to learn . . . And I'm going to get there . . . (Laughs). Seriously, I can get it a lot better in the next couple of years . . .

Q: Living the way you do? You don't take very good care of yourself do you?

MICK: No. Nor do you. But I do think I can work on my voice, I just need to practice.

Q: Do you think that people still put things on you that they see, or they want to . . . like the whole Mrs. Trudeau thing in Canada. Do you see yourself as a sort of innocent bystander for that one?

MICK: Really, really.

Q: There you were, minding your own business . . .

MICK: There I was, not even on the same floor . . .

Q: And an international incident ensues . . . Do you take any responsibility for that?

MICK: Absolutely none for that one.

Q: Well it's what people think the Rolling Stones are. You don't have that English male thing about having a little woman around, cooking . . .

MICK: Oh give me a break. I mean really, this propaganda about women that's been done against me . . . I can't bear . . . I can cook perfectly well myself and I don't need to go home. I mean I can go out and eat somewhere around the *corner*, probably better than I can eat at home.

Q: I always thought you had this sort of inner need for a person to take care of you, you know, a more conventional type relationship . . .

MICK: Not at all. I suppose I did have it years ago. Maybe eight, nine, ten years ago . . . I thought I did, or

would, or ought to, or something but I don't have it anymore.

Q: You never suffer? Never get lonely?

MICK: Of course I get lonely. But I don't want a relationship with a woman where I'm in "charge" and I expect fidelity and all that. I never require that of anyone and I don't want it required of me. But I won't be unkind . . . Look, everything seems to be vaguely all right. I mean it could be a lot worse.

Q: So you think your life is in order?

MICK: I think it's in order as much as it possibly can be. Under the present circumstances. [*Starts to sing part of "Shattered," the line that goes "sex and sex and sex and sex."*]

Q: Sex? Is that still important to you?

MICK: Sure. I'm sexually motivated . . .

Q: Sex gets people into so much trouble . . . (*laughter*).

MICK: Yeah, dangerous . . . (*grins*).

Reminiscing one day about Mick Taylor:

MICK: He was never very well dressed. I could never get him to wear the right clothes onstage. That doesn't mean to say that I don't love him, or that I don't miss him—I do. But he's very young, and he has a lot of ideas. This isn't the kind of band where you can follow those kinds of ideas through.

Q: Are there a lot of ideas that you want to do that you can't within the context of this band?

MICK: Well, not really—because I don't have that kind of imagination. Besides, I'm incredibly lazy.

Q: We *would* start talking about clothes. What did you think about that *Soho Weekly News* article about heroin? Didn't you think they made it look terribly glamorous? It seemed quite irresponsible.

MICK: Yeah. Well, one of the things I was pointing out in a recent interview was that people think of heroin as a glamorous drug whereas really it's very expensive and not very good. Yet, it gets a laugh now on the Johnny Carson show. Well, I don't know if it's there yet. I don't really watch the Johnny Carson show, but do you know what I mean? Cocaine . . . I'm *sure* I've seen it on the Johnny Carson show . . . okay? They talk about it. So I thought there was this glamorizing of it by the magazines and TV, and that was what the danger was going to be with heroin. I made a remark that *High Times* should publish heroin prices, because they publish the prices of all these other drugs that you never see . . . pills . . .

but not heroin, which apparently quite a lot of people take. And I said it was hypocritical.

And then I couldn't *believe* that cover of the *Soho* when it came out—with that beautiful blond girl, and the heroin . . . because it's not like that at all. And even the *inside* piece, was all about these people who could sort of *handle* it on the weekend, you know what I mean? And it isn't like that at all . . . It is not a recreational drug. I don't think there is such a thing as a recreational drug, but anyway, heroin certainly isn't it.

In order to promote this glamorous story about this drug that's now *happening* in New York, what they hang it on is, that it's cheaper than ever, it's better than ever, and it's *cheaper* than coke, and it's *better* than coke. It's insane, it's like advertising that it's cheaper than coke, so someone is going to want to run out and try it because it's cheaper . . . and

better . . . I think it's really irresponsible.

Q: All right, next. Now tell me, do you really want to tour? I mean, do you want to get back up on that stage again? Do you miss it?

MICK: Yes. Desperately. No. I do, yes. I really want to get up there. Whether Bill can get up there or not is another matter. He said he was going to retire, didn't he? In two years. He named the date. We've got two years to find another bass player.

Q: What's kept you from being bored, though?

MICK: That's a good one. Um. I'll take *heroin*. I'd better buy it now while it's cheap (*laughs*).

Q: Do you feel that most of your life you've been busy doing something that you don't really know what it is?

MICK: Yeah, really. I'm not interested in defining it.

LISA ROBINSON

MAGIC, MUSIC AND DRUGS

Keith Richard has lived with Anita Pallenberg for twelve years. They have two children, Marlon (eight) and Dandy (six). When we visited them at their country house in Westchester County, Dandy was in England with Keith's mother, but Taryn Phillips (John and Genevieve Waite's six-year-old son) was there visiting Marlon. Keith and Anita have a great relationship with their kids. When Marlon staggered into the living room at 10 a.m., rubbing his eyes, Keith made him breakfast.

Before the interview, I asked Keith if he had read William Burroughs' statement: "I think I am in better health now as a result of using junk at intervals than I would have been if I had never been an addict." (*Junky*, 1953: asked recently if he still stood by this, W.S.B. answered, with a sanguine nod, "Certainly.")

Keith had actually taken the apomorphine cure with Dr. Dent's notorious assistant, Smitty: "Dr. Dent is dead, see, but his assistant whom he trained, this lovely old dear 'oo's like a mother hen called Smitty, still runs the clinic. I 'ad 'er down to my place for five days and she just sort of comes in and says: ''ere's your shot dear, there's

a good boy.' Or, 'You've been a naughty boy. You've taken something, yes you 'ave, I can tell.'"

We did the interview by Keith's swimming pool.

"This is the first time I've sat beside a swimming pool during the summer in four years," he said.

Q: Did you ever read De Quincey's book on the opium eater?

KEITH: It's one of those books that I started. I'd also started *Diary of a Drug Fiend*, Aleister Crowley's book on the twenties. And some Arthur Machen stuff: *White Powder* was a great story. That's where a guy has a friend who changes slowly as he takes this white powder. From a happy-go-

lucky fellow, 'e becomes morose and, you know, *withdrawn*. Nobody sees him, until one day there's this foul black liquid starts dripping through the ceiling of 'is friend 'oo lives below. They go up there and 'ee's not to be found, you know. That's 'im. This black drip.

Q: There are some incredibly beautiful passages in De Quincey's book where he describes taking off.

KEITH: I've read some nineteenth-century descriptions of smoking marijuana and it's as if they were talking about the most incredible acid.

Q: I was reading David Niven's autobiography a while ago where he talks about smoking a lot of grass with Errol Flynn in Hollywood in the thirties. David says he never got off.

KEITH: Oh, right, they never do, do they? (*putting on a stiff upper-class accent*) "I don't see what they get out of this. No effect at all." Like they never think of the possibility that they are just too insensitive to notice. Or they just never took the time to notice. I'm sure Errol Flynn got off!

Q: Do you pay a lot of attention to taking care of yourself physically, considering the amount of work you have to do?

KEITH: I don't pay that much attention to it, just because I've never had to. I'm very lucky in that everything's always functioned perfectly, even under the most incredible strains and amounts of chemicals. But I think a lot of it has to do with a solid consciousness of it in a regulatory system which serves me. I never take too much of anything. I don't go out for a big rush or complete obliteration. I sometimes find that I've been up five days, and I'll collapse and just fall asleep, but that's about the only thing that I do to myself and I only do that because I find that I'm capable of doing it.

Q: Have you ever been in a dangerous situation with drugs?

KEITH: No. I don't know if I've been extremely lucky or if it's that subconscious regulatory thing I've gotten because I'm not extremely careful, but I've never turned blue in somebody else's bathroom. I mean, I consider that the height of bad manners. I've 'ad so many people do it to me and

it's really not on, as far as drug etiquette goes, to turn blue in somebody else's john. You suddenly realise that somebody's been in there for like an hour and you 'aven't 'eard a sound and I think it's such a drag, because, you know, I think it's a drag when people do it to me, thumping on the door: "Are you all right?"

"Yeah! I'm having a fucking crap!"

But people do do it. I mean, if somebody's been in the john for hours and hours I'll do it and I know 'ow annoying it is when I 'ear the voice comin' out: "Yeah, I'm all right!" But, I mean, sometimes I'm glad I've done it because, you know, we've knocked the door down and there's somebody going into the last stages of the colors of the rainbow and that's really a drag.

The ambulance comes and . . . cleans everything up. Because you can't pretend 'e's just fallen ill or something.

Q: Is music magic to you?

KEITH: In the way that magic is a word for something that is power that we don't fully understand and can enable things to happen. I mean, nobody really understands about the effect that certain rhythms have on

people, but our bodies beat. We're only alive because the heart beat keeps going all the time. And also certain sounds can kill. It's a speciality of the French for some reason. The French are working with huge great speakers which blow down houses and kill laboratory technicians with one solitary blast. I mean, the trumpets of Jericho and all that. I've seen people physically throw up from feedback in the studio. It's so loud it started their stomach walls flapping. That's the most obvious aspect of it. But on another level, if you go to Africa or Jamaica, you see people living to that rhythm. They eat, talk, walk, fuck, sleep, do everything to that rhythm. It's magic in that it's an unexplored area. Why, for instance—zoom in 'ere—should

rock and roll music suddenly appear in the mid-fifties, catch hold, and just get bigger and bigger and bigger and show no signs of abating?

Q: Do you feel that it was your destiny to be a musician?

KEITH: Well, when I used to pose in front of the mirror at 'ome, I was hopeful. The only thing I was lacking was a bit of bread to buy an instru-

ment. But I got the moves off first and I got the guitar later.

Q: Is the guitar an instrument you can get further and further into?

KEITH: Yeah, it is. I'm sure Segovia is still learning a few licks here and there. I think most guitar players feel that they're always just learning still. Nobody ever feels that they've reached anywhere near covering the whole thing. It's still coming up with surprises. Although that's not *the* most important thing to me. It's never been a function in our band to do one thing or another. We're all doing all of it, you know. That's what happens and that's what interests me about it, it's not who's playing virtuoso. I'm interested in what people can do in terms of an overall sound and the intensity of it that can be done on that level. I mean, five people produce one thing out of five separate things going on. After all, what's the point of dissecting everything and putting parts under a microscope and ignoring the rest?

Q: Do you get very high off the response to your records when they're particularly effective in some way?

KEITH: Yeah, sometimes, you try to, but it's not always that immediate. You put a record out and then you get the feeling everybody's disappointed with it. Then two years later you bring another record out and you suddenly realize that they're all holding this other record up and saying "If only it was as good as this one." And I know it's not because we're ahead of our time because that's not ever what we're trying to do, it's not avant-garde, no, that's not it. It's just that when you've been around as long as we have, people have got their own fixed idea of what they want from the Stones and its never anything new, even though they do really want it, they still compare it with this big moment in the backseat of a car fifteen years ago and it's never as good as then. There's so much nostalgia connected with it that you can't possibly fight, so you have to sometimes let the record seep into their lives, let them have a good time with it first. Because a lot of the time with records it's the experiences that people have been through while that record's been playing that makes it special to them. (*making a face and putting on mock upper-class British accent*) "It's our song darling." So that sort of shit. And the longer you've been around, the harder it is to fight that one, 'cos you got so much other stuff which is somebody else's song darling. And although they're interested and they'll buy the new record, it doesn't mean as much to them as the one they heard that magical night when they screwed fifteen chicks.

Q: Do you feel the records continue to make progress?

KEITH: Everybody's blinded by the technology of it at the moment.

Technology is useful. But also I feel that just because you have 24 tracks it takes 24 times longer to make an album, because it's all such a decision-delaying process. I mean, in the old days, whatever you laid down on tape in the studio was just about it. Now you've got every instrument all split up on tape spread over three different tracks. I mean everybody says we'll do two or three solos new and we'll decide later, which means that you're in a completely different frame of mind and you don't even remember what you were trying to do when you actually come to decide what it is that you were doing in the first place.

Q: So do you write a song that you're really into and then take it into the studio and it comes out in a way that isn't fulfilling your original intention?

KEITH: I've got two thoughts about that. I don't think just because you write a song that you necessarily know what it should sound like. 'Cos, after all, if you're gonna give it to a band to play, then I find it a bit dictatorial to say "Well this is the song and this is how it goes and everybody's gonna play this." Because if you're gonna share this song and 'ave it played by everybody else you give it to them and it changes. I prefer to write a song as little as possible. I'd rather do the bare bones of it and give it to the rest and say, "Well, what do you make of that?" I find that much fairer.

Q: Do you think of songs as short stories?

KEITH: Some of them. I mean, things like "Hand of Fate" particularly, we got into a story, others are just connections, almost stream of consciousness. One line doesn't really connect to what's gone before. People say they write songs, but in a way you're more the medium. I feel like all the songs in the world are just floating around, it's just a matter of like an antenna, of whatever you pick up. So many uncanny things have happened. A whole song just appears from nowhere in five minutes, the whole structure, and you haven't worked at all.

Q: Have you thought at all about doing a concert tour like Dylan's *Rolling Thunder*. Is it totally impossible for you to do that still?

KEITH: No. I think that's the way things have really gotta go. I can't see going around forever playing bigger and bigger baseball parks and superdomes. I think audiences have gone about as far as you can go with it. In fact I think a lot of people probably

don't go because they just can't stand to go to those places, you know.

See, rock and roll keeps half these stadiums in America in the black. If it wasn't for that, half of them would just be closed down. Yet none of them are built with any consideration for playing music in. They're ice hockey stadiums, tennis courts, everything but rock and roll. I mean, also, there's audiences in South America, nobody goes there. Behind the iron curtain they're screaming out for somebody to come and see them. It's not all the bands' fault. They'd go there if it was made a lot easier to get there. It's not easy to get to these places. You've got everything working against you, from the sort of agent-manager flim-flam syndrome of "why should we send them to South America where nobody knows how to put on a tour and its miles

away, when we can stick them in the Garden for six nights and make a fortune." There's no P.A. on the whole of the South American continent that's worthy of the name, so that means that one has to be shipped there. There's every reason not to go there, except that the audiences are there and they're crying out to see people that they keep reading about. I mean they buy thousands of magazines just to see some crappy pictures of Mick and Bianca on the middle-page spread, you know . . . the middle-aged spread.

Q: Have you been forced to become a businessman as well as a musician?

KEITH: Only for short periods of time. Once a year I go through the little folder. This has come in, this has gone out. This is a projection of next year. And then I wonder why bother

Keith jams with Jim Carroll.

to read it anyway, because it hasn't made the slightest bit of difference to my day, or the next day. What's important is that I keep on doing what I do, not how much money it's making.

Q: Do you hang around with each other or does the group completely separate?

KEITH: These days everybody just fragments too, so suddenly you're alone from all these people who you've been incredibly close to for two or three months. Sometimes Ronnie and I are with each other for five or six days on the trot. Other people have been to sleep six times and we've seen six dawns. You can't even remember the last time you slept because you've got this memory . . . It's funny, you know, when you sleep everything is so neatly put into compartments of that day and that day, and I did that on that day, but if you stay up for five or six days the memory goes back into one long period with no breaks at all and days don't mean anything anymore. You just remember either people or specific events.

Q: If you all keep in good shape, do you think you have another fifteen years?

KEITH: Oh yeah. I hope so. There's no way to tell. We know a lot of the old black boys have kept going forever. A lot of the old roots boys, the old blues players, and as far as we're concerned they're virtually playing the same thing. They kept going till the day they dropped. They still are. B. B. King's close to sixty. Jimmy Reed died last year and he was going to the end. Chuck Berry's still going. Muddy Waters just had one of his biggest albums ever, Howling Wolf kept going to the very end, Sleepy John just died last month, he was preparing to go on a European tour . . . I mean, Elvis was the one that I would have said, but he happened to have went early. It's a physical thing. There's no denying that there's a high fatality rate in rock and roll. Up until the middle sixties the most obvious method of rock and roll death was chartered planes. Since then drugs have taken their toll, but all of the people that I 'ave known that 'ave died from so-called drug overdoses 'ave all been people that've 'ad some fairly serious physical weakness somewhere.

Q: Do you ever get worried that they'll finally get you?

KEITH: Well, I mean if they haven't done it by now, no. I mean, 'cos it must be fairly obvious to everybody now that they've 'ad a go with trying. If they try again I don't see any real way they can get away with it just because they have been trying to get me and it never works that way.

VICTOR BOCKRIS

Thursday, September 29, 1977, 3 p.m., the Factory board room overlooking unique Union Square. Three Rolling Stones, Mick Jagger, Keith Richard and Ron Wood, arrive for tea (Moët et Chandon) accompanied by Earl McGrath, President of Rolling Stones Records, which recently released *Love You Live*. Andy Warhol is assisted during this interview by *Interview*'s European Editor, Catherine Guinness, and towards the end, Victor Hugo, the Venezuelan artist.

KEITH: (reading thoughtfully, *Daily Express*) "Kids ruin Elton's new restaurant."

RON: Yeah, Rolling Stones wreck restaurant. . . .

MICK: They all went for a meal.

AW: *Did you? When was that?*

KEITH: Stuck chewing gum all over the—

MICK: Did you? You naughty boy. Is it a chichi restaurant?

RON: But anyway it wasn't that. The food wasn't any good.

KEITH: The food was useless.

RON: So we left what we thought it was worth.

MICK: No, you told me that. They said eighty quid and—

KEITH: We left thirty and it wasn't enough.

MICK: How many people?

KEITH: Three?

MICK: That's a bit cheap. You can't get a meal for a fiver, even a bad one.

EARL MCGRATH: Where?

RON: In Covent Garden.

MICK: It's called Friends. We're gonna advertise it.

AW: *Are you going away Keith?*

KEITH: Am I going away? We all are, yes.

MICK: We're all going to Paris, France.

KEITH: We're all going to make a record.

RON: The trouble is none of us has told the other when.

MICK: Look, we're gonna meet there on Wednesday . . .

CATHERINE: *Why record in Paris?*

MICK: We haven't recorded there yet.

KEITH: We go where it's available.

MICK: Nobody will have us.

AW: *Does it make a difference where you record?*

MICK: These days most studios are the same to be honest, so—

KEITH: They're like Holiday Inns.

CATHERINE: *Do you remember your first meeting with Andy?*

MICK: With Andy? Wasn't it at Jane Holzer's?

AW: *Baby Jane Holzer's.*

MICK: At a party. Do you remember, Keith? You were there.

AW: *It was the first time you were in New York.*

KEITH: I don't know who she is.

MICK: And it was our first party when we came to new York. Now he's going to remember.

CATHERINE: *Was it a good party?*

MICK: Well, everyone seems to remember it, even Keith does now. Everyone was there. Everyone was there.

KEITH: I thought that was well worth remembering.

MICK: But Andy and I never spoke to each other again for about seven years.

CATHERINE: *Why?*

MICK: I don't know. But then he did . . . for some reason. We had to work together, let's see, from 1963 to 1969.

AW: *When I had to photograph your zipper for the cover of* Sticky Fingers.

MICK: Yeah, that's when we had to talk to each other . . . again.

KEITH: I met Murray the K on this ridiculous—

MICK: Oh, the weirdest thing was when Murray the K was really down on his luck and he'd just started up this new radio thing. I was just gonna go on stage, and he had this Uher tape recorder and he says, "Mick, I'm back in the business and I've got this syndicated show and I just want you to say a few words just for old times, you remember Murray the K, ha, ha." And just then the strap breaks on his Uher and it goes smashing to the ground and I said, "Well, that's the last word."

KEITH: Murray. Poor old Murray.

EARL: Do you know that Ahmet used to call him up and say, "Could I speak to Murray The K. It's Ahmet The E."

MICK: It's like Anouk Aimee tripping over the curb in last month's *Interview*.

AW: *She said she always trips.*

MICK: "I always do things like that." What a silly girl then. Is it camp enough, this interview? I always want to get into the feel of it, you know. A bit.

CATHERINE: *Do you think you're being too serious?*

MICK: No, we're just too butch.

CATHERINE: *It's a bit butch, it's true.*

AW: *Is it true that original melodies are running out?*

MICK: I don't believe in original melodies. There are only so many computations of eight notes.

CATHERINE: *Which is rather a lot. I think it's eight to the power . . .*

MICK: Eight to the power of eight.

AW: *Where do you think the new music is coming from?*

MICK: You gotta ask Keith, he's a musician.

AW: *Do you think punk rock is new?*

MICK: Come on punk rock questions, come on get your answers.

KEITH: It ain't.

RON: It's a good breather, isn't it?

MICK: Yeah. I'll breathe out for that one.

KEITH: Punk rock?

MICK: Some's rubbish and some's great. I think in England it's much more of a real thing than it is here, I think, here it's kind of like an association. In London you got all these kids that are really out of work, you know, they got nothing else to do but play in rock groups. Rather similar to us. . . .

KEITH: It's always been the same. . . .

MICK: No matter what Johnny Rotten and Sid Vicious do, they can't be more disgusting than the Rolling Stones are in an orgy of biting.

CATHERINE: *Have the Sex Pistols tried to beat you up?*

MICK: Oh no. They've stopped short of violence. I think even Sid Vicious is basically a nice guy, but Johnny Rotten keeps talking bad about me. He'll get his rotten teeth kicked in one day.

KEITH: They're fucking just asking for it if they always insist on catching public transport on the way home from their gigs.

MICK: They still live with their mums you know. Johnny Rotten says, "I still live with my mum, in a block of flats."

KEITH: He moved to the slums, right?

MICK: He's not revealing it though.

KEITH: I think his mum kicked him out. . . .

CATHERINE: *So how's Margaret Thatcher doing these days?*

MICK: Far better than Margaret Trudeau.

CATHERINE: *That's right.* The Daily Mail, *which is rather left wing, as you would agree, Mick, had a big thing praising her.*

MICK: It might be left wing to your father, but it's certainly not left wing to me. How's your father these days? He got kicked out of The Monday Club, didn't he?

CATHERINE: *No, he resigned, he was. . . .*

MICK: He was kicked out, come on, give up, resigned!

KEITH: Given the boot . . . come on.

AW: *How many hotels have you been kicked out of?*

MICK: Oh, not many, about three hundred.

CATHERINE: *What was your biggest bill for damages?*

EARL: $8,000 at The Bristol in Vienna.

MICK: And we didn't pay, I hope.

AW: *Why? Because you gave them so much publicity?*

MICK: It was Ahmet's fault.

AW: *Ahmet did it all?*

MICK: No, you see, he said I'd quieted down somewhat. . . .

EARL: So they waited until the last night of the tour and they tore *my* room apart.

MICK: HA HA HA HA HA. It was rather nicely done, in sort of imitation Empire style with those little cabinets with little paintings and shit—"No, not the chandelier!"

AW: *If you want to be seen you can put your chin up more and if you want to disappear—you can wear a wig.*

KEITH: Exactly. Like walking through the Plaza lobby when the Zeppelin are staying there—you're automatically under scrutiny, everybody's looking for a rock star.

MICK: If you walk through any hotel lobby where some other group is staying you're asking for it.

RON: It's full of short men in raincoats making statements for their group's managers.

AW: *Do managers all have the same look?*

MICK: They all look like Brian Ferry.

AW: *Do you sign autographs if people ask you?*

KEITH: Oh yeah. It's such a small thing, and it's obviously important to them in some way.

AW: *Do you play your guitars every day, Keith?*

KEITH: Just about.

RON: We build up towards playing every day, but it takes a few days to generate it— it just happens.

MICK: But I don't think there's anything wrong with having sex, you know.

CATHERINE: *At what age?*

MICK: Any age.

AW: *I think that five's too young.*

MICK: To have sex? Rubbish. This is really sort of taboo in society—people never thought that children had any sexual ideas at all; in fact, children are highly sexual. They don't have to fuck each other but they obviously have sexual ideas. Everybody who has had a child knows that. Freud was the first person that dared to say that children had sexual ideas and they almost stoned him into the ground for that. It was absolutely taboo.

CATHERINE: *He said that they had ideas that he interpreted as being*

sexual ideas.

MICK: I can't remember the exact text, Catherine.

CATHERINE: *It's true though.*

MICK: The whole thing that came out was that he said children had sexual ideas; and everyone else, until then, had just brushed it under the carpet and ignored the whole fucking

thing. I mean, little boys have erections; and everyone knows that—who has had children, or boys.

CATHERINE: *How old were you?*

MICK: I can't remember. Who can remember their first wet dream? Can

you remember yours. Andy? How old were you?

AW: *I must have been . . .*

MICK: Andy was late, a late learner.

CATHERINE: *But I mean five or six?*

KEITH: Yup.

CATHERINE: *I think eleven.*

MICK: Children have erections before that.

KEITH: My little boy has hard-ons all the time. When they wet their nappies they have it.

MICK: I mean, all the games that kids play at various ages—you've got all sorts of sexual orientations about taking girls' clothes off and looking at each other.

CATHERINE: *Ah, that's what you think.*

MICK: What do you mean, Catherine? What other interpretations can you possibly put on it—if you want to see a girl's navel?

AW: *What was that book they did with all photographs of naked kids?*

MICK: It was called, it was called. . . .

EARL: *Show Me.*

MICK: It really was a piece of shit. I hated it. That was just for adults to turn on.

AW: *Have you ever been to porn movies?*

MICK: I've been to some, but I don't really like them very much. They don't turn me on very much. I like to go to *films.*

CATHERINE: *Have you seen Pasolini's Salo?*

MICK: No I haven't actually, but a

friend of mine told me all about it.

KEITH: That's what everybody says. Nobody's seen Pasolini.

CATHERINE: *I have.*

MICK: What's it about Catherine?

CATHERINE: *It's about four ugly men doing all the most perverted things they could possibly think of to about twelve beautiful teenagers.*

KEITH: Girls and boys?

CATHERINE: *Girls and boys.*

MICK: That film caused a lot of stir in London. The police seized it.

KEITH: They had *The Texas Chainsaw Massacre* playing down the street.

MICK: But you see what Keith means is that it is so violent and it's playing.

AW: *Censors are the same all over*

—*they have such a contradictory way of judging things. . . .*

VICTOR: *Please excuse me. Who does their hair?*

MICK: Keith and Ronnie? They do it themselves. They're always cutting it off in my bathroom and making a mess.

AW: *They do their own hair? But hairdressers are really important now. Why don't you have one travelling with your group?*

MICK: What a camp suggestion, Andy! I wish Anouk Aimee was here to fall over the curb with me. . . .

AW: *We were in Fort Lauderdale and this guy told me the bathroom was clear, so I went in . . .*

MICK: The bathroom was what?

AW: *Clear. So I went in and—*

MICK: This is a *clear* bathroom.

AW: *So I went in and four other people came in after me and it was so embarassing because one guy said to another "You're peeing next to. . . ,"
And that guy turned to me and said, "Are you who I think your are?"*

MICK: "Are you who I think you are?" Oh my God, that's my unfavorite line of all.

AW: *But do people follow you into bathrooms just so they can say they peed next to Mick Jagger?*

MICK: I don't know. I never ask them what they're doing there. I just address them civilly and tell them what the bathrooms are for. I mean, they're not for hanging around and making social comments as far as I'm concerned.

CATHERINE: *Would you say that the bathroom's usually fuller when you leave than when you arrive?*

MICK: It all depends whether I piss on them or not.

VICTOR: *In the movies they showed of your tours, you look very much like Bianca.*

MICK: No, *she* looks like *me,* man.

VICTOR: *No. All your gestures are like hers.*

MICK: Did you know her before you knew me?

VICTOR: *Yes. I've known her for years.*

MICK: Well I existed before her. I came first.

AW: *They're both from South America.*

MICK: She's from Central America. She's not from South America.

VICTOR: *It's the same thing. Close.*

MICK: It may be worse, Victor. I've been to both places.

VICTOR: *You look very, very much like her. Every year you look more like her.*

MICK: Maybe next year's gonna be different.

VICTOR: *Are you divorcing her? Are you divorcing Bianca?*

MICK: No! Not as far as I know.

VICTOR: *Do you get off with her?*

MICK: Do I get off with her?

VICTOR: *On her?*

MICK: That's rude!

VICTOR: *No, because in the movies you look beautiful like her.*

MICK: Well I'm glad I'm as beautiful as my beautiful, fucking wife.

AW: *She is beautiful.*

MICK: She's very cute. And she's very beautiful.

AW: *She's photogenic.*

MICK: She's photogenic.

AW: *She's a good dancer.*

MICK: She's a good dancer. What else can I say?

AW: *She has really soft skin.*

MICK: She has really soft *and* beautiful skin.

VICTOR: *What soap does she use?*

MICK: She never uses any soap.

AW: *She takes a bath after she does her make-up.*

MICK: Then she takes a bath. And she's very quick.

AW: *It's a great system. She gets all made-up and then she hops in her hot bath. Do you put your make-up on before your bath?*

MICK: Are you kidding? I haven't had a bath and I can't bother to take my make-up off.

VICTOR: *Why do you look clean?*

MICK: You don't have to bathe every day to look clean. It's just an illusion.

ANDY WARHOL

JAG-AHR OF THE JUNGLE

Look back, it was 1965. Pa was shouting from the tv room. "jesus christ! jesus christ!" I flew up those stairs pumping in 3-D. Bad black widows . . . water moccasins . . . red snake long as a fire hose. see our house was built on a long swamp. on easter a boy died. he sank in the quick mud and the next morning he floated up like ivory soap. mama made me go to the wake. the afternoon was hell hot, mosquitoes and steam were rising from the swamp. the world series was on. the women sat around the casket. all the men sat around the tv.

Which brings me back to pa. I ran in panting. I was scared silly. there was pa glued to the tv screen cussing his brains out. A rock'n'roll band was doing it right on the ed sullivan show. pa was frothing like a dog. I never seen him so mad. but I lost contact with him quick. that band was as relentless as murder. I was trapped in a field of hot dots. the guitar player had pimples. the blonde kneeling down had circles ringing his eyes. one had greasy hair. the other didn't care. and the singer was showing his second layer of skin and more than a little milk. I felt thru his pants with optic x-ray. this was some hard meat. this was a bitch. five white boys sexy as any spade. their nerves were wired and their third leg was rising. in six minutes five lusty images gave me my first glob of gooie in my virgin panties.

That was my introduction to the Rolling Stones. they did Time is on my side, my brain froze. I was doing all my thinking between my legs. I got

shook. light broke. they were gone and I cliff-hanging. like jerking off without coming.

Pa snapped off the tv. but he was too late. they put the touch on me. I was blushing jelly. this was no mamas boy music. it was alchemical. I couldn't fathom the recipe but I was ready. blind love for my father was the first thing I sacrificed to Mick Jagger.

Time passed. I offered up everything I didn't have. every little lamb. I can tie the Stones in with every sexual release of my late blooming adolescence. The Stones were sexually freeing confused american children, a girl could feel power. lady glory, a guy could reveal his feminine side without being called a fag. masculinity was no longer measured on the football field.

Ya never think of the Stones as fags. In full make-up and frills they still get it across. they know just how to ram a woman. they made me real proud to be female. the other half of male. they aroused in me both a feline

sense of power and a longing to be held under the thumb.

The Aftermath album was the real move. two faced woman. doncha bother me. the singer displays contempt for his lady. he's on top and thats what I like. then he raises her as queen. his obsession is her. "goin home." what a song. so wild so pump pumping. do it down in the basement. don't come til the last second. cockpit. cover you like an airplane. stones music is screwing music.

They rechanneled hot rivers at 78 speed. they were a guide for every shifty white kid. who could get behind the sun tanned soul of Jan and Dean? look back on the T.A.M.I. show. Leslie Gore was auntie mama. the spastic moves of Gerry and the Pacemakers. god bless the marvelous majorette precision of Motown. the T.A.M.I. shows saving grace was pure spade. until the last precious moments with the Rolling Stones. On that silver screen they were bigger than bed. my head spun my pussy dripped my pants were wet and the Rolling Stones redeemed the white man forever.

No wonder the Christian god banned the image. jealous bastard. he must have foreseen the black and white movie. who can reject the power of that image? real or 3-D the magic leaks thru. if you got it, and they had it.

I seen them live in 1966. In the heart of the february freeze. Frank Stefanko picked me up in a towtruck. we cruised thru every redlight in south phillie. It was my first white concert. Now at the Roxy the spades danced on the ceiling. But this was different. These blonde screamers were after more than a party.

Mick ripped off his flowered shirt and did a fandango. satisfaction, tambourine on head he strutted like some stud. virgin fell off her folding chair and broke her leg. I sussed it all out.

this was no tv this was real. I could enter the action. I got set to out stoneface Bill Wyman. the cornerstone of the stones. relentless as Stonehenge as a pyramid. any hard edged kid took to him. He was on stage right to catch some spit from Mick. Then hell broke. handkerchiefs folded like flowers. a million girls busting my spleen. oh baudelaire. I grabbed Brian's ankle and held on like a drowning child. It seemed like hours. I was getting bored. I looked up. I yawned. Bill Wyman cracked up. Brian grinned. I got scared. I squeezed out and ran. like the altar boy who busts his nut to peek in the sacred chalice. once achieved what next? I left without my hat. I was soaking wet. sweat was freezing on my face.

The politics of speed. Between the Buttons came out. Thats when I zoomed in on Brian. I got obsessed with him. Focused on him like some sick kodak Brian between the what? Look at that cover. look at him. he's exposed, he's cold as ice. his powdery skin. his shadow eyes. a doomed albino raccoon. I seen them do Ruby Tuesday on tv. Mick was on top he was the prince. decked in a mirrored shirt and shingled hair. he made his first public ballet bow. Brian was crouched down. he seemed covered with a translucent dust. mr. amanda jones.

By 1967 they all but eliminated the word guilt from our vocabulary. Lets Spend the Night Together was the big hit. Its impossible to suffer guilt when you're moving to that song. The Flowers album was for loners and lovers only. It provided a tight backdrop for a lot of decadent fantasy. And by 67 fantasy had already got the best of me.

I never considered the Stones drug music. They were the drug itself. They took up where Martha and the Vandellas left off. Real heatwave dancing music. thru demon genius they hit that chord. basic as Charlies drum beat, as primitive as a western man could stand. find the beat and you dance all night. dive into Gimme Shelter full volume. Its always been easy to let it loose to the Stones, cause they're so cool. so worthy.

Plenty of body shot. they had their brain shot too. Remember "We Love You?" the beat was hidden. it was far from western but when it needled ya you were shot up but good. madly intoxicating. erotic and extending. Like the Satanic Majesty. Real search party music. hang your lantern high. brain operation. Then they backed it up with Beggars Banquet. Pure hump hump. Get that trojan.

Body and brain. They spell cocaine, the inner search light. speed and slow motion. perfect snow job. the results are alchemical. and if you can't afford it the Stones are it. Sticky Fingers. Exile on Mainstreet. Stick your nose in the speakers and get frostbite.

It was July 2. The doctor thought I was bats. He gave me morphine for the pain. He whispered sweet dreams.

That night stretched like a cloud. A hypnotic. I was aware of the droning of bees. In the garden the blonde woman was preparing a mixture of pollen and pure honey. Keith was twisting her arm. He had a leather erection. Mick was writhing. some dizzy ritual. The pollen made me wheeze. I laid in the grass and puked. The dew was cooling my hot leg. Someone grabbed my ankle. bruising it. I was saved. I was suffocating in my own warm vomit. I gulped sweet oxygen and turned. Brian was still holding on. I wanted to speak to him but I got caught up in the lace border of his cuff. I traced the delicate embroidery until it stretched across my field of vision like queen anne's lace.

It was morning. It was dazzling. It was July 3rd. By night fall the whole world knew that Brian Jones was dead.

I went home to America and threw up on my fathers bed.

I was antique. He had returned to light and I was holding baby hair.

Brian was a length ahead. He was gonna dig up the great African root and pump it like gas in every Stones hit. But it wasn't time yet. Unlucky horoscope. Imagination and realization were ticking on separate timepieces.

But Brian was in a hurry. Running neck and neck with his vision was his demon. He would soon as stick his dick up the baby dolls ass. Shove pins in the heads of innocents. Torn between evil energy and pure spirit. Bad seed with a golden spleen. The Stones were moving toward a mortal mergence of the unspoken moment and the hot dance of life. But they were

moving too slow for Brian. So slow he split. In too.

Death by water. Just a shot away from the heart of Ethiopia. Rising to original heights. Up and over Adams apple sauce. There are blonde hairs raveling in the Stones vital breath. ha ha. Brian got the last laugh.

And the sacrifices continue. moving toward the perfect moment. the miracle of Altamont. The death of the lime green spade. Not shocking. Necessary. The most graceful complete moment. Compare his dance of death with Micks frenzied movement. Micks spastic magic. Unlucky motor.

Give history a chance. St. Meredith. his image in pure copper rising over the speedway. Our jesus of Brazil.

Look back Altamont. Our Rome. water babies. no flow. no one. gimme gimme. a private piece of the action. some footage. some tail. hold it to the ego like gold plate. no collective act.

And Mick was no flashing priest. A pretty sailor thrown in a cell of sissy athletes. All panting into anarchy. They pluck up Mick like the old fairy tale. Split the goose that lays the slow

golden eggs. shake that magic maker. extract that diamond tooth.

That's the western movement. Thats the way of rock n roll. At my first school dance Jo-Jo Rose got stabbed. U.S. Bonds was lip-synching "Quarter to Three." Nobodies erecting monuments to Jo-Jo Rose. Nobody's blaming U.S. Bonds neither.

Blame Mick Jagger? For what? for performing thru theory not grace. The alchemy was not there. The performer and the audience have got to be as intimate as the killer and his victim. Like in Performance. Takes two to make the radio. Contact pill. If you can see it you can get it. Brian dreamed of it. Mick failed at it.

But you know he's redeemed. Mick did it. This is no stylistic trick. Tuesday night July 25 1972 at Madison Square Garden. A sacred peep show. Pope don't bless my flashlight. I found my own way.

Born to be. Born to be me. Got my ticket for free. What would I wear? Keith Richards gear? bone in the ear? Naaa. Lay the flash aside. Dress like Don't Look Back. Just the right dark

glasses. Blow my last buck to be cool. grab that taxi. adjust my shades and light a Kool. Pat my flask of Jack Daniel's. I get there. Completely solitaire.

My seat juts out. Overlook the ground floor. Left handed stage view. Nobody can get in my way. Nothing but ramp and space. A box seat. Tuesday was the off night. The double show day. Rock stars make their own labor laws. Inhuman work load. No party. No hip chicks. Just fans. Everyone a stranger. Good. I could play at being a cool and perfect stranger myself. I sat there feeling incognito hot shit. Then my stomach started feeling funny. Detached jello. Regulate my breath. Be a breathing camera. The hungry eye.

Something snapped. I'm no screamer. I swear. When the roller coaster crashes. I hold my breath. I refuse to let loose. It's a matter of pride. But I cracked. My tear ducts burst. They were there in 4-D. Fell on one knee. Couldn't see. My brain cracked like an egg. The gold liquid spurted all over the stage. Mick bathed in it. Keith got his feet wet. Then I calmed quick. It was like coming without jerking off. They hadn't even finished brown sugar and I was cool as a snake. Physically for me the concert was over. Like hearing the punchline then sitting thru the long drawn out joke.

The rest was pure head motion. Like viewing any ancient ceremony. Pass the sacred wafer. Transfixed my open laughter. My brain was open as a loft. No mere image. I was ashamed. They were just men. Charlie raised over like King Drum. Bill in red velvet. His bass way up. His classic dignity. Mick Taylor completing the triangle. The maypole.

Mick and Keith wove their magic round. Keith a drunken kid. He was moving so good. Thin raunchy glitter. I don't care what anyone says. He's the real rolling stone. He got the silver. Basic black guitar. Like a convertible. Like heartbreak hotel. His plexiglass one got stolen.

Not without sacrifice. He was loosing his grip. He introduced the band. A long silence before Keith. Death rattle. Did he introduce Brian Jones? Freeze that moment. I got no Maysley video to look back on. What was he saying? The silence was anything but golden. Does the lion drown underwater? Or does he swallow the golden fish? Brian swimming thru the crowd. I looked down. They were modulating. Jagger was apologizing. Incoherent. drooling. the heat. the drink. I was in shock. My heart stopped thisshort. from stopping.

PATTI SMITH

12
SESSIONOGRAPHY, THE STONES IN THE STUDIO 1962–1981

Note: Personnel at the sessions includes all members of the Rolling Stones (plus Ian Stewart) unless stated otherwise. Additional personnel are listed.
*Indicates unreleased track.
†Mobile Recording Unit

1962

Curly Clayton Sound Studio, London
OCTOBER
Engineer: Curly Clayton
Personnel: Mick Jagger, Keith Richards, Brian Jones, Tony Chapman, Ian Stewart

Soon Forgotten*
You Can't Judge A Book*
Close Together*

1963

IBC Studios, London
JANUARY 28–FEBRUARY 2
Engineer: Glyn Johns

Diddley Daddy*
Road Runner*
Bright Lights, Big City*
I Want To Be Loved*
Honey, What's Wrong?*
Crackin' Up*

R. G. Jones Studio, London
APRIL
(Soundtrack for a 20 minute documentary on the Stones filmed by Giorgio Gomelsky)
Engineer: R. G. Jones, Jr.

Pretty Thing*
It's Alright, Babe*

Olympic Studios, London
MAY 10
Producer: Andrew Oldham and Eric Easton
Engineer: Roger Savage

Come On

I Want To Be Loved
Love Potion No. 9*
Pretty Thing*

Decca Studios, West Hampstead London
JULY/SEPTEMBER
Producer: Andrew Oldham

Poison Ivy (two versions)
Fortune Teller
It Should Be You*

Kingsway Studios, London
SEPTEMBER 14–15, OCTOBER
Producer: Eric Easton

You'd Better Move On
Money
Bye, Bye Johnnie
I Wanna Be Your Man
Stoned

Kingsway Studios, London
NOVEMBER
Producer: Eric Easton

Poison Ivy
Fortune Teller
Talkin' About You
You Better Move On

1964

Regent Sound, London
JANUARY–FEBRUARY
Producer: Andrew Oldham
Engineer: Bill Farley

Little By Little
Route 66
I Just Want To Make Love To You
Honest I Do
Mona (I Need You Baby)
Now I've Got A Witness
I'm A King Bee
Carol
Tell Me (You're Coming Back)
Can I Get A Witness
You Can Make It If You Try

Walking The Dog

Regent Sound Studios, London
LATE FEBRUARY
Producer: Andrew Oldham
Engineer: Bill Farley
Additional personnel: Phil Spector, Gene Pitney, Graham Nash

Not Fade Away
And The Rolling Stones Met Phil And Gene*
Mr. Spector And Mr. Pitney Came Too*
Andrew's Blues*

Regent Sound, IBC Studios, London
MAY
Producer: Andrew Oldham
Engineer: Bill Farley

Under The Boardwalk
Congratulations
Good Times, Bad Times
Time Is On My Side (1st single version)
Grown Up Wrong
Off The Hook
You Can't Catch Me
Susie Q

Chess Studios, Chicago
JUNE 10–11
Producer: Andrew Oldham
Engineer: Ron Malo

If You Need Me
Empty Heart
2120 South Michigan Avenue
Confessin The Blues
Around And Around
It's All Over Now
Down The Road Apiece
Reelin' And A Rockin'*
Down In The Bottom
Tell Be Baby*
Hi-Heel Sneakers*
Stewed And Keefed*
Look What You've Done
I Can't Be Satisfied
Don't Lie To Me

RCA Studios, Hollywood
OCTOBER 27
Producer: Andrew Oldham
Engineer: Dave Hassinger

Heart Of Stone
Down Home Girl
Hitch-Hike
Everybody Needs Somebody To Love
Pain In My Heart
Oh Baby (We Got A Good Thing Goin')

Chess Studios, Chicago
NOVEMBER 5, 6, 8
Producer: Andrew Oldham
Engineer: Ron Malo

Little Red Rooster
Surprise, Surprise
Time Is On My Side
What A Shame

1965

RCA Studios, Hollywood
JANUARY 10–11, FEBRUARY 17–18
Producer: Andrew Oldham
Engineer: Dave Hassinger
Additional Personnel: Phil Spector, Jack Nitzsche

The Last Time
Play With Fire

Chess Studios, Chicago
MAY 10–11
Producer: Andrew Oldham
Engineer: Ron Malo

The Under Assistant West Coast Promotion Man
That's How Strong My Love Is
Mercy, Mercy
Try Me*
Fanny Mae*
Key To The Highway*
Get Back To The One You Love*
Leave Me Alone*
Go On Home*

RCA Studios, Hollywood
MAY 12–13
Producer: Andrew Oldham
Engineer: Dave Hassinger

Satisfaction
The Spider And The Fly
Cry To Me
One More Try
Good Times
My Girl
I've Been Loving You Too Long
Tracks of My Tears*

RCA Studios, Hollywood
DECEMBER 3–8
Producer: Andrew Oldham
Engineer: Dave Hassinger

19th Nervous Breakdown
Sad Day

1966

RCA Studios, Hollywood
MARCH 3–8
Producer: Andrew Oldham
Engineer: Dave Hassinger

Flight 505
High And Dry
It's Not Easy
I Am Waiting
Long Long While
Lady Jane
Out Of Time
Paint It Black
Stupid Girl
Under My Thumb
What To Do

RCA Studios, Hollywood
DECEMBER 3–8
Producer: Andrew Oldham
Engineer: Dave Hassinger
Additional personnel: Jack Nitzsche

Take It Or Leave It
Doncha Bother Me
Sittin' On A Fence
Mother's Little Helper
Think
Sad Day
Ride On Baby
Going Home
Lookin' Tired*

Olympic Studios, London
AUGUST–SEPTEMBER
Producer: Andrew Oldham
Engineer: Glyn Johns

BETWEEN THE BUTTONS sessions
Can't Believe*
English Summer*

RCA Studios, Hollywood
AUGUST 7
Producer: Andrew Oldham
Engineer: Dave Hassinger

BETWEEN THE BUTTONS (early sessions)
  Have You Seen Your Mother, Baby,
    Standing In The Shadow?

Who's Driving My Plane

Olympic Studios, London
NOVEMBER
Producer: Andrew Oldham
Engineer: Glyn Johns

Dandelion
Ruby Tuesday
English Summer*
Gold Painted Nails*

RCA Studios, Hollywood
NOVEMBER–DECEMBER
Producer: Andrew Oldham
Engineer: Dave Hassinger

BETWEEN THE BUTTONS sessions
(continued)
Let's Spend The Night Together

1967

Olympic Studios, London
LATE JULY
Producer: Andrew Oldham
Engineer: Glyn Johns
Additional Personnel: John Lennon,
Paul McCartney

We Love You

Olympic Studios, London
JUNE–SEPTEMBER
Producer: The Rolling Stones
Engineer: Glyn Johns
Additional personnel: Nicky Hopkins,
Steve Marriott

THEIR SATANIC MAJESTIES REQUEST
sessions

1968

Olympic Studios, London
MARCH 1–JUNE
Producer: Jimmy Miller
Engineer: Glyn Johns
Additional Personnel: Al Kooper, Dave
Mason, Ry Cooder, Nicky Hopkins,
London Bach Choir, Madelaine Bell,
Doris Troy, Nannette Newman (vocals
under the direction of Jack Nitzsche)

BEGGARS BANQUET sessions
Jumpin' Jack Flash
You Can't Always Get What You Want
Midnight Rambler
Sister Morphine
You Got the Silver
Memo from Turner
Family
Downtown Susie
Child Of The Moon
Silver Blanket*
Lady*
Hamburger to Go*
Did Everyone Pay Their Dues*
(first version of Street Fighting Man)

Redlands
(Keith's house in Sussex)
JULY
Producer: Jimmy Miller
Engineer: Glyn Johns

Still a Fool*
Hold On I'm Coming*
Rock Me Baby*

*Completed in 1969 at Electra &
Olympic Studios.*

BBC Studios, London
DECEMBER 10–11
Producer: Allen Klein
Engineer: Glyn Johns

THE ROLLING STONES ROCK AND ROLL
CIRCUS
Sympathy for the Devil
You Can't Always Get What You Want
Yonders Wall*
Salt of the Earth (live vocal, recorded
track)
Jumpin Jack Flash
Route 66
Confessin' the Blues
Walking Blues
No Expectations

1969

Olympic Studios, London
MAY
Producer: Jimmy Miller
Engineer: Glyn Johns
Additional Personnel: Mick Taylor

Honky Tonk Women (single version)
Toss the Coin*
Old Glory*

Olympic Studios, London
JUNE–JULY
Producer: Jimmy Miller
Engineer: Glyn Johns

Additional material for LET IT BLEED
Live with Me
Gimme Shelter
Jiving Sister Fanny
I'm Going Down
Try a Little Harder
I Don't Know Why

Elektra, Hollywood
NOVEMBER
Producer: Jimmy Miller
Engineer: Glyn Johns
Additional Personnel: Byron Berline
(fiddle on Honky Tonk Women)

Country Honk (LP version)
Gimme Shelter (Merry Clayton
overdubs vocals)
Live with Me

Muscle Shoals Studios, Alabama
DECEMBER 1
Producer: Jimmy Miller

Brown Sugar

You Gotta Move
Wild Horses

1970

Olympic Studios, London and **MRU,**†
Stargroves (Mick's house in Newbury)
EARLY SUMMER
Producer: Jimmy Miller
Engineers: Glyn Johns, Chris Kimsey,
Jimmy Johnson
Additional Personnel: Ian Stewart,
Jack Nitzche, Ry Cooder, Nicky
Hopkins, Bobby Keyes, Jim Prices,
Paul Buckmaster, Rocky Dijon, J.
Dickinson (with Mick on guitar, Bill
Wyman on electric piano and Jimmy
Miller on percussion)

Balance of STICKY FINGERS sessions

1971

Leeds University
APRIL 13

Live broadcast over the BBC

MRU, Nellcote *(Keith's house in the
south of France)*
JULY–NOVEMBER
Producer: Jimmy Miller
Engineers: Andy Johns, Glyn Johns,
Joe Zaganno, Jeremy Gee
Additional Personnel: Nicky Hopkins,
Bobby Keyes, Jim Prices, Mac
Rebennack, Billy Preston, Bill
Plummer, Clydie King, Vanetta "plus
friend," Al Perkins (steel guitar), Amyl
Nitrate (percussion), Jerry Kirkland
(backup vocals), Tammi Lynn, Shirley
Goodman, Joe Green, Kathi McDonald
(on this album Keith plays bass, Mick
guitar and harmonica, and Jimmy
Miller percussion)

EXILE ON MAIN STREET sessions (then
tentatively titled *Eat It* or *Jungle
Disease*)

Elektra, Hollywood
NOVEMBER–DECEMBER
Producer: Jimmy Miller
Additional Personnel: Nicky Hopkins

Vocal overdubs and EXILE tracks
mixed
  Travellin' Man*
  Leather Jacket*
  Potted Shrimp*
  I'm a Country Boy*
  Blood Red Wine*
  Cocksucker Blues*

1972/1973

Dynamic Sounds, Jamaica
NOVEMBER 1972 and MARCH 1973
Producer: Jimmy Miller
Engineers: Keith Harwood, Andy
Johns, Glyn Johns
Additional Personnel: session
musicians

GOAT'S HEAD SOUP sessions
Save Me*
Through the Lonely Night*
Chris Cross*
Tops
After Muddy and Charlie*
Jamaica*

1974

Musicland, Munich
MARCH, APRIL, DECEMBER
Producers: The Glimmer Twins
Engineers: Andy Johns, Keith Harwood
Additional Personnel: Billy Preston,
Nicky Hopkins, Ray Cooper, Ed
Leach, Charlie Jolly, Blue Magic,
Kenny Jones, Willie Weeks, Ron Wood

If You Can't Rock Me
Ain't Too Proud to Beg
It's Only Rock 'n Roll (But I Like It)
Till the Next Goodbye
Time Waits for No One
Luxury
Dance Little Sister
If You Really Want to Be My Friend
Short and Curlies
Fingerprint File
Drift Away*

Musicland, Munich
MARCH 25, 29, 31, APRIL 2, DECEMBER
12, 15
Producers: The Glimmer Twins
Engineers: Keith Harwood, Glyn Johns,
Phil McDonald, Lew Hahn
Additional Personnel: Ron Wood,
Nicky Hopkins, Billy Preston, Wayne
Perkins, Ollie Brown, Harvey Mandel
(with Mick on string synthesizer, guitar
and piano, Keith on bass, piano and
backup vocals)

Hot Stuff
Hand of Fate
Cherry Oh Baby
Hey Negrita
Fool to Cry
Crazy Mama
Worried About You
Slave

1975

MRU, Rotterdam
JANUARY 23
Producers: The Glimmer Twins
Engineers: Keith Harwood, Glyn Johns,
Lew Hahn
Arranger: Arif Mardin
Additional personnel: Billy Preston
(with Mick on "foot")

Melody
Shame, Shame, Shame*

1977

Pathé Marconi, EMI studios, Paris
MAY–AUGUST
Producers: The Glimmer Twins
Engineers and Mixing: Chris Kimsey
Additional Personnel: Sugar Blue, Ian
McLagan, Mel Collins, "1 Moroccan, 1
Jew, 1 WASP" (percussion)

SOME GIRLS sessions
Claudine*
Summer Romance* (first version)
I Can't Help It*
Hang Fire
Do You Think I Care*
When She Held Me Tight*
Everlasting Is My Love*
Munich Hilton*
Black Limousine
Fiji Gin*
Rotten Roll*
Where The Boys All Go
Start Me Up

1978–80

Pathé-Marconi, EMI Studios, Paris;
Compass Point Studio, Nassau,
Bahamas. Mixed at **Electric Ladyland**,
The Hits Factory and **The Record
Plant**, New York
Producers: The Glimmer Twins
Engineer: Chris Kimsey
Additional Personnel: Bobby Keyes,
Nicky Hopkins, Sugar Blue, Michael
Shriere, Max Rom

EMOTIONAL RESCUE sessions
We Had It All*
Ain't No Use Cryin
Petrol*
Jah Is Not Dead*
Linda Lu*
Gangster's Maul*
It's A Lie*
Bulldog* (a.k.a.: Little T & A)
Glass Eye*
Tall And Slender Blondes*
Wish A Woman*

1981

Electric Ladyland and **Atlantic Studios**,
New York
Producers: The Glimmer Twins
Engineer: Chris Kimsey
Additional Personnel: Sonny Rollins
and Pete Townshend

TATTOO YOU sessions
Heaven
Neighbors
Waiting On A Friend

(Other TATTOO YOU tracks were
recorded during sessions for BLACK
AND BLUE, SOME GIRLS and EMO-
TIONAL RESCUE, but were re-recorded
and re-mixed between January and
June, 1981.)

TOM BEACH AND JAMES KARNBACH

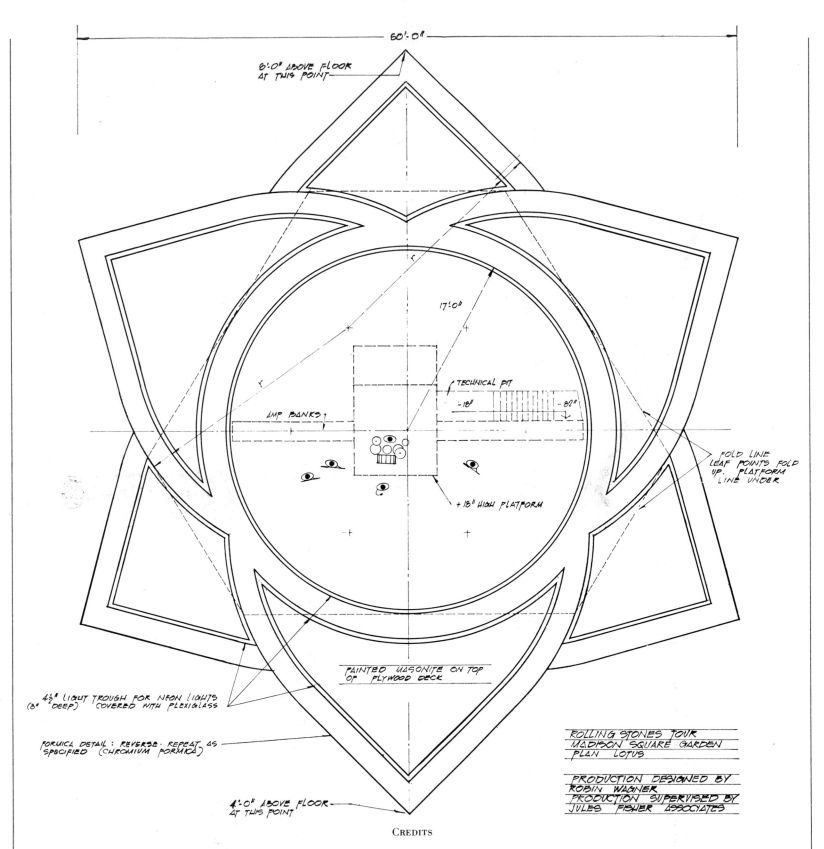

CREDITS